BENEATH THE FOOTNOTE

O. Lawrence Burnette, Jr.

BENEATH THE FOOTNOTE

A
Guide
to the
Use and
Preservation
of American
Historical Sources

THE STATE HISTORICAL SOCIETY OF WISCONSIN
MADISON   MCMLXIX

To

E. T. B.

for patience

PREFACE

HISTORY PRESUMES to understand all things, but it is uncomfortable in understanding itself. Like a disturbed adolescent, it seems hung up on philosophical questions it cannot answer from its own experience and too embarrassed to ask for help. It has adjusted to the problem of its ultimate meaning and purpose by denying that it has any, but from time to time misgivings about the adequacy of its methodology prick its conscience.

Anxiety about the historical method rippled through the ranks of European historians about 1900, and among their American colleagues a generation later. Since the 1930's numerous works on historical methodology have been published in America, and courses in historiography have appeared in academic curricula even at the undergraduate level. Clearly, the profession in our own time is again worrying about its inner workings, about its process of discovering and proving truth if not about its philosophical frame of reference. However, even during self-analysis, American historians have insisted upon their familiar methodology and interpretive analysis. As a result, their efforts have been more descriptive than analytical.

American history has a strong prejudice for substance over procedure, and it trains its students in historical methodology through practical application rather than abstract theory. It expects the mechanical processes of history to become second nature, like breathing. The profession justifies this arrangement by citing its impressive productivity and by suggesting analogies with the Anglo-American system of legal proof.

Parallels do exist between the methods of law and history, but they are not exact. In law, evidence is received from a wit-

ness questioned under oath and required to defend his testimony
under cross-examination. Because the proper development of
evidence is crucial to the legal process, the "best evidence" rule
has been formulated by which greatest weight is given to the
best available testimony by the witness theoretically most competent to supply it. The most conspicuous exception to the
rule is the *prima facie* precedence given an original writing,
official record, or other authenticated document. Authoritative
as he is, Wigmore on evidence does not apply directly to history.
Historians deal almost entirely in documentary evidence, none
of which enjoys *prima facie* standing. History's eye witness
generally cannot be called for cross-examination, and there is
a lively traffic in hearsay evidence. The salvation of history's
methodology is that its sources do not testify with finality and
its judgments are ever subject to review.

American historians have become involved in complex problems of historical documentation so infrequently that with im-
punity they have been able to ignore its theoretical aspects. In
the broadest and classical sense, documentation means any accepted process of historical proof based upon any kind of physical evidence, whether written, graphical, or archeological. That
definition has been handed down by the classical authorities
and accepted by the modern ones, and it leaves room for the
contemporary American impatience with theory. There is general agreement that historical documentation consists of three
steps: 1) location and collection of probable sources of historical information; 2) criticism of the probable sources to test
for genuineness and authenticity; and 3) criticism of authentic
sources for the extraction of credible information. Theory knows
the first step as the science of heuristics and the latter two as
historical criticism in its various aspects. Contemporary American practice covers the same ground with different labels.

Even though the rules of legal evidence do not strictly apply
in the court of history, the American historical tradition has
pragmatically extracted four general principles as the heuristic
equivalent of the "best evidence" rule. These principles assume
that the best historical evidence is that produced closest in time,
most objectively disposed, most confidentially related, and most
expertly witnessing to the facts to be established. Proceeding
from these basic premises, American history has adopted a classi-

fication of sources based upon the form of transmission of evidence as the functional equivalent of theoretical heuristics and historical criticism.

Since American history thinks of methodology in terms of categories of evidence and the associated criteria of evaluation, it is probably wiser to attempt to rationalize and explain the existing system rather than supplant it. The present study is offered as a contribution to the care and use of the primary sources for American history, as a guide for neophyte, fledgling, and amateur historians to the extensive world beneath the footnote. It is not intended as a finding aid. Rather, it is concerned with the origins and evolution of those institutions and practices involved in the care and use of the primary forms of American historical evidence. The availability and priority of certain of those forms from generation to generation may also help to explain the changing styles in America's historical understanding of itself, but that would be the fascinating subject of yet another study.

This work has intruded upon many years, acquaintances, and friendships, and the list of its creditors is too long to enumerate. Specific acknowledgment can be made to only a few. Professor Thomas Cary Johnson first introduced the author to the pleasures and importance of the "history of history" while he was a graduate student at the University of Virginia. Dr. Alice E. Smith of the State Historical Society of Wisconsin first suggested the need for a work on the theory and practice of American historiography, and other colleagues in the Society provided encouragement and assistance to complete and publish this study. The basic plan of the work was borrowed from the fertile thought of Sir Hilary Jenkinson, the master of modern archival science, and it was further influenced by the writings of such contemporary archivists as Ernst Posner, T. R. Schellenberg, and Lester J. Cappon. The contributors to the *American Archivist* have provided quantities of grist for this mill. Classes of students at the University of Wisconsin and at Birmingham-Southern College have ground down many of the idiosyncrasies of the first drafts of the manuscript. Colleagues in the College have contributed selflessly of their respective talents and insights, and the administration of the College has generously supplied financial assistance to bring the study to completion. Mrs. Marshall Carney has made editorial contributions in addition to being a model typist.

To all the named and nameless who have contributed, this work is obliged for whatever merit it may have. As always, the author alone assumes responsibility for all wherein it has gone astray.

                                    O. LAWRENCE BURNETTE, JR.
Birmingham-Southern College
Fall, 1968

CONTENTS

Preface   vii

  I. American National Archives   3

 II. State and Local Archives in America   43

III. Quasi-Public Archives   74

 IV. Business Archives and Records   104

  V. Manuscript Collections at the National Level   130

 VI. State and Local Manuscript Collections   167

VII. Quasi-Public Manuscript Collections   193

VIII. Private Manuscript Collections and Collectors   229

 IX. Newspapers as Historical Evidence   265

  X. Records of the Mass Culture   285

 XI. Aural and Graphical Documentation   316

XII. Preservation and Dissemination of
     Historical Evidence   340

     Bibliography   379

     Index   438

AMERICAN NATIONAL ARCHIVES

A RCHIVES have existed since there have been governments and other institutions to create and preserve written records, but the systematic use of archival sources in written history is a fairly recent development. The European school of scientific historiography of the nineteenth century was rooted in the rich soil of the European national archives, and the subsequent experience of historians in using this category of source material has shaped the canons and practices of the profession in the use of almost all other forms of historical documentation. These canons, together with an interest in the archival sources from which they were derived, when imported into America profoundly influenced the institutional character of American archives and their use by scholars in the writing of the nation's history.

It is far easier to trace the derivation of the term "archives" than to construct a satisfactory modern definition. From the Greek word archeion, which once meant seat of government, the term came to mean the storehouse where the records of government were kept and, by extension, the accumulation of records themselves. Thus, from the beginning, "archives" has had the dual meaning of both a building and a body of records. In American usage, archives might be defined as the essential whole of the verbal or graphic documentation accumulated by any organic institution or person in the course of activities, but subsequently preserved for some purpose other than that simu-

3

lating creation, under circumstances reasonably guaranteeing the integrity of the records.[1] It is not necessary that the records be the creation of a government; private individuals as well are quite capable of producing records which may become archives.

Until modern times, archives generally consisted of such materials as papyrus, rag paper, parchment, vellum, inks of gall and iron, linen or silk thread, leather, wood, beeswax and resin, and shellac. Hence, the principal dangers to preservation have generally been vermin, fire, water, and misplacement. Some purposeful and continuing policy of preservation has generally been necessary to save these relatively impermanent materials from destruction.

The scheme of archival arrangement prevalent in the Western world is rooted in the classical practice of filing incoming correspondence with the replies sent, and the practice was adopted, perfected, and spread throughout Europe by the Catholic Church in the Middle Ages. Prior to the eighteenth century secular records were usually cared for haphazardly as a part of the royal treasury. Thereafter, the ecclesiastical practices

[1] The definition is that of the present author. See also those of the archival authorities. Arthur H. Leavitt translates the Dutch *archief* as "the whole of the written documents, drawings and printed matter, officially received or produced by an administrative body or one of its officials, in so far as those documents are intended to remain in the custody of that body or of that official." Leavitt (trans.), Samuel Muller, J. A. Feith, and R. Fruin's *Manual for the Arrangement and Description of Archives* (New York, 1940), 13. Hilary Jenkinson, on the other hand, defines archives as composed of documents which were "drawn up or used in the course of administrative or executive transaction (whether public or private) of which itself formed a part; and subsequently preserved in their own custody for their own information by the person or persons responsible for that transaction or their legitimate successors." Jenkinson, *A Manual of Archive Administration* (London, 1940), 11. The Italian archivist Eugenio Cananova (1867–1951) in his manual *Archivistica* defined the term as "the orderly accumulation of documents which were created in the course of its activity by an institution or an individual, and which were preserved for the accomplishment of its political, legal or cultural purposes by such an institution or individual." Quoted in T. R. Schellenberg, *Modern Archives: Principles and Techniques* (Chicago, 1956), 12–13. Schellenberg's own definition is, "those records of any public or private institution which are adjudged worthy of permanent preservation for reference and research purposes and which have been deposited or have been selected for deposit in an archival institution." *Modern Archives*, 16. Thus, it appears that all of the authorities in varying degrees of emphasis incorporate three components in their definitions: (1) organic and purposeful creation; (2) purposeful preservation; and (3) integrity of custodianship.

have been adopted almost universally as national archival agencies have been established.

Archival science in modern Europe originated in France and has enjoyed extensive development there to the just pride of French scholarship and bureaucracy. The records of the Old Regime were probably as poorly kept as those of other contemporary governments, but the privileges substantiated by those records became embroiled in the French Revolution. One of the results was the reformation in 1794 of the royal records and the establishment of the national archives. Unfortunately, the child was ill-conceived and grew misshapenly until reformed along more naturalistic principles.

The difficulty of the *Archives Nationales* lay in the training of its first two directors, Armond-Gaston Camus and Pierre-Claude-François Daunow. Both were librarians and sought to impose an arbitrary schematic classification system upon the records in their care. Chaos resulted. Record groups (*series*) were established by subject without regard to the office of origin or the natural order of creation or arrangement of the records.

The first major reform of the *Archives Nationales* was undertaken by the historian François Guizot, who served as Minister of Public Instruction from 1832 to 1839 and as head of the cabinet from 1840 to 1848. The reformation consisted of a new principle of arrangement, grouping the records by the creating agency, or *fonds*, rather than by subject. Guizot's reforms were later amplified and formulated into the archival principle of *respect des fonds*, keeping intact all records originating from a given agency but permitting various modes of arrangement within a given *fonds*.[2] Other than the principle of *respect des fonds*, French influence upon American archival practices has been largely negative—an example of errors to be avoided.

The political disunity of Germany until late in the nineteenth century did not prevent its scholars from making invaluable contributions to Western historiography and archival science. The Prussian State Archives in Berlin took an early lead over other German provincial institutions, and as the political

---

[2] Schellenberg, *Modern Archives,* 170–172. See also, Theodore R. Schellenberg, "European Archival Practices in Arranging Records," National Archives, *Staff Circular,* No. 5 (July, 1939).

power of Prussia expanded so did the influence of its archival tradition. In addition to generous state support and a strong academic orientation, chief among the German archival contributions was the principle of provenance, or *Provenienzprinzip*. Formulated by Heinrich von Sybel and Max Lehmann, the principle rigorously insisted upon the retention or rearrangement of archives in the same order in which they were created. American archival practice has generally adopted not only the German principle of provenance but also reliance upon registers as guides to archival arrangement as well as abstracts of the individual documents.[3]

The third national tradition which has heavily influenced American archival practice is that of Great Britain. The British public records tradition dates well back into the Medieval period and was a secular application of chancery practices of the Catholic Church, but innovations in the form of "rolls," or abstracts of fiscal and administration documents, began to appear in the thirteenth century. Frequently, it was rolls rather than records that survived to become grist for the historian's mill.

The English institution of the rolls series, which satisfied the requirements of legal evidence and obviated the necessity of reference to original documents, postponed archival reform until well into the nineteenth century. In 1838 the pressure of historians and the national archival shame to which successive Parliamentary commissions had pointed finally resulted in the creation of the Public Records Office, which adopted a modified form of the principle of provenance as the basis of arrangement.[4] The English records tradition is reflected in America more in the creation of records than in their preservation as

---

[3] Schellenberg, *Modern Archives*, 173–174; Schellenberg, "European Practices," 7–8; Ernst Posner, "Max Lehmann and the Genesis of the Principle of Provenance," in *The Indian Archives*, 4:133–141 (July–December, 1950).

[4] Schellenberg, *Modern Archives*, 175–176; Schellenberg, "European Practices," 9–10; C. R. Cheney, *English Bishop's Chanceries, 1100–1250* (Manchester, England, 1950), vii–98; Henry G. T. Christopher, *Paleantology and Archives* (London, 1938), 160–175; Charles Johnson, *The Public Record Office* (London, 1918), 3–47; Charles F. Mullett, "The 'Better Reception, Preservation, and More Convenient Use' of Public Records of Eighteenth-Century England," in *American Archivist*, 27:195–218 (April, 1964); Charles Johnson, "The Public Record Office," in James Conway Davies, ed., *Studies Presented to Sir Hilary Jenkinson* (London, 1957), 178–195.

archives, and it may be traced most clearly at the state and local level rather than in the federal government.

EARLY FEDERAL ARCHIVAL DEVELOPMENT

DESPITE ample European experience as guidance, until the creation of the National Archives in 1933 the records of the government of the United States were in worse condition, were less accessible, and were less used than those of any comparable nation in the Western world. The condition of the archives of many of the American states in the nineteenth century put to shame those of the central government and stimulated historians to sponsor a number of abortive attempts at reform.

In 1789 Charles Thomson, secretary of the Confederation government, turned over all of the Continental and Confederation records in his care to the new administration, which placed them in the care of the new Department of Foreign Affairs (soon renamed the Department of State). When the War Department was subsequently created its organic act stipulated that military records of previous governments be entrusted to its care, and the same procedure was followed in the creation of the Treasury Department. Thus, an incipient national archives was frustrated at the very inception of the federal government. The Department of State retained possession of the nucleus of the national archives including such documents as the journal of the Continental Congress, diplomatic correspondence prior to 1789, and the priceless originals of the Declaration of Independence, Articles of Confederation, and the Constitution. Until 1903 these records shared the fortunes of the Department and formed the basis of its manuscripts library, from which has emerged the National Archives.[5]

In the first half of the nineteenth century the influence of such documentarians as Jared Sparks resulted in several projects for the publication of state papers and for the purchase of the private correspondence of the Founding Fathers—in lieu of the

---

[5] Carl L. Lokke, "The Continental Congress Papers: Their History, 1789-1952," in National Archives *Accessions*, No. 51 (June, 1954), 1-7.

establishment of a national archives. This collection and publication made selected portions of the national historical source
base more widely available and powerfully stimulated the national historical tradition; however, it also obscured the need for
a national archives organized along the best European lines.
In the latter half of the century the new professional historical
organizations and the expanding Library of Congress began to
agitate for the centralization and professionalization of the national archives. The Department of State and the federal bureaucracy systematically opposed the move as striking at their proprietary control of their own records.

Ironically, the federal government expended far more care
and money in the preservation of the archives of the Confederacy
than it spent on its own records in the nineteenth century. Immediately after the fall of Richmond in April, 1865, General
Order Number 60 directed all Union field commanders to forward to Washington all captured Confederate records of whatever nature. Secretary of War Edwin Stanton was especially interested in preserving this documentation in order to establish
a "war guilt" and to prove the suspected complicity of Jefferson
Davis in the assassination of President Lincoln. The collection
of Confederate records, popularly called the "Rebel Archives,"
consisted of over 400 boxes, hogsheads, and barrels and was entrusted, under armed guard, to the care of Professor Francis
Leiber and his staff. In sifting for evidence of "war crimes,"
the clerks organized the mass of papers according to the principle of provenance, thereby effecting a re-creation of the Confederate archives. In all probability, these records were the only
portion of those held by the federal government in the last
century which could qualify for the term "archives."[6]

The Civil War also occasioned another pioneering effort at
federal records management, the success of which probably delayed the establishment of a national archives. Following the
war thousands of pension applications flooded into the War Department, each claim requiring verification by reference to the

---

[6] Carl L. Lokke, "The Captured Confederate Records under Francis Leiber," in
American Archivist, 10:277–319 (October, 1946); Dallas Irvine, "The Archives
Office of the War Department: Repository of Captured Confederate Archives,
1868–1881," in *Military Affairs*, 10:93–111 (Spring, 1946).

numerous hospital rosters. Fred C. Ainsworth, a young army doctor heading the Record and Pension Division, broke the logjam by creating a name-index card file which abstracted the information contained in over 19,000 bound volumes of hospital records containing the medical records of over 7,000,000 Union veterans. Ainsworth worked hand-in-glove with the pension lobby to expand the concept of "carded records" to other archival series, relieving in an "unprofessional" but commonsense way a records problem of enormous proportions.[7]

After the Civil War all of the federal offices were cluttered with the records the war had generated, but there was no authority to dispose of the surplus paper. To the contrary, an act of February 26, 1853, made it a felony to destroy any federal record, and all of the urgent pleas from offices about to be swamped by their papers went unheeded by Congress until 1889. In that year Congress reluctantly granted the Postmaster General permission to dispose of the file of money-order applications which occupied most of the basement of the Postoffice Department building. Congress was fully aware of the magnitude of the records crisis in the federal bureaucracy, but rather than seeking a solution through the creation of a central archives, it experimented with makeshift forms of records control.[8]

The National Archives came into existence gradually, and it is difficult to assign a date to its establishment. The concept was well over 100 years old when it was realized, and precedents abroad were surely not lacking. But providing such cultural services at government expense seemed basically un-American, and the same fate befell the idea as had befallen John Quincy Adams' suggested national university. Nor was the government impressed with its own need for a better ordering of its records. As has been true of so many steps of cultural progress in America, only a self-interested group of sufficient potency could prod a lethargic government into action. The campaign was long and tedious.

---

[7] Mabel Deutrich, "Fred C. Ainsworth: The Story of a Vermont Archivist," in *Vermont History,* 27:22–33 (January, 1959); Siert F. Riepma, "A Soldier-Archivist and His Records: Major General Fred C. Ainsworth," in *American Archivist,* 4:178–187 (July, 1941).

[8] Harold T. Pinkett, "Investigations of Federal Record Keeping, 1882–1906," in *American Archivist,* 21:163–192 (April, 1958).

The first serious discussion of institutionalizing the federal archives was rooted in the need to provide storage for noncurrent records. The idea was put forward in the decades following the Civil War, and, with minor modifications, it was essentially the only program during the ensuing thirty years which sought to lift the archives out of their slough.

In 1877 President Rutherford B. Hayes sent to Congress a report regarding the security against fire of the federal buildings in Washington. This report raised the secondary question of the security of noncurrent records against destruction. The mass of papers was not only at risk, it was itself part of the fire hazard. To the natural suggestion that the noncurrent material be destroyed, the President reacted characteristically. "Every paper worthy at any time to be recorded and placed in the public files," he declared, "may be of value at some future time, either in a historical, biographical, or pecuniary way, to the citizen or the nation." Instead of destruction, the President recommended that federal buildings and noncurrent records be made more secure by the erection of a "fire-proof building of ample dimensions . . . for the accumulation of the archives of the government no longer required for constant use."[9] It is not clear what, if anything, the President had in mind beyond simple warehouse storage. In any event, his recommendations were received without action by Congress.

In 1878, following the report of President Hayes, the Secretary of War endorsed a proposal of the Quartermaster General for the construction of an inexpensive, fireproof hall of records—a warehouse for storing noncurrent army records but open as well to all other federal departments. A typically American solution to the problem of office crowding, the suggestion ignored entirely European archival experience. Had the proposal been approved by Congress, the opportunity of establishing an archives might have been lost, and it is entirely possible that the net result would have been only the centralization of inadequate care for the federal archives. Although the concept of a hall of records provided for ready access to the documents, any one of them

[9] G. Philip Bauer, "Public Archives in the United States," in William B. Hesseltine and Donald R. McNeil, eds., *In Support of Clio: Essays in Memory of Herbert A. Kellar* (Madison, 1958), 63–64.

being subject to recall, there was no provision for the essential ingredient of a professional archives establishment, a competent staff with legal as well as physical custody of the records under their control. Demonstrating a lack of awareness of larger implications, the recommendation was repeated for several years and received support on several occasions from the Secretary of the Treasury. It was found by Congress to be politically unpopular (rather than archivally unsound), and no other action was taken.[10]

Congress did not see fit to relieve the problem of records storage, and the mass of files continued to grow. Temporary solutions varied from department to agency, according to the available space and the character of the files, but no general solution was attempted prior to the passage of the first Records Disposal Act of 1889. That legislation, growing out of the Cockrell Commission Report, provided the first legal basis for the orderly disposal of certain classes of bulky and insignificant federal records. Under its provisions, such records series as the postal money order forms in the Post Office basement were nominated for destruction, subject to approval of a joint committee of Congress. This *ad hoc* procedure, coupled with the receptiveness of the new Library of Congress Manuscripts Division to receive federal records and individual documents of exceptional significance, drained off the pressure for a more complete solution of the records problems, until pressure was generated from outside the government.

Preliminary plans for a federal hall of records were drawn in the 1890's, and in 1903 a bill was finally enacted which authorized the purchase of a site and the construction of the building. President Theodore Roosevelt was interested in the project, but, just as all seemed to augur well for its success, Congress began to lose interest. Speculation by a group of Washington real estate operators inflated the cost of the proposed site and cast an unsavory pall over the entire project in the minds of some members of Congress. As Senator Elihu Root said years later, "Nobody seemed to take interest enough in the subject to have the building put up after the land was bought." The lack of

[10] *Ibid.,* 64–65.

interest was not quite as general as it might have seemed, however. Lathrop Withington, a most remarkable private citizen of Newburyport, Massachusetts, took upon himself the personal task of seeing that the United States endowed itself with a proper agency for its archives. He prevailed upon Senator Henry Cabot Lodge to introduce a bill modeled after the organic act of the British Public Records Office. The legislation would have converted the still-pending and rather modest hall of records into a fully independent and institutional national archives. Unfortunately, the bill was sealed in committee by Senator George P. Wetmore of Rhode Island, out of deference to Ainsworth R. Spofford, for years head of the Library of Congress and then head of its Manuscript Division. Spofford, according to Withington, had a "mania for retaining in his hand a monopoly of all literary matters in Washington." Spofford's services in the development of the Library of Congress into a national research library had been great, but there was some truth in Withington's charge. In any event, Spofford had powerful friends in Congress, he was opposed to any agency which might weaken his beloved library, and Withington's plans were lost with him when the *Lusitania* went down.[11]

Withington may have been somewhat premature in his plan for a national archival institution, for Congress was as yet only reluctantly committed to the idea of warehouse storage for non-current records, and even that idea lacked implementation. Into the breach stepped another memorable propagandist, J. Franklin Jameson, and he brought with him the concerted support and professional prestige of the American Historical Association. Educated at Harvard and Amherst and the recipient of the first doctorate in history from Johns Hopkins, Jameson had created a solid reputation as a professor at Brown University. He had developed an interest in the federal records as a rich primary source as early as his graduate days in Baltimore, and he longed for a chance to devote his full time to promulgating and popularizing their use. His opportunity developed in 1905, when he was called to Washington to become director of the

[11] Fred Shelley, "The Interest of J. Franklin Jameson in the National Archives, 1908–1934," in *American Archivist*, 12:99–130 (April, 1949).

Department of Historical Research of the Carnegie Institution. For the next quarter of a century Jameson, more than any other single individual, became the moving force in the establishment of a national archives.[12]

In his new position, and with the benefit of his friends and colleagues through his executive leadership of the American Historical Association, Jameson was in an especially favorable position to direct and lead the campaign for the fulfillment of the congressional promise of a records building. He concentrated first on the building itself, calling it an archives, a hall of records, or whatever Congress would agree to build, believing that once the physical plant was constructed, professional guidance could determine its operational character. Jameson opened the long campaign in 1908 by drafting a statement on the numerous legislative and executive recommendations which had been made regarding a records building over the past thirty years, and he submitted his own survey of space requirements for the building. Secretary of the Treasury George B. Cortelyou followed the precedent of his predecessors in expressing the greatest support for the project within the Cabinet, and, through Cortelyou, Jameson made a strong appeal for a congressional appropriation in the 1910 annual message of the President. Jameson's plans were outlined in a letter to Charles D. Norton, secretary to President William Howard Taft, in November, 1910. His immediate goal was "the thin edge of the wedge, by providing at first simply a proper archive *building*, into which departments might turn all papers which they were content to regard as not needed in their own buildings, and in which papers might be held as deposits, subject to regulations framed by the department, with respect to storage and accessibility to officials and the public."[13] It seems perfectly clear that Jameson's plans involved a bit of purposeful deception. He would seek merely a building and, once transfer had occurred, a proper archives, such as those in which his Carnegie agents toiled in Europe, would be led into being. At his urging the Americal Historical Association formally approved Jameson's plan for the hall of

[12] Waldo G. Leland, "John Franklin Jameson," in *American Archivist*, 19:195–202 (July, 1956).
[13] Shelley, "J. Franklin Jameson," 106–107.

records and appointed a committee to press the issue. In addition to Jameson, the committee consisted of John B. McMaster and Admiral Alfred T. Mahan.[14]

The occasion of the AHA convention in New York in 1909 and the tenth anniversary of the establishment of the Public Archives Commission were seized as an opportunity to generate support for the construction of an archives building in Washington. The Public Archives Commission had been created to bring pressure for reform of the archives of the various states, and it had met with fair success, especially in a number of southern states. Now its views would be raised to the broader federal horizon.[15] A memorial documenting the long history of congressional and executive concern with the matter was addresssed to both houses of Congress. Since 1881 no less than forty-two archives bills had been introduced, and Congress appeared to be delaying implementation of a principle it had previously approved. Speeches of Congressmen and Senators began to echo the impatience of the nation's historians.[16] In true professional style, the historians commissioned and circulated a documented article describing the frustrating history of the archives movement.[17]

The program of "education" by Jameson and the AHA began to convert a number of influential Congressmen, who became as much interested in the details of the proposed building as in construction of any building. Sidestepping the idea of a memorial and still operating on the premise that a plain, large building would be most flexible for its ultimate purpose, Jameson received the support of Senators George P. Wetmore and Miles Poindexter and drafted for them H.R. 11850, introduced by Representative Morris Sheppard of Texas in 1911. The bill directed the Secretary of the Treasury to prepare plans and

[14] *Ibid.,* 105–106.
[15] Waldo G. Leland, "The First Conference of Archivists, December, 1909: The Beginnings of a Profession," in *American Archivist,* 13:109–120 (April, 1950).
[16] Shelley, "J. Franklin Jameson," 108–109; R. D. W. Connor, "Our National Archives," *Minnesota History,* 17:1–19 (March, 1936).
[17] Written by Charles O. Paullin and entitled "History of the Movement for a National Archives Building in Washington, D.C.," the article was printed in the *Congressional Record,* vol. 53, part 14 (appendix), pp. 1116–1119 (1916). It was later reprinted as 62 Cong., 2 sess., *Senate Documents,* vol. XXVI, no. 297.

costs estimates for an archives building, essentially a hall of
records, of 1,500,000 cubic feet, expandable to 4,000,000 cubic
feet, shaped as a solid cube with no light wells, requiring a total
area of about 40,000 square feet.[18] President Taft endorsed the
proposal in a message of February 2, 1912, and a receptive Congress incorporated the idea in the Public Building Act of 1913.
By this legislation, approval was given to the principle of the
building and to the plans sketched by Jameson, but no appropriation was made for construction.[19] Before new pressure could
be applied to Congress, the greater emergency of World War I
diverted the attention of all parties. The hostilities in Europe
delayed the prior inspection of European archival establishments
which had been stipulated in the Public Building Act of 1913
as necessary before construction could be undertaken.

While the nation's historians continued to support the proposed construction of a hall of records, under Jameson's leadership they increasingly referred to the project as the national
archives building. This subtle shift in phraseology was indicative of a deliberate shift in concept, from that of a warehouse
storage of noncurrent records to a central archival agency after
the European model, having both legal and physical custody
of the archives of the federal government. Jameson apparently
conceived the distinction as one of degree, which could be
bridged by the slow but inexorable process of bureaucratic evolution. A hall of records might be constructed, but from about
1912 on, so far as Jameson was concerned, it was the national
archives which would occupy the building. To popularize the
new concept he engaged in a lobbying campaign remarkably
similar to that which ultimately brought the physical building
to reality. In short order Jameson secured the invaluable support of such patriotic organizations as the Sons of the American
Revolution and the Daughters of the American Revolution.[20]

Under the leadership of Jameson, the AHA took the lead
in expressing its concern for the institutional character of the
agency which would ultimately care for the federal archives.
As early as 1909 Waldo G. Leland presented a paper entitled

[18] Shelley, "J. Franklin Jameson," 109–110.
[19] *Ibid.*, 111–112.
[20] *Ibid.*, 112–113.

"American Archival Problems" which recommended the adoption of the principle of provenance as the only feasible scheme
of archival management of federal records whenever they might
be institutionalized. The point was reiterated and expanded
in 1912 in a subsequent paper entitled "The National Archives:
A Programme." The latter article was given wide circulation
as a Senate Document in 1915, so that it may be said federal
archival principles were well established long before the institution took form.[21]

Jameson and the AHA were not timid in pressing the archival
concept in Congress while simultaneously lobbying for a records
library. As early as December, 1906, they had introduced a
Senate bill providing for the creation of a "Board of Records
Commissioners," which would have sole legal custody of all
federal records over eighty years old. After surveying and appraising these older records, the commissioners would transfer
that portion selected for permanent preservation to the "national
archives," where they would be cared for by a professional
archival staff. The bill also provided for the recruitment of
ancient state records into the national archives.[22] Such a radical
proposal ran counter to the vested interests of the government
clerks in their files, who found ways to communicate their opposition to Congress, blocking any legislation in that direction.
If any centralization of the government's records were to be
undertaken, the executive departments reluctantly favored a
hall of records in which they would retain at least legal title
to their transferred records.[23]

The expressed concern of American historians for the establishment of a national archives was accomplished primarily
through the Public Archives Commission of the AHA, created
in 1900. In its early years, the commission concentrated almost
exclusively on state archives, but by 1909 it began to exert its
influence upon the national scene as well. Headed by such
leaders as Herman V. Ames, Jameson, Victor Hugo Paltsits,
Gaillard Hunt, and Waldo G. Leland, it preached the gospel

[21] Schellenberg, *Modern Archives*, 181–182.
[22] Bauer, "Public Archives," in Hesseltine and McNeil, eds., *Clio*, 67–68.
[23] Robert H. Bahmer, "The National Archives After Twenty Years," in *American Archivist*, 18:195–205 (July, 1955).

of provenance and the cultural necessity of a national archives. It slowly but effectively succeeded in overcoming the hostility of the civil service and the Library of Congress to the creation of a potential rival.[24]

The Annual Conference of Archivists was not held in 1915. Instead, a session was planned in conjunction with the AHA, meeting in Washington for purposes of stimulating a drive for a national archives. Senator Poindexter, a friend of the movement, presided over a session attended by over 400 delegates at the Continental Memorial Hall.[25] The session resulted in the usual flood of memorials and petitions to Congress, and the cause was given additional urgency by a report in the same year of the fire marshal of the District of Columbia. His report called attention to the total of 250 fires in the government buildings in Washington in the years between 1873 and 1915.[26]

Another spectacular fire in 1921 in the Census Office did as much as anything to revive the interest of the nation in archives following the war, and Jameson soon found himself commanding the powerful support of economists, political scientists, and the American Legion. In 1923 the Hearst papers joined the crusade, and finally President Calvin Coolidge was moved to recommend anew the construction of an archives building. The building was incorporated in the Public Buildings Act of 1926, an omnibus act aimed at filling in the federal triangle along Pennsylvania Avenue. By the Act a building commission was directed to fix the priority of construction of several needed office buildings, assign sites, and supervise preparation of the plans.[27]

The congressional building commission was committed to assigning a high priority to the archives building. To aid it in its many decisions, the commission appointed an advisory committee, of which Jameson was the most active and influential

[24] For a discussion of these points see Bauer, "Public Archives," in Hesseltine and McNeil, eds., *Clio,* 65–66; Charles M. Andrews, "Archives," in American Historical Association *Annual Report* of 1913, 262–263; Shelley, "J. Franklin Jameson," 102–103; Dunbar Rowland, "The Adaptation of Archives to Public Use," in AHA *Annual Report* of 1912, 269–273; and Worthington C. Ford, "Manuscripts and Historical Archives," in AHA *Annual Report* of 1913, I:78–79.

[25] Victor H. Paltsits, "An Historical Résumé of the Public Archives Commission from 1899 to 1921," in AHA *Annual Report* of 1922, I.157.

[26] Connor, "National Archives," 17–19.

[27] Bahmer, "National Archives," 196–197; Shelley, "J. Franklin Jameson," 119–120.

member. Before a site could be determined and plans could be drawn, the approximate size had to be determined, as the increment of records during the recent war had thrown all previous calculations into error. When the suggestion was advanced of two buildings, a hall of records for semi-current and an archives for older records, Jameson was the first to squelch the idea. Instead, he argued for one building of approximately 3,000,000 cubic feet, which could be expanded. Such a building would permit the inevitable accession of all older records, plus a selective and progressive transfer of a portion of more recent ones, providing space in the national archives for about thirty years.[28]

Jameson's inventory of federal records revealed that approximately 108,000 cubic feet of records prior to 1861 existed and should be retained complete. Another 923,000 cubic feet of records, part of which should be retained, existed from the period 1861 to 1916; another staggering 2,500,000 cubic feet of paper had been created since 1917. With proper selection this total mass should be reducible to 3,000,000 cubic feet to be accessioned over thirty years. Therefore, it was conceived that the new federal archives building would be full by about 1960 with records created up to 1930.[29]

The original site allotted the building was the same which had been previously advanced, the block bounded by Twelfth, Thirteenth, B, and C streets. The claims of the Commerce Department to that site proved too strong, however, and a second block had to be considered, that bounded by Ninth, Tenth, B Street, and Pennsylvania Avenue. The fact that the square lay almost in the bed of a little stream and that it presented no opportunity for future expansion gave pause to some of the partisans, but Jameson counseled them to accept the site in good grace.[30]

With the size and site established, the architect proceeded to draft a building unique to Washington. Pre-eminently a permanent building for a highly specialized purpose, yet not a library, the design took on monumental proportions. Within a classic exterior, the latest, most scientific devices were incor-

---

[28] Bahmer, "National Archives," 196–197.
[29] Shelley, "J. Franklin Jameson," 125–126.
[30] Ibid., 121–122.

porated. Each stack was a sealed room, accessible only to the staff. The building was well protected against fire and was air-conditioned ("re-conditioned") throughout. The cornerstone for this temple of history, which would cost the nation over $12,000,000, was laid by President Herbert Hoover on February 20, 1933.[31]

Once the physical building of the archives was under way, the advisory committee under Jameson turned its attention to problems of the legal powers and duties of the institution in order that the national archives should be in a position to begin operation immediately upon completion of the building. A hastily drawn bill (H.R. 8910) was introduced by Representative Sol Bloom of New York; with modification, it became the National Archives Act of 1934. The Act placed the direction of the new archival agency in the hands of an archivist appointed by the President (with the consent of the Senate), and it placed the agency outside the jurisdiction of any government department, answerable only to the President and to Congress, thus giving it the greatest possible independence to serve all three branches of the federal government. That the act escaped the mire of partisan politics and that the initial appointment of R. D. W. Connor set a high professional level was, in large measure, a reflection of the personal interest of President Franklin Delano Roosevelt in the new agency.[32]

The appointment of R. D. W. Connor as the first Archivist of the United States was a particularly fortunate choice. A native of North Carolina and educated at the state university, Connor had been instrumental as a young man in forming the North Carolina Historical Commission. As its secretary for many years, he knew firsthand how to walk the tightrope of an academic career in the service of a state. As leader of an outstanding state archival establishment, he had played an active role in bringing the need for a national archives before Congress. He was nominated for the national post by the AHA, and, as a sound scholar and a Southern Democrat, he typified a part of the brain trust which the New Deal recruited and called to

[31] Connor, "National Archives," 16–19.
[32] Shelley, "J. Franklin Jameson," 128–129; Ernst Posner, "The National Archives and the Archival Theorist," in *American Archivist*, 18:207–216 (April, 1955).

Washington.[33] After many years of frustration and false starts, the national archives was off to a most auspicious beginning.

OPERATION OF THE NATIONAL ARCHIVES

THE NATIONAL ARCHIVES was the coddled infant of the federal administration when it began operation in 1934, and the extra care and attention given it resulted in rapid and sound growth in an indigenously American pattern. For better or for worse, few European precedents for organization and operation were imported, the agency working out its own solutions. Its achievements in the short years since 1934 have been truly impressive, and the eclectic path of its development has placed it among the most respected of such institutions in the world. In the course of its struggle to produce a peculiarly American solution to the federal archival problem, it has evolved a workable balance between providing efficient service to the government while vastly enlarging the opportunity for private research. In fact, the very availability of materials in the National Archives has changed the character of American historiography, and even greater changes are foreseen. In its service to the federal departments, the National Archives has played an increasingly significant role in the creation and management of the federal records, mediating between current administrative practices and the future needs of history.

Before the National Archives could begin to accession any records, it had to make an exhaustive inventory of what was available for transfer in terms of the volume and complexity of the existing records. Furthermore, it had to develop an understanding of the character of the federal files of records, for, until it proved itself, the various departments would remain suspicious of its power and jealous of their records. The legal powers conferred by Congress on the National Archives would be meaningless unless the agency could prove its ability and usefulness.

The federal records in 1934 were still being produced and

---

[33] Waldo G. Leland, "R. D. W. Connor, First Archivist of the United States," in *American Archivist*, 21:277–303 (July, 1958).

maintained under recommendations of the last inquiry into records practices, the Taft Commission of 1910. This most recent layer of federal records, by far more voluminous than all the earlier records combined, rather than being folded was now being filed flat or in vertical folders. Both outgoing and incoming letters were being filed by self-indexing subject classification, a decimal-subject being in general use. Loose-filed carbon copies had replaced the bound volumes of press copies of outgoing correspondence, and the practice of abstracting correspondence in registry volumes had been discontinued. In short, the government's record practices approximated those which private business had found to be most efficient at the least expense.[34]

An inventory of records was the first major project in opening the National Archives. A corps of deputy records examiners worked its way through the various departments and agencies in Washington; a WPA project known as the Survey of Federal Archives Outside of Washington (SFA) made a parallel study of federal records in the field. On the basis of these actual inventories and appraisals, negotiations were undertaken with the departments involved for the selective transfer of record groups to the new archival establishment.[35]

While federal records were being recruited from their cellar and attic files, Archivist Connor and his small staff were studying the problem of organizing the agency for maintaining and servicing these growing collections. The principal issues to be resolved were the arrangement and description of the archives, the development of organization policy, the creation of a finding-aids system, and the development of policies governing use.

Arrangement and description was inevitably based upon the long-established principle of provenance, but, in contrast with European practices, the National Archives would be dealing with records series produced by agencies still functioning. More than archival theory demanded that the records be kept in the order produced. What, then, would be regarded as the "record unit," into which the total accumulation would be divided?

[34] Bess Glenn, "The Taft Commission and the Government's Record Practices," in *American Archivist*, 21:277–303 (July, 1958).
[35] Bauer, "Public Archives," in Hesseltine and McNeil, eds., *Clio*, 68–69.

An arbitrary decision was ultimately made, with due regard for the principle of provenance and the estimated size of types of records, to organize the archives primarily according to record groups, each group generally containing the records of a federal bureau or its equivalent. Within record groups, the material would be left in records series, in the form and order produced. The form varied from files by subject matter, to case histories, to files of material of physical uniformity. Series, in turn, were recognized as comprising file units, bound volumes, folders, dossiers, individual documents, and the like.[36] Record groups were assigned serial numbers, generally coinciding with the order of acquisition of such material by the National Archives. By 1950 the number of record groups had grown to 266.[37]

The rate of acquisition was slow at first, but by July, 1938, documents were arriving at the rate of 50,000 cubic feet per year, taxing the capacity of the archives staff to process them. As the inflow of records warranted, the holdings were divided into several divisions such as foreign affairs, defense, and labor. The tasks of disposal, classification, cataloging, and reference were centralized in functional units. The resulting duplication of effort and overlapping of responsibility gradually diminished, however, as the several deputy archivists, with general policy outlines, assumed semi-autonomous control of the records groups under their supervision.[38]

The war threat of 1940 brought new awareness of the need to safeguard the nation's archives. The consequent increase in

---

[36] Schellenberg, *Modern Archives,* 180–181.

[37] U. S. National Archives, *Your Government's Records in the National Archives* (Publication 51-4), (Washington, 1950). As an example of the organization and description of the archival holdings, the archives of the State Department are divided into two record groups: RG 59, General Records of the Department of State, and RG 84, Records of Foreign Service Posts. RG 59 is largely composed of diplomatic correspondence exchanged in Washington with foreign powers, and includes about 14,000 cubic feet of papers. RG 84 is the internal body of State Department paper, largely letters of instructions and reports to and from the foreign service staff. It contains about 26,000 cubic feet (figures of 1950). Component record series within RG 59 embrace the chronological sequence of diplomatic exchanges with the various national powers, retaining the order and form of the creation of the files in the State Department. See also, Schellenberg, *Modern Archives,* 179ff.

[38] Wayne C. Grover, "Federal Government Archives," in *Library Trends,* 5:390–401 (January, 1957).

size and rate of deposits, plus the enormous expansion of the government's records during the war emergency, resulted in an accelerated schedule of filling the archives building. By 1946 the building was over three-fourths full, occupied mainly by records of the expiring temporary agencies of World War II, for which the National Archives was the only trustee, and by general archives over fifty years old.[39]

The finding-aids program of the National Archives early became a necessity. The mass of records, even if self-indexing, lacked guides to the general groups and series likely to contain information being sought by the scholar. Registration sheets were prepared as records first arrived at the National Archives. In two pages or less of description, a historical survey of the role and function of the agency creating the records was presented, together with inclusive dates and an indication of relationship with other existing record groups. Secondly, preliminary inventories, indicating the agencies' own imposed order in the component record series, were published on a continuing basis. By 1956 over 100 such inventories had been produced, and others were projected. Lastly, special aids were occasionally produced. These aids represent the only attempt to index pertinent research material by name, place, and subject. Two large, ambitious guides have been produced relating to material on Latin America and on material of interest to genealogical research.[40]

From its founding the National Archives has followed the most liberal policy of access and use consistent with its dual functions of service to the government and service to the greatest number of researchers and investigators. Any restrictions placed upon record series are imposed at the time of accession and are mutually agreeable to the contributing agency and the archives staff. All such restrictions are scheduled to expire at some definite time, all subject to a general rule that nothing shall remain restricted beyond fifty years unless the Archivist specifically determines that the national interest demands it. The soundest justification for restricted access to archives is the

[39] Bauer, "Public Archives," in Hesseltine and McNeil, eds., *Clio*, 69.
[40] *Ibid.*, 68–70; Grover, "Federal Government Archives," 394–395.

possibility of compromising the military security of the nation, although military documents are generally not transferred to the Archives until they have been declassified. A second sensitive category is the documents of diplomacy, for good relations between nations are facilitated, even in the modern era, by preserving the privilege of private communication. The time limit imposed by tradition upon the privileged documents of the State Department is generally twenty-five years, but the fortunes of diplomacy often make possible the earlier clearing of restrictions. A third category of restricted information contained in the federal archives is that relating to business and finance. Public disclosure of some of the information collected from business firms for statistical purposes by the government might undermine the very foundation of the competitive enterprise system. In recognition of this possibility, access to confidential information filed with an agency of the government was restricted by the Federal Reports Act of 1942 to those other agencies with statutory authority to require the same information. Such confidential information as is contained in income tax returns of individuals and corporations, therefore, is indefinitely restricted and is not available to public inspection even if transferred to the Archives. Similarly, that category of personal information which the government requires to be furnished (or which it creates), as in the case of raw census returns, records of military and government service, medical records, etc., is regarded as confidential, not to be made available to public inspection during the lifetime of the subject. An exception to the rule of personal privacy are those records relating to the official conduct of public officials who are accountable to the public in the discharge of their duties.[41]

That body of archives which is available to the public is accessible for public or private use, for any legal purpose without discrimination. Any document open to use may be called to the search room for examination under such supervision as will protect its physical and moral integrity. If special circumstances warrant, as in consulting a bulky volume of records, a researcher may be admitted to the stack area for a direct search. Loan

[41] Schellenberg, *Modern Archives,* 225–230.

of documents is rare and is limited to government agencies and to established private research institutions, and then only upon conditions which will guarantee the safety of the records. The necessity for a loan of documents can generally be avoided by taking advantage of the wide range of reproduction services available at the National Archives. These services are available to government agencies free on demand and to all others at cost. The informational services of the Archives staff are quite extensive, providing information *about* the records rather than making them available. This service is willingly extended within the limitations of staff time and in relation to the seriousness of the project which poses the question but is denied when the requested information is already in published form or when it requires special research.[42]

The halcyon days of the New Deal provided the proper climate for the rapid growth of the National Archives, but the growth was largely quantitative rather than qualitative. The personal interest of the President, the active encouragement of the historical profession, and the increasing respect of Congress and the federal hierarchy combined to overcome many of the problems with which older archival establishments were still struggling. Soon after the archives building was completed and long before more space was actually needed, the projected expansion in the inner court was completed as a PWA project. All these factors plus the accelerated transfer of records, however, failed to alter the essential character of the archives. The institution remained true to its original concept until forced to come to grips with the records problems of World War II. This development and the attendant changes in the structure and character of the federal government have done much to alter the concept and functions of the National Archives.

American archivists were ill-prepared for war in 1941, never having been forced to face anything more serious than the biennial battle for appropriations. With the cultural stability of the world threatened, many archivists reappraised the materials under their charge as being so ill-organized and ill-cataloged as to be incapable of withstanding the shock of dislocation. In

---

[42] *Ibid.*, 231.

1940 the National Archives and the Society of American Archivists established a committee to advise agencies on the procedures for protection of archives from war hazards, but the external and temporary threat of war pointed up the more general inadequacies of American archival economy. The National Archives staff was hard pressed to handle reference requests from other government agencies who, in their frenzied efforts to discover the successful precedents and solutions of every problem in World War I, quadrupled the number of such requests. And the mountain of paper generated during the war presented the National Archives with the essentially new problem of records in the mass. The agency was forced to develop an archivally anomalistic concept of *destroying* portions of records in order to cope with the surviving portion. It is highly significant that 1945 marked the publication by the National Archives of a manual entitled, *How to Dispose of Records: A Manual for Federal Offices.*[43] The National Archives and the archival profession in America had entered a new stage of development.

The boom in production of federal records brought the National Archives into a new phase of its operation and service, that of records management. For purposes of discussion, "records management" may be defined as the process of selectively reducing to manageable proportions the bulk of records indigenous to modern civilization in such a way as permanently to preserve those of future cultural value without impairing the substantive integrity of the mass for purposes of research. Fortunately, the crisis which produced the problem also provided some experience in its solution. Many staff members of the National Archives, given wartime assignments to records sections of temporary agencies, developed programs of records disposal at the end of the war, certain that the National Archives could not house and maintain the paper mountain which they had seen building.

Since records are grist for the archivist's mill, his concern for the circumstances of their production is a legitimate one. It has been suggested that the study of the methods and tech-

---

[43] Philip C. Brooks, "Archives in the United States During World War II, 1939–1945," in *Library Quarterly,* 17:263–280 (October, 1947).

niques of modern file rooms is the modern equivalent of the science of diplomatics. Theoretical considerations aside, the practical problem of bulk in modern records makes inevitable the archival concern in their creation, else archivists are in danger of being hoisted with their own petard. In addition, the professional archivist is the one career officer of the government best able to make a meaningful appraisal of the secondary values in archives and thereby to protect the interests of the future historian.

It would seem that the frightening rate of records production has altered the National Archives from a records-keeping to a records-destroying agency. The historian is properly unimpressed with figures in justification of destruction of documentation, but consideration of these figures does lead to some sober thoughts about the capacity and the willingness of the nation to care for its records. Each year the government produces about four times the record capacity of the present Archives building, or about 4,000,000 cubic feet, and about 30 per cent is currently scheduled for permanent preservation. Even if only 20 per cent of the current yearly production of 4,000,000 cubic feet were saved, the residue would still amount to 800,000 cubic feet, quite a staggering volume. If the bulk were reduced to the minimum storage requirement by microfilm, consider the costs. At $15.00 per cubic foot, the yearly microfilm bill would amount to $12,000,000. If only one per cent of the current records production were saved, the yearly microfilming bill would still amount to $600,000, and the accumulation of microfilm alone would fill an archives building every 25 years![44]

The problem of federal paper had already attracted the attention of the National Archives before it was attacked more directly and externally by the first Hoover Commission in 1947. It is improbable, however, that the National Archives could have effectively adopted and implemented policies without the bipartisan and prestigious leadership of the commission.

Early in its existence, the Hoover Commission undertook a study of the management of federal records. Recognizing the special problems inherent in the question and aware of the self-

[44] Grover, "Federal Government Archives," 100–101.

proclaimed successes of records programs in certain private businesses, the commission contracted with the National Records
Management Council to provide a task force headed by Emmett
J. Leahy. Stripped to its bare essentials, the report submitted
in October, 1948, factually observed that current records of the
federal government constituted 18,500,000 cubic feet and cost
more than $1,200,000,000 annually to make and keep. The
reduction of that staggering sum appeared a tactical objective
for the commission, and the Leahy task force made three speci
fic recommendations: the creation of a Federal Records Bureau
embracing all record-keeping and record-management functions
of the government; the enactment of a Record Management
Act giving authority for the creation, preservation, management,
and disposal of records; and the appointment of records management officials for each department or agency to implement a
records program under a new Federal Records Administration.[45]
The commission accepted and endorsed the report in principle,
going one step farther and recommending the creation of a
Records Management Bureau within the newly proposed Office
of General Services. It is significant to note that the commission's solution of centralization was in direct contrast to the
decentralization urged in all other cases.[46] The National Archives protested its subjugation to another executive department as well as the proposed fragmentation into separate divisions of its former and new functions. Congress was in a re-
forming mood, however, and the recommendations of the Hoover Commission were made law in 1949 over the objections of
the National Archives.

The reorganization through the new Division of Records
Management re-emphasized the management of current records
by promulgating the requirement that all operating federal departments and agencies schedule the retention and eventual destruction or retirement of their current records. With various
time stipulations, these schedules divided the current records
of the government into three classes: those to be retained permanently; those to be preserved for a definite period of time

---

[45] Robert W. Krauskopf, "The Hoover Commission and Federal Record Keeping,"
in *American Archivist*, 21:371–400 (October, 1949).
[46] *Ibid.*

and judged then to be of no further value for research; and those to be destroyed within a relatively short time. A large percentage of federal records fell into the second category, and a new concept (as "new" as the hall of records) was conceived to provide storage for these intermediate records. Under the supervision of the Records Management Division, regional record centers were established in Boston, New York, Washington, Atlanta, Chicago, Fort Worth, Denver, and San Francisco, supplemented by a specialized center in St. Louis for personnel records of separated federal employees. Additional General Services Administration depositories were established in Kansas City and Seattle for disestablished federal agencies. These, too, were designated to become records centers when funds became available. The centers have been established mainly in metal warehouses, and they have been a real savings to the government. Annual reference to the records in all the centers amounts to about 334,000 calls on a total of 1,500,000 cubic feet of records.[47] A system of records schedules and records centers having been virtually completed, the Division of Records Management next turned its attention to developing and implementing greater economy and efficiency in the creation and maintenance of current records.[48]

The Administrative Services Act of 1949 broadened the scope and functions of the archival service at the expense of the National Archives' independence from other executive departments. The Act created the National Archives and Records Service within the General Service Administration, which consolidated all government housekeeping functions. The reorganized Archives and Records Service was comprised of the National Archives, the Federal Register, the Roosevelt Library, and the Records Management Division as coordinate divisions. What the archives staff considered to be unnecessary fragmentation and subjugation of its functions was partially corrected in 1950 with the passage of the Federal Records Act, which established procedures for the creation, maintenance, and retirement of

---

[47] Herbert E. Angel, "Federal Records Management Since the Hoover Commission Report," in *American Archivist*, 16:13–26 (January, 1953); Krauskopf, "Hoover Commission," 383.

[48] Grover, "Federal Government Archives," 394–395.

federal records. Despite delegation of authority and administrative accommodation of the law, the National Archives has neither lost its identity nor sense of archival purpose by having its duties broadened to include those of records management.[49]

The archival act of 1949 established the Franklin D. Roosevelt Library as a coordinate division of the archives system, but the Library had come into being several years prior and had been operating under the supervision of the National Archives for some time. In 1938 President Roosevelt, apparently planning retirement from office in 1941, revealed his plan to dedicate his personal and presidential papers to the federal government. His action was the first and a praiseworthy break in the tradition established in 1789 that presidential papers were personal property, to be disposed of without regard to their significance to future historiography. Some questions were raised regarding the propriety of a separate establishment to house the documents, as many former presidents had found the facilities of the Library of Congress adequate to care for their collections. Roosevelt's interest was deep, and he persevered in his intention, conceiving the shape, design, and contents of the building to be erected on land donated at his Hyde Park estate. A national committee was appointed to raise the needed funds for the building and equipment, a total of about $367,000. Title to the site was transferred to the government, accepted by Congress, and placed under the charge of the National Archives. All during World War II the President gradually transferred his papers and mementos, but the task of separating private from official papers had not been completed at his death. By the terms of a memorandum, Samuel Rosenman and Grace Tully oversaw the completion of the task by employees of the National Archives.[50] The first presidential library was thus created and placed under the care of the National Archives, establishing a precedent for succeeding libraries.

The second presidential library was a short time in materializing, thanks to the special interest of President Harry S. Truman in history, albeit largely of the personal or biographical

---

[49] Krauskopf, "Hoover Commission," 383.
[50] Waldo G. Leland, "The Creation of the Franklin D. Roosevelt Library: A Personal Narrative," in *American Archivist*, 18:11–29 (January, 1955).

variety. The Truman Administration in slightly less than eight years generated 1,600 file drawers of correspondence and records in the White House, plus countless mementos. To protect the independence of the executive offices and the confidences involved in much of the correspondence, President Truman determined to take his papers with him, but the financial burden would have been too great for him to bear personally. The solution was the creation of the Harry S. Truman Library at Independence, Missouri, patterned after the Roosevelt Library, to house the papers of the President and his closest political associates. Under the provisions of an Act of August 12, 1955, the Truman Library was accepted by the government for care and supervision on a basis similar to that of the Roosevelt Library, with the provision that similar presidential libraries in the future could automatically be accepted for supervision by the government.[51] It is reasonable to expect a chain of such libraries to be developed across the country, the next links being the Eisenhower Library at Abilene, the Hoover Library at West Branch, the Kennedy Library at Harvard University, and the Johnson Library at the University of Texas.

The Roosevelt Library, and to an even greater extent the Truman Library, has caused many scholars to question the propriety of such separate establishments. Such dispersal of research material certainly makes for inconvenience even in the age of air travel, and such decentralization is undoubtedly more expensive than if presidential papers were centralized at public expense. Criticism has also been advanced that the libraries are conceived as much as personal memorials as workshops for scholars, and that their collateral purpose as tourist museums is incompatible with the functions of archival institutions. All these points have some validity, but those who express such criticisms may assume too great a proprietorship in what law and custom recognize as essentially private property. Former presidents are pulled in many different directions by considerations affecting their records. Generally they themselves desire to have continuing access to the papers, using their files as a

[51] David D. Lloyd, "The Harry S. Truman Library," in *American Archivist,* 18:99–110 (April, 1955); Richard S. Kirkendall, "A Second Look at Presidential Libraries," in *American Archivist,* 29:371–386 (July, 1966).

ready reference with which to defend themselves from political attacks. Their wish that the truth about their administration be publicized demands that their files be opened as freely and as promptly as is consistent with their obligations to their correspondents. These considerations seem to have been placed in equitable balance in the concept of presidential libraries under the care of the National Archives, but the justification of separate and permanent institutions appears yet to be established on the grounds of scholarly use and interest.

The Korean War launched the federal government on a new spiral of bureaucratic growth. A second Hoover Commission was accordingly established by Congress in 1953 to cut the government back to smaller size. As a part of its inquiry into the practices and organization of the government, the commission proposed a new investigation into the creation and maintenance of federal records, and Emmett J. Leahy was appointed to conduct the work. This time the area of inquiry was "Paperwork Management," a phrase coined to indicate a broader concern than the mere storage and disposal of records as included in the term records management. The Leahy committee recommended a new Paperwork Management Service entirely separate from the National Archives to simplify the form and reduce the volume of federal records. The commission again endorsed the principles of the report, but the President in 1955 declined to seek legislation to implement the committee's recommendations. Instead, he requested all federal departments to comply with its spirit, and, when Congress restored the National Archives to independent status in November, 1956, he reassigned the functions of record management to that agency. Insofar as possible, agency record offices were assigned the paperwork management functions contemplated in the Leahy request, and a new office manual, *Plain Letters and Form Letters*, was issued by the National Archives. A supplementary report of the Hoover Commission, aimed at reducing the paperwork required by the government of its citizens, was assigned to the Budget Bureau for implementation in the approval of forms.[52]

[52] Krauskopf, "Hoover Commission," 386.

The National Historical Publication Commission, long advocated by the American Historical Association, was provided for in the National Archives Act of 1934, but the commission did not become active until 1950. Its primary function has been to encourage the publication of useful historical works, especially source material. It has also assumed direction of the useful bibliographical text, *Writings in American History*, and in 1961 it published a guide to manuscript depositories in the United States, both archival and manuscript. It also proudly sponsored, under the editorship of Clarence E. Carter, the selection and publication of *The Territorial Papers of the United States*. An impressive publication program through microfilm was also quietly developed through the years at the National Archives. More than 7,000 rolls containing more than 5,000,000 pages of documents have been made available. In addition, a category of records not worth preserving in the original was filmed, and copies of these films can be obtained at the regular price of film publications.[53]

The National Archives conceives of itself as a service organization, and its conduct as such is exemplary. The agency is also a part of the federal bureaucracy, and its operations are constantly clouded by the fact. The staff is a devoted group, well trained in history and generally recruited from that field. Yet they seem impelled to establish their professional independence. Largely cut off from equal membership in the historical profession, and perhaps sensitive to their segregation, they have retreated into a sub-profession of their own, much concerned with techniques, methodology, and abstract theory, and little concerned with advancing the cause of historical knowledge. Forced to take a middle ground between the cultural significance and the practical utility of the records they service, they have not shown leadership in resolving the potential conflict between the two points of view. Only in the fields of records management and records appraisal have American archivists gone beyond their European counterparts and advanced the science of archival economy.[54]

[53] Bauer, "Public Archives," in Hesseltine and McNeil, eds., *Clio*, 72–73.
[54] Posner, "National Archives," 214–215.

APPRAISAL OF MODERN GOVERNMENT ARCHIVES

A PPRAISAL OF RECORDS relates to the evaluation and estimation of their permanent worth as sources of information in order that a logical and systematic selection for preservation or destruction may be made. The process is at best a subjective one, but the staff of the National Archives has evolved a system of theoretical considerations upon which to base their actions which incorporates a high degree of objectivity. The principles are broad and flexible, permitting their application to a wide range of modern, high-bulk records, both public and private. The system evolves from a theoretical basis of selection, to an identification of value in research, to a determination of the specific categories of records of greatest significance.

As practiced at the National Archives, the selection of records for permanent preservation as archives rests upon three conditions: the amount and nature of the information contained in them; the convenience of their arrangement; and the degree to which their textual substance is concentrated.[55] The criteria for selecting records for preservation and disposal are the same as preserving any official archives: a primary, or official, need to know about past official actions; and a secondary recognition of permanent cultural values inherent in such material.

Official use would be sufficient justification for keeping that portion of the records in question which from experience are known to have permanent utility for official reference. Fortunately, this small category of records is also of prime interest to nongovernment researchers. Were the selection to be made on the basis of official use alone, however, the choice would be too narrow and the resulting concept of the government's operations distorted. The primary, official interest in research must be taken in conjunction with the secondary or cultural interest in conducting any system of selection.

Permanent cultural values of archives always vary from nation to nation and from age to age, depending upon the nature of the

[55] G. Philip Bauer, *The Appraisal of Current and Recent Records* (National Archives Staff Information Circular No. 13, June, 1946), 7–8.

government and how it impinges upon the life of the nation. For example, in post-Revolutionary France, the primary reasons no longer existed for preserving most of the pre-Revolutionary archives. Revolutionary France recognized four classes of archives under their secondary value: useful papers, including the basic documents regarding the right of the state to confiscate properties; historical papers; feudal titles supporting feudal rights and privileges; and useless papers. The first two categories were marked for preservation, and the remaining two were marked for destruction. The ill-considered and hasty appraisal of records under this value system later resulted in an ultra-cautious disposal system when the French archives were reformed. In 1921 regulations codified the procedure of appraisal of French records, greater emphasis being placed upon indefinite preservation to satisfy chance interest in the future. Only material which has been summarized in print or has outlived a purely temporary significance may now be disposed of without question.[56]

German archival institutions fell heir to the accumulation of the government registry offices, and they followed the usual practice of throwing away the oldest records first to make room for the newer. Gradually, however, German archivists came to regard public records as evidence of organic growth, and they began to keep everything. In the modern period they have come to the point of removing worthless papers from an archive group without feeling that they are impairing its integrity. In fact, such weeding of registry files is conceived to be the process whereby the files are converted to archives.

German archival appraisal standards were profoundly influenced by the pronouncements in 1901 of H. O. Meissner, former head of the Prussian Privy State Archives. His archival philosophy was contained in five general rules, some so general as to be obvious: old age is to be respected absolutely, for records become more valuable as time makes them more scarce; extremes of any type ought to be avoided; too great an abstraction is an evil; records created for some definitely temporary purpose are generally disposable, but the end product may be preserved; and

[56] Schellenberg, *Modern Archives,* 133–135.

records on organic growth and the development of policies of
a permanent nature generally ought to be preserved.[57]

British archivists generally followed a very flexible system of
records appraisal and resisted the formalization of a scheme until the wartime paper salvage program during World War II
brought them to the task. Adopting American practices, British
officials creating records are expected to pass upon their preservation for official reference. For informational value, those documents which show the history of the government, answer technical questions on operations, or meet the scholarly need for
information incidentally or accidentally contained in archives
are marked for preservation. The purely ephemeral are disposed
of as soon as possible. Indexes and registers are preserved for
any records which are discarded. In general, British appraisal
values stress a utilitarian standard: the greatest number of persons, things, or topics.[58]

In the United States, appraisal of archives has been further
refined to distinguish between evidential and informational
values in the secondary value.

Archives incorporate the evidence which the government needs
for the reconstruction of a knowledge of its development. This
category of material is, for the same purpose, of great interest to
the historian of politics and public administration. The keys
to selection of such evidential material are the position of an
office in the administrative hierarchy, the character of functions
performed by each office, and the character of activities carried
on under a given function by each office in the hierarchy.[59]

One category of records to be so selected primarily for its
evidential value is "policy records," keeping in mind, of course,
that it is often difficult to draw a distinction between records
of "policy" and "administration." Policy documents include
those relating to organization (showing status or changes in the
form of government), procedure (showing how the government
accomplished its tasks), and official statements (showing how
the government accounted for its operation, usually on a formal
and fixed internal basis). A second category of evidential rec-

[57] *Ibid.*, 135–136.
[58] *Ibid.*, 137–138.
[59] *Ibid.*, 140–143.

ords includes those of operation (showing the routine of daily business, samples being usually sufficient for most purposes). A third category of evidential records is the government's house-keeping records (showing how it managed its personnel, finances, property, and other material affairs). In general, all house-keeping records except personnel records can be safely destroyed after their legal life has expired, for they contain little of evidential value. Lastly, the category of publications and publicity records is valuable for insight into how the government projected itself to the public, for without such knowledge of the government's intent, other records are frequently meaningless.[60]

The broad range of human activity reflected in archives is an indication of the array of evidential values inherent in such records. Assignment of priorities to these evidential values can be accomplished by categorization of use. For instance, they have application to the citizen-to-government relationships which are becoming more numerous and complex. Only from government records comes the documentation supporting land titles, rights to pensions and citizenship, eligibility for certain types of licensed employment and the like. Secondly, government archives are frequently the only permanent source of documentation for a vast complex of citizen-to-citizen relationships such as royalty rights, wage disputes and settlements, rate and tariff schedules, and price regulations. Thirdly, the government unilaterally has need of the evidence contained in its records for its official and administrative needs and for its corporate purposes touching its own best interests. It needs documentary evidence to answer claims made against it, to find and establish precedents giving continuity to its actions, and to protect itself against politically disloyal employees.[61]

Evidential values in archives are intentionally present. Informational values, on the other hand, reside therein accidentally or incidentally. Informational values, therefore, are often unsuspected or may not be apparent, and the appraisal of records on the basis of this criteria is correspondingly more difficult. Enough illustrations come to mind of incidental information which has been discovered from ancient records to suggest the

[60] *Ibid.*, 145–146.
[61] *Ibid.*, 116–117.

possibility of similar discoveries in the future from contemporary documentation, but chance future significance is not alone sufficient justification for preservation. In appraising informational values in records, therefore, two considerations apply among American archivists: old age is respected, and the burden of proof rests upon the affirmative for preservation. It has become accepted practice to retain all documentation prior to 1861, for that date marks a sharp demarcation in the American development as well as a demarcation between a period of scarcity of documentation and one of a surplus.[62] Some of the more obvious subjects which require and have been supplied informational values from archives are the science and history of public administration, diplomatic history, national history, economic history and theory, demography, biography and genealogy, technology, and physical science.[63] The categories of records incorporating informational values are those relating to persons, corporate bodies, and places.

Records of informational value to persons may be of value to the persons concerned or of interest to third parties. As a general rule, it is assumed that the government has an obligation to preserve records of concern, but not of interest or curiosity. Personal records in federal custody relating to citizenship, property, and military service are preserved for as long as there is a reasonable expectation the concerned individual may request reference. The government, having discharged its primary obligation, may thereafter retire the records. Fortunately, most documentation for vital statistics, such as birth and death certificates, is in the custody of the several states, and attempts to transfer the burden of archival responsibility to the federal government have been resisted.[64]

The government requires more, but owes less, archival service from and to its corporate citizens than its personal citizens. It may be assumed that corporate bodies can bear a greater burden of caring for their own documentation. The government, therefore, can be expected to preserve only records relating to corporate agencies which are unavailable elsewhere. The special

[62] *Ibid.*, 148–150.
[63] *Ibid.*, 115–116.
[64] *Ibid.*, 148–150.

nature of corporate documentation makes sampling of it inapplicable. Therefore, it should be preserved as a class or not at all.[65]

Government records incidentally relate to places and may be so organized, but that incidental relationship is not in itself justification for preservation. As a general rule, if information is of general and wide interest to the whole population, as the original plat for the city of Washington, it should be kept. If it is of only local interest, as a plat of a World War II army base, it may be safely transferred to the locality, or retired with the base.[66]

The objective of any scheme of records appraisal is the definition of some mutually exclusive categories for preservation and disposal, preferably in some order of priority. At the National Archives these categories have been reduced to four. In descending order, they are records for official reference, protection of private rights, scholarly research, and satisfaction of private interest and curiosity.

The primary justification for the maintenance of archives should always be understood to be that of the official business of the government, regardless of the scope of the secondary purposes and values involved. Despite the passage of time, the government has need of continuing reference to such records as minutes of boards and commissions, summary reports of chiefs of departments and agencies, and major orders of the highest authorities. Usually these records are highly concentrated, well organized, and of very small bulk. Beyond these obviously identifiable records is supporting documentation which is often as necessary for official reference as the policy documents themselves. The government, too, needs to know how and by whom basic policies have been implemented. In quasi-judicial agencies, policy is not made but is evolved through specific cases, so that the case files of such agencies as the National Labor Relations Board and the Federal Trade Commission are necessary to an understanding of the operation of the agency. Other types of records of frequent reference by the government are

---

[65] *Ibid.,* 158–160.
[66] Bauer, *Records Appraisal,* 8–12.

those pertaining to budgets and budget planning, and investigational studies and reports.[67]

Legal documentation for all manner of private rights is buried in the federal archives. Such information as age, citizenship, marital status, degree of financial need, findings of quasi-judicial bodies, condition of health, place of residence, and receipt of licenses is available on almost every resident. Such a mass of information cannot be retained forever *in toto,* and preservation must be in reasonable proportion to expense and probable use. As a general rule, therefore, each federal agency creating such personal documentation is responsible for its preservation for as long as it may be needed during the lifetime of the subject. Thus, the Bureau of Immigration and Naturalization is responsible for documenting naturalization until the death of the citizen. The federal government and its archives have so far resisted the temptation to develop permanent dossiers on its citizens, for the demand for such service is a fiction, and the practice smacks of totalitarian procedures.[68]

Scholars are varied in their documentary demands upon the government, and sometimes they have been unreasonable. Fortunately, most of the documentation they desire will have been preserved for other purposes, but how much can the nation afford to save of what the scholar alone wishes to keep? Some rough guidelines may be developed. Files on individual cases, closed without appeal and giving rise to no change in policy, would be excluded from preservation except for an historical interest in the person, corporation, or organization involved. Especially selected archives of historical interest may be retained without violating the integrity of the collection. Material such as rate schedules filed with the Interstate Commerce Commission may be treated similarly. On the other hand, personal and agricultural financial data might well be sampled because of the lack of any other basis of preservation. The needs of biography are among the most difficult to serve, and we can only hope that

[67] *Ibid.,* 13–17.
[68] *Ibid.,* 16–19.

today's important people are those in whom future biographers will be interested.[69]

A dramatic case study of the scholarly use of the federal archives may be seen in the historiography of the Civil War. By a recent count, over 100,000 books have been written on the tragic conflict. While coping with the flood freshened by the Civil War centennial, the Centennial Commission's executive director commented that the greater part of the literature, for lack of original research, made no contribution to knowledge. Instead, he called for a better ordering of archival and manuscript resources so that historians could get on with their unfinished business of interpreting the war and its impact upon the nation.[70]

Records required for the satisfaction of private interest and curiosity are the most diverse and bulky of all those of the federal government, and, in proportion to the serious use made of them, they are extremely costly to maintain. Every government agency has information of interest to someone, but the categories of most frequent reference include population schedules of the census, veterans' records, Selective Service records, and wage and claims records of the Bureau of Old Age and Survivors Insurance (OASI). How much of these bulky records should the government be expected to retain? Population schedules exist only to support statistical summaries and are now subject to destruction after they have served their original purpose, despite the protest of genealogists. Veterans' records relating to special benefits require special handling, but intermediate storage for 150 years should serve all reasonable calls for reference. The annual cost of $300,000 for preserving the records of Selective Service seems unjustifiable, but even more so is the expense of maintaining an OASI file after the death of a claimant. In both cases destruction of the records soon after the government's interest in the material has expired is indicated.[71]

In the last analysis, the identification of classes of records for

[69] *Ibid.,* 13, 16–19.
[70] James I. Robertson, Jr., "The Civil War Centennial—Archival Aspects," in *American Archivist,* 26:11–18 (January, 1963).
[71] Bauer, *Records Appraisal,* 13, 19–22.

destruction upon application of appraisal values is nothing more than a recognition of the fact that modern government creates more records than it can reasonably maintain. A combination of documentary birth control and euthanasia is indicated in order that truly significant documents may be given an opportunity to fulfill their destiny.

The United States of America was the last great power to institutionalize its national archives. Within thirty years of this event, however, the size, professional competence, and institutional prestige of Clio's temple in the nation's capital had taken at least an equal position among similar establishments and, in many instances, had become the world leader. These accomplishments might be considered one of the material monuments of the American Historical Association and its members, brought into being by the generous support of a nation lately awakened to its archival heritage.

vv

II

vvvvvvvvvvvvvvvvvvvvvvvvvvvvvvvvvvvvvvvvvvvvvvvvvvvvvvvv

STATE AND LOCAL
ARCHIVES IN AMERICA

THE TWIN, uniquely American principles of federalism and home rule have given to the archives of state and local governments a legal importance and historical significance surpassing those in any other nation. The legal value of such documentation has long been recognized; it forms, in fact, the basis of the American system of law. The historical significance of such local documentation, however, was largely overlooked until well into the twentieth century. Even recently, local documentation has been more apt to be used exclusively for local historiography. Granting that state and local documentation has received less professional care and ordering, and that it lies scattered in disarray all over the nation, its richness and wide availability commend it to American historians. Their neglect of this mass of local documentation has contributed to the possibility of a misunderstanding of the nature of American development and to the context of nationalism in which American historiography has flowered. It is not too much an exaggeration to observe that America had no uniquely national historiography until the mass of state and local documentation was employed. As Turner's study of the frontier pointed out, it is in the regional and local particulars that the historical differences between American and European experience become obvious. So long as the national development of America was compared with the pattern of national history in Europe, only historical continuity and similarities were emphasized.

43

It is a curious fact that although national historiography was becoming appreciated in the nineteenth century, little was done to recapture and utilize the national documentation for it. Rather, a selective search was made among the accumulated mass of state and local documents for that evidence which supported the scientific history in the national framework. This selective search resulted in incomplete collections of manuscripts, rather than in archives on any level, but throughout the nineteenth century the archives of the states enjoyed far better care than those of the federal government. In America at least, archival interest and utilization proceeded from the state to the national level, to the point of ignoring local documentation in recent years of historical writing. Fortunately, a rediscovery of local resources has been in process since the turn of the century.

For the sake of convenience, a consideration of public archival materials for American history below the national level can be arbitrarily divided into state archives and those of local governmental units, usually counties and municipalities. Because the distinction is often difficult to draw and a number of characteristics are shared, the following discussion of the utilization of, and the development of finding aids for, state and local archives has been consolidated.

STATE ARCHIVAL PROGRAMS AND LEGISLATION

IN A VERY REAL SENSE, the American states predate the federal government, their records-keeping practices evolving out of European and colonial practices, considerably tempered by the informal character of state governments. State records have traditionally been close to the people, their legal significance being of far greater importance than their cultural values. Their keepers, too, have been of a different order, for there were relatively few state bureaucracies in the nineteenth century. Records keepers were generally entirely subservient to politicians and members of the bar. Only as the cultural values of state records came to be recognized were steps taken to make the records more accessible to the public.

The study of colonial records-keeping remains a fruitful subject for historical inquiry, but what work has already been done reveals a general picture of neglect and decay, and an amiable laxity of official conduct. As Governor Arthur Dobbs of North Carolina once complained, whenever officers "died, all papers die with them."[1] In colonies lacking a stable seat of government, the plight of public records was even more serious. Even when regular provision was made for the creation and preservation of records in colonial America, fire undid about one-third of the best intentions.[2]

The archival reforms of the French Revolution had little effect on the American tradition of public records. Instead, Americans took up the European fad of publishing archives, a movement which had been popularized in England by Thomas Rymer (1641–1713) and in America by Ebenezer Hazard in his famous American State Papers proposal. In nineteenth-century America, documentary publication floated on the same tide of patriotic fervor which in Europe witnessed the publications of the British Record Commission and of *Monumenta Germaniae*. The states responded to these pressures more slowly than did the central government because most of the extant records of the states were available only outside the country.[3]

The archival publications of the Public Record Commission in Britain (1800–1836), aiming at faithful reproductions of the original documents, were "carried out to the pecuniary advantage of the officials, though at an unreasonable cost to the Nation." The resulting Parliamentary inquiry cooled the public ardor for documentary publication, but America failed to profit by the British example. Alexis de Tocqueville commented that Americans cared little for their original records and predicted that in

[1] J. G. de Roulhac Hamilton, "Three Centuries of Southern Records, 1607–1907," in *Journal of Southern History*, 10:9 (February, 1944).

[2] Ernst Posner, *American State Archives* (Chicago, 1964), 8–9. This work appeared while the present study was in progress, and the author wishes to acknowledge his great indebtedness to it. The genesis of the Posner study is described in Ernst Posner, "The Study of State Archival Programs," in *American Archivist*, 26:305–306 (July, 1963).

[3] Lyman H. Butterfield, "Archival and Editorial Enterprise in 1850 and 1950: Some Comparisons and Contrasts," in *Proceedings of the American Philosophical Society*, 98:160 (June 15, 1954), as quoted in Posner, *American State Archives*, 10–12.

a hundred years it would be more difficult to write a history of
the United States than one of medieval France.[4]

From time to time there was interest in preserving state archives; it could hardly be said to have become a movement, however, until a generation after the Revolution. At that time, it
had a specific purpose only incidentally related to the general
state concern for education. That concern did not become sufficiently wide to generate action until the twentieth century.

The search for "materials for history" in the early 1800's was
almost exclusively confined to public documents in the possession of the various states and in the parent archives of Europe.
Initially stimulated by the popularization of the Revolution, the
search for historical documentation by the 1820's also became
caught up in the contemporary scramble for internal improvements and the rivalry among the states for prestige. North Carolina was a case in point. Its promoter of internal improvement
and history, Archibald DeBow Murphy, simultaneously proposed a vast network of canals in the Old North State, to be
constructed with federal funds, and advocated a broader documentation of the state's history to prove his contention that the
federal government had previously slighted the state out of her
fair share of federal bounty. History here was being used shame-
lessly to shore up local pride and to lay claims upon the central
government. When Murphy's private search for state historical
documentation became financially burdensome, the state legislature came to his aid with an appropriation. The project was
considerably broadened when federal authorities suggested the
possibility of additional documentation from the Plantation Office in London. Murphy's promotional history was never written,
but his valuable collection of materials and his example became
the foundation of the North Carolina Historical Society.[5]

Murphy's interest in state records, although certainly not the
first, was among the earliest for purposes of historical documentation. In the colonies there had been but little interest in archives, for colonial history had been generally the province of

[4] Hubert Hall, *British Archives and the Sources for the History of the World War*
(London and New Haven, 1925), 214; Alexis de Tocqueville, *Democracy in America*
(2 vols., New York, 1945), I:69; both quoted in Posner, *American State Archives*,
12–13.

[5] David D. Van Tassel, *Recording America's Past* (Chicago, 1960), 103.

uncritical scholars without recourse to documentary evidence. Nevertheless, several colonial administrations recognized the future value of their records. In 1639 the General Court of Massachusetts directed the inferior courts to keep more extensive records of their judgments, both for the better administration of justice and for evidence of the evolution of the colony. In 1729 Maryland directed that all public records in private hands be surrendered, one of the first attempts to correct the loose security protecting state records in America. Most of the public documents of the colonies were those supporting some legal rights embracing such documents as land grants, deeds, wills, and licenses, and access was generally granted only upon payment of fees. Records of colonial legislatures and governors, on the other hand, were generally regarded as closed to the public, and the rising demand for inspection of such privileged material was met by a policy of selective access. The Revolution quickened popular interest in such documents and demonstrated the point that they were the property of the people, but the states were not moved to make adequate provision for the care and maintenance of their older records.[6]

In the various states the older records were usually left in the care of the agencies which had created them, although some states provided for the transfer of old, noncurrent records to the care of the secretary of the commonwealth. No American state maintained any separate depository, and every state lost records to the energetic collecting policies of Peter Force, Jared Sparks, and others.[7] Only desultory measures were undertaken in New Jersey, New Hampshire, and Georgia for the better care of archives and recovery of strays.[8]

What little archival activity the states did undertake was aimed at restoring extant older records rather than preserving and defending more contemporary records. In 1818 New York began translating its Dutch colonial records, which ultimately totaled twenty-four folio volumes and were deposited in the office of the secretary of state. In 1881 these volumes, with some older

---

[6] Bauer, "Public Archives," in Hesseltine and McNeil, eds., *Clio,* 49–50.

[7] John H. Moore, "Jared Sparks in North Carolina," in *North Carolina Historical Review,* 40:292 (July, 1963); Posner, *American State Archives,* 13–14.

[8] Bauer, "Public Archives," in Hesseltine and McNeil, eds., *Clio,* 51–53.

archives, were transferred to the state library to form the nucleus of the state's archives, but no provision was made for the care and preservation of local records. A large number of them failed to survive the neglect of the nineteenth century.[9]

Massachusetts had a somewhat better record of caring for its state and local records. Between 1836 and 1846 it retained the Reverend Joseph Barlow Felt to arrange and bind the colonial and revolutionary records of the commonwealth. Unfortunately, this amateur archivist adopted an arbitrary system of topical arrangement, utterly destroying any system of fonds or provenance which may have existed. The effort, though misdirected, was successful in salvaging 241 volumes of documents which might otherwise have perished. No more records were compiled until 1891, when a card index was made abstracting the personal information on muster and militia rolls of the Revolution and Civil War. Massachusetts also extended its protection to land records. In 1884 a commission on public records was created to supervise the care of local records, with generally good results.[10]

Other states also participated in the mania for locating and preserving documents of the Revolutionary period. In 1847 the Senate of South Carolina directed its clerk to arrange and prepare for public use all those records in his care dating from 1782. The task was completed in 1848. A general resolution providing for the collection and preservation of the documents of the Palmetto State was passed in 1849, disastrous fires of 1843 and 1844 in the offices in Columbia being cited as justification for central fireproof storage for the records. Under legislative patronage, J. S. Green in 1850 began to collect, arrange, and index the colonial and Revolutionary papers of the state.[11] His work laid the foundation for one of the most extensive archives of any of the original states.

In contrast to the emerging archives in New York, Massachusetts, and South Carolina, the archives of Pennsylvania were notoriously inaccessible, scattered, and subject constantly to pillage. In 1851 a select committee of the legislature reported that the

[9] Ibid., 53–54.
[10] Ibid., 54–55.
[11] Ibid., 55.

state's noncurrent records were useless in their present condition and were fast perishing from abuse and neglect. The uncompromising report resulted only in a meager appropriation for classifying and binding a small portion of the records, which were transferred in 1885 to the state library for reference. Little was done to put the material in order for reference or research until the end of the century.[12]

The states were little interested in their archives throughout the nineteenth century, but what little interest existed usually took the form of publishing rather than preserving archives. Constant demand for archival reform was characteristically seized as the justification for extensive programs of documentary reproduction. The fundamental situation which had given rise to the initial complaint was left unrelieved, however. With reason to be ashamed of its care of the original archives, Pennsylvania was the leader in the program of publishing such documents as its *Votes and Proceedings of the House of Representatives* (1682–1776), its series of *Colonial Records* (seventeen vollumes by 1860), and its *Pennsylvania Archives* (in seventeen volumes). Similar, but less ambitious, projects were undertaken by New York, Massachusets, Rhode Island, Virginia, Maryland, and North Carolina.[13]

In 1826 began the raid of the American states on the archives of Europe. The year was the semi-centennial of the Declaration of Independence, its significance further punctuated by the simultaneous deaths of Adams and Jefferson. With interest in American documentation rising at fever pitch and with the example of documentary publication in England, France, and Germany before them, several of the states embarked upon ambitious programs of re-creating, so to speak, their colonial archives by making transcripts of official papers in Europe. In 1824 Georgia had commissioned Joseph Y. Bevan to arrange its archives, and he discovered large gaps which obviously could be filled only by reference to the British archives. The peace treaty of 1783 had contained no provision for supplying America with documentation of her colonial past, and the British government was in no mood at the time to grant favors to America. Despite

[12] *Ibid.,* 55–56.
[13] *Ibid.,* 57–59.

these obstacles, patient diplomacy opened the files of the Board of Trade to the agents of Georgia, and the incident suggested similar possibilities to other states.[14] Soon a small army of quasi-diplomatic agents were dispatched by the states to the European archives to make transcripts of material relating to their colonial history.

Following the example of Georgia, New York dispatched an archival agent to England, Holland, and France in 1839, and he brought back eight manuscript volumes ultimately published in fourteen printed ones. Because of smaller financial resources, New Jersey had to be content with preparing a card index of British documents pertaining to the state. Later the material was transcribed and published as a part of the series entitled *New Jersey Archives*. In 1891, advancing its long-standing interest, the South Carolina Public Records Commission sent an agent to London to copy all pertinent colonial records. Some thirty-six manuscript volumes of transcripts resulted.[15] Indeed, it appeared that the "documania" of the early years of the century had given way to a "transcriptmania" in the latter, equally detrimental to the more contemporary records produced since the stirring days of the birth of the nation.

After spurting ahead of the federal government in the early years of the nineteenth century, the states later floundered in their concern for their archives. It required outside pressure to restore their earlier enthusiastic interest and to generate interest in newer areas which had not previously expressed concern for the preservation of public records as historical evidence. The chief vehicle for this pressure, the Public Archives Commission of the AHA, was created in 1899.

Although the centennial of the Revolution in 1876 produced some local stirrings of archival reform in New England, the emergence of the school of scientific history in the late nineteenth century provided the real stimulus for archival consciousness in the nation at large. The influence of the Germanic tradition of historical scholarship and of the seminar methodology was enormous and was best exemplified at Johns Hopkins University and in the work of Herbert Baxter Adams. One of Adams'

[14] Van Tassel, *Recording America's Past*, 104–105.
[15] Bauer, "Public Archives," in Hesseltine and McNeil, eds., *Clio*, 58–59.

students, Woodrow Wilson, later recalled that "those professors wanted to set everybody under their authority to working on what they called 'institutional history,' to digging, that is, into the dusty records of old settlements and colonial history."[16] "Institutional history," in the parlance of scientific history, led to local documentation for national institutions, which, in turn, led to the demand for institutionalization of the state and local archives.

J. Franklin Jameson was the link between the historical interest in local documentation and state archival reform. He put forward a specific proposal in 1895, which developed into the Historical Manuscripts Commission of the AHA. In 1899 a parallel group, the Public Archives Commission, was raised—with a sweeping program of surveying the archives in all of the states, and an appropriation of $500 for postage. The first report of the commission, filed in 1900, included archival surveys of ten states. By 1910 the commission had obtained forty-six archival surveys from thirty-two states, two cities, and the Philippines.[17]

Although the Public Archives Commission contributed signally to the fight to secure a national archives, it was conceived as a medium for transmitting the professional concern of the nation's historians for the plight of state archives. For the first several years of the twentieth century, the commission conducted a very active and effective campaign for more professional care of the state and local documentation for American history. The success of this movement was exemplified by the formation of archival programs in the South.

Due to the inherent and incipient southern nationalism, southern public archives have, on the whole, fared better than the private records of the region, but the destruction of records which occurred is still appalling. Numerous statehouse fires in Alabama, Virginia, North Carolina, and South Carolina destroyed tons of state papers; even more destructive than fire, however, were the years of official neglect of the records. Southern

---

[16] W. Stull Holt, ed., *Historical Scholarship in the United States, 1876–1901: As Revealed in the Correspondence of Herbert B. Adams* (Baltimore, 1938), 90n., as quoted in Posner, *American State Archives*, 16–17.

[17] Posner, *American State Archives*, 18–19.

county records, containing relatively more significant documentation than those of other sections, have fared worse than the state records, and southern municipal records have fared worst of all.[18]

The degree to which the southern states have overcome their archival tardiness, and the characteristic pattern of state "departments of archives and history," is a reflection of the efforts of one nonprofessional friend of archives in one state, Thomas McAdory Owen of Alabama. In 1898, fired by a determination to place the states' interest in its past upon a firm and documentary basis, Owen as a young lawyer assumed control of the moribund Alabama Historical Society. From that vantage point he lobbied for the establishment of a state department to care for the state archives and to promote the study of the state's history. With the creation of an investigative commission which he headed, Owen ensured the creation in 1901 of the Alabama Department of Archives and History, of which he became the first head.

The Alabama agency was given a broad statutory mandate of clear title to the state archives and was assigned the duty of collecting historical material of all kinds and the responsibility for the "diffusion of historical knowledge." In short order Owen set about collecting not only manuscripts, museum pieces, and newspapers, but as well "relics and personal belongings of eminent Alabamians, as library desks or tables, chairs, knives, dirks, dueling pistols and other firearms, stock, knee or shoe buckles, drinking cups, watches, chains, snuff boxes, and canes."[19]

In 1903 Mississippi adopted the Alabama formula for expressing its interest in its past, establishing a regional pattern. Arkansas and West Virginia followed suit in 1905. In 1907 North Carolina created a department which was soon to take first place among such state agencies. All the southern states before World War I had adopted some such measures, and the regional lag in state archival administration had been eliminated. Typically, the southern departments of archives and history com-

[18] Philip M. Hamer, "The Records of Southern History," in *Journal of Southern History*, 5:3–17 (February, 1939).

[19] Peter A. Brannon, "The Alabama Department of Archives and History," in *Alabama Historical Quarterly*, 24:1–15 (Spring, 1962); Thomas McAdory Owen, "State Department of Archives and History," in AHA *Annual Report*, 1904, 237–257; Posner, *American State Archives*, 19.

bined the triple functions of maintaining custody of noncurrent public records, collecting unofficial records of the state's history, and taking other action to promote the study and writing of the state's history.[20]

Laudable as was the creation of state departments of archives and history, it is well to remember that the selective acquisition of some old state records does not constitute an archive. Nor is the legislative opinion which holds archivists to be glorified file clerks or librarians conducive to archival growth and excellence. Unfortunately, these erroneous concepts have to varying degrees entered into the departments of archives and history, impairing their usefulness and promise. The peculiar nature of state archives, the deleterious effect of one-party politics, and a real or professed lack of funds have combined to make strong and competent state archivists in the South the exception to the rule. In general, archivists have not been given clear legal title to the documents transferred to their care. Home rule and local sovereignty have also made efforts to extend the protective care of the states over the archives of the local governmental units largely ineffectual, though there is an increasing recognition that such extension is necessary and desirable.[21]

The existing variation in state archival establishments is due to the cultural development of the various states. It is no more to be expected that they should all adopt the same machinery for maintaining their historical documentation than that they adopt uniform mechanics of government. The older states of the Northeast, where historical societies developed early but on an exclusive pattern, generally entrusted their archives, if to any agency other than the creating, to the state library. The states of the Middle West, however, have more democratic historical societies which frequently have been made trustees of

---

[20] Hamer, "Southern History," 10–11.

[21] Margaret C. Norton, "Scope and Function of a State Archives Department," in Society of American Archivists, *Proceedings,* 1936–1937, pp. 75–76. The opinions expressed are those of the present author. For additional commentary on state archival operation and reform, see: A. M. Patterson, "State Archival Agencies' Services to Other State Agencies," in *American Archivist,* 26:315–318 (July, 1963); Frank B. Evans, "The State Archivist and the Academic Researcher—'Stable Companionship'," in *American Archivist,* 26:319–322 (July, 1963); Kenneth W. Richards, "The State Archivist and the Amateur Researcher," in *American Archivist,* 26:323–326 (July, 1963).

the state's archives. The southern states, on the other hand, having few historical societies of any kind, exclusive or democratic, were forced to evolve their own state governmental agencies for caring for their archives. Each of these basic arrangements has its advantages and disadvantages, and, insofar as the primary purpose of proper archival management is served, it would seem the part of wisdom to permit the luxury of variety to the states.

That variety almost defies generalization, however. As of 1957, seven states had some form of independent history, archives, or records commissions, parts of the state government but outside the executive branch. The archives of nine states were operated under the supervision of the state library, while five others were functions of the office of the secretary of state. Ten states, all in the Middle or Far West, had transferred their archives to state historical societies, and two had seen fit to lodge them in state departments of education. Five states had no formal archival system at all, and the remaining states had irregular arrangements of varying kinds.[22] The variety and scope of state archival establishments are illustrated by the following chart:[23]

DIRECTORY OF STATE ARCHIVAL AND RECORDS MANAGEMENT AGENCIES, 1964

State	Agency and Location	Annual Budget	Record Holdings
Alabama	State Department of Archives and History, War Memorial Building, Montgomery	$ 23,800*†	192,000 cu. ft.
Alaska	None (Function by Secretary of State, Juneau)	————	————
Arizona	Department of History and Archives, State House, Phoenix	6,500*†	3,000 cu. ft.

*Archives only.
†Professional salaries only.

[22] Mary G. Bryan, "Trends of Organization in State Archives," in *American Archivist*, 21:31–42 (January, 1958).

[23] Prepared from information contained in William T. Alderson, comp., *Directory of State and Provincial Archivists and Records Administrators, 1963* (mimeographed, Nashville, 1963); and Posner, *American State Archives*, Appendix B and D, 372–373, 375–376.

State	Agency and Location	Annual Budget	Record Holdings
Arkansas	History Commission, Old State House, Little Rock	N.A.	1,200 vols.
California	Archives and Central Records Department, Sacramento	119,987	18,000 cu. ft.
Colorado	State Archives, State Historical Society, Denver	105,847	8,000 cu. ft.
Connecticut	Archives Department, State Library, Hartford	32,000	7,000 cu. ft.
Delaware	Public Archives Commission, Hall of Records, Dover	151,090	15,285 cu. ft.
Florida	None (Function by State Library, Tallahassee)	——	——
Georgia	Department of Archives and History, Atlanta	102,520*	1,350 cu. ft. 60,000 vols.
Hawaii	Board of Commissioners of Public Records, Iolani Palace, Honolulu	114,995	4,450 cu. ft.
Idaho	State Historical Society, Boise	N.A.	2,000 cu. ft.
Illinois	Archives Division, State Library, Springfield	269,279	80,000 cu. ft.
Indiana	State Library, Indianapolis	47,000	3,000 cu. ft. 15,000 vols.
Iowa	State Department of History and Archives, Historical Building, Des Moines	15,000	24,000 cu. ft.
Kansas	State Historical Society, Memorial Building, Topeka	31,000*	5,70
Kentucky	Historical Society, Old State House, Frankfort	43,515	
Louisiana	Department of Archives, Louisiana State University, Baton Rouge	90,920	
Maine	None	——	
Maryland	Hall of Records Commission, Annapolis	180,00	
Massachusetts	Archives Division, Secretary of Commonwealth, State House, Boston	6	
Michigan	Historical Commission, Lansing		
Minnesota	State Archives, Minnesota Historical Society, St. Paul		
Mississippi	Department of Archives and History, War Memorial Building, Jackson		

State	Agency and Location	Annual Budget	Record Holdings
Missouri	None (Function by State Historical Society, Columbia)	———	———
Montana	None	———	990 cu. ft.
Nebraska	State Historical Society, Lincoln	7,500*†	6,000 cu. ft.
Nevada	None	———	Insignificant
New Hampshire	State Historical Society, Concord	19,065	200 cu. ft.
New Jersey	Department of Archives and History, State House, Trenton	46,437	10,000 cu. ft.
New Mexico	History and Publications, Museum of New Mexico, Santa Fe	65,000	764 cu. ft.
New York	Division of Archives and History, Education Building, Albany	70,800	40,000 cu. ft.
North Carolina	Department of Archives and History, Education Building, Raleigh	285,000	7,000 cu. ft.
North Dakota	State Historical Society, Liberty Memorial Building, Bismarck	20,000	520 cu. ft.
Ohio	State Historical Society, Columbus	25,540*	12,250 cu. ft.
Oklahoma	State Historical Society, Oklahoma City	37,000*	N.A.
Oregon	State Archives, State Library, Salem	50,607*	8,400 cu. ft.
Pennsylvania	Public Records, Pennsylvania Historical and Museum Commission, Harrisburg	72,495*	13,500 cu. ft.
Puerto Rico	Institute of Puerto Rican Culture, General Archives, San Juan	59,400*	11,700 cu. ft.
Rhode Island	Department of State, State House, Providence	34,410	350 cu. ft. 870 vols.
South Carolina	Archives Department, World War Memorial, Columbia	107,132	20,000 cu. ft.
South Dakota	None (Function by State Historical Society, Pierre)	———	small quantity
Tennessee	Division of Archives, State Library and Archives Building, Nashville	43,260*†	60,000 cu. ft.
Texas	State Archives, Austin	71,449	30,000 cu. ft.
Utah	State Historical Society, State Capitol, Salt Lake City	43,250	1,000 cu. ft.
Vermont	Public Records Commission, State House, Montpelier	32,813	500 cu. ft.

State	Agency and Location	Annual Budget	Record Holdings
Virginia	Archives Division, Virginia State Library, Richmond	91,800†	4,000 cu. ft. 63,000 vols.
Washington	State Archives, Department of Public Instruction, Olympia	23,720	45,000 cu. ft.
West Virginia	Department of Archives and History, State Capitol, Charleston	10,000	3,500 cu. ft.
Wisconsin	Division of Archives and Manuscripts, State Historical Society, Madison	69,280*	23,500 cu. ft.
Wyoming	State Archives and History Department, Cheyenne	90,000	1,250 cu. ft.

An example of state archival development may be seen in a more detailed examination of the experience in Wisconsin. Curiously enough, more attention was paid to the archives of other states than to his own by the redoubtable Lyman C. Draper. Under his leadership, the State Historical Society of Wisconsin made no move to institutionalize or to organize the state archives. In fact, no one made such a move until prodded by the Public Archives Commission in 1899. In 1900 the society moved into its spacious new quarters, and, in the same year, Professor O. G. Libby of the University of Wisconsin made a report on the archives of the state. He confined his report to a listing of holdings and made no recommendation for a central archival agency.

In 1905, in a second report by Professor Carl R. Fish, the society first indicated its interest in being designated the state's archival agent. The records at that time were reported to be in surprisingly good condition, needing only to be made more readily available for reference. The archives having fortunately survived the Capitol fire of 1904, Fish urged their transfer to the more efficient care of the society. Reuben Gold Thwaites formally presented the society's request in 1906, and in the next year the legislature designated the society as the trustee of the state. The society was passively to receive what might be transferred to it by the various state departments. After the initial transfer of some high-bulk record series, Thwaites lost interest in the archival program, and it languished for several years. In 1914 his successor, Milo M. Quaife, seeking to justify the construction of a new building or an enlargement of the existing one, advanced a new plan for all the state's archives to be transferred to the society. The legislature was deaf to the scheme.[24]

The lack of interest of the Wisconsin legislature in archival reform turned Quaife, instead, to securing transcripts of European archives touching upon Wisconsin, and to securing transcripts from the Indian Office in Washington regarding policy in removing and managing the Indians of Wisconsin. Both of these projects resulted in an accumulation of over 35,000 pages of transcripts, but the establishment of a Wisconsin archives was not thereby advanced. Quaife had not forgotten the plan, however, and in 1917 he hired a young high school teacher in Milwaukee, Theodore C. Blegen, to make a survey of the state archives. Blegen unfavorably compared the Wisconsin archives with those of Europe and the other American states, and he recommended transfer for full supervision by the society together with a new building to house them. The legislature remained unimpressed.[25]

Quaife's successor, Joseph Schafer, took a new tack to popularize the richness of state and local archival material through his famous *Domesday Book* plan following World War I. His intention was to present systematically and completely all the information from public sources affecting every farm in the state. Scholars applauded this ambitious program, but the state failed to provide the financial support. With the failure of the Domesday plan came another postponement of the establishment of the state's archives. Not even the stimulation of the Federal Historical Records Survey was sufficient to revive the state's archives, most of the funds being spent on indexing federal census records of 1840 to 1870 rather than inventorying archival material.[26]

The Wisconsin centennial in 1946 gave added significance to

[24] Donald J. Lisio, "The Development of Wisconsin Archives" (Unpublished research paper of February, 1961, in the possession of the present author), 2–6.

[25] *Ibid.,* 7–12. See also Theodore C. Blegen, *A Report on the Public Archives* (Madison, 1918).

[26] Lisio, "Development of Wisconsin Archives," 7–12.

the state's archives, and the society's director, Clifford L. Lord, with the support of Governor Walter S. Goodland, seized the opportunity for a new effort toward archival reform. Legislation was passed in 1947 again naming the society the archival agent of the state, the opening wedge in a new building drive. As a result of legislative politics, a committee appointed to review the expanded space requirements of the society was directed to withhold its report until 1949. It reported precipitately in 1948, recommending expansion of the society building to care for the archives at an approximate cost of $1,500,000. The legislature did not act.[27]

The 1947 act also established a Committee on Public Records, composed of the attorney general, the state auditor, and the director of the historical society. The function of the committee was to pass upon all requests of state departments to destroy records. Without the space adequately to house them, the society might still impose its archival interest upon original records, but it was given no power to order destruction or to requisition state records. Under the supervision of Archivist Jesse E. Boell, a modern archival and records management program was implemented, fortunately rejecting Lord's plan to arrange the archives chronologically according to subject. In 1949 a critical shortage of space and a desire to extend state archival service to the more significant local archives suggested the establishment of five regional depositories in the libraries of state colleges and smaller cities about the state. In addition to relieving the space shortage in the central archives, the regional plan has been adjudged a qualified success.

Suspicion of society self-interest in management of the archives prompted the Wisconsin legislature to transfer archival administration from the society to an executive department in 1957, only to be restored to the society in 1959. In the 1959 transfer, however, the records management function was retained by the executive office. In sum, in the few years since the archives program of Wisconsin got its laggard start, it has become recognized as one of the best of its type in the nation; but the controversy surrounding the charge of self-interest on the part

[27] *Ibid.,* 12–14.

of the state historical society and relative legislative indifference to the records management function presents a somewhat clouded future for the agency.[28]

The federal archival establishment has become something of a professional standard in the United States; in contrast, the bewildering variety of the state archival systems defies a neat systemization. The archival system in some states was drafted and is staffed by inexperienced politicians rather than professional archivists, and uniformity of organization would probably raise the level of care and service. Towards that end, the Society of American Archivists has consistently promoted the adoption of a model archives act. This model act is based on no single existing state system, but on the principle that an archives should be an agency with permissive authority to collect and administer noncurrent records in such a way that they are in the most capable hands, are most free from political interference, and are most readily available to research. It is the consensus that the care of an independent agency or supervision by a self-governing historical society are the best organizational formats for the proper administration of state archives. Realizing the impracticality of implementing such uniformity in archival organization, the uniform archives movement has instead concerned itself with an effort to stipulate how any archival agency should function, regardless of its form. The uniform legislation sponsored by the SAA, therefore, is concerned with such matters as definition of public archives, definition of records management functions of archivists, establishment of minimum standards of paper and ink, establishment of penalties for damage or destruction of archives, authority to recover archival strays, authority to re-create missing archives, establishment of minimum standards of fireproof storage, authority to make duplicates with the force of originals, and provision for destruction of archives. No state has yet passed the model act without significant local alteration.[29]

[28] Ibid.

[29] Albert Ray Newsome, "Uniform State Archival Legislation," in American Archivist, 2:1–16 (January, 1939); Society of American Archivists, Committee on Uniform Legislation, "A Proposed Model Act to Create a State Department of Archives and History," in American Archivist, 7:130–133 (April, 1944).

LOCAL ARCHIVES IN AMERICA

L OCAL UNITS OF GOVERNMENT—counties and municipalities—probably come closer to the American's fireside than
those of the state or national level, yet in a routine, matter-of-
fact way. Devoted almost exclusively to the service functions of
government, they provide police and fire protection, education,
public health, sanitation, and welfare services. They promote
community order by planning, building codes, and roadway maintenance; they are bastions for the protection and enforcement
of title to property, real and personal. Most importantly, local
governments are the effective agents for administration of justice through the courts. Whenever citizens are involved in any
of these basic questions of public service, administration, and
law, the pertinent documentation is contained in the records
of the locality, either county or municipality.

The American local unit of government inherited from its
colonial predecessor a wide range of records matching the range
of activities, but without a tradition of professional archival care.
Local governmental records have been largely created and maintained by dedicated but untrained servants. To them, current
records have been species of private property, to be created and
organized for administrative convenience. Old records have also
been regarded as a nuisance to be piled into basements or attics
in the hope that the forces of nature would accomplish what the
law and bureaucratic indecision refused to do. Save in specific
exceptions, as with deeds, wills, and similar legal papers, the
"courthouse gang" has been unaccustomed to public interest in
their archives, and for the most part this vast accumulation of
documentation has been preserved only for its primary purposes.
Its secondary cultural values have been largely unrealized.

County government in America remained relatively unchanged
in form following the Revolution, perpetuating the American
adaptation of the English county government. Largely outside
of the unifying control of state governments, county records
took on a bewildering array of various forms and physical conditions during the nineteenth century. As the population grew
and expanded westward, county organization grew more complex,
or divided amoeba-like into multiple entities, and each evolu-

tion in a county organization brought a corresponding change in county archives. The transfer and assumption of duties between counties and the rising urban centers also brought further confusion to land records, so that one of the first problems in the utilization of land records is to identify the various record series.

The natural erosion of records has kept within bounds those local records which survived from the last century, and happily the extant records are, for the most part, the very ones which the historian most desires Plat books and tax rolls, deed and will books, marriage licenses, county budgets and ordinances, and departmental reports have generally been saved at the expense of such ephemeral and more bulky files as tax returns, closed court cases, disbursement vouchers, and police reports.

The gradual assumption in the twentieth century of an increasing proportion of the functions of local government by municipalities and states has further prevented the county courthouse from being crushed by the weight of its own paper, for its production of records in proportion to the expanding population has been declining. For the most part, the body of county records still is archivally amorphous, but where records are found in usable condition, their bulk and organization do not generally pose a problem to researchers. Finding and initially inventorying pertinent records for a specific research project is still the most difficult task in using local archives.

The difficulty of locating and using local archives in historical research contributed to sporadic demands for archival reform. Prior to the 1930's scholars had not been vocal in these demands because they understood that such a project clearly would be possible only on a national scale drawing upon the resources of the federal government. The mere fact that there are more than 3,000 county units, plus the cities and towns in the nation, places a survey of their archives in the class of a major and encompassing project. Desirable as the undertaking was, it had to await the Depression emergency before it could be justified, and then as make-work for unemployed white-collar workers.

The Historical Records Survey was unique among the relief programs of the New Deal. Using an untrained corps of office workers, in five years it amassed an incredibly large collection of information, opened the records of local governments to general public use, made available the material for rewriting local history upon a sound documentary basis, and vastly stimulated good records-keeping practices. A plan to have the nation's unemployed stenographers, typists, file clerks, and teachers make a systematic survey of local archives was drawn up by Robert C. Binkley and adapted by Harry Hopkins in June, 1935. An excellent choice of Luther H. Evans as director of the project got it off to a good start in November, 1935. Its purposes were to locate and inventory local records, study ways of preserving them from further decay, make recommendations to cover their filming, classifying, and cataloging, and facilitate their use in research. An initial appropriation of $1,195,000 was allotted to the program, far less than Evans had requested. He characteristically decided to begin work on county archives with an eye for demonstrating the worth of the program and generating local political support for it.[30]

Evans' first and most difficult task was to organize his force of untrained workers, artfully creating the equivalent of a staff of trained historical researchers. In January, 1936, he published a procedural *Manual for the Survey of Historical Records,* attempting to reduce to routine practice the highly subjective evaluation and description of archives. His workers were directed first to prepare a complete list of archival depositories within their jurisdiction, seeking the permission of the custodian in each case before attempting to make an inventory of records. Records examiners were then dispatched in pairs to the courthouses of the land, becoming familiar first with the most recent records in each category before cataloging those records and working their way back from the present day.

No more than 3,000 Historical Records Survey workers were employed in any one month, but the teams somehow covered every courthouse in the nation. Some 3,066 workers inventoried the records to be found therein, and accomplished the whole task with a margin of error which is estimated not to exceed 15 per cent. The rough inventory forms describing each identified records series went directly to the state headquarters of the

---

[30] David L. Smiley, "The W.P.A. Historical Records Survey," in Hesseltine and McNeil, eds., *Clio,* 3–13.

survey, where other workers edited the information with inventories of standard form. WPA regulations prohibited printing of the inventories, but some were printed at local expense, and others were mimeographed in survey offices.[31] World War II brought an end to the program before it had completed its work, but by 1942 twenty-eight volumes of inventories of state archives, 628 volumes of county archives, and 180 volumes of municipal archives had been published. The material for the remaining local archives which had been gathered was deposited for safekeeping in state archives, state universities, historical societies, and other agencies until a more propitious time might see the completion of the heroic task. These plans never materialized.[32]

The large number of published guides and tenfold quantity of unpublished material produced by the Historical Records Survey has not yet received the attention and use it deserves, yet the survey can be considered nothing less than a success. For one point, it conclusively proved that high standards of accuracy were compatible with mass team scholarship, which suggests many opportunities for relieving scholars of the drudgery of routine. Secondly, it at least called attention to local documentation for American historical scholarship, and stimulated a greater demand for better archival care at the local level of government.[33] The survey never built any courthouse annexes, yet its work did much to bring about that end. In Tennessee, for example, one-fourth of the courthouses were provided with ample fireproof records vaults as a result of the survey findings of inadequate protection. The permanent improvement in records-keeping practices and care of local archives by the simple expedient of comparison has immeasurably improved the condition and research accessibility of records all over the country.[34]

Bad as was the case of county archives in the last century,

---

[31] Ibid., 14–23. The survey was expanded in 1937 to embrace an inventory of Early American Imprints, under D. C. McMurtrie. Subsequent projects listed portraits, surveyed the records of 235,000 church congregations, and undertook a Historical American Buildings Survey.

[32] Sargent B. Child, "What Is Past Is Prologue," in American Archivist, 5:217–227 (October, 1942).

[33] Smiley, "Records Survey," in Hesseltine and McNeil, eds., Clio, 23–27.

[34] Child, "What Is Past Is Prologue," 226–227. See also, Herbert A. Kellar, "An Appraisal of the Historical Records Survey of the Works Progress Administration," in A. F. Kuhlman, ed., Archives and Libraries (Chicago, 1940), 44–59.

that of the records of cities was probably even worse. The American city rose and expanded under conditions of social and political disgrace, and its indigenous documentation was accumulated without regard for the principles of archival economy. Widespread graft and corruption in the cities possibly made city administrators more reluctant to create or maintain documentation, and urban history had a serious shortage of documentation before the reform era forced popular attention upon the problem. Only within the last several years has there been a concerted effort to reform the archives of the American city on anything approximating the scale of that of the state and federal governments. Examples of the cases of Philadelphia and New York will suffice.

The modern city of Philadelphia began to take on its metropolitan character in 1854 when twenty-eight boroughs, districts, and townships were consolidated into a city government, centralizing the municipal records of the area. Some records were lost in the transfer, more in the move to the new city hall in 1888. Even more were lost, however, as a result of official neglect and corruption which began to infect the growing city. By 1904, Lincoln Steffens in *The Shame of the Cities* singled out Philadelphia as the worst-administered city in America, casually touching upon the derelict state of the official records of the city. But the Muckrakers sought more spectacular reforms than those of municipal archives, and little was done to correct the situation until 1950. In that year Joseph C. Clark, the city controller, determined to modernize completely the operations of his office, including a reform of its records functions. After a careful inventorying and sorting of material which had not been touched for years, Clark's staff found that the bulk of the records in its care could be reduced by 60 per cent, with corresponding savings to the city. This dramatic success had a bearing upon the new Home Rule Charter which the city was then drafting, and popular interest supported the inclusion of a Department of Records, embracing a Forms Control and an Archives Division. Operations were begun in 1952 and proved so successful that the independent office of Recorder of Deeds was transferred to the department as its third, or Documents, Division. Although the records management divisions of the Philadelphia program have emphasized forms control and reduction of permanent records by microphotography, the great success of these activities has carried along the archival program and given the city one of the most highly praised archives in the nation.[35]

Upon reorganization, the archives of Philadelphia were found to have totalled some 200,000 cubic feet, of which over half could be, and were, destroyed at a saving of over a third of a million dollars. The current accumulation of archives is proceeding at an orderly rate and is within the capacity of the city's resources. Having put its own archival house in order, the city was threatened with being overwhelmed by the documentation of the courts of record in the city. These courts were not under the provisions of the charter but were furnished office and filing space at city expense. The Court of Common Pleas, for example, processed 50,000 cubic feet of records and was accumulating new ones at a rate that threatened to fill the entire city hall within a few years. To meet this paper explosion, the city archives sponsored legislation to permit the court to dispose of part of its files and to employ the staff of the municipal archives to supervise a reduction to a more manageable size. Rounding off an admirable pioneering program, the Philadelphia Archives has published *A Guide to the Municipal Archives.*[36] Its example for other large cities is a commendable one.

The nation's largest city took no regard for its archives until Mayor Fiorello La Guardia in 1939 appointed an archives committee to study and make recommendations for reform. The sad conditions reported were not new, but the personal interest of the mayor procured an appropriation in 1943 of $500,000 for a central archives building. With that sum, the city bought the Rhinelander Building on Williams Street, only one block from city hall, which contained about 2,000,000 cubic feet of space convertible to records storage. Until the end of World War II the chief function of the records staff was paper salvage. In 1948 Mayor William O'Dwyer reestablished the archives committee, which urged the creation of a permanent agency with legal custody of the archives. An *ad hoc* agency as a branch of the

---

[35] Charles E. Hughes, Jr., "The Philadelphia Program," in *American Archivist,* 21:131–142 (April, 1958).

[36] *Ibid.,* 139.

Municipal Reference Library was soon constituted, and its functions have largely been those of records management, legal custody remaining in the creating agency and the records remaining closed to the public. The archives division proper has legal custody only of those records transferred to it, to date mainly those of the mayor's office since 1898. Both the records center and the archives division are exempt from the supervision of the New York State Division of Archives and History.[37]

The relatively modest archives program of the City of New York in 1959 cost only $73,000 out of a total city budget of over $2,000,000,000, and approximated 100,000 cubic feet, with at least 2,000,000 cubic feet of city records aging to become archives in the future.[38] The archival program of the city was, therefore, protected only by the cofferdam of records management.

APPRAISAL AND USE OF STATE AND LOCAL ARCHIVES

THE PUBLIC ARCHIVES of the states and localities should be subject to the same considerations of appraisal and use as govern those of the federal government, but their general applicability has not yet been recognized in all divisions of government, and exceptions are pleaded for certain types of subarchives. Until localities recognize the secondary, or cultural, value of their archives, local variations in the conditions under which they are appraised, opened for use, and used must be expected.

The principles of what to keep and what to dispose of in state archives reflect the diversity of state archival systems and the purposes motivating their establishment. There are no laws providing for the disposal of records in twenty-one states, where presumably it is a criminal offense to select any official records for destruction. In three states the law permits the selective destruction of specific records series, while another three states provide for the destruction of records upon approval from nonarchival agencies. The remaining majority of the states author-

[37] Jason Horn, "Municipal Archives and Records Center of the City of New York," in *American Archivist*, 16:311–320 (October, 1953).
[38] James Katsaros, "Managing the Records of the World's Greatest City," in *American Archivist*, 23:175–180 (April, 1960).

ize destruction of records only after appraisal by a competent archival authority. In addition to these general provisions, several states have legalized the destruction of records after they have been photographically reduced.[39]

On the premise that cities are actually public service corporations and that their records contain a higher percentage of permanent archives than any other level of local government, a different standard has been urged for the appraisal of municipal records. If the experience of the New York archives can be accepted as a guide, as much as 16 per cent of the total volume of records needs to be retained for permanent archival reference. The question of housing the large percentage of nonpermanent, nonarchival records, however, poses a problem almost as difficult as that of appraisal, and the generally accepted solution has been that of microfilm. Microfilm, however, may at times be an uneconomic solution, unjustified by any degree of public convenience or necessity. The case of the city records of Portland, Oregon, may be cited in example. That city recently filmed 2,200 cubic feet of noncurrent, nonarchival records at a total cost of $63,826, or about $25 to $30 per cubic foot. Microfilming can be justified as a method of preserving and storing such a category of records only if the costs of microfilm do not exceed the estimated yearly storage expense of the original document ($1.00 to $1.25 per cubic foot) times the estimated useful life of the records. In other words, the useful life of the Portland records should exceed twenty to twenty-two years to justify their being microfilmed.[40]

Although the principle has been irrefutably established that public records are public property, the law is not so emphatic as to the public accessibility of archives. Generally speaking, in the absence of statute law, the common law grants to operating departments of government discretion in supervising selective admission to the "public" portion of the records, provided that the right of personal privacy is always respected and that any use of the records is in the public interest. It is with this generally

[39] Christopher Crittenden, "The Disposal of Useless State Archives," in *American Archivist,* 7:165–173 (April, 1944).
[40] Thorton W. Mitchell, "Municipal Archival Programs," in *American Archivist,* 23:181–183 (April, 1960).

restrictive legal position that most state and local governments
protect themselves from the disruptions of public access to their
records, until access is granted by statute as a part of archival
reform. Even after reform, public access to state and local archives is more restricted than access to the federal archives. In
the federal system the primary, official function of archives has
been integrated with their secondary, cultural values. On the
state and local level, the primary function often takes precedence
over and restricts the extent of the secondary usage.

The laws and practices governing public access to archives and
records vary so widely that it is difficult to generalize upon them,
but it is certainly true that the fight for more liberal access has
been largely waged by the press. It fully understands that its
access to public records is generally based on administrative privilege rather than legal right, and this attitude might well be
adopted by scholars wishing access to the same material. While
it is true that the extent and freedom of access are widening under
the constant criticism of "secrecy in government," the increasing
liberality of the law is due to the operation of a cultural lag
rather than any contemporary legal thought. Where access is
granted selectively by administrative action, four principal points
are usually considered. Is the record in question "public" or
privileged? If a "public" record, is it traditionally open for inspection? Is inspection restricted to persons or purposes? Is it
possible in a given instance to enforce the presumed right of public inspection?[41] The significance of these considerations to the
scholar desiring access to local archives is that enlisting the interest and support of the local records keeper is more productive than quoting the letter of the law.

As the Historical Records Survey confirmed, the courthouses
of the 3,000 counties in the United States contain a bewildering
array of primary documentation for American historiography.
The one record series common to all, and one of high significance
to the writing of history, is that of land tenure and transfer.
Because evidence of the chain of title to the original owner is
a legal necessity, county governments have assumed the obligation of publicly recording and preserving every transfer of real

[41] Harold L. Cross, *The People's Right to Know: Legal Access to Public Records
and Proceedings* (New York, 1953), 5–13.

estate within their jurisdictions. The Middle West has further
refined the system by the additional service of a professional
abstracter, who cross-indexes all transfers of real estate by township and section, thereby providing at once a complete history of
the transactions affecting a given tract of land and greatly simplifying the work of the scholar. Another local land record of
prime significance for documentation are the surveyors' note-
books made in running the rectangular surveys in the Middle
West. These notes contain not only a description of the natural
terrain before settlement, but also an indication of the sites of
Indian and squatter settlements, and an excellent guide to soil
types. Prepared in triplicate, one copy was deposited in the
General Land Office in Washington, one remained in the local
land office, and one was deposited in the Surveyor General's
Office.[42]

Although land records in the office of the recorder of deeds
are undoubtedly the core of county records for historical research, other county offices contain often-overlooked documentation of importance. The records of the county court, or legislative and administrative board, contain minutes of its proceedings, the records of general administration, reports of vital statistics, records on road construction and maintenance, entries of
expenditures on public health and welfare, and documentation
for the wide variety of other service functions of local government. The file of the circuit court serving the county usually
contains a fairly complete file of cases tried before it, and probate court files contain documentation relating to the wills,
inheritances, orphans, and other public works of the county.
The records of the treasurers and commissioners of revenue
jointly reflect the economic growth of the area and its public
expenditures, most of which has always been for public education, as reflected in the files of the superintendent of schools and
the school board. Only by intelligent use of these varied record
series can the history of a county and its internal operations be
written.[43]

If counties and their records are numerous, municipalities
are, by comparison, legion. There are over 16,000 city and town

[42] Donald Dean Parker, *Local History* (New York, 1944), 51–54.
[43] *Ibid.*, 54–57.

governmental units in the United States, each with its own records. As a general rule, most of the officials of these municipal units are part-time public servants and employees, and the records created by them are correspondingly meager. Yet in the twentieth century there has been a trend towards more uniformity and intensity in municipal records keeping, laying the foundation for excellent documentation for urban history.[44]

Archives of state and local governments have not been more widely used in research because of the dual difficulties of locating and isolating a particular document out of a mass of papers scattered in so many depositories and often so inaccessible. The remedy for these difficulties is the development of a system of finding aids based upon an accurate inventory and description of the holdings of each unit of government.

State finding aids are as diverse as the records to which they relate. One of the most common forms, unfortunately, is the memory of a staff retainer. The most elementary written finding aid in general use is the inventory of holdings, or the shelf list, but it is generally not available to the public outside of the archives building, necessitating a personal trip to verify holdings. The accession number system, prevalent in Great Britain, is not much used in America despite its advantage of filling the shelves without the necessity of leaving space for future accessions of similar material. As a finding aid system it is completely arbitrary and requires a close knowledge of the organization to find specific materials. Lists of holdings, similar to those issued by the National Archives, have been issued from a number of state archival establishments, but the lack of uniformity in reporting and arranging the entries leaves something to be desired. Calendars, on the other hand, were formerly the delight of scholars, and when published often eliminated the necessity of reference to the original document. The high cost of preparing and publishing such guides has made them obsolete except in the case of series of very high significance and very low bulk. Indexes, usually of personal names, are the modern equivalent of calendars. If they are done thoroughly, however, the index often grows larger than the original body of records. Only in the case of specific materials for specific purposes can such massive proj-

---

[44] *Ibid.*, 62–63.

ects as the Ainsworth carded records be justified. Otherwise, scholars using state and local archives must rely upon self-indexing schemes or learn to be patient with the nature of their sources.[45]

Inventories of the Historical Records Survey are by far the most important single class of finding aids to state and federal archives. That portion of the guides which has been published is readily available in most research libraries; the unpublished guides are to be found in typescript on deposit in the designated central historical library of each state. These guides have long awaited the reference use for which they were intended, and a growing familiarity with them on the part of scholars will greatly facilitate research.

Special guides to state and local archives are beginning to appear as the result of a demand for such material. A revision of the valuable topical guide to New York City materials for early American history was published in 1953[46] and stands as a model for other large metropolitan collections. Its companion tool for early state archives and manuscripts was published in 1950.[47] Probably the most ambitious step yet taken to centralize the finding-aids program for state and local archives was a publication in 1961 by Philip M. Hamer for the National Historical Publication Commission.[48] Although this work is of great help in identifying the general nature of the archives in various agencies, until something approximating a union list of archives is created, scholars must continue to rely upon personal mobility and strong constitutions to serve as their finding aids.

The establishment by the American Historical Association in 1964 of an *Ad Hoc* Committee to Collect the Basic Data of American Political History suggests another means by which the use of state and local archives in national historiography may be facilitated. Despite the obstacles involved in locating and using such documentary evidence, American historians have begun

---

[45] William J. Van Schreevan, "Information Please: Finding Aids in State and Local Archival Depositories," in *American Archivist,* 5:169–178 (July, 1942). Cf. Ainsworth records, *supra,* Chapter I.

[46] Greene and Morris, *Guide to . . . Early American History,* 208–211, 331–333.

[47] William Sumner Jenkins and Lillian A. Hamick, *A Guide to Microfilm Collections of Early State Records* (Washington, 1950).

[48] Hamer, *Guide to Archives.*

to employ it for studies in such fields as popular voting, legislative voting, and demography. Giving national coordination to the search for the most pertinent local archives, the immediate goal of the *ad hoc* committee was the collecting of all county election returns since 1824 for all federal elections and statewide contests. Within the first year, the goal was 90 per cent realized, which strongly suggests that concerted effort by the historical profession may reduce the obstacles in state and local archives to manageable and usable proportions.[49]

[49] Samuel P. Hays, "Archival Sources for American Political History," in *American Archivist*, 28:17–26 (January, 1965).

vvv

III

vvvvvvvvvvvvvvvvvvvvvvvvvvvvvvvvvvvvvvvvvvvvvvvvvvvvvvvvvvv

QUASI-PUBLIC ARCHIVES

O NE OF THE BASIC TRENDS in the rise of civilization
has been the institutionalization of modern society, and this
trend has precipitated a concurrent evolution in the process of
modern historical documentation. There was a time when the
history of a state could be safely (if not solely) based upon the
records of its government and its few great leaders, but in the
modern world there has evolved a whole spectrum of institutions
which variously separate and converge the members of society,
and which largely determine the nature of the social fabric by
the network of ties and associations which they foster. It would
be foolish, if not impossible, to base a history of the United
States solely upon the resources of the National Archives and the
private papers of the Presidents. Not even the outlines of the
nation's development could be correctly drawn, for the connecting threads between the state and the individual supplied by
organized institutions would be missing.

To the alarm of rugged individualists, *individuals* have largely ceased to exist in modern society. Social existence has come
to mean membership in some quasi-public group, be it a labor
union or a professional organization, a church or a club, a na-
tionality faction or a racial minority, a formal political party or
an informal pressure group, or an upper, upper-middle, upper-
lower-middle, or lower social class. Americans have lost their
individual identities to gain status and satisfaction as group participants and conformists, and American history is increasingly

74

revealed in the records of its groups. These institutions have become so intimately clothed with the public interest that they must perforce expect public interest in their records and archives. The time is coming, and is now here, when such quasi-public documentation is regarded as public property held in private trust. For the most part, scholars have already made good the public claim to such material.

Of primary concern in American historical documentation are the archives of religious denominations, colleges and other educational institutions, labor organizations, and other social, cultural, and political institutions. These archives are here considered as a composite grouping, with the parallel category of business records receiving separate treatment elsewhere.

RECORDS OF QUASI-PUBLIC INSTITUTIONS

OTHER THAN a common principle of co-operative action through social organization, the myriad of quasi-public organizations in contemporary America defies generalization as to character, purposes, and history. The historian's earlier concern with such diverse groups was the substantive history of the group itself, but he has come to seek in the records of social organizations the documentation for the new dimensions of social history. No matter how local, each group is nationally significant in some degree, and so are its records.

Over 260 religious bodies were listed in the 1960 *Yearbook of American Churches*, and no one pretends that this list is complete. To a characteristically high degree, they all seek to perpetuate themselves partially through a reconstruction of their past, hence they are all actively interested in records preservation. This task has been principally delegated to the various denominational seminaries, which, until the recent development of co-operative professional and library standards, often defended denominational orthodoxy and exclusiveness from the ramparts of anti-intellectualism and a close provincialism. Such well-organized churches as the Roman Catholic, Episcopal, and Presbyterian have long stressed good denominational records of a comprehensive nature. The liturgical churches, such as the Lutheran and Episcopal, have tended to develop strong holdings

of material relating to liturgies and canon law, while the non-
liturgical Baptists, Disciples of Christ, and other free churches
seldom have archives outside their working papers of administration. Those American churches traditionally associated with
later ethnic arrivals have compiled records far removed from their
purely ecclesiastical functions, more properly illustrating their
secondary function as cultural acclimatizer.[1]

In addition to a denominational exclusiveness regarding church
records, an earlier historical emphasis upon economic determin-
ism retarded the development of social and cultural history and
impaired the professional historian's interest in the supporting
documentation for it. The interest in American religious subjects can be almost dated from a 1907 address by J. F. Jameson,
"The American Acta Sanctorum," in which he made a plea for
the study of the religious past as an aspect of cultural history.
By 1920 the field had become a respectable province for historical study, and it provided a growing number of topics for
doctoral dissertations. The use of American religious history also reflected denominational demands for professional, scholarly
treatments of their past. All of the better denominational colleges boast well-trained scholars in their chairs of history, and
these men have exercised a powerful constructive influence upon
the care and preservation of church records, previously the exclusive domain of retainees, antiquarians, and amateurs.[2] It will
be observed that the character and organization of each denomi-

---

[1] Roscoe M. Pierson, "Denominational Collections in Theological Seminary and
Church Historical Society Libraries," in *Library Trends*, 9:213–230 (October, 1960);
Parker, *Local History*, 82; August R. Suelflow, "The Struggle of Church Archives
for Respectability," in *American Archivist*, 24:403–408 (October, 1961). The libraries of religious denominational institutions have been professionalized through
the Amercan Theological Library Association, the American Society of Church
History, and other similar groups. Having overcome their professional inferiority
complex, these librarians are no longer apologetic in collecting denominational
material. Thus, there is a theological library equivalent of the ecumenical movement.

[2] William Warren Sweet, "Church Archives in the United States," in *American
Archivist*, 14:323–331 (October, 1951); see also Sweet, "Church Archives in the
United States," in *Church History*, 8:43–53 (March, 1939). Of course, the circumstances under which church records were created were not always ideal for their
preservation, but where they have been preserved they often are the earliest
sources of community history, predating official archives and newspapers. See
Parker, *Local History*, 80–82.

nation largely determines the nature and accessibility of its archives.

The Roman Catholic Church in the United States has inherited the long tradition and the canonical obligations of records keeping common to the universal church, but its status as a non-established church in the United States has precluded the famed archival network which it has evolved in Catholic lands.

Catholic archives are divided into the two basic classes of ecclesiastical archives of the church proper, and corporate or institutional archives of clerical or lay orders, societies, and organizations. Canon law governs the creation and maintenance of the former, but the latter are regarded as private collections, outside the authority of canon law, although often preserved as carefully as the archives of the church proper. The ecclesiastical archives of the church in America fall into three basic groupings of archdiocesan, diocesan, and parish records, reflecting the basic structure of church organization. Within archdiocesan or metropolitan archives are included communications to and from the Holy See, acts of provincial councils, certain types of documents relating to suffragan dioceses, records of consecration of bishops, appeals from suffragan tribunals, and other similar administrative series accumulated by the chancery of an archdiocese. Diocesan or episcopal archives likewise include documents to and from the Holy See, acts of diocesan synods, minutes of episcopal *curia*, records of ordinations and matrimonial dispensations, deeds to diocesan real property, reports of the spiritual and material condition of tributary parishes, reports of the diocesan school superintendent and diocesan bounties, and all official administrative records pertaining to the bishopric. Parish or parochial archives document the origin and development of individual churches and contain the official letters to and from bishops, confirmations, marriages, and summaries of the spiritual and material condition of the parish.[3]

Because the earliest Catholic dioceses in America generally grew up to become metropolitan sees, they are the most important record centers. Baltimore has the oldest, but New York

[3] Thomas F. O'Connor, "Historical and Archival Activities of the Roman Catholic Church in the United States," in American Association for State and Local History, *Church Archives and History* (*Bulletin*, vol. I, no. 10, April, 1946), 287–295.

has by far the best-organized collection of records, due largely to the interest and work of Archbishop Michael Corrigan, 1885–1902.[4] The archives of Detroit, Cincinnati, New Orleans, and Vincennes, incomplete as they are, are especially important for the role of the church in the development of the West, and they have fortunately survived the perils of several reorganizations and have been brought together at Notre Dame University in a special collection known as the Catholic Archives of America. Their archival existence is a tribute to the foresight and initiative of Professor James Farnham Edwards, who taught history at Notre Dame in the early twentieth century.[5] Catholic archival development has had twin traditions: archives for the administrator and archives for the historian. The former has been emphasized in theory, but the latter has excelled in practice. Diocesan records have freely passed into and out of private hands, and it was Professor Edwards who conceived the plan of centralizing the orphan archives or those which could better serve scholarship than administration.[6]

The work of Professor Edwards and Archbishop Corrigan also stimulated the codification of the law of archives in the Code of 1918. Pertaining only to ecclesiastical archives, the code defined archives of two classes, common and secret, the latter being confidential records touching matters of conscience or the canonical process. All bishops were thenceforth required to keep archives in a safe and orderly manner, to secure the return of archival strays, and to protect their records against theft or unlawful entry. It has been established that the archives of the church exist primarily for administrative purposes, and even the common class may be opened to public inspection and research only upon application to the bishop or his diocesan chancellor. Au-

---

[4] O'Connor, in AASLH, *Church Archives and History*, 291–295. The historical derivation of other dioceses traces to the creation of the diocese of Spanish Louisiana in 1793, which came under the jurisdiction of Baltimore after the Louisiana Purchase.

[5] *Ibid.*, 296; Sweet, "Church Archives," in *Church History*, 46–47; Mabel E. Deutrich, "American Church Archives—An Overview," in *American Archivist*, 24:396–397 (October, 1961); Thomas T. McAvoy, "Catholic Archives and Manuscript Collections," in *American Archivist*, 24:409–414 (October, 1961).

[6] Henry J. Browne, "The American Catholic Archival Tradition," in *American Archivist*, 14:127–140 (April, 1951).

thenticated copies of any document will generally be provided at cost.[7]

Most Catholic corporate archives are still family secrets in the possession of their creators. The only central depositories, other than Notre Dame, are at St. Louis University (western Jesuit archives) and in the American Catholic Historical Association at Catholic University of America in Washington, D.C.[8]

The Protestant Episcopal Church, although hierarchical in structure, has not developed the institutionalized network of archives characteristic of the Roman Catholic Church. In theory each diocese has, or once possessed, its own archives, but they have become scattered to such a degree that the only workable collections are those which have been aggressively collected. One of the principal collections is at Church Mission House, 281 Fourth Avenue, New York City, covering the church in the colonial period. The Church Historical Society, founded in 1910, formerly administered an archival establishment at Episcopal Divinity School in Philadelphia which was national in scope. In 1940 it was designated as the official depository, and in 1956 it was transferred to the Theological Seminary of the Southwest in Austin, Texas. Among more than 6,000 cubic feet of holdings is a complete file of General Convention journals and many journals of diocesan conventions. Other Episcopal collections of national or regional significance are housed at various Episcopal seminaries about the nation, particularly at Trinity College (Hartford), Maryland Diocesan Library (Baltimore), Massachusetts Diocesan Library (Boston), and Virginia Diocesan Library (Richmond).[9]

Presbyterian archives are well cared for, reflecting the characteristic organization of the denomination. The polity of Presbyterianism, a system of graded courts, is the foundation for the systematic preservation of records. Each local congregation is ruled by a session, or consistory, which in turn sends delegates

---

[7] O'Connor, in AASLH, *Church Archives and History*, 301–304.

[8] *Ibid.*, 296; Pierson, "Denominational Collections," 230.

[9] Sweet, "Church Archives," in *Church History*, 48; Pierson, "Denominational Collections," 229; Deutrich, "American Church Archives," 401; Dorman H. Winfrey, "Protestant Episcopal Church Archives," in *American Archivist*, 24:431–433 (October, 1961).

to the regular meetings of a presbytery, or classis, usually encompassing a major portion of a state. Presbyteries are grouped to form synods, generally with boundaries coterminus with states. At the national level is the General Assembly, exercising supreme legislative, judicial, and executive control over the denomination. The Presbyterian Church in the U.S.A. assumed corporate form in 1706 with the creation of the first presbytery; in 1716 the first American synod met. Following the establishment of national independence, the General Assembly was constituted in 1789. Under its direction the extant records of the church have been given professional care, probably the best of any Protestant denomination.[10]

The ruling body of the Presbyterian Church has regarded the function of keeping its archives as worthy of a special department in the offices of the General Assembly, located in the Witherspoon Building in Philadelphia. In addition to this central depository, which includes the records of the church from its founding, there are smaller regional depositories at Presbyterian theological seminaries at San Francisco, Auburn (New York), McCormick (Chicago), and Princeton.[11]

The Presbyterians were among the Protestant denominations deeply split by the Civil War, and the southern branch was organized at Augusta, Georgia, in 1861. After the fall of the Confederacy, the southern branch assumed the title of the Presbyterian Church in the U.S., leaving off "of America" for distinction from the parent body with which it has hitherto refused to join.

The southern branch continued its separate development, sharing the traditions of the larger family, among which is an emphasis upon church records. With more modest financial resources, the church did not benefit from the professionalization of its archives until Dr. S. M. Tenney, the "Draper of Southern Presbyterianism," began to collect manuscript records. Out of this private effort grew the establishment in 1926 of the Historical Foundation of the Presbyterian and Reformed Churches, at Mon-

[10] Thomas H. Spence, Jr., "The Historical Foundation of the Presbyterian and Reformed Churches," in AASLH, *Church Archives and History*, 259–262.

[11] Pierson, "Denominational Collections," 229; Deutrich, "American Church Archives," 401.

treat, North Carolina. Housed in a stone building, the agency now holds over 1,000 volumes of original presbyterial, synodical, and session records, a remarkably complete file of property deeds, and a quantity of records from Presbyterian educational institutions. An excellent collection of printed volumes and records completes the material for this religious group, renowned for its high regard for its own history and church records in general. Additional "southern" Presbyterian archives are located at the denomination's seminaries in Richmond, Virginia, and Louisville, Kentucky.[12]

The Methodist Church began its separate existence in the United States in 1784, and its growth has paralleled in microcosm the American society within which it has come to be a major religious factor. Springing from deep English roots in the eighteenth century, it divided in the nineteenth and reunited in the twentieth. Despite its hierarchial organization, it has never established a central archival repository matching its General, Jurisdictional, and Annual Conferences.[13]

The Methodist Church has manifested interest in its own history through a multiplicity of historical societies, each aspiring to collect some locally accreditable church archives, and most of them affiliated with the Association of Methodist Historical Societies, located at Lake Junaluska, North Carolina. Outside the framework of the National Conference, major archival collections are to be found in society depositories in New York, Boston, Philadelphia, Baltimore, and Atlanta. The library of the Methodist Publishing House in Nashville, Tennessee, also boasts a major body of Methodist archives.[14] The fragmentation of the archives of Methodism has recently spurred the National Conference to action to overcome the worst aspects of the difficulty. A National Methodist Historical Society has been formed for the purpose of establishing a national Methodist archives and drawing

[12] Spence, in AASLH, *Church Archives and History,* 263; Thomas H. Spence, Jr., *Historical Foundation of the Presbyterian and Reformed Churches* (Montreat, North Carolina, 1956), 1–15, 61–75; Sweet, "Church Archives," in *American Archivist,* 329; Deutrich, "American Church Archives," 401.

[13] William E. Lind, "Methodist Archives in the United States," in *American Archivist,* 24:435–440 (October, 1961).

[14] Pierson, "Denominational Collections," 229; Sweet, "Church Archives," in *American Archivist,* 329.

to it the various major collections now scattered about the country.[15]

The Disciples of Christ, the youngest major church in the United States, is greatly interested in its historical development, the interest stimulated by the celebration of the sesquicentennial of its founder, Alexander Campbell. Small collections of its archives have been in existence for some time at Transylvania University in Lexington, Kentucky, and at Disciples Divinity House, an affiliate of the University of Chicago. More recently another regional depository has been established on the West Coast at Culver-Stockton College in California. By far the most important collection of archives for the church, however, is that held by the Disciples of Christ Historical Society in Nashville, Tennessee.[16]

The archives of the Congregational Church reveal the denomination's principal emphasis upon educational and missionary endeavors. The American Board of Foreign Missions was founded in 1810, the first major overseas expansion of American Protestantism. Since that time the board has supervised the work of over 4,500 regular missionaries and about 1,000 short-term appointees; thereby a large volume of highly illuminating correspondence has been accumulated. Originally housed in the library of the American Congregation Association, the archives have since been transferred to the Andover-Harvard Library and are available for scholarly research. They are particularly valuable as documentation of American cultural expansion as the first wave of American imperialism, the development of Congregationalism at home and abroad, and the "tainted money" philanthropy controversy of 1910.[17]

The Boston collections are supplemented by those in the Chicago Theological Seminary. Here are located the archives of the American Home Missionary Society, the Church Building Soci-

---

[15] Sweet, "Church Archives," in *Church History*, 49–50; Deutrich, "American Church Archives," 400; Edwin Schell, "Methodist Records and History at the Grassroots in Northern Virginia," in *American Archivist*, 27:381–386 (July, 1964).

[16] Sweet, "Church Archives," in *American Archivist*, 330; Sweet, "Church Archives," in *Church History*, 47–48; Pierson, "Denominational Collections," 227; Deutrich, "American Church Archives," 398–399.

[17] Mary Walker, "The Archives of the American Board for Foreign Missions," in *Harvard Library Bulletin*, 6:52–68 (Winter, 1932).

ety, and other organs and prominent members of the church. The denominational holdings at the American Congregational Association in Boston must now be supplemented also by those of the Historical Society of the Evangelical and Reformed Church at Lancaster, Pennsylvania, since the recent merger of the two denominations. Other Congregational collections are located at the Congregation Library in Boston, Congregational House in Hartford, Grinnell College, Dartmouth College, and Oberlin College.[18]

The historical interest of the Church of Jesus Christ of Latter-Day Saints in its past is distinctive and unique, and, as an outgrowth of it, American history and its documentation is the beneficiary. The church traces its origin to 1823, when Joseph Smith claimed to have had revealed to him a set of golden plates upon which was inscribed the Book of Mormon. Thus, from the very beginning, the keeping of records has been the tradition of the Mormon faith. As it has spread by vigorous missionary activity, each unit has been required to keep systematic records and to report to a central office. More than 1,000 wards, over 100 stakes, and over 40 missions each report through hierarchical channels to the office of the church historian in Salt Lake City, where there is prepared a master day-by-day journal of the church as a whole. The worldwide scope of the church gives its archives international significance, and their secular value was proved during World War II when hundreds of photographs and firsthand descriptions of war areas were supplied to American military intelligence units.[19]

Mormons believe in the principle of vicarious work for the dead, the living standing as proxies in performing baptism, ordination, marriage, and other rites for those who died "without the law." As the basis for this temple work, the Genealogical Society of the Church of Jesus Christ of Latter-Day Saints has over 13,000,000 file cards on the forebearers of contemporary members of the church. The belief that its members should

[18] Sweet, "Church Archives," in *American Archivist*, 330; Sweet "Church Archives," in *Church History*, 47; Pierson, "Denominational Collections," 227; Deutrich, "American Church Archives," 398.

[19] Pierson, "Denominational Collections," 228; Virgil H. Peterson, "Behold There Shall Be a Record Kept Among You," in AASLH, *Church Archives and History*, 272.

know and revere their forefathers has given further impetus to
the church's genealogical interest and organized program. In
1938 the church began its famed microfilm project, casting a
broad net to film the original records of genealogical interest
from Europe and the older parts of America. A continuing project, it has made over 200,000 rolls of microfilm, corresponding
to more than 200,000,000 pages of original unpublished records.
At an average of 300 pages per volume, this material equalled
that contained in more than 700,000 bound volumes.[20]

Three copies of each roll of film were made, the negative and
one positive print going to Salt Lake City, and one positive print
to the owner of the original records in appreciation for its cooperation. By this co-operation many counties in eastern states
had their oldest wills, deeds, land records, court records, marriage banns and licenses, tax and military rolls, and similar records duplicated on film at no charge. The copies in Salt Lake
City constitute an incomparable collection for local American
history. The material is kept in proper physical conditions, is
exactingly cataloged, and is open for the use of the public. Together, the church historian's office and the library of the Genealogical Society constitute the largest and best-supported center
for the study of any American religious body. In addition, the
official records are invaluable in documenting the economic and
social history of the West, especially the role of the church in
railroad building and early industrial development.[21]

The Deism of the Revolutionary generation produced pro-
found changes in American Protestant sectarianism, and the
changes have been reflected in the records left by the churches
and sects. During the crisis of the Revolution the Church of
England was politically suspect, and its records were left to be
scattered. The Methodist Church rapidly moved to take the
social position formerly held by the Anglican organization in
many areas of the United States. The Baptist Church, long regarded as radical by the more conservative of the colonials, became quite respectable during the Revolution and with the

<hr>

[20] Deutrich, "American Church Archives," 399–400.

[21] Peterson, in AASLH, *Church Archives and History,* 278–279; Pierson, "Denominational Collections," 227; Archibald F. Bennett, "The Record Copying Program of
the Utah Genealogical Society," in *American Archivist,* 16:227–232 (July, 1953).

Methodist Church enjoyed a tremendous cycle of growth and expansion. The first great wave of national expansion took place under the sway of a religious revival, fully capitalized upon by the Baptists and Methodists, but this growth was at the expense of a wide irregularity in records-keeping practices. During the nineteenth century, as the maturing denominations began to be more conscious of their origins and their early records, they began to institutionalize their archives at some affiliated college or seminary.[22]

The Baptist Church is a case in point. Due to its loose organization, it has failed to produce a large body of centralized archives, and the sectional split during the Civil War further scattered those papers which would have ultimately qualified as archives.

Under the auspices of the American Baptist Historical Society, founded in 1853, one of the leading Baptist archival collections has been built at Crozer Theological Seminary at Chester, Pennsylvania. This depository contains about 500 volumes of Baptist periodicals, a virtually complete file of state reports, 3,000 sets of minutes of Baptist Associations in the United States and foreign areas, manuscript letters of prominent clergy and laymen, numerous church record books, a complete file of Northern Baptist Convention annual reports, Foreign and Home Missionary Society reports, and miscellaneous material. An even larger and more valuable collection of Northern Baptist archives has been brought together in the American Baptist Historical Society on the campus of Colgate-Rochester Theological Seminary in Rochester, New York. Other Baptist archives are located at Southern Baptist Theological Seminary in Louisville; Furman University, Greenville, South Carolina; Baylor University, Waco, Texas; Franklin College, Franklin, Indiana; University of Richmond, Virginia; Bethel Theological Seminary, St. Paul; and Andover-Newton Theological School, Newton Center, Massachusetts.[23]

The exclusive archival agency for the Southern Baptist Church was formerly the library of its theological seminary in Louisville,

[22] Deutrich, "American Church Archives," 387–390.
[23] *Ibid.*

Kentucky, containing the manuscript record books of many individual congregations and the minutes of the Southern Association. Recently, however, the Historical Commission of the
Southern Baptist Convention in Nashville has undertaken an
aggressive collecting program through microfilming local church
records and centralizing the films in its Nashville offices.[24]

The organizational complexity of the Lutheran Church in
America is reflected in the decentralization of its archives. Dis-
counting small splinter factions, there are three large, loosely-knit
bodies of Lutherans in America: the Synodical Conference, American Lutheran Conference, and the United Lutheran Church.
The numerous archival depositories document the various shifts
which have produced the basic organizational structure.

The Synodical Conference was formed in 1872 by a union of
the Missouri Synod and the Wisconsin Synod. The former, established by German Lutheran immigrants in the 1840's, has remained strictly orthodox and has designated Concordia Historical Institute in St. Louis as its archival depository. The smaller
Wisconsin Synod, the outgrowth of Lutheran settlement near
Milwaukee in the 1850's, has established its archives at the Lutheran Theological Seminary at Thiensville, Wisconsin.[25]

The American Lutheran Conference, the church of the Scandinavian Lutheran, was formed in 1930 by the union of a number of constituent groups. The American Lutheran Church, a
merger of German and Swedish synods of Ohio, New York, and
Iowa, established its archives at Wartburg Theological Seminary
at Dubuque, Iowa. The Swedish Lutherans were principally
members of the Augustana Synod, whose main archives are at
Augustana College Library, Rock Island, Illinois, supplemented
by smaller holdings at Gustavus Adolphus College, St. Peter,
Minnesota, and Upsala College, East Orange, New Jersey.[26]

The United Lutheran Church, a merger in 1917 of several

[24] Pierson, "Denominational Collections," 226; Sweet, "Church Archives," in
Church History, 45–46; Belden Menkus, "The Baptist Sunday School Board and
Its Records," in *American Archivist*, 24:441–444 (October, 1961).

[25] Mabel Deutrich, "Archival Developments in Lutheran Churches in the United
States," in *American Archivist*, 15:127–138 (April, 1952).

[26] Deutrich, "Archival Developments," 130–135; Deutrich, "American Church
Archives," 400.

smaller groups, is largely comprised of the Dutch Lutheran congregations. Their archives are located at the Lutheran theological seminaries in Philadelphia and in Gettysburg.[27]

American Judaism has had its records centralized at the American Jewish Archives, located on the campus of Hebrew Union College-Jewish Institute of Religion in Cincinnati, Ohio. Founded in 1947, the American Jewish Archives has become a major center for research in American Jewish history. Broad in appeal, the collection recognizes the role of the United States in the contemporary world and the role of international Jewry in influencing American development and policy. While the material is drawn principally from the twentieth century, some of it goes back to the Revolution. In addition, there is a growing collection of American Jewish periodical literature, mostly on microfilm. A smaller but quite significant collection of Jewish historical documentation is located at the Jewish Theological Seminary of America in New York City.[28] A more recent develop ment is the establishment of a collection by the American Jewish Historical Society on the campus of Brandeis University at Waltham, Massachusetts.

Other Protestant churches have archival arrangements as varied as those of their larger cousins. The Friends Library in Philadelphia is an outstanding example of a central repository, housing in a fireproof building Quaker material dating from 1742. Particularly conscious of their history, local meetings have also generally provided for the care of their archives, such as the example of the Joint Archives of the two New York Yearly Meetings, kept in the Quaker Meeting House, Rutherford Place, New York City. A unique Quaker archival collection is also housed in the library of Swarthmore College.[29]

The American Moravian Church has two provinces in the United States, each with a very extensive set of records. The

[27] Deutrich, "Archival Developments," 135; Sweet, "Church Archives," in *Church History,* 49; Pierson, "Denominational Collections," 228.

[28] Pierson, "Denominational Collections," 228; Jacob R. Marcus, "The American Jewish Archives," in *American Archivist,* 23:57–61 (January, 1960); Deutrich, "American Church Archives," 397.

[29] Sweet, "Church Archives," in *Church History,* 48; Deutrich, "American Church Archives," 399.

archives at Bethlehem, Pennsylvania, contain material dating
back to 1457; those in Winston-Salem, North Carolina, contain
material dating from 1753. The Moravian Provincial Archives
at Bethlehem is built around a collection of some 7,000 volumes
relating to the history of the church. Added to this nucleus has
been a fine group of paintings, a large body of manuscript music, and over 500,000 pages of original archives from the various
congregations, stemming from the strict reporting system instituted by the founder, Count Zinendorf. While a good deal of
the material is repetitive, nevertheless it constitutes one of the
most complete bodies of documentation for tracing the social
and political development of a culturally homogeneous group
in America.[30]

In 1953 the General Conference of the Seventh Day Adventist
Church decided to establish its central archives in the conference
headquarters at Takoma Park, Maryland. The records date back
to the formation of the church at Battle Creek, Michigan, in
1863, and now embrace statistical and related records documenting the denominational growth, correspondence of the secretary
with administrative officers since 1863, and official records of
the Conference since 1863. All three groups are adequately indexed, but only the first is open to public use. A systematic records management program has been instituted in the various
Adventist offices, and the church archives promises to become
one of the best organized and most useful of its kind in the country.[31]

A shining example of church archival reform is provided by
the United Church of Canada. Formed in 1925 by a merger of
Congregational, Methodist, and Presbyterian bodies, all with
poor records habits, the new denomination has established a
central archives at Victoria University in Toronto. The agency
receives individual church records as well as those of the organization. Each conference of the church also has its own library

---

[30] Sweet, "Church Archives," in *Church History*, 50; Pierson, "Denominational
Collections," 226–230; Deutrich, "American Church Archives," 400; Kenneth G.
Hamilton, "The Moravian Archives at Bethlehem, Pennsylvania," in *American
Archivist*, 24:415–423 (October, 1961).

[31] Jason Horn, "Seventh Day Adventist Archives," in *American Archivist*, 17:221–
224 (July, 1954).

and keeps such records as it may feel capable of caring for.[32]

Among the smaller American denominations, the common practice has been to place archives in the care of one or more colleges or seminaries under the control of the denomination. For example, the central archives of the Christian Reformed Church are located at Calvin College, Grand Rapids, Michigan. The Evangelical and Reformed Church has placed its records at Franklin and Marshall College, Lancaster, Pennsylvania, and at Eden Theological Seminary, Webster Groves, Missouri. The archives of the Mennonite Church are at Goshen College, Goshen, Indiana, with smaller groups at other Mennonite colleges throughout the Midwest. The New Brunswick Theological Seminary in New Jersey houses the records of the (Dutch) Reformed Church in America. The archives of the Unitarian-Universalist Association are located at Meadville Theological School in Chicago and at Crane Theological School, Tufts University, Medford, Massachusetts.[33]

The organizational archives referred to above by no means contain all of the religious archives in the country, for many groups of such records have been "adopted out" to collecting institutions not connected with the creating denominations. State historical societies have been active in collecting church archives, especially in Massachusetts, Pennsylvania, Wisconsin, and Minnesota. University libraries have also been active in the field, the largest collections having been compiled by the University of Chicago, Union Theological Seminary, and Duke University.[34]

The libraries of institutions of higher education have long been active in the collection of religious manuscript materials, but only recently has the concept of institutional archives become widespread. Jared Sparks began the movement by gathering all available Harvard records and depositing them in the library.

[32] E. C. Kyte, "Archives of the United Church of Canada," in *American Archivist,* 13:229–232 (July, 1950).

[33] Deutrich, "American Church Archives," 398–402.

[34] Sweet, "Church Archives," in *Church History,* 52–53; Suelflow, "The Struggle of Church Archives," 403–408; Melvin Gingerich, "A Manual for Church Archivists," in *American Archivist,* 24:455–450 (October, 1961); Pascal Marie Varieur, "The Small, Limited, or Specialized Church Archives," in *American Archivist,* 24: 451–456 (October, 1961); Edmund L. Binsfield, "Church Archives in the United States and Canada, A Bibliography," in *American Archivist,* 21:311–332 (July, 1958).

Dartmouth records have been housed in the library since 1870, and Librarian Melvil Dewey instituted an archival section in the Columbia University Library. All of these projects were prompted by historical rather than administrative motives, and all later suffered under library management, becoming confused with manuscript collections in those institutions. As the organic archives of a corporate entity, their proper preservation requires firm administrative backing as well as warm support from the faculty. Recognizing its records as the organic archives of a corporate entity, Harvard University reformed its archives in 1930. Similar action followed at Montana State University, Fisk University, and Brown University. Archives are generally placed within the library, although that is not necessarily the best place for them. Other institutions have recognized the inherent conflict, and have constituted their archives as separate divisions, responsible directly to the president, although they may be conveniently housed in the institution's library.[35]

College archives were surveyed in 1962, resulting in a report of a bewildering array and a steady growth of archival agencies. Almost 120 had separate archival divisions. In seventy other colleges, archives-keeping was a function of the library or an appointed faculty member. In fifty-four institutions reporting, individual offices continue to keep their own records, and thirty-one institutions reported that they made no provision at all for archives. The report recommended certain immediate reforms: employment of a trained archivist where the size of the institution warranted; integration of archives as part of the administrative scheme, not as an appendage of the library; establishment of archives independent of the library; and restriction of archives to the materials of the sponsoring institution.[36]

[35] John Melville Jennings, "Archival Activity in American Universities and Colleges," in *American Archivist*, 12:155-163 (April, 1949); Clifford K. Shipton, "College Archives and Academic Research," in *American Archivist*, 27:395-400 (July, 1964); Anne MacDermot, "University Archives in the Boston Area," in *American Archivist*, 23:407-417 (October, 1960).

[36] Dwight H. Wilson, "Archives in Colleges and Universities," in *American Archivist*, 13:343-350 (October, 1950). See also Ernst Posner, "The College and University Archives in the United States," in *Miscellanea Mercati* (Vatican City, 1952), 363-374; Philip P. Mason, "College and University Archives: 1962," in *American Archivist*, 26:161-166 (April, 1963).

The treatment of theses as official administrative documents in schools offering graduate programs poses a special problem. If such a view leads to placement in the archives, the archives are apt to become overburdened by frequency of consultation, for, as thesis librarians can testify, theses *are* consulted. Actually the field of theses is the juncture of a number of lines of interest. As "unpublished" books, theses are rightfully library materials. As "potential" books they are in a category which university presses attempt to publish with high selectivity. The university archivist frequently will find his custody of the thesis collection his entree to the wider academic community, and it should be so used. Only as archival materials are used, and only when archival collections are enlarged by faculty and administrative support can they be regarded as serving their primary purpose.[37]

The historically decentralized nature of the labor movement in the United States has produced a volume of records far exceeding that of other nations. This decentralization has had its disadvantages, however. The files of American labor are scattered throughout the country, most of them poorly housed, and the bulk of them relatively inaccessible to researchers. These records represent probably the largest single category of primary research material for American history which remains to be explored and utilized.

There exists an amazingly varied number and type of labor organizations, often having little association with one another, but all presumably possessing their own records. Strictly speaking, therefore, the "archives of labor" is a misnomer, for no such clearly identifiable body of records exists. According to the list of labor organizations, theoretically there are archives for 109 international unions, 50 state and territorial federations, and 821 city central federations of the American Federation of Labor. In addition there should be records for the 33 member unions of the former Congress of Industrial Organizations, 40 state industrial committees, and 247 city and county labor councils. To these groups there must be added 73 railroad brotherhoods and other independent unions, and 75,000 "locals" of the entire

---

[37] Horn, "Adventist Archives," 321.

movement. This potential inventory of archives poses a staggering descriptive and narrative task ahead.[38] And not all of the documentation for American labor history is to be found in labor's own records!

Government archives, both federal and state, are an obvious and important source for labor history, and the Committee on Labor Union Archives of the Society of American Archivists has been primarily concerned with calling attention to these records. In federal archives, material on the American labor movement spans the range from the creation of the Bureau of Labor in 1884 to the myriad functions of several labor agencies of the present day. The documents of the Department of Labor are largely published and are of lesser significance as historical sources than the unpublished files of such agencies as the Wage and Salary Stabilization Boards (to 1953), the Federal Mediation and Conciliation Service (from 1913), and the National Labor Relations Board (since 1933). In addition, the special concern with labor problems of the NRA and WPA is well documented in their files. Unfortunately, state and local governmental archives relating to labor are mostly in dead storage and are unidentified.[39]

National union records constitute by far the largest and most important category of documentation for labor history, and the pattern of labor's development has been reflected in the nature and quantity of its records. American labor has traditionally been concerned primarily with waging skirmishes for specific economic advantages rather than battling for general political and social power; the records of wage contests, therefore, have been considered of no further value after a successful settlement. Consequently, labor unions have neglected their records, and collecting institutions have been slow to enter the field. Frequent breaks in organizational continuity have also impaired the research value of labor archives. From time to time, such material

[38] Vaughn D. Bornet, "The New Labor History: A Challenge for American Historians," in *The Historian*, 18:1–24 (Autumn, 1955); William J. Stewart, "The Sources of Labor History: Problem and Promise," in *American Archivist*, 27:95–102 (January, 1964).

[39] Paul Lewinson, "The Archives of Labor," in *American Archivist*, 17:19–24 (January, 1954).

has also been considered to be personal property and has shared the fate of the personal files of the leaders of the movement. The American Historical Association in 1953 expressed concern over the operation of these factors upon labor archives, particularly the scattering effect of institutional collecting. Why should American labor put its records out for adoption, further destroying their archival integrity? Why should not labor assume the care of its own archives as an obligation of the movement? The mixed status of the archives of the AF of L, the United Mine Workers, the United Steelworkers, and the International Ladies' Garment Workers illustrates the results of the conflicting pressures which have operated upon this significant body of primary documentation.[40]

The AF of L archives and library were formerly in the organization's Washington headquarters and were organized in four parts: the AF of L Library, the Samuel Gompers Room, the Central File Room, and the active office files. Of these, the first three are of interest to historians. The library, in its new headquarters near the White House, contains only printed works bearing on the history of labor, but a large portion of the archives was recently transferred to the State Historical Society of Wisconsin. This body of records embraces the bulk of the correspondence of Samuel Gompers and William Green, strike files, and legislative files, all of which have been largely overlooked by labor historians.[41]

The great research potential of the AF of L files is not, unfortunately, characteristic of the records of other labor organizations. Prior to the merger of the two principal labor unions, the CIO regarded itself as too young to create archives, but presumably a portion of its files is still intact. Brighter promise of what small labor groups can do are the examples of the UMW and the ILGWU. The former is developing an archives of the papers and speeches of John L. Lewis in its headquarters building in Washington, which may develop into the vehicle for

---

[40] Henry J. Browne, "Raiding Labor's Records," in *American Archivist*, 17:262–264 (July, 1954).

[41] Bornet, "New Labor History," 1–22; Lewinson, "Archives of Labor," 22; F. Gerald Ham, comp., *Labor Manuscripts in the State Historical Society of Wisconsin* (Madison, 1967), 10–12.

an institutional archives. The latter has preserved its own archives in the research department of the New York headquarters.[42]

Collections of union records have been made by a number of non-union institutions, and the practice is continuing despite labor's re-evaluation of the advisability of putting its archives out for adoption. An excellent collection, including a portion of the Gompers Papers, is held by the New York Public Library. Personal collections of Terence Powderly, John Hayes, and John Mitchell are in the library of Catholic University of America in Washington. The largest institutional collections are those built around the John R. Commons Collection at the State Historical Society of Wisconsin, at the Tamiment Library in New York, Wayne State University, and at the Labor-Management Documentation Center at Cornell University.[43]

It has been observed that Americans are "joiners," and the necessary documentation for a wide range of quasi-public activity lies in the archives of the organization to which they belong. Most manuscript libraries, faced with the multiplicity and often secret nature of these groups, have not exercised an aggressive collecting policy in this field. This policy ignores the importance of many of these organizations and denies a basic American social trait. Precisely because such material was produced for purposes other than historical documentation, its historical value is correspondingly high.

Most quasi-public agencies are highly decentralized even though they may have a central headquarters and an elaborate organization. Ultimately, the burden of activity is upon local leaders and members. Financial considerations generally preclude a centralized collection of archives, and the local branches are left to dispose of their own records. Therefore, the field is a fertile one for collecting agencies, and an enumeration of the possible sources is more suggestive than descriptive.

Social and civic groups command the loyalty of millions of Americans and help to knit together the varied threads of the social fabric. American men regularly congregate in meetings of

---

[42] Lewinson, "Archives of Labor," 22.
[43] *Ibid.;* Leone W. Eckert, "The Anatomy of Industrial Records," in *American Archivist,* 26:185–187 (April, 1963).

Rotarians, Kiwanians, Civitans, Lions, Optimists, and a host of fraternal bodies. Their wives constitute the membership of women's clubs, leagues of women voters, junior leagues, and innumerable auxiliaries. Veterans have their own powerful organizations such as the American Legion, Veterans of Foreign Wars, and Disabled American Veterans. Patriotic societies, such as the Daughters of the American Revolution, Society of the Cincinnati, and the Union League reckon their membership by the hundred thousands, and their influence by even greater numbers. In an earlier day the National Grange of the Patrons of Husbandry commanded considerable economic and political influence.[44] All these groups have records of varying degrees of completeness and will become better known and more frequently used as sources of historical documentation.

Foundations have assumed a vital role in American life, for their continuity as well as their funds constitute a powerful force in characterizing the development of America. A list of foundations too long to enumerate covers an unbelievable range of humanitarian, economic, intellectual, and social concerns. Their files are a blueprint for the institutionalization of good works and are increasingly the documentation from which a segment of American social history will be written.

Political parties have increased in size and power with the growth of government, but their indifference to record-keeping has resulted in a large vacuum in the documentation of American political history. The Democratic National Committee was organized in 1844, the Republican counterpart in 1856, but virtually all their records prior to 1928 have been destroyed. Regrettable as this fact may be, it is a natural outgrowth of American politics. Both national parties live from hand to mouth and cannot afford the luxury of retaining records after they have served their useful life. Both organizations have frequently moved their headquarters, and party officials are often happy to use such occasions to destroy reams of confidential papers. The Republican party's records are largely decentralized, under the control of eleven separate operating divisions. Democratic party

[44] Helen T. Finneran, "Records of the National Grange in Its Washington Office," in *American Archivist*, 27:103–112 (January, 1964).

records, on the other hand, are about 85 per cent centralized in the national headquarters.[45]

Among the papers retained by the Republican National Committee are correspondence and receipts for contributions and expenditures (destroyed after ten years), transcripts of meetings of the national and executive committee (from 1928), records of the last several party conventions, press releases for the past five years, correspondence regarding policy from 1928, field reports for the past five years, selected political studies made by the research division since 1936, confidential records and reports since 1928, and housekeeping records.

The Democratic National Committee's holdings virtually parallel those of the Republicans but are not quite so complete. The principal records are correspondence and receipts for contributions and expenditures since 1946, policy correspondence since 1946 (weeded), patronage correspondence since 1946, confidential reports and plans since 1946, and housekeeping records.[46]

So long as political parties view their records only as the literary remains of election defeats and victories, the records will continue to receive inadequate treatment. Organized public opinion is needed to persuade both major parties to be as solicitous of history's concern with their records as some of the minor parties have shown themselves to be. Specifically, both parties should establish central records offices having general records management control. Both should rigidly enforce their own rules that their records are the property of the party, not to be disposed of to any other agency or individual. As necessary, systematic transfer of archives should be made to some centrally located, nationally prominent agency such as the Library of Congress. Within the obvious limitation of partisan politics, records and archives should be opened as freely and as quickly as possible, including the freedom to microfilm. Each national committee might well give thought to the idea of building a selected permanent archives of its own through a microfilm program.[47]

Causes and movements became a part of the American social

---

[45] Donald R. McCoy, "The Records of the Democratic and Republican National Committees," in *American Archivist*, 14:313–322 (October, 1951).

[46] *Ibid.*, 317–318.

[47] *Ibid.*, 320–321.

scene following the Revolution, but they were informal organizations and left little documentation until the ferment over slavery and women's rights embroiled the nation. The earliest peace groups were founded after the War of 1812, and the Swarthmore Peace Collection is an excellent illustration of some of the problems and rewards in pursuing such material. The Swarthmore Collection contains three divisions: *large* bodies of documents gathered by individuals or institutions, kept in provenance; *small* bodies of documents, arranged alphabetically by name of author; and "Collective Documents Group B," all foreign material, arranged by country and alphabetically by author. The Swarthmore experience has demonstrated that the principal problem of movement archives is their lack of natural form or provenance; hence an order has to be reconstructed for them. Emphasis in archival arrangement must be placed upon ultimate origin rather than immediate donor possession. There is a continuing influx of such material, and collecting institutions are advised to be bold in weeding and discarding.[48]

ADMINISTRATION AND USE OF QUASI-PUBLIC ARCHIVES

THE SPECIAL CHARACTER of quasi-public archives and the circumstances of their creation pose a special problem in their administration and use. For one consideration, they are likely to be housed in non-archival institutions, under the care of file clerks, operating officials, or librarians rather than archivists. Even if open to the public, they are likely to be held in a place generally unfrequented by scholars. Their remoteness from the main stream of scholarship makes bibliography of great importance as a tool for research.

The recent trend toward the establishment of presidential libraries has alarmed a number of institutions which have tradi-

---

[48] Ellen Starr Brinton, "Archives of Causes and Movements: Difficulties and Some Solutions Illustrated by the Swarthmore College Peace Collection," in *American Archivist*, 14:147–154 (April, 1951); Robert S. Gordon, "Suggestions for Organization and Description of Archival Holdings of Local Historical Societies," in *American Archivist*, 26:19–40 (January, 1963).

tionally collected manuscript sources. While the concept of personal archives is archivally sound, in practice the collection of the papers of America's great figures has been allotted to such agencies as the Library of Congress and the several nationally oriented historical societies. There was only muttering when the first of the presidential libraries was established under the National Archives system, but there was general objection to the sweeping provision in the Presidential Archives Act of 1955 authorizing the libraries to accept for deposit "other papers relating to and contemporary with any President or former President of the United States." The American Association for State and Local History has led the opposition. Declaring itself as not opposed to presidential libraries as such, but only to their unchecked expansion in collecting, the issue has yet to be amicably settled. Opponents of such expansion also fear the establishment of a precedent of creating in the home state of each former President a library-archives-museum. Considerations of cost and personality cult aside, such a practice is described as an evasion of the Archives Act of 1934, for considerable amounts of nonarchival material have become housed without the sanction of law in the presidential libraries. In attempting to recreate the documentation for the "era" of each President in turn, considerable duplication is inevitable. On the other hand, the decentralization of source material is welcomed by other scholars.[49]

In defense of presidential libraries, their existence is acknowledged to be a response to the wishes of the various Presidents and to be a recognition of the fact that traditional methods of manuscript collecting will not suffice for the high bulk of a modern President's papers. Such presidential libraries as already exist are going concerns, and it is rather pointless to speculate on what they should and should not collect. More to the point is the question of the future development of such institutions. So long as retiring Presidents retain title to their official archives, the public may have to humor their wishes or see the papers disappear forever. Some reasonable compromise between a desire for presidential archival independence and a demand for the

    [49] James H. Rodabaugh, ed., *The Present World of History: A Conference on Certain Problems in Historical Agency Work in the United States* (Madison, 1958), 35–42.

creation of a federal archival monopoly is surely possible. As archival institutions of a peculiarly quasi-public nature, it has been suggested that presidential libraries restrict themselves to original research material, housing only those printed volumes as are necessary to use intelligently the manuscript sources. It is the scope of manuscript collecting for the federally-sponsored libraries which seems to be the crux of the problem. No one seems particularly concerned if the papers of a cabinet member or a close political associate gravitate to a presidential collection, but it is the broad language of the act of 1955 which disquiets the collectors of manuscripts. They view an aggressive, federally-supported organization as a threat to the free competition between institutions for manuscripts.[50]

Not all presidential libraries are embroiled in the controversy. It is confined to the libraries in existence or planned for Herbert Hoover, Franklin D. Roosevelt, Harry S. Truman, Dwight D. Eisenhower, John F. Kennedy, Lyndon B. Johnson, and presumably their successors. Earlier presidential archives, not supported by the federal government, are different cases.

The Adams Family Papers are unique; no other American family archives has been preserved with such fidelity over such a long period. In 1956, at the expiration of a former arrangement, the Adams Manuscript Trust selected the Massachusetts Historical Society as the depository for the papers, retaining, however, absolute and literary rights in the material. The archives may be said to be "complete," and additions are made only to fill gaps in personal correspondence. The material is now being microfilmed and sold to other institutions on subscription, and a long-range policy of publication of the papers, on several interest levels, is going forward. Until the papers are processed they remain closed, but scholarly access is selectively granted, subject to the retention of literary rights pending publication.[51]

The Hayes Memorial Library at Spiegel Grove, Ohio, houses the papers of President Rutherford B. Hayes. Built in 1914

[50] *Ibid.*, 47.
[51] *Ibid.*, 42; Buford Rowland, "The Papers of the Presidents," in *American Archivist*, 13:195–211 (July, 1950).

and now under the management of the Ohio Historical Society, it was the first separate presidential library. Open to the public, it contains over 75,000 pieces of documentation, but it has not displayed the magnetic power to attract other contemporary collections, for most of the surviving ones had been placed before the Hayes Library was established.[52]

The Hoover Library at Stanford University is also unique among modern presidential libraries. Seeking to institutionalize the principal interests and the problems of Herbert Hoover's era, the name of the library has been changed to the Hoover Institution on War, Revolution, and Peace, and the agency has adopted a collecting policy as broad and as dynamic as its name. In essence, the Hoover Institution is a manuscript collection, privately supported, the papers of President Hoover having been removed to the presidential library at West Branch, Iowa. No objection has been raised, however, to the addition of such diverse items as General Joseph Stilwell's China diary and the papers of Senator Ernest Lundeen of Minnesota. It is this broad collecting policy, if adopted by federally-supported agencies, that has raised the fears of inequitable competition.[53]

The problems posed by the chain of presidential libraries suggest the question of how best to preserve the archives of institutions. In general, are the larger purposes of scholarship better served by quasi-public institutions assuming their own archival functions, or is it more practical for such material to be collected as manuscripts by traditional historical agencies? The solution to this question involves a basic conflict between archivists and manuscript librarians.

The character, situation, and resources of quasi-public institutions are so varied that it is hazardous to assign an inflexible archival rule to them all, but a consideration of the multiple purposes of records and archives suggests the form of such a rule. In the first instance, the records of such institutions are presumed to be of some continuing interest to the organizations themselves, for their corporate nature requires a long and well-documented memory. Most such institutions have their headquarters in a major center of population or in an academic community

[52] Rowland, "Papers," 205.
[53] Rodabaugh, *Present World of History*, 37–40.

so that records are relatively accessible in their original location. Therefore, it would seem that both administrative and scholarly interests reinforce the proposal that institutions retain their own records *if* they are willing and able adequately to care for and service them as a trust for posterity. If any of these elements be or become lacking, it would then seem desirable to encourage the deposit of the institutional archives in an established manuscript agency, with due regard for the proper choice of agency. The relative ease of travel having drastically revised some formerly valid criteria for placing manuscript materials, it would seem wise today to place a greater emphasis upon complementing collections rather than on geographical location or any other considerations. Collecting agencies would thus be free generally to follow a sound policy of building to strength rather than riotously competing for what is available, or passively taking what is offered. There is already a national disposition in the direction of complementary collections, and the world of scholarship should further encourage it.

When an institutional archives is accessioned into a manuscript collection, it is generally treated as far as possible according to archival procedures. Its archival integrity is thereby respected, and its natural provenance is not disturbed to conform with some external arrangement. There need be nothing anomalous about an archives within a manuscript collection.

The problem of unique manuscript archives within a library of printed materials raises entirely different questions of policy and administration, for the incompatibility of the materials is obvious to both archivists and librarians. In the first place, such an arrangement should be approved only if more acceptable alternatives do not exist. Physically speaking, the condition of most library stacks is not conducive to the proper preservation of manuscript materials.[54] Professionally speaking, librarians are generally not trained to give proper care and service to archival materials.[55] Therefore, if it is necessary physically to house ar-

---

[54] Arthur E. Kimberly and J. F. G. Hicks, Jr., *A Survey of Storage Conditions in Libraries Relative to the Preservation of Records* (National Bureau of Standards, Misc. Publication No. 128, Washington, 1937).

[55] American Library Association, Committee on Public Documents, *Public Documents . . . with Archives and Libraries* (Chicago, 1934–1938); A. F. Kuhlman, ed., *Archives and Libraries* (Chicago, 1940).

chives in a library, as is the case with most college archives, the manuscript material should be handled entirely apart from that of the library, preferably by a separate staff trained in archival work.

Apart from the problem of professional care and arrangement, one of the greatest difficulties in utilizing quasi-public archives in historical research is the problem of locating them. This most voluminous category of documentation has had the fewest number of bibliographical guides prepared. Outside of the established agencies, researchers are thrown largely upon their own resources and initiative in tracing the location of the archives they seek. A thorough knowledge of the internal structure of organizations and a ready approach to key individuals will be invaluable in the search. The few published guides to certain classes of archives will, of course, provide clues for information the archives themselves do not contain.

The *Guide to Church Archives*, pioneered in 1910 by the Carnegie inventory of all materials in official hands, listed all unpublished materials for church history, both archives and manuscripts. One conclusion from a casual perusal of the *Guide* is that church archives are where you find them, for even official papers have been scattered into museums not even remotely connected with the denomination which created the records. The *Guide* is silent on the large mass of archives which has strayed into entirely private hands.[56]

The Carnegie *Guide* was spotty and incomplete, yet it remained the only tool of its kind until the Historical Records Survey in the 1930's undertook to inventory church archives from the local level up. This ambitious project had completed its coverage of about one-fourth of the nation's 64,000 church units when it was terminated. The bulk of its unpublished inventories was listed in one of its final reports in 1943.[57] A few of these inventories were published under non-federal auspices, principally ones on the Roman Catholic Church of New Hampshire, the

---

[56] W. H. Allison, comp., *Inventory of Unpublished Material for American Religious History in Protestant Church Archives and Other Repositories* (Washington, 1910).

[57] See U. S., *W.P.A. Technical Series, Research and Records Bibliography*, No. 7, Revised, April, 1943.

Moravian Church of Wisconsin, and various Baptist bodies in New Jersey.[58]

The latest and most complete bibliography of church archives was published in 1958,[59] and it should serve as a model for others on such classes of archives as colleges and universities, the labor movement, and other quasi-public organizations of national significance. The production of such bibliographies of archival classes would greatly facilitate the study of the institutions, make them more conscious of their archival responsibility, and be a step preparatory to the completion of the long-desired national union catalog of manuscript research materials.

[58] Parker, *Local History*, 82.
[59] Binsfield, "Church Archives," 311–332.

vv

IV

vvvvvvvvvvvvvvvvvvvvvvvvvvvvvvvvvvvvvvvvvvvvvvvvvvvv

BUSINESS ARCHIVES AND RECORDS

IT WAS ONCE OBSERVED that the United States has two capitals—one in Washington and one in Wall Street.[1] This truism dramatized the interrelationship between government and business in a modern, capitalistic state; it also pointed to the increasing significance and utility of business archives and records in writing the history of modern America.

The records of American business and government were first brought into significant conjunction through efforts to regulate business for the public good. Until congressional committees and regulatory commissions began to subpoena corporate records in order more effectively to control business, such records were regarded as a form of proprietary secret, closed alike to public inspection and scholarly use. In an age of rugged individualism, American corporate business grew to maturity behind a protective screen of closed books and locked files, thereby breeding a mutual distrust between itself and historical judgment. In no small measure, the fact that American corporations refused for so long to acknowledge any public right or interest in their records is reflected in the unfriendly judgments which historians have rendered upon them. The earliest historians of American business were political reformers, not objective scholars. Given their preconceptions, the limited documentation available to them, and the generally uncooperative attitude of business lead-

---

[1] Oliver Wendell Holmes, "The Evaluation and Preservation of Business Archives," in *American Archivist*, 1:173–174 (October, 1938).

ership, the judgments of these historians were almost foregone conclusions.

It remained for developments in economic theory to transmute an intellectual concept of business history, thereby placing a new set of values upon the archives and records of American business. Classical economics led the historian of business into a concern for the components of production: the development of transportation and technology; recruitment and management of a labor force; and the perfection of a sales organization. Marxian economics, on the other hand, led the historian of business into a preoccupation with the materialistic contribution of labor to the exclusion of the financial support of the great capitalists. Nineteenth-century English economic thought, with its imperial overtones, added the dimension of national welfare to business history and led business historians into a search for new connections between political policy and corporate operations. German scholarship in the late nineteenth century finally institutionalized the study of business history by seeking to place it upon a "scientific" basis and approaching it inductively rather than deductively.[2]

Despite a broadened concept of business history in Europe, the world of nineteenth-century business records is a wasteland. Only after 1900 did European business, starting in Germany, begin to appreciate the value of its records. The Rhenisch Westfälische Wirtschaftsarchiv was established in 1906 as a depository for the archives of several large German firms. In France, since 1931 public archives have solicited and received the records of corporations which are in the process of liquidation. The popularization of corporate histories, beginning about 1930, has also called attention to business archival resources in Europe.[3]

The German approach to business history was transmitted to America by such pioneers in economic history as Richard Ely and Edwin F. Gay, but it was N. S. B. Gras who took the first step in the establishment of academic study of business history by placing emphasis upon the marketplace as the focus of eco-

[2] Henrietta Larson, *Guide to Business History: Materials for their Use* (Cambridge, 1948), 6–18.
[3] Étienne Sabbe, "The Safe Keeping of Business Records in Europe," in *American Archivist*, 18:31 (January, 1955).

nomic activity. In 1916, when Gras became the first occupant of
the Straus Professorship of Business History in the Graduate
School of Business Administration at Harvard, the discipline acquired intellectual respectability.[4]

Business history is now defined as a study of past economic
activity concerned with the administration of the combinations
of labor, natural resources, and capital in the production and
exchange of goods or services with a profit motive.[5] Therefore,
records of whatever nature and origin which contribute to the
development of a broad, integrated understanding of past business activity are grist for the business historian's mill. Business
records formerly of interest or use only to their creators are
now of vital significance to historians concerned with topics which
transcend those of a purely business nature.

In rebuttal of the traditional contention over the bulky nature of corporate archives, it should be recalled that the essence
of American business development has been the operation of small
entrepreneurs, who have left few records. The mercantile capitalists of the eighteenth and nineteenth centuries generally left
large accumulations of papers, mostly business and personal correspondence, which rests unseen and unused in private hands.
The mature industrial capitalist, who flowered in the nineteenth
century, left the record of his activity in the records of his institutions, but the records are often so bulky as to degrade their
value for research.[6] The paradox of poverty in abundance is
the principal difficulty in locating and using business records
in historical research.

THE FORM OF CORPORATE RECORDS

ALTHOUGH the modern corporation took its form and
achieved its dominant position rather late in American economic development, it has become, willy-nilly, the historian's
best source for business documentation and the focus of his attention. Corporate form is a curious hybrid of military and

---

[4] Larson, *Guide to Business History*, 6–18.
[5] *Ibid.*, 3–5.
[6] *Ibid.*, 22; Thomas D. Clark, "The Archives of Small Business," in *American
Archivist*, 12:27–35 (January, 1949).

bureaucratic characteristics (both of which it once pretended to disdain as inefficient), and the nature of the records it produces is in large measure conditioned by the form it has assumed. Modern corporate archives generally consist of discrete records series created by component offices discharging the myriad aspects of modern business activity. An analysis of the structure of a typical modern corporation may therefore facilitate an understanding and evaluation of the records it produces.

Relatively little variation exists in the basic structure of the thousands of corporations operating in the modern business complex. The typical form can be graphically represented by the following organizational chart (Figure 1).[7]

The stockholders in the aggregate are the ultimate source of authority in the modern corporation, at least in theory. The diffusion of ownership and the professionalization of management, however, have reduced the active role of stockholders to the ratification of policies, acts, and decisions made in their name by the board of directors and the management. The regular accounting of this effective delegation of authority contained in corporate reports represents the only series of corporate records to be regularly printed and distributed. Because such records are public, they are designed to represent the corporation in the best possible light consistent with the law; hence their use for historical research is limited to the documentation of major trends, stockholder relations, and information of an incontrovertible and statistical nature.

The directorate of a modern corporation generally consists of a majority of "inside" or management personnel; hence it is not strictly a deliberative or representative body. Its function is generally analogous to that of a board of trustees, enjoying almost plenary authority by leave of the stockholders so long as the enterprise enjoys good financial health. The deliberations of the directors are of the most vital historical significance, but the increasing specialization of management personnel and the complexity of corporate functions have often brought a further delegation of authority to the executive committee of the board. In the committee's daily and continuing sessions, the fortunes of the modern corporation are made or lost, and the commit-

[7] Adapted from A. A. Berle, *American Corporations* (New York, 1946).

FIGURE 1. STRUCTURE OF TYPICAL, INTEGRATED CORPORATION

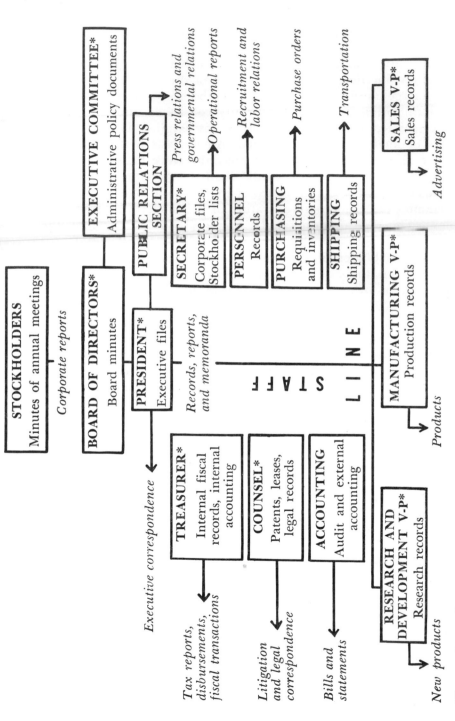

STOCKHOLDERS
Minutes of annual meetings

Corporate reports

BOARD OF DIRECTORS*
Board minutes

EXECUTIVE COMMITTEE*
Administrative policy documents

PRESIDENT*
Executive files

PUBLIC RELATIONS SECTION

Press relations and governmental relations

Records, reports, and memoranda

Executive correspondence

SECRETARY*
Corporate files, Stockholder lists

→ *Operational reports*

PERSONNEL
Records

→ *Recruitment and labor relations*

PURCHASING
Requisitions and inventories

→ *Purchase orders*

SHIPPING
Shipping records

→ *Transportation*

SALES V-P*
Sales records

→ *Advertising*

STAFF | LINE

TREASURER*
Internal fiscal records, internal accounting

Tax reports, disbursements, fiscal transactions

COUNSEL*
Patents, leases, legal records

Litigation and legal correspondence

ACCOUNTING
Audit and external accounting

Bills and statements

MANUFACTURING V-P*
Production records

→ *Products*

RESEARCH AND DEVELOPMENT V-P*
Research records

→ *New products*

***Key people,** usually management members of the Board of Directors, who produce records of greatest historical significance.

tee's records, however sketchy, are the key to reconstructing the history of the corporation.

Although it is manifestly impossible for the president of a large corporation personally to make all those policy decisions which the historian would hope to find recorded in the files of the executive office, still it is those files which will prove most productive for an understanding of the managerial development of the enterprise. The executive office is the channel of communications between the operating divisions and the board of directors, and copies of the myriad reports and memoranda passing through it remain in its files. Even with the decentralization of authority which characterizes larger corporations, the office of the president still must carry the burden of correspondence at the highest executive level. Furthermore, through the increasingly significant appendage to the president's office, the public relations section, the modern corporation seeks to communicate with and influence the public at large.

The office of the corporate treasurer, entrusted with the permanent financial records of the organization, is the depository of those several records series which relate to the fiscal health of the firm. From this office emanates financial correspondence with outside agencies in the form of tax reports, disbursements, and exchanges. Here, too, are created and preserved the financial books of the corporation. The more common of such books and statements are journals, ledgers, daybooks, trial balances, and balance sheets. Machine methods of bookkeeping have streamlined a number of accounting forms and practices, but most of these records will appear in corporate treasury records.

The corporate secretary has traditionally been regarded as the custodian of the permanent records of the organization, but this function is more correct in a legal than in an historical sense. In actual practice, the office of the secretary is apt to preserve only those records required of the corporation by law, such as stockholder lists, minutes of the directors, and similar records series, leaving other records of equal or greater historical value to be preserved by other officers, if at all. A 1957 survey revealed that 44 per cent of corporate secretaries acknowledged primary responsibility for the supervision of the total records program of their firms; an additional 33 per cent acknowledged a secondary responsibility for records management. In the remaining 23 percent of American corporations responding to the questionnaire, preservation of corporate records presumably was regarded as a function of some office other than that of the secretary.[8]

New concepts of records management have had their principal impact upon corporate records through the secretaries, and the 1957 survey indicated that this new science has been applied in American business firms to identify three classes of records: those records for immediate use only; records of a limited life; and longer-term and permanent records. Included in the first category are bulletins, memoranda, informal exchanges, and such papers that ought never to be incorporated in the files. The second category comprises "working papers" which, after they have served their purpose, may be disposed of. Only the third category is regarded as deserving the care and expense of preservation, an expense which approximates $25.00 per cubic foot per year, or about $2.00 per cubic foot per month.[9]

Perhaps the practical usages adopted by American business firms will serve as a rough approximation of what has been subjectively regarded as important and worth the cost of continuing care. Schedules of retention of various classes of records in a number of corporations in 1951 revealed the following pattern:[10]

PATTERN OF CORPORATE RECORD RETENTION SCHEDULES

Type of Record	Number of Corporations/Retention Period			
	1–3 Years	4–10 Years	Over 10 Years	Permanent
Cancelled stock certificates	1	30	27	180
Cancelled bonds	5	14	6	82
Proxies—routine meetings	94	83	4	71
Cancelled dividend checks	5	152	16	55
Cancelled pay checks	30	172	8	32
Bank statements	85	130	8	20

The problems of form, preservation, and use of corporate records result primarily from the high-bulk, mechanically-pro-

---

[8] Frank H. Case, "The Corporate Secretary Looks at Records Management," in *American Archivist,* 23:419 (October, 1960).

[9] *Ibid.*

[10] Case, "Corporate Secretary," 424–425.

duced records of the modern age. Time was, not so many years ago, when the production of records did not exceed the reasonable ability to care for them, and a larger percentage was preserved. The circumstances of records creation also affected their form. Before 1890 business records of all kinds were generally kept in bound volumes, literally the "books of the firm." As the volume of correspondence grew, card files were gradually developed as an index to the bound volumes. In some offices, an abstract of routine correspondence was transferred to an index card, somewhat relieving the necessity of retaining the bulky original file. The use of carbon paper after 1897 and the introduction of the typewriter facilitated the keeping of correspondence to such an extent that the system of binding volumes began to crumble of its own weight. The evolutionary development of record forms led to the introduction of the vertical file, designed to provide alphabetical or topical self-indexing.[11]

The scholar and manuscript librarian also find older business records in the form of docket files of folded letters, often already vandalized for their stamps and covers. Since except in extraordinary cases the philatelic details of business correspondence are of no significance to the researcher, it has been suggested that *all* remaining stamps and covers be removed and sold, thereby reducing the bulk of material. Beyond this step, the materials might be left in their original file form, for there is generally some rationale behind their internal order.[12]

The physical bulk of business archives has posed a continuing problem for the depositories normally accustomed to collecting more compact groups of personal papers. Of course, the lag in the systematic collection of business archives may also be a reflection of the scholarly interest in business today, but it is sometimes a moot point to determine whether records stimulate scholarship, or vice versa.

The earliest systematic collection of bulky American business records began in 1916 at the Harvard Business School Library. This program was largely restricted to the records of defunct manufacturing concerns in New England. Impetus was given the

[11] Holmes, "Evaluation of Business Archives," 176 177.
[12] Robert W. Lovett, "Some Changes in the Handling of Business Records at Baker Library," in *American Archivist*, 19:39 (October, 1956).

movement by the establishment of the Business History Society in 1925 (now inactive) and the building of Baker Library in 1927. These pioneering efforts have made multiple contributions. In addition to providing a scientific basis for the study of American business history, they have pointed up to business firms the importance of adequate records and have helped them to improve the status of their records and to anticipate the future requirements of the business historian.[13]

A recent experience at the Baker Library in processing a typical collection of business records will illustrate some of the problems involved in making such material available for research. The Stevens Mill Company was one of the oldest textile enterprises in North Andover, Massachusetts, its operations dating back to 1813. After its bulky but incomplete records were acquired by the library, the material lay for some time in its large wooden boxes—untouched, unsorted, and further deteriorating. When the records were finally processed in 1961, the Baker Library staff found that the material defied the neat categorizations of traditional manuscript collections, and its original internal order was no longer apparent. Therefore, procedures had to be improvised. The records were first separated into items for immediate disposal, cancelled checks, docket-folded items, and non-docketed material. Ultimately, out of the latter two categories there was recreated the original records series of daybooks, journals, cash books, bill books, ledgers, trial balances, labor time books, payroll books, payroll recapitulations, purchase orders, and inventories. Thus by persistence and ingenuity was a mass of disorganized paper transformed into a highly significant collection of some sixty cubic feet.[14]

Before the concept of company archives was born in 1938, the burden of preservation of business archives lay exclusively upon the few institutions dedicated primarily to the collection of business records. These institutions included the Baker Library at Harvard, the McCormick Historical Association Library in Chicago, and those general manuscripts depositories which recog-

---

[13] Robert W. Lovett, "Care and Handling of Non-Government Archives," in *Library Trends*, 5:381–382 (January, 1957).

[14] Nina L. Edwards, "The Stevens Mill Records—Triumph Over Chaos," in *American Archivist*, 26:59–62 (January, 1963).

nized the unique value of business records. At the University of Virginia Library an excellent collection of records of the early iron industry was almost accidentally collected and preserved. Similarly, at the University of North Carolina, a superb collection of plantation records of the Old South was built up, perhaps without appreciating that they constituted one form of business records. At Duke University a parallel collection of industrial records for the New South was created.[15] More recently, the nucleus of a promising collection bearing upon business history was established in 1945 at Cornell University by the New York State School of Industrial and Labor Relations. This unique collection and institute was dedicated to solving the problems of labor-management relations and came into being through the efforts of Senator Irving M. Ives. Although the collection of primary documentation was incidental to the program of academic research of the institute, with the proper support such a depository could become a center for the study of those corporations with particularly good (or difficult) records of labor relations.[16]

In other sections of the nation centennial celebrations have often stimulated a new interest in economic history and have led to the collection of business archives for research. For instance, the centennial of statehood provided the impetus for the Wisconsin Manufacturers Association to undertake a survey of its constituent firms to uncover business records for historical research. The project was organized by the State Historical Society of Wisconsin and a faculty committee of the University of Wisconsin, with support from the Rockefeller Foundation. Once the firms had been coded by the Standard Industrial Classification Code, a prime list of 4,000 was circularized, requesting them to indicate the existence and availability to scholars of ten different types of business records. The project was regarded as a statistical success; 46 per cent of the firms responded to the questions, and over 225 indicated willingness to open their records to qualified researchers. The survey has provided innumerable leads for the subsequent acquisition by the State His-

---

[15] Oliver Wendell Holmes, "Some Reflections on Business Archives in the United States," in *American Archivist*, 17:295–296 (July, 1950).
[16] Eckert, "Industrial Records," 185–190.

torical Society of Wisconsin of important collections of business archives.[17]

Business history as a field of professional interest, and its records as a source of historical documentation, has not fully overcome the prejudice of research institutions against this category of historical documentation. As recently as 1957 a survey indicated that only nineteen state archival agencies, twenty-four state historical agencies, fourteen state universities, five private universities, seven other historical societies, and seven other libraries collected or accepted business records.[18] Even those institutions which reported an interest in business records were selective, discriminating as to age, region, topic, or over-all bulk to avoid being swamped by the unmanageable. Of those institutions collecting business records, twenty-four selected as to date (usually restricting themselves to the nineteenth century or earlier), fifty-four restricted themselves mainly to the records of their region, twelve collected the records of certain specific business fields only, and twenty-nine discriminated openly and frankly on the basis of bulk alone.[19]

Some of the problems inherent in business records follow them into the depositories and continue to plague the curators and the scholars who try to use the records. The high bulk of the material suggests that weeding based upon informed use might be practical.[20] Forty institutions reported that they did weed business collections; eighteen did not.[21] Almost the same division reported the preservation of printed records with business archives. Forty agencies disposed of printed material, and seventeen did not.[22] Secrecy in business records posed yet another problem. A total of thirty-four agencies reported general restriction on the use of their business collections, while fourteen reported their collections were generally open.[23] The problem

[17] Robert P. Thomson, "The Business Records Survey in Wisconsin," in *American Archivist,* 14:250–251 (July, 1951).

[18] Robert W. Lovett, "Business Records in Libraries," in *American Archivist,* 20:255 (July, 1957).

[19] *Ibid.,* 255–266.

[20] Jack King, "Collecting Business Records," in *American Archivist,* 27:387–390 (July, 1964).

[21] Lovett, "Business Records in Libraries," 256–257.

[22] *Ibid.*

[23] *Ibid.*

of literary rights in private, incoming letters has frightened other curators.[24] The sum of these problems may explain to some degree why thirty-nine of these same agencies reported their business records were used for scholarly and research projects, while ten agencies reported their business collections had not been used at all![25]

APPRAISAL OF BUSINESS RECORDS

THE UNEXCELLED EFFICIENCY of the modern business corporation in the production of records makes discrimination in appraisal all the more manadatory for the collector and user of these records. Otherwise, should everything be saved, the overburden of bulk will guarantee that little will be salvaged. Out of a study of corporate form and development, circumstances of creation and characteristics of records, legal requirements, actual experience, and common sense must a system of evaluation and appraisal of business records be developed. Such a system should be based upon an intelligent guess of what is most likely to be of value in years to come. The goal should be to identify and save the maximum amount of information consistent with the smallest physical bulk.

Fortunately, there is rough congruity between the functional, internal evaluation of corporate records and the external evaluation placed upon them. Corporate records generally fall into a scale of descending significance corresponding to the level of their creation within the corporate structure. Thus, in an approximate sense, minutes of the meetings of the directors are of greater significance than records of stockholders' meetings, which, in turn, are more significant than general accounting records, and so on down through property records, production records, sales records, general correspondence, and general miscellaneous records.[26]

Superimposed upon a corporation's internal evaluation of records are other, external factors which must be given considera-

[24] Seymour W. Connor, "The Problem of Literary Property in Archival Depositories," in *American Archivist*, 21:149–151 (April, 1958).
[25] Lovett, "Business Records in Libraries," 257–258.
[26] Lovett, "Non-Government Archives," 384–385.

tion in constructing a system of appraisal. Principal among these factors are the requirements and precedents of the law, the corporation's interest in fostering better public relations, and the legitimate interest of scholarship in business records as a source of documentation. These factors suggest the specific importance of a given series of business records and lead to a functional categorization of business records into groups which may be called administrative records, accounting records, production records, and general correspondence.[27] Even this categorization of business manuscripts will not serve as a final criterion for evaluation. Obviously, even among administrative records, not all can be saved, nor will historians willingly allow "general correspondence" to be consigned to the flames. A schedule by which specific records series are identified for permanent preservation, or preservation for an appropriate number of years, offers the best means of serving all interests in business records. Because of the scarcity of older business records and their relative lack of bulk, records produced before 1900 generally might be exempted from any records schedule.[28]

The most potent force contributing to the preservation of contemporary corporate records is not inertia, managerial enlightenment, or even the organized pressure of historians. It is the authority and the omnipresent threat of the United States Internal Revenue Service. Since 1913 American individual and corporate taxpayers have been forced to give a thought to the documentation required to support their annual tax statements, and the accumulation of information is, or will become, prime historical documentation. This long-standing obligation has been codified by *Regulation 94 Relating to the Income Tax.* Under the authority of the Revenue Act of 1936, each taxpayer is required to keep sufficient records to establish gross income, deductions, credits, and other amounts claimed, farmers alone being exempt. Whether or not the statute of limitations has ex-

---

[27] Ralph M. Hower, *The Preservation of Business Records* (Boston, 1941), 4–5; Arthur H. Cole, "Business Manuscripts: Collecting, Handling, and Cataloging," in *Library Quarterly,* 8:107–108 (January, 1938).

[28] This rule has been validated by the experience in 1951 of appraising a large collection of New England textile records at the Baker Library. See Robert W. Lovett, "The Appraisal of Older Business Records," in *American Archivist,* 15:231 (July, 1952).

pired, the government can, if it suspects fraud, require the production of records from any number of years past.[29]

In addition to fiscal records preserved for tax purposes, active corporations and business firms are under an obligation to preserve certain of their administrative records to satisfy legal requirements of their states of incorporation or those in which they conduct business—and scholarship may be the ultimate beneficiary. Stockholder records, such as stock and bond registers, reports to the stockholders, and minutes of stockholder meetings, generally qualify for permanent preservation. In addition, key managerial records such as directors' minutes, executive committee minutes, contracts, records of securities held, and insurance policies are generally awarded permanent preservation by requirement of statute or to maintain legal rights.[30] Despite variations in state corporate legislation, the categories of corporate records preserved for legal reasons are remarkably uniform, perhaps another illustration of the fact that American business has become largely blind to state boundaries.

Another category of legal documents created by business operations is usually preserved permanently by custom with the force of law. Likely to be included in this category will be the original charter and amendments, franchises, deeds, titles, leases, licenses, and mortgages. Even though these may be on record elsewhere, their collection and preservation by a business firm often is a boon to a historian attempting to untangle a web of legal transactions.

In addition to records which are permanently preserved in the company's own interest by the requirement of law or custom, there is a larger category of business records which should also be accorded permanent preservation because of their value for historical research. Those firms that are especially interested in their own development or in that of their industry may save this material on their own volition. If such a motive is absent, historical scholarship must register its own interests in the material and, if necessary, make arrangements for suitable care and preservation once the records are released by their creator.

Business historians are interested primarily in general develop-

[29] Holmes, "Evaluation of Business Archives," 182.
[30] Hower, *Preservation of Business Records,* 10–11.

ment and trends rather than specific circumstances and events. They are more concerned with reasons for developments than in the fact or the time of their arriving. Thus, historians of business or those using business records are most apt to be concerned with records of policy creation and implementation, with the papers of those individuals and officers who were vitally important in the management of corporate affairs. Therefore, all correspondence and memoranda of senior company executives should be saved permanently, excluding only printed material or that normally available elsewhere. General correspondence of officials next below senior rank should be shifted for more important items that illuminate and complement the files of higher officials. In addition, administrative reports of the various departments should be considered for preservation even though the essence of such information usually finds its way into the annual reports of the management to the board of directors and to the stockholders.

The growing importance and use of public relations in business have swelled the volume of such records. The historian of business is as much interested in the public context of a corporation as in its internal history and expects a complete and central file of all company publications of whatever nature. Likewise, public speeches and pronouncements by senior officials should be permanently preserved. A valuable supplement to such documents of the public relations of a business firm is a company diary or journal, kept by some competent and designated person as a contemporary sketch of the firm's history.[31]

By far the greatest bulk of business records are what may be termed operating or housekeeping records, those papers generated for internal circulation and use in the routine conduct of business. Their high bulk impairs their usefulness except as documentation for a history of a given firm, and the routine nature of their contents gives them utility only in filling out the bare bones of policy outline. Nevertheless, the complexity and decentralization of modern business organizations require the preservation of a certain amount of this category of intermediate documentation. An effective compromise between preservation

[31] *Ibid.*

in extenso and destruction *in toto* has resulted in maintenance of selected record groups for a certain number of years. This procedure serves the purpose of contemporary reference and the historical purpose of "seasoning." Properly seasoned, the material may be reviewed for ultimate disposition upon expiration of the initial period, usually from three to seven years.

Accounting records constitute the most critical category of operating papers to be preserved for a certain number of years. All main, original accounting records should unquestionably be preserved, but in various businesses these records will have varying forms. Some of the more common are daybooks, general and subsidiary journals, general and subsidiary ledgers, balance sheets, statements of income and expenses, budgets, records of departmental performance, and accounting manuals.[32]

Accounting terms have become so popularized that their exact meanings have become rather obscure. Therefore, a definition of some of the more common ones may be in order here. A business "journal" is a financial record of original entry in which sales, purchases, receipts, and like transactions are recorded, usually in double-entry form, indicating the running balance between income and expenditures. Original journal entries are regularly transferred to a "ledger," in which like categories of transactions are grouped under appropriate headings. Another form of original entry is a "daybook" in which each day's debits and credits (not necessarily restricted to cash transactions) are posted. Similarly, a "trial balance" is the transfer of all credits and debits in open accounts from a daybook into a double-entry ledger to test their total equality. A "balance sheet" is a summary statement of financial condition, giving assets, liabilities, and net worth.

Records of material operations relate to the mechanical processes whereby raw materials are converted into sold products through the component steps of purchasing, production, inventorying, advertising, and sales. Each step produces records which should be preserved for a determined seasoning period. Ledgers created in the purchasing department indicate the nature of goods bought, from whom, and for what prices. This statistical

[32] *Ibid.*

summary is substantiated by letters, specifications, and other reports to illustrate methods and policies governing the purchase
of supplies and materials. From the various production departments there should be preserved charts, graphs, diagrams, engineering drawings and blueprints, and photographs to show
plant layout, work flow, product design, and mechanical operations. Expository reports and statistics should be preserved to
document engineering functions, research projects, inspection
procedures, and the volume of production. The functions of
inventorying and warehousing should be illustrated by records
of controls applied thereto. All correspondence with outside
advertising agencies, all plans for advertising, and a file of all
advertising copy should be preserved to document the function
of sales promotion. From the sales department itself, there
should be preserved all summary figures on sales, market anal-
yses, dealer correspondence, price lists, discount schedules, catalogs, outlines of sales campaigns, and copies of all sales forms,
trade marks, and packaging.

The records of labor and personnel, which are not so voluminous as the records of material, are often more critical to a company's operation because of the general likelihood of legal questions arising out of them. The dossier of an individual employee
must be preserved intact during his employment and for several
years after employment has been terminated. More general personnel records are invaluable documentation in illustrating corporate personnel management and relations. Especially desirable are records of the number and categories of employees, rates
of attendance and turnover, rates of pay, and schedules of additional compensation and fringe benefits. From the personnel
department there should also be preserved for a certain number of years summarized information on practices and policies
on hiring, training, supervision, promotions, dismissals, hours,
vacations, union relationships, and employee publications.[33]

Business organizations which do not engage in manufacturing
generate categories of indigenous records to which may be applied a preservation schedule. Consider, for example, a recent
analysis of the preservation practice applied to the records of

[33] *Ibid.*

a life insurance company.[34] The obvious records designated for permanent preservation were abstract or history cards (documenting the full history of individual policies) ; account cards (documenting premium collections for each policy) ; dividend record cards; cancelled checks; cash books; minutes of directors meetings; main ledger; payroll; all records pertaining to company real estate; and all correspondence from the first twenty-five years of the company. Records designated for intermediate preservation included policy applications and medical reports (as long as policy is in force plus ten years) ; agents' accounts (fifteen years) ; agents' contracts (fifteen years after termination) ; bank deposit slips (ten years) ; commission vouchers (ten years) ; and mortgage loans (ten years after payment). Records retained for relatively short periods of time included policy loans (one year after payment) and policies returned (one year). Contemporary general correspondence is periodically "weeded" to about 5 per cent of the original bulk and awarded indeterminate preservation.

The practice (which evolved into a manuscript science following World War II) of scheduling specific record series for preservation and disposal has particular application to the high-bulk records of modern corporations. The principles and rationale of the practice have been more extensively discussed elsewhere in relation to the records of modern governmental units. Sufficient here should be an outline, expressed in the form of general rules, of the application to the records of business.

A cardinal rule in scheduling records is to give consideration, where possible, to archival factors in the creation and maintenance of current records. By such anticipation, the conversion of business records into archives may be greatly facilitated. All potential archival material should be labelled and filed as such from its inception to insure the automatic retention and conversion by classes; all records which can be predetermined to have no archival value should be destroyed as soon as they lose their current record value. No record should be retained beyond its

---

[34] Harold Larkin, "Retention of Life Insurance Records," in *American Archivist,* 5:96–97 (April, 1952). The company reported upon was the Connecticut Mutual Life Insurance Company.

current use, regardless of potential archival value, if it is duplicated in more compact form elsewhere. To insure that these
principles will be observed will normally require the establishment of a centralized control over all records released from current use and considered for archival conversion.[35]

On the basis of the factors and considerations outlined above,
the records of a business firm may be divided into four categories of descending order of archival priority. First are *vital
records*, those which are irreplaceable, the loss of which would
cause serious business interruption and inconvenience. For a
combination of operating, legal, and historical reasons they should
be permanently preserved in their entirety and awarded fireproof storage. Second is a category of *important records*, into
which the bulk of all corporate and business records normally
fall. These records are essential to continuous and convenient
operation, but they could be reproduced from vital records albeit
at considerable expense. For legal and operating reasons they
should be retained for a certain number of years. Then, on the
basis of historical evaluation, they should be further preserved,
destroyed, or sampled for preservation. While under temporary
preservation they should be given fire-resistant storage. A third
category of *useful records*, the loss of which would cause temporary inconvenience but entail no serious disadvantage, should
be destroyed after their legal and operating utility has expired,
usually a relatively short time after their creation. For historical reasons, such record series should be sampled before disposal
to illustrate aspects of the routine operations of the business
organization. While retained, useful records should be given
only secure storage. Lastly, all *nonessential records* of only secondary value to current operations, and having no permanent
value on any basis whatever, should be disposed of in their entirety as rapidly as created and given no storage whatever.[36]

Scheduling of business records according to the above formula still leaves large areas of subjective evaluation and guess
work, but those areas may be narrowed by reference to a num-

---

[35] Hower, *Preservation of Business Records,* 11–12.
[36] *Ibid.*

ber of specialized guides. The Interstate Commerce Commission, for example, publishes permissive rules of destruction for obsolete records of transportation companies under its supervision. Various industry associations have established guides for their constituent corporations, such as a 1923 code published by the National Electric Light Association and the 1935 *Protection of Records* issued by the National Fire Protection Association. Probably the most comprehensive and general guide for scheduling business records yet published is *The Preservation of Business Records* by Ralph M. Hower. This work was released in 1937 by the Business History Society.[37]

Records preservation techniques are not sufficiently refined to permit sampling upon a strict statistical basis. Even if such a basis were practical, the nature of business records and their historiographical usage might make it undesirable. The purpose of sampling business records is to provide some original evidence for generalizations about the routine conduct of business illustrated in documentation too voluminous to keep *in toto*. The predisposition of historians to literary concepts makes such a non-scientific approach inevitable, yet some safeguards need to be imposed upon sampling techniques to limit the inherent inadequacies of the process.

In the first instance, samples should be so taken as to provide year-to-year comparisons, but scholars should be cautious in basing generalities upon such selective evidence. Secondly, samples should be sufficiently large to reveal typical transactions in their entirety, otherwise the conclusions will most certainly be erroneous. Thirdly, samples should be chosen to relate approximately to equivalent dates and categories from year to year, to allow for seasonal variations. Fourthly, when space permits, all records of the series should be retained at five- or ten-year intervals, if possible, to coincide with the decennial census years. In all cases, a statement of the principles upon which the sample was based, the date, and the identity of the sampler should be made a matter of record with the preserved material.[38]

[37] Holmes, "Business Archives," 178–179.
[38] Hower, *Preservation of Business Records*, 22–23.

CORPORATE ARCHIVES MOVEMENT

T HE HESITANCY of established American manuscript depositories to solicit or accept business archives has posed a serious problem for researchers interested in the material. Two solutions have evolved. On the one hand, traditional depositories have slowly cast off their prejudice against business records and have begun to accord them a minimum standard of care. On the other, a combination of scholarly pressure, self-interest, and the recommendations of records managers has resulted in a new concept in maintenance of documentation, the corporate archives movement.

The Baker Library at Harvard University was the first agency in America to take for its purpose the deliberate creation of a body of business records for scholarly reference. Since other depositories discriminated against the records, the Baker project was established upon the premise that it was the responsibility of American business in general to care for its own archives. Working through the Business History Society, the Baker Library popularized the concept of a national center for business records, but the idea was soon recognized as impractical. Sheer bulk of documentation, which had closed other doors to business records, soon swamped the facilities of an institution devoted exclusively to their collection. The Baker Library was soon forced to retreat to the more restricted field of the business records of New England, but its pioneering work conclusively demonstrated that the collection of business records for historical research was possible and worthwhile. The lessons learned at Harvard could be applied either at other special regional depositories or at traditional manuscript libraries.[39]

Paralleling the American experience at the Baker Library, interest in British business records was stimulated through the organization of the Council for the Preservation of Business Archives in 1934. Here the plan was not to establish a separate depository for business archives. Rather, the council sought by consultation and co-operative effort to shepherd the retired records of older firms into established manuscript libraries and, in-

[39] Holmes, "Business Archives," 181–182; Cole, "Business Manuscripts," 94–95.

cidentally, to encourage the libraries to receive such deposits. The council also undertook to establish a central "Register of Business Archives," a card index to known collections in private or institutional custody which has served both as a finding aid and as a lead file for manuscript acquisitions. The council has also undertaken surveys of trade and regional collections to facilitate their use by scholars, always placing their emphasis upon the older records.[40]

The force of examples of business manuscript collecting on both sides of the Atlantic has been greatly encouraging, yet the harvest has been disappointingly small. The practitioners of business history continually point out that records are still in hiding. For example, it is known that about seventy-five companies manufactured steam engines for agricultural purposes between 1850 and 1920, yet no correspondence from any of them can be found in any public depository. Similarly, at least 125 companies have built tractors since 1900, yet there are no records available to the historians of agricultural mechanization. In the United States over 1,200 companies have built motor cars and trucks since the turn of the century, yet there are no records on public deposit anywhere, although certain personal papers of automobile pioneers have been made available.[41]

The continuing problems of business archives called forth the creation of the National Records Management Council by the Committee on Business Records of the American Historical Association in 1949. Patterned after the British council, the American group has made its principal contribution through studies and specific recommendations to individual firms on the subject of records retirement and deposit. It has published articles and bulletins on collecting and using the archives of business and has sponsored seminars at New York University for businessmen and historians. The council has been instrumental in launching, in addition to the Baker Library, the Southern Business History Center at the University of Florida, the Longwood Library at Kennett Square, Pennsylvania, and a similar depository at

[40] Holmes, "Business Archives," 183–184.
[41] Reynold M. Wik, "Adventures in Business Records: The Vanishing Archives," in *American Archivist*, 14:190–197 (July, 1951).

the University of Oregon for materials of the Pacific Northwest.[42]

The establishment of special depositories for business records and the increasing willingness of general depositories to accept business records are encouraging developments, but the problems inherent in such material remain unsolved for the most part. One of the most difficult problems of the user is the proprietary interests and restrictions which linger around business records. Especially is this the case in the question of literary rights in corporate archives. Who owns such rights? Presumably the company does, since the records were produced for hire. While a corporation's title to its own records would seem to be absolute, hedged only by legal provisions and general usage, historians and manuscripts custodians favor the prompt and complete transfer of all literary rights by the depositing corporation.[43]

The trepidation with which regular manuscript depositories approach business archives and the problems which have plagued even those agencies especially created to collect them have suggested yet another method of insuring the regular and systematic preservation of business records. This plan calls for the creation of a corporate archives within the corporate structure itself, established and maintained by corporate funds and administered by professional archivists. It is presumed that such agencies can be operated without a conflict between the corporation's interest in its own records and the interests of scholarship. The two largest and best known of such institutions, the archives of the Firestone Tire and Rubber Company and the Ford Motor Company, are proof of the applicability of the concept.

The archives department of the Firestone Tire and Rubber Company was established in March, 1943, in the company's principal office in Akron, Ohio. The stimulus of the war was undoubtedly critical in the decision. The Firestone Company had been founded in 1900 by Harvey S. Firestone, and its records throughout its early years had been carefully preserved upon the express wish of the founder. At the time of his retirement, the corporation files contained some 5,000 non-active file drawers and about 4,000 active drawers including the personal papers

[42] Lovett, "Non-Government Archives," 382–383.
[43] Robert W. Lovett, "Property Rights and Business Records," in *American Archivist*, 21:262–263 (July, 1958); Connor, "Literary Property," 143–152.

of the founder. The latter had been cataloged in 1937–1938 and were correctly regarded as the nucleus of the corporate archives.

Since designating the Firestone correspondence and inactive corporate files as an archives and placing it under professional supervision, the company has followed a continuing program of systematic organization. By 1953 the collection contained over 560,000 documents, 150,000 photographic negatives, and thousands of feet of microfilm. The materials are housed in metaledged boxes of the type in use in the National Archives, and they are effectively and extensively card-cataloged under "persons," "places," "occasions," and "products." Microfilm has been extensively used to preserve and reduce the bulk of material deteriorating from age. In association with the archives a corporate library of 25,000 volumes has been developed on the literature of rubber, plastics, economics, engineering, transportation, and other subjects of interest to the company. Out of this collection it is expected that biographies of the company's founders and histories of its development will be written.[44]

An even more ambitious corporate archives undertaking is that of the Ford Motor Company. The archives owes its existence to the observance of the fiftieth anniversary of the company in 1953. Prior to that time, the company records were located in the Ford Engineering Laboratory in Dearborn, where some 7,500 feet of floor space was allotted to them. Approximately one-half of the total space was required to house the noncurrent records of the company, one-fourth was devoted to office space, and the remaining one-fourth was assigned to the unique Oral History Project for recording the reminiscences of veteran employees of the firm. All the space was air-conditioned, and the records were in reasonably good order and condition.

In preparation for the anniversary observance, the company requested the advice and help of the National Archives in institutionalizing the company records. After a preliminary inventory in May, 1952, the Ford records were moved to Fairlane, the former Dearborn home of Henry Ford, founder of the company, and were consolidated with smaller collections of Ford's private correspondence under trained archival supervision. The

---

[44] William D. Overman, "The Firestone Archives and Library," in *American Archivist*, 16:305–306 (October, 1953).

original Ford Archives contained sixty-four collections totaling over 4,000 linear feet.

The Ford corporate records originally accessioned spanned the years from 1900 to 1947 and related to production, legal, auditing, public relations, sales, advertising, engineering, and executive affairs. In the years following, additional groups of records have been added, so much so that the combination archives-museum-library is severely taxing the capacity of the building, never designed for such use.[45] The materials have already seen extensive and effective use in the biography of Ford by Allan Nevins,

The natural justice of a corporation caring for its own archives and the prospect of generous corporate support are very appealing concepts to libraries struggling to cope with bulging collections infrequently used and to scholars concerned that for lack of an efficient depository, business archives will vanish. In the case of the Firestone and Ford experiments, the enlightened steps of management have been universally applauded by the historical profession, yet these examples raise other questions underlying the general problem and utility of corporate archives. Is it sufficient to rely upon the voluntary action of industrial corporations to insure the continued preservation of their archives, even after they have become institutionalized? Perhaps even more significant, upon the basis of the use derived from these two examples, can such expenditures be justified on a continuing basis? Might it not be less expensive and more efficient to create co-operative regional or industry-wide archives to which corporate records might be transferred, expenses of operation being shared *pro rata* by the co-operating firms?

While it may be safely assumed that the historical profession would prefer the conversion of corporate records into archives through regional or industry agencies, it is perhaps more certain that corporate pride and proprietary interests will continue to channel these materials into company archives. Two recent examples of intermediate size, the Bank of America and the Boeing Aircraft Corporation, will suffice to suggest the general trend. The establishment of the Bank of America Archives grew

[45] Henry E. Edmunds. "The Ford Motor Company Archives," in *American Archivist,* 15:99–101 (April, 1952).

out of its successful defense against an antitrust suit and its desire to publish its history in connection with the centennial of the state of California. The resulting collection is highly selective and emphasizes very heavily the legal, adminstrative, and public-relations aspects of the bank's development.[46] The Boeing archives came into being in 1955 similarly as a result of efforts to produce a history of the company's first forty years. Since the history of Boeing is largely a history of the engineering development and sale of its aircraft, over half of the 500 cubic feet of the Boeing archives relate to these topics.[47] One is tempted to conclude that the histories of the Bank of America and the Boeing Corporation would exaggerate the obvious qualitative differences between the two enterprises because of the administrative decisions underlying the creation of their respective archives.

No criticism of any particular corporation is intended, but a protective screen, albeit subtle and sophisticated, seems still to surround most American corporate business records. Business archives, when established within a corporation, are generally for corporate purposes rather than for the service of scholarship; when scholarly access to business records is granted, it is generally conceived as a gesture to public relations rather than as an obligation to public information. Relations between the business community and historians have improved since the mutual distrust of an earlier day, but there is still room for a broader realization of mutual interest in the creation and management of business archives and records.

[46] O. G. Wilson, "Bank of America's Archival Program," in *American Archivist*, 29:43–48 (January, 1966).

[47] Peter M. McLellan, "The Boeing Archival Program," in *American Archivist*, 29:37–48 (January, 1966).

MANUSCRIPT COLLECTIONS
AT THE NATIONAL LEVEL

THE DEFINITION OF ARCHIVES as the organic documentary residue of any government, institution, or person appears to leave very little to constitute manuscript collections. Admittedly, the distinction between archives and manuscripts is somewhat arbitrary, based upon the circumstances and purposes of collection rather than upon any inherent qualitative differences in collected materials. The essential distinction is that manuscript collections are fortuitous and take form after the fact of the historical events to which they witness. The form of a manuscript collection at times closely approximates that of archives and in American parlance is generally referred to as the "papers" or "records" of a person or agency. In the case of the result of the efforts of a collector who brings together papers without regard to their internal organic relationship, the body of materials is generally known as a "collection." In a third instance, the term "manuscripts" may refer to a collection of discrete writings acquired by a depository for its special pertinence to research, the entire collection reflecting some particular significance which the individual portions did not possess. The common characteristics of such materials are an essentially private nature, the lack of any obvious intent of publication, and the institutionalization or ordering at some time after the creation of the component parts.[1]

[1] Lester J. Cappon, "Historical Manuscripts as Archives: Some Definitions and

The origin of collecting personal letters as historical sources or as objects of literary curiosity is lost in antiquity. It is known that the early Christians copied and circulated for inspiration the private letters of St. Paul and others, and Medieval scholarship was often disseminated in the form of private correspondence. The first collections of such writings were made at the great European universities at Paris, Oxford, and Salamanca. From these Medieval origins, the largest manuscript collections today have come to rest in the British Museum, the Bibliothèque Nationale, and the Vatican Library.[2]

The modern historical scholar has come to depend upon printed books for basic knowledge and established interpretations, but he prizes historical manuscripts as one of the primary sources for discovering new truth and for constructing new interpretations. The observation that "libraries exist for readers; archives and manuscripts, for writers" seems especially true in the field of history. American historians are endowed with a gross tonnage of primary historical manuscripts outstripping that of any other national state, and with an active program of collection which continues to compound their embarrassment of riches.[3]

Directly underlying the American interest in and use of manuscript collections is the great English manuscript tradition which began in the sixteenth century. It is illuminated with the names of such great collectors as John Leland, Richard Gascoigne, Sir Hans Sloane, Robert Hurley, Earl of Oxford, Sir Thomas Bodley, Sir Robert Bruce Cotton, and the royal house itself. Most of the treasures of these collectors have come into the care of the British Museum or the Universities of Oxford and Cambridge, where they were discovered and applied to American historiography by Jared Sparks and other pioneer documentarians.[4]

Their Applications," in *American Archivist,* 19:104–109 (April, 1956); A. C. Clark, *The Descent of Manuscripts* (Oxford, 1918); William J. Wilson, "Manuscript Cataloging," in *Traditio,* 12:458–459 (1956).

[2] Charles Oman, *On the Writing of History* (New York, 1939), 66–75; Mary A. Benjamin, *Autographs: A Key to Collecting* (New York, 1946), 3.

[3] [Jared Sparks], "Materials for American History," in *North American Review,* 23:275 (October, 1826); R. W. G. Vail, "Manuscripts and Archives, Introduction," in *Library Trends,* 5:309 (January, 1957).

[4] An excellent guide to the "cream of British documentation for American His-

While the French have been primarily interested in establishing archival agencies, they have also contributed to American historiography by creating a number of central manuscript depositories and developing their own tradition of manuscript collecting. Chief among the depositories is the Manuscript Department of the Bibliothèque Nationale, an outgrowth of the old royal manuscript collection begun in the fourteenth century. The collection is now surpassed in size and prestige only by that of the British Museum, and it early attracted the attention of American scholars looking for source material on the American Revolution.[5]

THE ORIGINS OF MANUSCRIPT
COLLECTING IN AMERICA

A N INTEREST in historical manuscripts and their collection predates the emergence of the historical profession in America by over two hundred years. In early America, to an even greater extent than in Europe, collecting literary antiques was an avocation of the political, religious, and social elite rather than the work of professional scholars or even antiquarians. The Fathers of New England were a serious lot, particularly interested in their own past. Very early they began to collect and

---

tory" is Grace Gardner Griffin, *A Guide to Manuscripts Relating to American History in British Repositories Reproduced for the Division of Manuscripts of the Library of Congress* (Washington, 1946). See also, Charles M. Andrews and Frances G. Davenport, *Guide to the Manuscript Material for the History of the United States in the British Museum, in Minor London Archives, and in Libraries of Oxford and Cambridge* (Washington, 1908); and B. R. Crick and Miriam Alman, *A Guide to Manuscripts Relating to America in Great Britain and Ireland* (London, 1961). For the development of English manuscript collections, see Seymour De Ricci, *English Collectors of Books and Manuscripts* (Cambridge, 1930), 14–25; and Colton Storm and Howard Peckham, *Invitation to Book Collecting, Its Pleasures and Practices, With Kindred Discussions of Manuscripts, Maps, and Prints* (New York, 1947), 117–118.

[5] Waldo G. Leland, ed., *Guide to Materials for American History in the Libraries and Archives of France* (2 vols., Washington, 1932, 1943), I, II; Henry P. Beers, *The French in North America: A Bibliographical Guide to French Archives, Reproductions, and Research Missions* (Baton Rouge, 1959), 25; N. M. M. Surrey, *Calendar of Manuscripts in Paris Archives and Libraries Relating to the History of the Mississippi Valley to 1803* (2 vols., Washington, 1926, 1928), I, II.

preserve their own manuscripts to justify themselves before God if not before man. Numerous private manuscript collections took form in New England in the seventeenth and eighteenth centuries, many of them of considerable significance. When John Adams in 1774 undertook to prove the northern and western land claims of Massachusetts, he went first to the private collection of Thomas Prince rather than to the colonial archives.[6]

Another stimulus to manuscript collecting in New England was the Yankee practicality of capitalizing upon a market for published editions of historical documents. Prime among the breed of early documentarians was Ebenezer Hazard, who in 1774 issued a circular announcing his intention to publish the "American State Papers." Though vexed by the lack of public support and indifferent private subscription, Hazard's enthusiasm for collecting manuscripts proved to be infectious, particularly after turning his project into an apologia for the Revolution. No less a collector than Thomas Jefferson publicly endorsed Hazard's project as placing "beyond the reach of accident" the "valuable Historical and State Papers" of the American Republic.[7]

The distinction of being the first American collector of manuscripts for general scholarly use belongs to the indefatigable Jeremy Belknap. For twenty years he collected manuscripts for his *History of New Hampshire*, and after moving to Boston to become minister of the Federal Street Church he became the founder of the Massachusetts Historical Society in 1791. Belknap intended this first historical society in America to be "active," "not to be waiting, like a bed of oysters, for the tide to flow in upon us, but to *seek* and *find*, to *preserve* and *communicate*, literary intelligence, especially in the historical way."[8]

[6] Lyman H. Butterfield, "Bostonians and Their Neighbors as Pack Rats," in *American Archivist*, 24:149 (April, 1961).

[7] Philip M. Hamer, ". . . Authentic Documents tending to elucidate our History," in *American Archivist*, 25:3–4 (January, 1962); Lyman H. Butterfield, "Draper's Predecessors and Contemporaries," in Donald R. McNeil, ed., *The American Collector* (Madison, 1955), 2–3.

[8] Lucile M. Kane, "Manuscript Collecting," in William B. Hesseltine and Donald R. McNeil, eds., *In Support of Clio* (Madison, 1958), 30, Butterfield, "Draper's Predecessors" in McNeil, ed., *Collector*, 4–5; Walter Muir Whitehill, *Independent Historical Societies, An Enquiry into Their Research and Publication Functions and Their Financial Future* (Boston, 1962), 1–13.

While Belknap was institutionalizing the collecting of manuscripts at the Massachusetts Historical Society, a young disciple, William B. Sprague, was introducing and promoting the European hobby of autograph collecting. Sprague reasoned that the American equivalent of European nobility were the Revolutionary Fathers, and he began to collect a set of the autographs of the signers of the Declaration of Independence and the Constitution. Conveniently situated in northern Virginia, by 1830 Sprague had completed his first set of "signers." By his death in 1876 Sprague had collected over 40,000 manuscripts, most of which were sold at auction sales.[9]

Hazard, Belknap, and Sprague laid the foundations in America of collecting historical manuscripts, but Jared Sparks outdid them all as the master collector. As a young collegian, Sparks begged his friend Sprague for a "stick cut from a tree which overshadows the toomb of Washington." Instead of this remote momento, Sprague sent an authentic Washington autograph. Perhaps this incident helped to kindle Spark's passion for historical manuscripts, or perhaps it grew from his dedication to his goal of writing an epic history of the Revolution. In any event, his career as a manuscript collector overshadowed that as a minister, magazine editor, and publisher of source materials on the Revolution.[10]

The collection and preservation of historical manuscripts during the first half of the nineteenth century was almost solely the province of such individuals as Hazard, Belknap, Sprague, and Sparks and of the privately-supported historical societies which they created and endowed with their collections. The young American nation lacked the public institutions through which to preserve the manuscript sources of its history, and it was forced to rely upon such private agencies as were willing to serve as keepers of its past. Historical scholarship flourished under these handicaps, but it was stunted by a provincial nationalism and almost exclusive interest in the Revolution, a consequence of the activity of the early manuscript collectors.

[9] Butterfield, "Draper's Predecessors," in McNeil, ed., *Collector*, 11–12, 14–15.
[10] *Ibid.*, 15–16; [Sparks], "Materials," 277–286, 291.

MANUSCRIPT COLLECTIONS
AT THE LIBRARY OF CONGRESS

THE FOREMOST INSTITUTION in the collection and preservation of the manuscript sources of the American past without peer has been the Library of Congress. In particular, the evolution of its Division of Manuscripts has fundamentally altered the early manuscript tradition in America, and its undisputed preeminence has provided a new and powerful leadership for smaller agencies to follow in their collecting activity.

Founded largely through the efforts of Thomas Jefferson, James Madison, and Albert Gallatin after 1801, the Library of Congress was conceived as a private reference library for members of Congress to facilitate their functions as lawmakers. The collection consisted exclusively of printed materials, and its original emphasis was upon law and closely allied fields—history and political economy. By 1814 it had become a valuable if small collection, but it unfortunately was destroyed in the sacking of Washington by the British.

When the Capitol and the congressional library were rebuilt after the War of 1812, Thomas Jefferson's personal library of about 6,700 volumes was purchased in 1815 as the nucleus of the new collection. The manuscript material which formed a portion of the Jefferson purchase was the first such documentation to be acquired by the library. Included were draft copies of laws of Virginia, a copy of the manuscript of Jefferson's "Notes on Virginia," and other miscellaneous autograph notes. This modest beginning was expanded in 1829 with the purchase of Jefferson's second library, which included two volumes of manuscript records of the Virginia Company of London for the years 1619–1625, and four volumes of seventeenth-century transcripts which had been procured by Jefferson while he was in Europe.[11] After these early foundations were laid, little progress was made towards building a manuscript collection at the Library of Congress until after the Civil War. What interest the federal gov-

---

[11] Fred Shelley, "Manuscripts in the Library of Congress: 1800–1900," in *American Archivist*, 11:3–4 (January, 1948); Dorothy S. Eaton and Vincent L. Eaton, "Manuscripts Relating to Early America," in *Library of Congress Quarterly Journal of Acquisitions*, 8:17–28 (November, 1950).

ernment had in acquiring original manuscripts during this period ran along archival rather than manuscript lines.

During the period of documania and under the hysteria of acquiring the papers of the Revolutionary generation before it expired, Congress did purchase the papers of Washington (1834 and 1849), Madison (1837), Jefferson and Hamilton (1848), and Monroe (1849). In all these cases, however, the material was deposited in the library of the Department of State rather than in the Library of Congress. Under prevailing doctrines, federal purchase was held to convert these private papers into integral parts of the Revolutionary archives, which already reposed in the Department of State.[12]

After acquiring selected private papers to complement the national archives for the Revolutionary period and the early National period, the federal government rather passively contented itself with desultory attempts to publish selected portions of the Hamilton and Jefferson papers. Meanwhile, at the Library of Congress the book collection flourished, but the few manuscripts which had come into the library's possession languished.

Not everyone acquiesced in the neglect of original documentation at the congressional library. Ainsworth R. Spofford, who became Librarian of Congress following the Civil War, was shocked to discover the deficiency of manuscript material. Giving expression to his alarm, he observed that "it need only be added that the National Library now possesses not a solitary specimen of original autographs in the shape of letters or papers of our revolutionary generals and statesmen, to show how greatly this department of the collection would add to the value of that Library." Taking a personal interest and initiative, in 1866 Spofford secured the transfer of an important group of papers from the Smithsonian Institution, including the Dolley Madison Collection, a group of Loyalist papers, and the Henry Schoolcraft papers. Furthermore, Spofford was the prime mover in the purchase in 1867 of the Peter Force library.[13]

In Spofford, the manuscript collection at the Library of Congress at last had a champion to overcome the inertia of neglect.

[12] Shelley, "Manuscripts," 3–5.
[13] *Ibid.*, 6.

It soon began drawing the large and significant components which would make it world renowned by the turn of the century. The remaining immediate goal was the appointment of a professionally trained manuscript librarian to organize the collection for public use. In his 1875 annual report, Spofford called attention to the needs of the manuscript collection: "The increasing attention that is paid to these memorials of the past, and the new uses that are found for old documents, with the growth of the historical spirit in this country, give force to the suggestion now made . . . , that a competent historical scholar should be employed to put all these loose materials for history in order, and to prepare a thorough index to their contents, under the direction of the Librarian." In 1876 Congress responded to the plea with an appropriation of $3,400 for the employment of a "competent historical scholar," but none could be found at that price.[14]

Although Spofford could not secure a manuscripts librarian, he continued to acquire manuscripts as they became available. Largely due to his cultivation, Dr. Joseph M. Taner gave to the Library of Congress his unequalled collection of Washington papers in 1882 and continued to add other pieces until his death in 1896. Also in 1882 Congress appropriated funds for the purchase of the Franklin Collection from Henry Stevens. The books, pamphlets, and newspapers went to the Library of Congress, but the Franklin manuscripts were deposited, over Spofford's objections, in the State Department with the papers of the other Revolutionary Fathers. When in the same year the Marquis de Rochambeau offered his Revolutionary ancestor's papers to the United States, Spofford quickly organized the support of Senator George F. Hoar and the Joint Committee on the Library for a special appropriation of $20,000, which was approved on March 3, 1883.[15]

Spofford would have wished to have even more manuscript material, but his aspirations were seriously curtailed by the legislative formula which required a special act of appropriation for each major purchase of manuscripts. Furthermore, he was

---

[14] David C. Mearns, *The Story Up to Now: The Library of Congress, 1800–1946* (Washington, 1947), 109. See also, Paul M. Angle, *The Library of Congress: An Account, Historical and Descriptive* (Kingsport, Tennessee, 1958).

[15] Mearns, *The Story Up to Now*, 110; Shelley, "Manuscripts," 6–7.

embarrassed by the sub-professional care being given the materials the library had already acquired. To dramatize the needs of this special category of research material, Spofford in the late 1880's began to agitate for the construction of a separate manuscripts building and the reorganization of the staff to provide a separate department for manuscripts.[16]

Appeals to national pride in support of expanding and institutionalizing the manuscripts collection at the Library of Congress ultimately bore fruit. In 1888, while the new library building was under construction, Senator William H. Evarts for the Library Committee declared that the committee "deem it a proper time to recommend that a systematic effort be made to collect and preserve all manuscript papers which may be offered to the Government, and to make provision for the purchase of manuscripts deemed of special value." The committee further resolved that, upon opening of the new building, a "special curator or custodian, of the requisite qualifications, should be selected to have charge of the department of manuscripts, and they should be made available to public use, under suitable regulations for their protection."[17]

In the new building, occupied in the autumn of 1897, the plight of manuscripts was not much improved from the crowding and neglect they had received in the dark corners of the Capitol itself. Even worse, breach of trust reared its ugly head in the celebrated case of Philip McElhone and Lewis McKenzie, two employees of the manuscripts section. McElhone and McKenzie were convicted of stealing valuable individual manuscripts from the collection and selling them to a New York dealer. The scandal and subsequent public reaction led to the creation in September, 1897, of a Manuscripts Department with a professional chief, Dr. Herbert Friedenwald. The reorganization also provided for a small but competent staff to manage the manuscripts, initiating a long-overdue program of sorting, cataloging, and improvements in security.[18]

Herbert Friedenwald was preeminently qualified by training and experience for his appointment to the Library of Congress

---

[16] Shelley, "Manuscripts," 6–7.
[17] Mearns, *The Story Up to Now*, 110–111.
[18] Shelley, "Manuscripts," 11–16.

staff. A native of Baltimore, he had graduated from the Johns Hopkins University in 1890 and had gone on to the University of Pennsylvania to take his Ph.D. under John Bach McMaster. He had extensively used the papers of the Continental Congress at the State Department and had published a paper on "The Care of Manuscripts." Perhaps even more propitious for the future of the manuscripts collection, Friedenwald had that individual initiative and awareness of collecting opportunities which would take him far afield in search of manuscripts—to Cuba and Puerto Rico, for instance, immediately after the close of the Spanish-American War. So unprecedented was this junket that only transportation could be supplied at government expense. Other out-of-pocket expenses had to be borne by Friedenwald himself.[19]

Friedenwald placed the Manuscripts Department upon a sound professional basis, but his repeated requests for additional appropriations were ignored by Congress. The new building, the new Librarian Herbert Putnam, and the rising trend of professional interest in historical manuscripts all focused attention on the needs of the manuscripts collection. Putnam, in his first annual report in 1899, strongly endorsed Friedenwald's request for additional funds to purchase manuscripts. Still they were denied by Congress. In disgust, Friedenwald resigned his post in September, 1900, to return to the academic world, but he left behind a foundation upon which was to be built one of the great manuscripts collections of the world.[20]

The department Friedenwald headed had been raised to a full, co-ordinate division of the Library of Congress—but with no significant salary increase—just before his resignation. Putnam was hard pressed to build and retain the elite corps he wished for the library on the niggardly salaries available to him. In submitting his fiscal estimate for 1902 to the Secretary of the Treasury, Putnam observed that the position of Chief of the Division of Manuscripts had been vacant since September 1, 1900. Having noted the difficulty of filling the vacancy, he declared his intention of keeping it vacant "until the salary shall be placed at a sum which will enable me to secure for it

[19] Mearns, *The Story Up to Now*, 143–144.
[20] Shelley, "Manuscripts," 18–19.

a thoroughly adequate person. This division deals with the material which forms one of the two great divisions in a national library. . . . The interests involved are altogether too important to be entrusted to a second-rate person."[21]

Under the leadership of Herbert Putnam from 1899 to 1939, the Library of Congress indeed fulfilled its promise. It was Putnam who transformed the private reading club of Congressmen into a workshop for scholars, "universal in scope; national in service."[22] It was Putnam who saw the implications for America in the Report of the Historical Manuscripts Commission of Great Britain and who suggested, with Waldo G. Leland, J Franklin Jameson, and others, that similar action be taken in the United States through the newly-chartered American Historical Association and the Carnegie Institution of Washington.[23] These men envisioned a professional triumvirate in which the professional historians would create the demand for manuscripts, the Carnegie Institution would publish massive guides to manuscripts in the United States and abroad, and the Library of Congress would become the dominant factor in the collection and preservation of manuscripts at the national level. A golden age in American historical documentation was about to begin.

THE DIVISION OF MANUSCRIPTS
AT THE LIBRARY OF CONGRESS

THE PHENOMENAL GROWTH and transformation of the manuscript collection at the Library of Congress was not solely due to the effective leadership of Spofford, Friedenwald, and Putnam. It was also a result of the concerted support and guidance offered by the rising generation of professional historians who constituted the membership of the American Historical Association at the turn of the century. In 1895 the AHA had established a Historical Manuscripts Commission consisting

[21] Herbert Putnam to Secretary of Treasury, October 1, 1900, Librarian's Letter-book No. 7, f. 6, Library of Congress.

[22] U. S., Library of Congress, *Herbert Putnam, 1861–1955: A Memorial Tribute* (Washington, 1956), 34.

[23] Lester J. Cappon, "Reference Works and Historical Texts," in *Library Trends*, 5:369 (January, 1957).

of J. Franklin Jameson, Talcott Williams, Frederick J. Turner, William P. Trent, and Douglas Brymner, and its report the following year established guidelines for the development of the manuscript collection of the Library of Congress.[24]

The AHA manuscripts commission took as its model the report of the British Royal Commission on Historical Documents of 1869. Adapting to the American situation the essence of the British report, the American commission recommended first that existing agencies extend and upgrade their holdings. This view implicitly favored the expansion of the manuscript collection at the Library of Congress over existing or potential agencies which did not have the resources or prestige of the federal government upon which to rely. In addition to this implicit discouragement of proliferation of collecting agencies, the commission also noted that those papers in public or institutional hands were reasonably well cared for, while those in private or proprietary hands generally were not. Again, the object of this observation was to encourage the growth of established agencies such as the Library of Congress and to discourage the scattering of manuscripts into less competent hands.[25]

Herbert Putnam was quick to point out that the recommendations of the AHA manuscripts commission were already being implemented at the Library of Congress. Putnam conceived of the Library of Congress as a national library of record, whose duty it was to collect every literary memorial of national scope. As Putnam observed in reply to the manuscript commission's report, "It is pleasant to conjecture the National Library of the United States accumulating at Washington a collection of manuscripts which would accomplish for the student of American history what is accomplished by the Bodleian and British museums combined for the student of British history."[26] Noting with some misgivings that the materials for American history were already widely and perhaps irrevocably scattered, Putnam argued that manuscripts of a truly national interest ought by

---

[24] "Report of the Historical Manuscripts Commission," in American Historical Association, *Annual Report* (1896), I:467–480.

[25] *Ibid.*

[26] Herbert Putnam, "The Relation of the National Library to Historical Research in the United States," in AHA, *Annual Report* (1901), I:115–120.

original collection or by transfer be assumed to be the province of the Library of Congress. At the same time, he eschewed for the library the collection of material of purely local interest. The Library of Congress fortuitously had already built its collection around the Revolutionary period, principally through the acquisitions of the Peter Force, Washington, and Rochambeau collections. In addition to building to enhance this nucleus, Putnam proclaimed his intention to add significant national documentation of the post-Revolutionary period.[27]

When Herbert Putnam arrived at the Library of Congress, approximately 20,000 individual manuscripts were held in the various collections. By 1911 the collection had grown so rapidly that a redefinition of the library's collecting scope had to be made. It became especially necessary to exclude archival materials in order to maintain the Library's capacity to absorb manuscripts.[28] Putnam was also successful in securing private funds to finance projects and to purchase collections in areas for which congressional support was not forthcoming. Some of the larger grants made to the Manuscripts Division after precedents had been established under Putnam were: $192,671 from James Benjamin Wilbur in 1925 to reproduce manuscript sources in European archives; $72,697 in 1927 from William Evarts Benjamin for appointing a consultant in American history; and $31,285 from the estate of James Benjamin Wilbur in 1933 for cataloging and processing source material in American history.[29]

Although founded with a heavy emphasis upon the Revolutionary period, the collection at the Library of Congress developed in a more contemporary direction. Perhaps as much as 90 per cent of all recent acquisitions has been from the period since 1900—the period characterized by problems of high bulk. For example, some acquisitions from the contemporary period have been the papers of Woodrow Wilson, 1,300 boxes; Josephus Daniels, 960 boxes; Booker T. Washington, 1,200 boxes; and Gifford Pinchot, 3,300 boxes.[30] The preponderance of recent,

[27] *Ibid.*, 122.
[28] Mearns, *The Story Up to Now*, 171, 186.
[29] *Ibid.*, 202.
[30] Katherine E. Brand, "Developments in the Handling of Recent Manuscripts in the Library of Congress," in *American Archivist*, 16:99–104 (April, 1953).

high-bulk collections has forced the staff at the Library of Congress to modify traditional processes of cataloging and arranging, and to borrow techniques from archival science.

The rapidly expanding manuscript collections at the Library of Congress have been cataloged by a highly flexible system devised by Herbert Friedenwald during his tenure as head of the section. Modeled after that of the British Museum, the catalog scheme is organized geographically by countries and chronologically within national areas. There is also a "miscellany" category for manuscripts which do not fit conveniently within any of the formal classes.[31] In the category of American history, obviously the largest by far, the collection is organized into the six primary chronological periods of United States history, the papers of each individual being assigned to the period to which he most closely belonged.[32]

The number and bulk of collections processed at the Library of Congress have also had a bearing upon the cataloging procedure employed. For example, reference is seldom made to the manuscripts themselves in the process of cataloging. Instead, a register which supplies information for future cataloging and descriptive reporting is prepared as each collection is accessioned.[33]

The unique characteristics of manuscripts pose special problems in cataloging and use. As the Library of Congress has become the preeminent repository of manuscripts in the United States, so has the solution of these problems become a preeminent concern of the library. Especially difficult has been the establishment of the restrictions in the use of manuscripts made necessary by their fragile and unique character, conditions imposed by donors, or the policies adopted by libraries and archival agencies. At the Library of Congress policy and practice since the establishment of the Division of Manuscripts have favored the widest and freest possible use of the materials consistent with their safety and integrity. Generosity and magnanimity have char-

[31] Shelley, "Manuscripts," 17–18.

[32] Curtis Wiswell Garrison, "List of Manuscript Collections in the Library of Congress, July, 1931," in AHA, *Annual Report* (1930), I:123ff.

[33] Katherine E. Brand, "The Place of the Register in the Manuscripts Division of the Library of Congress," in *American Archivist*, 18:59–68 (January, 1955).

acterized the library's dealings with individual researchers and with other reference libraries.[34]

The Library of Congress has also been quick to adopt the techniques of microphotography in facilitating the collection and use of manuscripts. The special applicability of microfilm to newspapers and manuscripts has led to its wide employment, as in the case of the emergency copying programs in Europe just prior to the outbreak of World War II, which had posed continuing problems of cataloging.[35]

At the Library of Congress and elsewhere the single most difficult problem in using manuscript materials has been locating them, and a central union catalog of American manuscripts has long been the goal of scholars and collecting agencies. A recent example of the problems of locating manuscripts on even a local research topic will illustrate the point. In exploring the Yakima Indian War of 1855–1856, it was necessary for a scholar first to consult the records of the army located in the National Archives. In addition, the private papers of Commanding General John E. Wood, located in the New York State Library in Albany, had to be consulted. Additional information was secured from various collections in the Washington Historical Society, the Hudson's Bay Company Archives in London, and the Catholic mission archives in various church officies.[36]

In addition to cataloging systematically its own collections, the Library of Congress since the turn of the century has led a movement to publish guides of manuscripts holdings. A pioneer effort was the issuance in 1924 of a printed checklist which briefly described the major despository holdings of each state.[37] In 1944 the American Association for State and Local History published an inventory of its constituent agencies' holdings which extended the usefulness of a 1941 *Guide to Depositories of Manuscripts Collections in the U. S.* The Library of Congress contributed

[34] Howard H. Peckham, "Policies Regarding the Use of Manuscripts," in *Library Trends,* 5:361–368 (January, 1957).

[35] William J. Wilson, "Manuscripts in Microfilm: Problems of Cataloger and Bibliographer," in *Library Quarterly,* 13:216–226 (October, 1943).

[36] William N. Bischoff, "Tracing Manuscript Sources," in *Oregon Historical Quarterly,* 51:156–163 (September, 1950).

[37] U. S., Library of Congress, *Manuscripts in Public and Private Collections in the U. S.* (Washington, 1924), *passim.*

considerable support to this project. By the end of World War II a union catalog of manuscripts was planned, and the Library of Congress was selected as the central clearing house.[38]

In 1948 the historical profession took official notice of the proliferation of agencies collecting manuscript materials and, fearful lest the standards established by the Library of Congress might not be universally observed, directed an *ad hoc* committee of the AHA to speak in the name of the profession. Concerning arrangement, the committee recommended that whatever significant arrangement could be discerned in incoming groups of recent papers be retained, at least during preliminary stages of processing. When an external order had to be imposed, the committee generally recommended a chronological arrangement except in collections covering a very short period, in which case an alphabetical arrangement would be indicated. In very large collections, if groups of papers dealing with subjects susceptible of segregation are included, they are so segregated. Regarding the special problems of high-bulk manuscripts, the committee recommended that each acquisition be evaluated as soon as possible upon receipt, and that record groups of little or no foreseeable use be removed for microfilming or total disposal.[39]

The *ad hoc* committee on manuscripts also gave its attention to the matter of guides and finding aids, especially as complicated by the rise of mass documentation. The committee broke cleanly with tradition and insisted that the new age of historical documentation be recognized by scholars and archivists alike, recommending "that in the case of large groups of recent materials, indexing of individual manuscript items, however ideally desirable, be considered for practical purposes the exception rather than the rule; and that there be substantiated therefor descriptive sheets or memoranda."[40] The standards and policies previously established by the Library of Congress were also urged by the committee in other areas of manuscript librarianship. To charges of excessive competition in collecting, the committee made the obvious reply that the most important considera-

---

[38] Cappon, "Reference Works," 373, 376.
[39] American Historical Association, *Ad Hoc* Committee on Manuscripts, "Report," in *American Archivist*, 14:229–230 (July, 1951).
[40] *Ibid.*

tion was that valuable manuscripts be collected by some agency, where they would be most readily available to the largest number of users. To the growing protests against restrictions upon use, the committee recommended that only those security controls be employed as would be necessary to insure reasonable care against abuse, compromise, misplacing, and theft. Libraries were enjoined to make every effort to secure unrestricted access and dedication to public use of all literary rights.[41]

One of the most difficult problems involved in the use of manuscript material has been that of general access, including the privileges of duplication and of exclusive access during active research. For the alleviation of this problem, the *ad hoc* committee urged that scholars and agencies adopt an attitude of mutual consideration and forbearance which would permit a free and competitive access to all materials (save doctoral dissertations for five years) and photo-copying at the risk of the researcher.[42]

Even if the questions of access and literary rights in manuscripts could be resolved, the underlying problem of locating pertinent collections would still remain. While manuscripts have no special sanctity in themselves, and their use imparts no automatic superiority to historical scholarship, American historians are expected to make maximum use of them, or at least to exhaust the possibility of reasonable use. It becomes increasingly clear that this expectation cannot be realized unless there are developed some systematic bibliographical tools and finding aids, such as a national manuscripts register.[43]

The AHA had expressed interest in a union catalog of manuscripts as early as 1946, but the magnitude of the task seemed too great for its resources. T. C. Blegen in his *Grass Roots History* in 1947 suggested a plan for the project, but little was done to implement it until 1951, when the Library of Congress generously agreed to sponsor it.

The creation of the Union Catalog of Manuscripts has been planned in two steps. First, a nationwide adoption of Library of Congress rules of cataloging by all co-operating manuscripts

[41] *Ibid.*
[42] *Ibid.*
[43] Bell I. Wiley, "Historians and the National Register," in *American Archivist,* 17:325–330 (July, 1954). Wiley provides an excellent example, indicating how the register would facilitate the location of papers of Confederate Congressmen.

depositories has been encouraged. Secondly, as standardized catalog entries are forwarded to the Library of Congress for the Union Catalog, the library has agreed to print on cards and sell the entries for public distribution. The project began operation in May, 1952. Although the cataloging in the co-operating agencies has been slow, the project was well under way at the time of this writing, several volumes having been published. It is generally held that the Union Catalog is in the process of becoming a bibliographical tool even more valuable than that for printed books. It has also helped librarians overcome a certain nervousness in handling manuscripts. The prestige of listing has already called a number of collections out of private into institutional hands. In other cases, displaced manuscripts have been returned home through sale, exchange, or gift.[44]

PAPERS OF THE PRESIDENTS

THE PERSONAL PAPERS of the American presidents constitute the bedrock of manuscript documentation for the nation's historiography. As befits its status as the national library of record and research, the Library of Congress has at least some material from twenty-three chief executives, from Washington to Coolidge, a total of nearly two million manuscripts on "Presidential Row." Thus with rare exceptions, the Library of Congress until recently has preempted the field of presidential papers. Thousands of scholars have made the pilgrimage to Capitol Hill to worship and to work at this historiographical shrine and have given professional thanks for the convenience and comprehensiveness of the collection. Until recently, unfortunately, the Library of Congress lacked the funds to make this bedrock even more widely available.

In 1957 Representative Paul C. Jones (Democrat of Missouri) introduced a bill to establish, as it were, an extension division of the university of manuscripts in the Library of Congress. Signed into law by President Eisenhower on August 16,

[44] Robert H. Land, "The National Union Catalog of Manuscript Collections," in *American Archivist,* 17:195–208 (July, 1954); see also, Howard H. Peckham, "Manuscript Repositories and the National Register," in *American Archivist,* 17:319–324 (July, 1954).

1957, the new legislation gave the library the authority to prepare on conventional 35mm film reproductions of each of the
presidential collections in its care. These reproductions were
to be made available on loan anywhere in the country, and positive prints of any collection were to be made available at cost.
Each roll of film will carry provenance and other information
concerning the collection, and name indexes will be published
for each collection. All entries will be incorporated into the
National Union Catalog of Manuscripts.[45]

The plan for the filming of the presidential papers began
with the smaller collections and has worked through the larger
ones as time and funds have permitted. In the meantime, scholars needing to consult the larger collections of presidential papers have been obliged to make the trip to Washington.

A brief summary of the provenance and scope of "Presidential
Row" at the Library of Congress will suffice to illustrate the
riches with which the national library is endowed. Unless otherwise noted, all of the presidential papers are fully open to public use.

All but a small percentage of George Washington's papers
are in the possession of the Library of Congress. Fortunately,
the core of Washington's Revolutionary correspondence was
gathered and arranged between 1781 and 1783 by Lieutenant
Colonel Richard Varick, who served the General as recording
secretary. This same meticulous care for records carried over
to Washington's political career, and his papers were left in
good order at Mount Vernon.[46] From there they were transported
to Boston by Jared Sparks in 1826. In 1832 George Cochin Washington, Representative from Maryland and nephew of Justice
Bushrod Washington, sold the "public" portion of this collection
to the federal government for $25,000. After Sparks had completed
his work in Boston, 192 bound volumes and several boxes of
loose manuscripts were shipped to Washington for deposit in
the library of the Department of State. In 1849 the department

[45] Fred Shelley, "The Presidential Papers Program of the Library of Congress,"
in *American Archivist*, 25:429–434 (October, 1962). The legislation may be found
at 71 U. S. *Statutes* 368.

[46] John D. Knowlton, "Properly Arranged and So Correctly Recorded," in
American Archivist, 27:371–374 (July, 1964).

purchased the remaining "private" papers from the Washington heirs for $20,000. The combined collections remained at the Department of State until 1903, when they were transferred by Executive Order to the Library of Congress, there to be consolidated with the Washington items acquired in the purchase of the Peter Force library in 1867. Since 1903 several additional items have been acquired so that over 95 per cent of the surviving Washington papers are now at the Library of Congress.[47]

The bulk of the Thomas Jefferson papers were purchased by the government in 1848 from Thomas Jefferson Randolph for $20,000. From 1848 to 1903 they remained in the library of the Department of State, being transferred in 1903 to the Library of Congress. This collection comprises the originals, letter-press copies, or microfilm copies of over 90 per cent of the extant Jefferson material, and additions are constantly being made as they are discovered. In addition to the library's holdings, minor collections of Jefferson manuscripts are owned by the Massachusetts Historical Society, the Pierpont Morgan Library, the Pennsylvania Historical Society, the Buffalo Historical Society, the Yale University Library, the University of Virginia Library, the American Philosophical Society, and the Missouri Historical Society.[48]

The magnificent collection of James Madison manuscripts (a significant portion of those known) came to the Library of Congress in the main through purchases from Mrs. Dolley Madison and from the Chicago Historical Society. Madison had arranged his papers in preparation for publishing them, and they devolved to the widow upon Madison's death. She attempted to complete the arrangements for publication but finally sold a portion of the original papers to the government in July, 1838, for $30,000. A selection was published in 1840 as *The Madison Papers*. In 1848, Mrs. Madison, being in financial straits, sold a second installment of Madison's papers to the government for $25,000. Upon Mrs. Madison's death it was discovered that a portion of the second installment had been held back and bequeathed to John Payne Todd, a son by her first husband. Todd subsequently sold the papers to J. C. McGuire of Washington, who offered

[47] Rowland, "Papers," 195–196.
[48] *Ibid.*, 197.

the material to the government, but no appropriation was voted. The Todd portion of Madison's papers was ultimately sold through a New York autograph dealer to Marshall Field for the Chicago Historical Society. The government's claim growing out of the 1848 sale plus a bonus of $10,000 at last reunited all of the Madison papers at the Library of Congress in 1910.[49]

The papers of James Monroe are widely scattered, but the largest single collection is at the Library of Congress. Acquired in 1849 from the Monroe heirs for $20,000, the papers remained in the library of the Department of State until 1903, when they were transferred with the other Revolutionary manuscripts to the Library of Congress. Other Monroe collections are in the hands of Lawrence M. Hoes of Washington, D.C., and in the New York Public Library.[50]

Andrew Jackson, so deeply embroiled in public controversy during his lifetime, had a keen sense of history and preserved his personal papers with great care, anticipating that his biographer would need private documentation to overcome the partisan nature of much of the archival and newspaper documentation. At Jackson's death the personal papers were turned over to Francis Preston Blair, in whose family they remained until 1903 when presented to the Library of Congress. A small collection of personal items which had been retained by Andrew Jackson, Jr., was purchased by the library in 1911 for $18,000. A third collection of about 1,200 items, which had been entrusted in 1842 to Amos Kendall to support a Jackson biography, was thought for years to have been burned in a Washington warehouse fire. When they were again uncovered they were purchased by the library in 1932. The Jackson holdings of the library now constitute about half of the known material, the other half being widely scattered.[51]

The Library of Congress also has the principal collection of Martin Van Buren's papers. When the "Little Magician" died in 1862, the papers remained in family hands until 1904–1905, when they were presented to the library by Mrs. Smith Thompson Van Buren (widow of the President's son), Mrs. Ellen James

[49] Ibid., 197–198.
[50] Ibid., 199.
[51] Ibid., 199–200.

Van Buren Morris, and Dr. Stuyvesant Fish Morris. The papers were culled by Van Buren himself and by his heirs, and some of the items were burned. The Library of Congress collection must be used in conjunction with another set of Van Buren papers in the New York State Library at Albany.[52]

William Henry Harrison's brief tenure in the White House produced few historical manuscripts, and what little remained is believed to have been burned when fire destroyed the Harrison homestead at North Bend, Ohio, in 1858. Mrs. Benjamin Harrison gave a few discrete items to the library of Congress, and they now constitute a small but the best collection of Harrison manuscripts.[53]

John Tyler's papers were left to his widow and were largely destroyed in the burning of Richmond in 1865. The largest remaining collection of Tyler material was purchased by the Library of Congress in 1919 from Dr. Lyon G. Tyler, the President's historian son. Other items have been added from time to time as they have come to light.[54]

The major portion of the papers of James K. Polk is held by the Library of Congress, the first portion having been acquired for $10,000 in 1903 from Mrs. George W. Fall of Nashville, a niece by adoption. The celebrated diary, covering Polk's administration and the Mexican War, and a large quantity of papers collected by the Chicago Historical Society were purchased in 1910 by the Library of Congress for $3,500.[55]

Zachary Taylor's papers are widely scattered among descendants, but the Library of Congress has slowly gathered, largely by gifts, a small but important collection.[56] Likewise, the Franklin Pierce collection at the Library of Congress is small, but there exists none other to rival it. Pierce seems to have destroyed his papers before his death, and only a few items have survived by chance.[57]

The papers of the martyred President, Abraham Lincoln, were removed from the White House by Mrs. Lincoln and re-

[52] *Ibid.*, 200.
[53] *Ibid.*, 200–201.
[54] *Ibid.*
[55] *Ibid.*, 201.
[56] *Ibid.*
[57] *Ibid.*, 202.

turned to Illinois with her personal effects. They remained in Springfield, closed to all except John Nicolay and John Hay, who were authorized to use the papers in the biography they prepared. Robert Todd Lincoln succeeded to the ownership of the material and in his misguided historical zeal eliminated all "useless" documentation before depositing the papers in trust in the Library of Congress on May 7, 1919. On January 23, 1923, by deed of gift the President's son conveyed the Lincoln papers to the library, subject to their remaining closed for a period of 21 years following his own death, which occurred on July 26, 1926. The papers were duly opened on July 26, 1947,[58] in ample time to support the flood of histories of the Civil War stimulated by the centennial observance from 1961 to 1965.

The closest student of Andrew Johnson, Howard K. Beale, reports that the Reconstruction President suffered from writer's cramp and that he wrote little. However limited the Johnson autographs, the Johnson papers are voluminous. They reveal a politician far more capable than the popular image of a well-meaning but weak victim of circumstances. The papers also suggest the strong possibility that Johnson enjoyed the counsel of such competent men as George Bancroft.[59] The Johnson papers were created orderly, but they were dispersed into several hands following Johnson's return to Tennessee. The Library of Congress, in acquiring the collection in several parts from the heirs, rescued most of it from destruction or oblivion. The first lot was acquired in 1904 from the grandson of the President, Andrew Johnson Patterson, of Greenville, Tennessee. A second lot was obtained in 1931 from Patterson's widow. The collection includes virtually all of the incoming correspondence, but the letter books of outgoing correspondence were lost by a person to whom the family loaned them for reading.[60]

There is no large body of letters of U. S. Grant since he engaged in little correspondence. Many of his letters were returned to the senders, and many were supposedly destroyed by Grant in his old age. The Library of Congress has a small col-

---

[58] *Ibid.,* 203.
[59] William A. Dunning, "A Little More Light on Andrew Johnson," in Massachusetts Historical Society *Proceedings,* second series, 19:397–405 (November, 1905).
[60] Rowland, "Papers," 204.

lection presented by the President's grandson, U. S. Grant, III, and a few scattered pieces have been added by purchase.[61]

Throughout his career, James A. Garfield carefully preserved his personal papers, letter books, manuscript journal, and other memoranda. Following his death, all of these papers were returned to Ohio and preserved at the family home in Mentor. After thirty years they were opened to Professor T. C. Smith of Williams College, whose president was Harry Garfield, the son of the late President. After Professor Smith had concluded his use of the material, it was presented to the Library of Congress in 1930–1931 as a gift of the Garfield children. The collection is restricted and can be used only by permission of the Garfield family.[62]

Most of Chester A. Arthur's manuscripts were destroyed by the President himself, but the Library of Congress has a small collection donated by Chester A Arthur, III. An auxiliary collection of Arthur papers was later obtained from Mrs. L. R. Mitchell, whose father, J. C. Reed, helped President Arthur prepare his state papers.[63]

Grover Cleveland accumulated a large collection of personal papers, but they were left in great disorder. They were stored with Colonel Daniel Lamont, the President's secretary, through whom Robert McElvoy had access to the papers in writing the Cleveland biography. Afterward, through arrangements with Mrs. Preston, the President's widow, the first group of Cleveland papers was deposited at the Library of Congress in 1918. Additional deposits were made in 1923 and 1924 to swell the library's collection of Cleveland papers to over 30,000 pieces.[64]

The papers of Benjamin Harrison were deposited in the Library of Congress beginning in 1915 by the President's widow and his daughter, Mrs. James R. McKee. In 1933 the deposit was converted into a gift, permanently securing a voluminous collection for public use.[65]

The papers left by William McKinley were presented in 1935 to the Library of Congress by George B. Cortelyou, the executor

[61] *Ibid.*, 204–205.
[62] *Ibid.*, 205 206.
[63] *Ibid.*, 206.
[64] *Ibid.*, 206–207.
[65] *Ibid.*, 207.

of the former President's estate, who also served as McKinley's personal secretary during the administration. The collection is full, but it has been disappointing to many users. McKinley was among the most laconic of the Presidents.[66]

As befits a President with historiographical aspirations in his own right, the papers of Theodore Roosevelt were presented to the Library of Congress by the former President himself in 1917, and the collection has been subsequently increased by additional pieces. It is now regarded as complete,[67] a monument to the presidential patron of the Division of Manuscripts.

The voluminous collection of William Howard Taft papers, estimated at over 900,000 pieces, was begun as a deposit by the ex-President at the Library of Congress in 1919. Additions have since been made by other members of the family. Access to the Taft papers is granted upon application to the surviving literary executor of the Taft estate.[68]

The Woodrow Wilson papers, given to the Library of Congress in 1939 by Mrs. Wilson, are one of the largest and most distinguished of the library's collections, consisting of over 180,000 pieces. Before deposition in the library, the collection was in the hands of Ray Stannard Baker while he was writing the Wilson biography. The collection is divided into six primary categories: executive or official file; confidential file; personal file; peace conference file; papers relating to the period from retirement to death; and the presidential letters and documents.[69]

Shortly after he retired, President Coolidge directed that some fifty file boxes of correspondence be transferred to the Library of Congress, but the material remained under his control with respect to access and consultation. Following the President's death, Mrs. Coolidge continued to exercise these controls, but the papers are now fully open to public use.[70]

In summary, of the twenty-three presidential collections at the Library of Congress, nine have been acquired through purchase for a total of $170,000. The remaining fourteen collections have

[66] *Ibid.*, 207–208.
[67] *Ibid.*, 208.
[68] *Ibid.*
[69] *Ibid.*, 208–209.
[70] *Ibid.*, 209.

come into public hands as gifts or deposits with amazingly little restriction upon their access and use. This generous precedent has secured for the nation a veritable treasure of historical documentation, valuable in its own right and for its magnetic ability to attract the supporting collections of lesser public figures associated with these Presidents. The price of such a treasure trove, however, has been haphazardness in collection and vagueness in disposition. Furthermore, the burgeoning collections of the modern Presidents have threatened to saturate the library's capacity to absorb the mountain of paper produced in the President's name by an expanding army of staff members and office machines.[71] The desire of Franklin D. Roosevelt for a better system through which to bequeath to posterity his literary estate was the basis for a new concept of presidential libraries supported by public funds.

On December 11, 1938, readers of the Sunday newspapers learned that President Roosevelt had, at a luncheon attended by distinguished historians, librarians, and archivists on the previous day, announced a plan to donate his huge collection of papers, books, art objects, and momentoes of office to the people of the United States, and to build a library and museum to house them at his family estate at Hyde Park, New York. The three men who must bear most praise or blame, as the case may be, for the concept of a presidential library were Judge Samuel Rosenman (the literary guardian of the papers of Roosevelt), Frank Walker (the fund-raiser for the building), and R. D. W. Connor (whose National Archives staff was to furnish the professional care for the material). Conspicuous by his absence at the original planning session was any representative of the Library of Congress, but this intentional omission was blunted when Waldo G. Leland was invited to serve on the planning committee after the project was announced. The President had scored on an end run against the logical expectation of the eventual deposit of his papers at the Library of Congress. What he presented to the scholarly world and the library staff late in 1938 was an accomplished fact.[72]

---

[71] R. D. W. Connor, "The Story of the Franklin D. Roosevelt Library," in *American Archivist,* 3:84–85 (April, 1940).

[72] Leland, "Roosevelt Library," 11–18.

Roosevelt's motivation in projecting a special presidential library has been and will continue to be subject to debate, although the record is fairly clear. Archivist Connor, who was one of those closest to the President in formulating the plan, declared that it sprang unselfishly from the President, whom he declared to be "the nation's answer to the Historian's prayer." Connor repudiated the charge that the President sought a personal monument, and stated that Roosevelt earnestly demurred at naming it for himself, much preferring "Hyde Park Library."[73] Leland, on the other hand, originally was highly suspicious of the proposal and opposed it until he was convinced that the material was lost to the Library of Congress in any case. The custom of depositing presidential papers at the Library of Congress was strong, but the precedent and legal right of a President to dispose of his papers as he wished was even stronger.

The special character of the papers of the President arises from the Constitutional independence of the office. The inviolability of papers has been the outward form of many substantive Constitutional controversies involving the President and Congress, such as the one in 1886 regarding President Cleveland's removal of a district attorney in Alabama. To the demand of the Senate for the file in the case, the President replied:

> I regard the papers and documents withheld and addressed to me or intended for my use and action purely unofficial and private, not infrequently confidential, and having reference to the performance of a duty exclusively mine. I consider them in no proper sense as upon the files of the [Justice] Department, but as deposited there for my convenience, remaining still completely under my control. I suppose if I desired to take them into my custody I might do so with entire propriety, and if I saw fit to destroy them no one could complain. . . .[74]

Faced with such a sweeping and resolute statement of the principle of the privileged nature of executive documents, the Senate retreated, and the principle that a President has the unlimited right to dispose of his papers in whatever manner he sees fit became established beyond all question.

[73] Connor, "Roosevelt Library," 86–87.
[74] *Ibid.*, 82–83.

The committee appointed by President Roosevelt to perfect the plan for his proposed library necessarily adjusted its thinking to his preconceived ideas. On the basis of a rough inventory of approximately 6,117 linear feet, or about 4,774 cubic feet of material, a building costing approximately $450,000 was planned. The President took a keen personal interest in the project, issuing instructions to facilitate the transfer of material to Hyde Park when the library was ready to receive it. He directed that all papers be kept intact and that nothing be destroyed before being removed to the library and evaluated by trained archivists. He was especially interested in plans for the museum to house his numerous momentoes, "the part for the people" as he put it, and approved a twenty-five-cent entrance fee to help support the library. He personally planned a study in the library, to which he apparently expected to retire in 1941 and live out his days writing his memoirs. To the realization of the building fund he personally pledged the income from his writings, about $7,500 per year. He could, of course, have subscribed the entire cost of the building himself, but he preferred it to be built by popular subscription so that the people would understand that it and its contents truly belonged to them. A dinner on February 4, 1939, which opened the drive for funds, netted about $400,000 from 28,000 persons. The legal basis for transfer of the Hyde Park plot and library building to the United States was introduced in April, 1939, and passed by Congress by a strict partisan vote. The property was first assigned to the National Park Service and title conferred on July 24. On July 4, 1940, the completed building was turned over to the United States, and material began to flow from Washington to be processed by a staff from the National Archives.[75]

The death of the President on April 12, 1945, created a problem of special urgency for the Roosevelt Library. More than half of the total body of the Roosevelt papers, about 2,500 cubic feet, had not yet been transferred to Hyde Park. Instead, they were left in the hands of the literary executors of the estate. No provision had been made in the President's will for carrying out his intentions regarding the library, and special permission

---

[75] Leland, "Roosevelt Library," 21–27.

from the probate court had to be secured to permit the transfer of the remaining papers. The delicate matter of restrictive access in the interest of national security, international relations, and personal confidences had fortunately been anticipated in a presidential memorandum of July 16, 1943, to the director of the library. By this memorandum, Judge Samuel Rosenman, Harry Hopkins, and personal secretary Miss Grace Tully were authorized to screen the papers in case of the President's personal inability to complete the task.[76]

After processing, the Roosevelt papers were found to be remarkably complete and to be by far the largest (about 4,400 cubic feet in all) single manuscript collection to be institutionalized and opened to public use. About 85 per cent of the total collection was open to the public from the first day of access. In accordance with the criteria established by the President, those papers which are closed to the public relate to applications and recommendations for positions, derogatory remarks concerning individuals, investigative reports, personal and family affairs, information that could be used to harass individuals, information prejudicial to national security, reflections upon friendly powers, and confidential matters of a personal nature involving the President. All of the restricted papers are periodically reexamined, and all are expected to be opened within twenty-five years of the President's death.[77]

The government itself, or more exactly, the editorial staff of *Foreign Relations*, has had most frequent recourse to the Roosevelt papers since the library was established. A number of private scholars have also used the papers, including the Roosevelt biographers, but full utilization of the Roosevelt papers on a scale comparable to that of the other presidential papers in the Library of Congress still lies in the future. The sheer size and range of the collection discourages the traditional type of utilization. It should also be remembered that the Roosevelt papers do not contain transcripts of the personal or telephone conversations upon which President Roosevelt greatly relied in conducting the affairs of his office.[78]

---

[76] *Ibid.*, 28–29.

[77] Rowland, "Papers," 210–211.

[78] Herman Kahn, "World War II and Its Background: Research Materials at the Franklin D. Roosevelt Library," in *American Archivist*, 17:150–155 (April, 1954).

Implicit in some of the opposition to the establishment of the Roosevelt Library was the fear that all subsequent Presidents might be encouraged through this precedent to establish separate presidential libraries at public expense. Such a development, some thought, would needlessly scatter prime national documentation about the country without any corresponding benefits. The worst fears of these critics appeared to be realized when plans were announced late in President Truman's second term of office for the construction of the Truman Library in Independence, Missouri.

President Truman's eight years in the White House produced some 1,600 file drawers, or over 3,500,000 separate manuscript pieces, an acquisition of staggering proportions for any manuscripts repository. Again, as had been the case with the Roosevelt material, the argument of the necessity of a special agency to insure reasonable care was put forward. Additionally, President Truman, a hearty politician in good health when he retired, intended to use his remaining years preparing his memoirs and expected his official papers to be conveniently available. To accommodate the huge collection, a one-storey, air-conditioned, contemporary structure was constructed at an estimated cost of $1,750,000.[79]

In addition to the archival concepts borrowed from the Roosevelt Library, the Truman Library was formulated to serve the popular interest in the American Presidency. According to Daniel D. Lloyd, the head of the firm which designed the building, the library symbolized Mr. Truman's "deep interest . . . in the archival and historical professions and the sciences of preserving and expounding our national history." It was also Truman's desire that the library "serve as an active center of study and research, not only for his own period in the Presidency, but also for the whole range of contemporary events, bringing new resources and facilities for such study into fruitful use in the mid-region of our country."[80]

The convenience and wishes of President Truman ultimately overcame all criticisms of his removing his papers from Washing-

[79] Lloyd, "Truman Library,'" 99–110.
[80] Philip C. Brooks, "The Harry S. Truman Library," in *American Archivist,* 25:25–27 (January, 1962).

ton. After the building at Independence was under construction, a Joint Resolution of August 12, 1955, authorized the Adminstrator of General Services (then the functional executive officer of the National Archives) "to accept for deposit . . . the papers and other historical materials of any President or former President of the United States, or of any other official or former official of the Government, . . . subject to restrictions agreeable to the Administrator as to their use; and . . . to accept for . . . the United States, any land, buildings, and equipment offered as a gift to the United States for the purposes of creating a Presidential archival depository."[81]

Hearings on the joint resolution relating to presidential libraries were held before a special subcommittee of the Joint Committee on Government Operations. These hearings called forth testimony from a stellar list of witnesses. The Archivist of the United States, Dr. Wayne C. Grover, testified regarding the ease of operating the Roosevelt Library and outlined the special problems that handling of such high-bulk collections as the papers of modern Presidents would impose upon the traditional manuscripts depositories. Grover discounted the dangers of decentralization, listing the number of works based upon research at Hyde Park. Additional statements in support of the resolution were received from Basil O'Connor, president of the corporation to finance and build the Truman Library, from historian Henry Steele Commager, and from the secretary of the AHA, Boyd C. Shafer. The arguments most frequently advanced cited the Constitutional uniqueness of presidential papers, the material benefits to the government, the academic desirability of decentralizing such documentation, and the relative security against nuclear destruction. The estimated expense of operating a presidential library was set at the hearings at $150,000 per year, of which about one-third might be recovered from admission fees from tourists.[82] Opponents of the plan stressed the inconvenience of decentralization and the evils of the "cult of personality" perpetuated at public expense.

[81] 69 U. S. *Statutes* 695; Brooks, "Truman Library," 28.

[82] Elizabeth Buck, "General Legislation for Presidential Libraries," in *American Archivist,* 18:337–341 (October, 1955).

The Truman Library was dedicated and transferred to the government on July 6, 1957, and has since become an increasingly popular and significant attraction for tourists and scholars. The museum of political cartoons and objects associated with President Truman was opened in September, 1957, and has since averaged at least 100,000 visitors each year. Two staff members from the National Archives spent four years arranging Truman's papers, following the pattern set at the Roosevelt Library for separating confidential material from that immediately open to the public. Research rooms were opened on May 11, 1959, and about one hundred scholars each year have used the material there. As the library acquires the papers of the political associates of President Truman, the rate of usage will undoubtedly increase.[83]

In addition to assembling complementary manuscript collections of political associates, the Truman Library has also embarked on a program of collecting auxiliary printed and audiovisual material. A book collection program with emphasis upon President Truman, the Presidency, and foreign affairs was inaugurated in 1958 by a grant from the Rockefeller Foundation. From a core of 9,000 volumes collected by Truman while in the White House, the collection soon grew to over 50,000 volumes. One notable single acquisition was the personal library of the diplomatic historian, Samuel Flagg Bemis. Audio-visual material has found its way into the library and has been much used by radio and television producers.[84]

To allay the fears and criticism of encroachment upon multiple collecting fronts, the Truman Library has found it expedient to define its collecting policy. First, as a federal agency, the library pledges to avoid direct competition with state and local agencies in the acquisition of manuscripts of less than national significance. All of its acquisitions have, in theory, some definite connection with the Truman Administration. Secondly, it promises to concentrate its collecting on national and international affairs, particularly those of the Truman period. Thirdly, as an archival agency, the library pledges itself primarily to the col-

[83] Brooks, "Truman Library," 29.
[84] *Ibid.*, 32.

lection of original source materials rather than that material
which has been or probably will be published.[85]

Mr. Truman's personality pervades the library which bears
his name. His health permitting, he works in his office in the
library, but he keeps aloof from its operation. Another expression of the former President's keen historical perspective has
been his co-operation in the establishment of the Harry S. Truman Library Institue for National and International Affairs,
which makes grants-in-aid for research and study in the Truman
Era.[86]

While a few manuscript librarians may still grouse about "unfair competition," the system of presidential libraries seems to
have become thoroughly established with the creation of several
additional ones, the Eisenhower Library at Abilene, the Hoover
Library at West Branch, the Kennedy Library at Cambridge, and
the Johnson Library at Austin. Scholars have adjusted to the system, and some have even come forward to praise it. On the basis
of experience with the existing libraries, it has been suggested that
popular interest in the Presidency has been more closely integrated with scholarly research pursuits through such libraries, each
mutually supporting the other. In addition, the presidential libraries have become centers for research in special fields as exemplified by the outpouring of publication from research at
Hyde Park and Independence. Lastly, the decentralization of
materials inherent in scattered presidential libraries has been regarded by some scholars as a contribution to the historian's convenience rather than as an added burden.[87]

While a system of presidential libraries supported by federal
funds and administered by the National Archives may be a
new concept, it is not without parallels in private or proprietary
libraries and collections. Perhaps the oldest such institutionalization of presidential papers is the Adams Family Papers, in-

[85] Buck, "General Legislation for Presidential Libraries," 341. See also, Harry
S. Truman Library, *Acquisition Policy of the Harry S. Truman Library* (Independence, Missouri, 1958).
[86] Brooks, "Truman Library," 32.
[87] Herman Kahn, "The Presidential Library—A New Institution," in *Special
Libraries,* 50:106–113 (March, 1959); Richard S. Kirkendall, "Presidential Libraries
—One Researcher's Point of View," in *American Archivist,* 25:441–448 (October,
1962).

cluding the papers of Presidents John Adams and John Quincy Adams. Originally housed at various homesteads of the family, the papers were consolidated and placed in the Stone Library at Quincy, Massachusetts, by Charles Francis Adams in 1859–1870. There they remained under lock until after World War II, serviced by the Massachusetts Historical Society under an agreement with the Adams Trust. Although the trust is self-perpetuating, the trustees have reversed a former policy of highly restrictive access to one of systematic publication in cooperation with the Harvard University Press and Time, Inc. Several series of Adams material are being published under the editorial direction of Lyman H. Butterfield. First, a microfilm edition of the bulk of the papers is being issued for research libraries which wish to hold a duplicate of the collection. A selection of the famous diaries, family letters, and correspondence is being published in over eighty volumes by the Harvard University Press, and *Life* magazine is serially publishing essentially the same information.[88]

The papers of Millard Fillmore might well have been institutionalized after the fashion of the Adams papers but for an outrage committed against them. When President Fillmore retired he took with him all of his official papers, presumably planning to use them as the basis of his memoirs or for other historical purposes. Fillmore's son, unfortunately, did not have the sense of family pride and historical responsibility exhibited by the Adams' descendants, for the younger Fillmore directed in his will that "at the earliest practicable moment" all of the Fillmore correspondence be burned or otherwise destroyed. Following his death in 1889 his wishes were apparently carried out. In 1908, however, enough Fillmore material was discovered in an attic in Buffalo to comprise seventy bound volumes. This material was placed in the Buffalo and Erie County Historical Society, where it is available for scholarly use.[89]

James Buchanan saved everything and, after his retirement, occupied himself with arranging his papers. In contrast to the tragedy of Fillmore's papers, those of Buchanan have been used

---

[88] Rowland, "Papers," 196–197; Donald H. Mugridge, "The Adams Papers," in *American Archivist*, 25:449–454 (October, 1962).

[89] Rowland, "Papers," 201–202.

by three biographers. In 1897 they were presented to the Historical Society of Pennsylvania by the nieces of the late President.
The collection runs to some 25,000 items, covering Buchanan's
legal, diplomatic, and political career, and there are no restrictions upon its use.[90]

In 1916 the Rutherford B. Hayes Memorial Library at Fre-
mont, Ohio, was built and opened by the state of Ohio in fulfillment of the conditions which accompanied the grant by Colonel W. C. Hayes, son of the President, of the main body of his
father's papers. The main collection consists of almost 300 bound
volumes of over 75,000 manuscript items, plus other contemporary and family collections. It is administered by the Ohio
Historical Society, and the material is open to the public.[91]

After the death of Warren G. Harding in 1923, his widow
placed an undetermined number of private papers at the Harding
Memorial Association in Marion, Ohio. There they remained
closed both to the public and to scholars. While in Marion no
provision was made as to when and under what conditions the
papers would ever be opened, but in 1963 historians were grat-
ified by the announcement that the papers had been presented
to the Ohio Historical Society. The Society, in turn, bent every
effort to open the materials before the Harding centennial in
1965.[92]

Herbert Hoover bears the distinction of having left not one,
but two, manuscript repositories as literary extensions of his wide
range of public service. While directing relief operations in Europe during and after World War I, Hoover first conceived the
idea of collecting the papers and manuscripts that came through
his hands. In 1919, he proposed that his alma mater, Stanford
University, accept and care for the collection. Since then, the
collection reflecting Hoover's deep interest in world peace has
been greatly augmented by other manuscripts and printed mate-

[90] *Ibid.*, 202–203.
[91] *Ibid.*, 205. See also, Ohio State Archaeological and Historical Society, *An Index and List of the Letters and Papers of Rutherford Birchard Hayes* (Columbus, [1933]); Watt P. Marchman, "The Rutherford B. Hayes Memorial Library," in *College and Research Libraries*, 17:224–227 (May, 1956); Watt P. Marchman and James H. Rodabaugh, "Collections of the Rutherford B. Hayes State Memorial," in *Ohio History*, 17:151–157 (July, 1962).
[92] Rowland, "Paper," 208–209.

rials for the study, transcending all national boundaries, of war, revolution, and peace in the twentieth century, not only in Europe and America but in Russia, the Far East, and Africa as well. The Hoover Institute and Library at Stanford has become a center for research in a broad range of social studies, especially in comparative scholarship, supported not only by the Hoover Estate but by the Ford Foundation also. The Herbert Hoover Presidential Library was established in 1962 at West Branch, Iowa, to house the Hoover manuscripts relating to his service as Secretary of Commerce and as President, together with minor supporting collections of other figures associated with him in his public career.[93]

In response to the increased use of electronic means of communication by contemporary Presidents, the federal government in 1954 launched a new serial publication entitled *Public Papers of the Presidents of the United States* to capture in print a category of presidential statements which might otherwise be lost or be beyond verification in the future. The instructions establishing the serial provided that only "oral utterances by the President," or "writings subscribed by him," be included and that they be drawn exclusively from the public domain by virtue of press release or otherwise. Communications to Congress, public addresses, transcripts of press conferences, public letters, messages to heads of state, miscellaneous statements, and formal executive documents are examples of included material. Executive orders and proclamations are specifically excluded since they are already issued in the Code of *Federal Regulations*.[94]

Despite all the support extended American historiography at the national level through the Library of Congress, the presidential libraries, and other depositories, a union check list of manuscripts is still one of the most needed research tools of the American historian. So widely scattered is the documentation from nationally significant figures that a single scholar often

[93] *Ibid.*, 209–210; C. Easton Rothwell, "Resources and Records in the Hoover Institute and Library," in *American Archivist*, 18:141–150 (April, 1955); Wayne C. Grover, "The Herbert Hoover Library and the Presidential Library System," in *Palimpsest*, 43:387–392 (August, 1962).

[94] Warren R. Reid, "Public Papers of the Presidents," in *American Archivist*, 25:435–440 (October, 1962).

must despair of coping with it. The parallel efforts[95] of the American Historical Association, the American Association for State and Local History, and the Society of American Archivists are in process of bearing fruit, but until the National Union Catalog of Manuscripts becomes a reality, researchers must continue to rely upon temporary and incomplete guides.

[95] R. A. Billington, comp., "Guides to American History Manuscript Collections in Libraries of the United States," in *Mississippi Valley Historical Review,* 38:467–496 (December, 1951).

VI

STATE AND LOCAL
MANUSCRIPT COLLECTIONS

THE AMERICAN historiographical tradition has been shaped by three primary forces, each a product of its time and each contributing a characteristic aspect to the pattern of development. Without minimizing the role of archival agencies and other passive repositories of documentary sources, the positive contributions to the shaping of American historical scholarship have come primarily from the school of the amateur or vocational historian, from the newer school of the scientific historian, and from a network of state and local historical societies.

The decline of the influence of the amateur historian in the late nineteenth century has been more than compensated for by the proliferation and growth of professional history and historical societies in America. Although the field of historical scholarship has become populated by more than 1,000 historical societies[1] and by more than 10,000 academic historians, relations between these two major factions has not always been sweetness and light. Their petty antagonisms are as nothing, however, compared to their joint achievements. The greatest contribution (not always willingly received) by the historian to the societies has been a sense of purpose and direction in the

[1] American Association for State and Local History, *Directory of Historical Societies and Agencies in the United States and Canada, 1967–1968* (Nashville, 1967); S. K. Stevens, "The Present Status of Organizations and Aid for Local History in the United States," in *Proceedings of the Conference of State and Local Historical Societies* (1939), 21–31.

support of scholarship. The American historian, on his part, is indebted more to historical societies than to any other type of institution for the collection and preservation of the truly significant portions of primary sources of his field.

STATE HISTORICAL AGENCIES
AND THEIR MANUSCRIPT COLLECTIONS

THE GENERAL COMPLEXION of the historical societies in America is radically different from that of the early nine-teenth-century organizations which generally restricted member-ship to the wealthy, the socially elite, the locally patriotic, the culturally pretentious, and the genealogically preoccupied. Pro-fessional historians have penetrated the older societies and con-verted them to their own purposes, and they have helped in the creation of new societies with democratic and scholarly outlooks more in harmony with their own. Through two centuries, his-torical societies at the state and local level have carried on the yeoman and often noble functions both of supporting historical scholarship and of collecting and preserving the manuscript sources upon which that scholarship is built. The collective holdings of these organizations contribute significantly to the documentation available for the history of any modern state and are second in significance only to manuscript sources at the national level.[2]

The association of gentlemen in the interest of cultivating the past led to the establishment of European historical societies before the eighteenth century. The Society of Antiquaries of London was formed in 1572, was dissolved by James I, and was revived in 1707. The Royal Society of Antiquaries of Scotland dates from 1780, and the Hakluyt Society from 1846. On the Continent, the Academy of Inscriptions in France, the Royal Academy of History in Spain, and the Royal Danish Society all carried forward the ideals of historical scholarship and the prac-tice of collecting historical manuscripts.[3] The Old Regime and

---

[2] *Supra,* Chapter V.
[3] Julian P. Boyd, "State and Local Historical Societies in the United States," in *American Historical Review,* 40:10–37 (October, 1934).

all of its historical appurtenances died with the French Revolution, and Napoleon created a commission to study which areas of history needed exploration and how that study and its support could be institutionalized. The ensuing report was thoroughly reviewed in the *American Monthly Register,* for Americans recognized parallel cultural problems in the French Revolution and their own. When the new French historical society was formed, it corresponded with the founders of the pioneer American societies for their mutual encouragement. In 1821 Heinrich Friedrich Karl, Baron vom und zum Stein, sponsored a new historical society in Prussia and appointed the historian Georg Pertz to collect and edit documents from the Carolingian period. These efforts resulted in the publication of the first volumes of *Monumenta Germaniae historia,* a model project for many American historical societies in the nineteenth century.[4]

State and local historical societies first developed in the post-Revolutionary American scene as an aftermath of the patriotic groundswell that accompanied the birth of the nation, and these societies sprang up first in the urban centers of wealth and culture in New England and the Middle Atlantic states—in Boston, New York, and Philadelphia. The South had few urban centers, and there were few southern historical societies until the region's self-consciousness caused it increasingly to look backward to its former glory and power. Because the upper Middle West was peopled largely by New Englanders who carried with them their cultural traditions but not their social exclusiveness, they early formed historical societies supported by public appropriations. By contrast, all of the early eastern societies were private organizations, more by necessity than by choice, contrary to popular opinion. Not until the sons of the founders began to endow the societies their fathers had established did those agencies begin to achieve their larger promise. Most of the eastern societies normally took as their province the colonial and Revolutionary periods, while the newer western societies stressed the territorial origins of their own areas, early statehood, and the history of the triumphant nation to which they owed their very existence.[5]

[4] Van Tassel, *Recording America's Past,* 105.
[5] David D. Van Tassel and James A. Tinsley, "Historical Organizations as Aids

The principal contribution of the early historical societies was the collection and preservation of all manner of historical material for future use—books, pamphlets, newspapers, and manuscripts—but some contemporary and practical use of these collections reinforced the zeal of the founders. Jared Sparks and George Bancroft both relied heavily upon the manuscript collections of the existing historical societies, and recourse was made often by the federal government to private collections in the various societies in substantiation of boundary and other claims arising from the colonial and Revolutionary periods.[6]

The collection policies of historical societies in the early nineteenth century were always quite broad. They usually embraced the entire history of their constituent area, and the societies got some surprising monstrosities for their pains. With the proliferation of societies and a new concept of scientific history later in the century, such items as two-headed calves, Egyptian mummies, and "cabinets of curiosities" became obsolete. As history turned away from a primary concern for economics, sociology, anthropology, and archaeology, so did the historical societies.[7] By this time, however, the institutional character of such societies was largely set, and their diverseness was baffling to a new generation of historians, searching where they could for sources to support their studies of the growth of the nation and its political and social subdivisions.

A distinguished American national history was the first fruit of the alliance between scientific history and the western historical society movement. The historical societies predated scientific history, but they were infiltrated by the new generation of German-trained scholars. The state societies grew to their greatest prestige and influence where they were most closely associated with the departments of history of their respective

---

to History," in William B. Hesseltine and Donald R. McNeil, eds., *In Support of Clio* (Madison, 1958), 131–138; Dixon Ryan Fox, "Local Historical Societies in the United States," in *Canadian Historical Review*, 13:263–267 (September, 1952).

[6] Leslie W. Dunlap, *American Historical Societies, 1790–1860* (Madison, 1944), 123. See the action of the Massachusetts Historical Society in resolving in 1828 to "afford every facility" to the commission in settling the Maine-New Brunswick boundary dispute.

[7] Van Tassel and Tinsley, "Historical Organizations," in Hesseltine and McNeil, eds., *Clio*, 129–130.

state universities. The marks of their maturity, of having out-grown the sterility of antiquarianism, was the systematic collection of manuscripts and their dissemination either as edited documents or as monographic studies.[8]

Having achieved scholarly acceptance, the state historical societies have gone on to democratize and popularize themselves and the history they serve. They have learned to woo the public in order to expand the basis of their support, to preach the "gospel of salvation through a knowledge of the past to all who are capable of receiving it." Through popular historical magazines, historic tours, restorations, pageants, anniversary celebrations, and the like, the state historical societies have sought to "bring history to the people," hopefully without sacrificing the more scholarly services rendered to the academic community.[9]

To the cloistered historian, the number and variety of historical societies have come to resemble a maze. There are treasures to be found therein, but a guide is often needed. At the request of four of the oldest and most distinguished of the historical societies—the Massachusetts Historical Society, the American Antiquarian Society, the Historical Society of Pennsylvania, and the Virginia Historical Society—a grant was made in 1958 by the Council on Library Resources, a subsidiary of the Ford Foundation, to the Boston Athenaeum and to its director, Walter Muir Whitehill, to produce a guidebook with emphasis specifically upon the collecting and publishing functions of societies.[10] The resulting publication[11] was an invaluable basis for generalizations about the organization and holdings of various types of state and local historical societies.

Within the present chapter, historical societies are considered as either state or local in character. The former, of which there is at least one in each state in the union, devotes itself to the study of the history of a given state and region. The latter,

---

[8] H. Hale Bellot, "Some Aspects of the Recent History of American Historiography," in Royal Historical Society *Transactions,* fourth series, 28:138–148 (1946).

[9] Theodore C. Blegen, "State Historical Agencies and the Public," in *Minnesota History,* 9:123–134 (June, 1928).

[10] Walter Muir Whitehill, "In My Father's House Are Many Mansions," in *American Archivist,* 24:133–139 (April, 1961).

[11] *Independent Historical Societies: An Enquiry into their Research and Publication Functions and their Financial Future* (Boston, 1962).

varying in popularity from section to section, confines itself to the history of a subdivision of a given state, usually a county or a city.

State manuscript collections may be further classified according to the source of financial support and to the character of the holding institution. A group of private societies has grown up along the eastern seaboard; the oldest and best example of this group is the Massachusetts Historical Society. Among public societies, the State Historical Society of Wisconsin has set the pattern. A third group of state or regional historical associations is more professional in character, but such agencies possess relatively few manuscripts in their own right. A fourth group of state manuscripts collections rest in archival agencies, especially in the southern states, while a fifth group of state manuscripts collections is held by a few major metropolitan public libraries. Regardless of the degree of openness of membership of these societies or the precise nature of their organizational control, the manuscripts of all these agencies are considered as public and are open to qualifed scholars and researchers. This policy is in contrast to the quasi-public character of the collections of a number of church and cultural organizations, proprietary and institutional libraries, and college and university libraries which will be discussed in another chapter.[12]

Any attempt to classify the large number of manuscript collecting agencies, more-or-less public in nature and operating at the intermediate level of geographical interest, is bound to err and perhaps to offend. If for no other reason, there is enough competition and local pride involved to make comparisons and conclusions a hazardous undertaking. Rather, the principal purpose of the following chart is to illustrate the variety and surprising scope of many of the state manuscript agencies in America.[13]

---

[12] *Infra,* Chapter VII.

[13] The obscure origins and fitful development of many of the state manuscript agencies renders somewhat arbitrary the assignment of any date of establishment, classification as to type, and evaluation of holdings. Local pride may prompt other claims, but the information here presented is regarded as the most authoritative available and is compiled from: AASLH, *Directory of Historical Societies;* Whitehill, *Historical Societies;* and Posner, *American State Archives.*

DIRECTORY OF MANUSCRIPT COLLECTING AGENCIES
AT THE STATE LEVEL, 1964

State	Agency and Location	Estab-lished	Type	Significant Holdings
Alabama	State Department of Archives and History, War Memorial Building, Montgomery	1901	D	Alabama
Alaska	State Historical Library, Juneau	1900	D	Alaska
Arizona	Department of History and Archives, State House, Phoenix	(1864) 1937	D	Arizona [scant]
Arkansas	History Commission, Old State House, Little Rock	1905	D	Arkansas
California	California Historical Society, San Francisco	1886	P	California
	California State Library, Sacramento	1854	D	Far West
Colorado	State Historical Society, Denver	(1879) 1927	S	Colorado, Western Railroads
	Western History Department, Denver Public Library, Denver	[1930]	L	Rocky Mountains
Connecticut	Connecticut Historical Society, Hartford	1825	P	Genealogy, Colonial and Revolutionary
Delaware	Historical Society of Delaware, Wilmington	1864	P	[scant]
District of Columbia	Columbia Historical Society, Washington	1894	P	Genealogy, Colonial and Revolutionary
Florida	Florida Historical Society, Gainesville	(1856) 1902	P	Spanish Florida
Georgia	Georgia Historical Society, Savannah	(1839) 1920	P	Georgia
	Department of Archives and History, Atlanta	1918	D	Georgia
Hawaii	Hawaiian Historical Society, Honolulu	1892	P	Hawaii, Pacific
Idaho	State Historical Society, Boise	(1881) 1907	S	Idaho
Illinois	Chicago Historical Society, Chicago	1856	P	Chicago, Midwest

Key: P — private agency; S — state or public-supported society or agency; A — association; D — department of state government; L — metropolitan public library; ( ) — founding date of a preceding agency.

State	Agency and Location	Estab- lished	Type	Significant Holdings
	Illinois State Historical Library, Springfield	1889	D	Illinois, Lincoln, Civil War
Indiana	Indiana Historical Society, Indianapolis	1830	P	Northwest, Indiana
	Indiana Historical Bureau Indianapolis	(1915) 1925	D	Indiana
Iowa	State Historical Society of Iowa, Iowa City	1857	S	Iowa
	State Department of History and Archives, Historical Building, Des Moines	1892	D	Iowa
Kansas	State Historical Society, Memorial Building, Topeka	1875	S	Kansas
Kentucky	Filson Club, Louisville	1884	P	Trans-Alleghany, Ohio Valley
Louisiana	Louisiana Historical Association, New Orleans	1889	A	Louisiana [scant]
Maine	Maine Historical Society, Portland	1822	P	Maine
Maryland	Maryland Historical Society, Baltimore	1844	P	Lords Baltimore, Maryland
Massachusetts	Massachusetts Historical Boston	1791	P	Massachusetts, New England, Adams Family
	American Antiquarian Society, Worcester	1812	P	New England, Printing
	New England Historic Genealogical Society, Boston	1845	P	Genealogy, New England
	Boston Public Library, Boston	1822	L	New England
Michigan	Historical Commission, Lansing	1913	S	Michigan
	Burton Historical Collection, Detroit Public Library, Detroit		L	Midwest
Minnesota	Minnesota Historical Society, St. Paul	1849	S	Minnesota
Mississippi	Department of Archives and History, War Memorial Building, Jackson	1902	D	Jefferson Davis, Mississippi
Missouri	Missouri Historical Society, St. Louis	1866	P	Missouri, Miss- issippi Valley
	State Historical Society, Columbia	1898	S	Recent U.S.

State	Agency and Location	Estab-lished	Type	Significant Holdings
Montana	Montana Historical Society, Helena	1865	S	Montana, Rocky Mountains
Nebraska	State Historical Society, Lincoln	1878	S	Nebraska, Midwest
Nevada	Nevada Historical Society, Nevada	1904	S	Nevada
New Hampshire	State Historical Society, Concord	1823	P	New Hampshire
New Jersey	New Jersey Historical Society, Newark	1845	P	New Jersey
New Mexico	Historical Society of New Mexico, Santa Fe	(1859) 1880	P	New Mexico, Spanish Southwest
New York	New-York Historical Society, New York	1804	P	New York, Colonial and Revolutionary
	New York State Historical Association, Cooperstown	1899	A	Social history
	New York Public Library, New York		L	United States
	Division of Archives and History, State Library, Albany	1859	D	New York
North Carolina	Department of Archives and History, Raleigh	1903	D	North Carolina
North Dakota	State Historical Society, Liberty Memorial Building, Bismarck	1884	S	North Dakota
Ohio	Cincinnati Historical Society, Cincinnati	1844	P	Ohio, Ohio Valley
	Western Reserve Historical Society, Cleveland	1867	P	Slavery, Civil War, Cleveland
	State Historical Society, Columbus	1885	S	Rutherford B. Hayes, Ohio
	Cleveland Public Library, Cleveland		L	Cleveland, Great Lakes
Oklahoma	State Historical Society, Oklahoma City	1895	S	Oklahoma
Oregon	Oregon Historical Society, Portland	1898	S	Oregon, Pacific Northwest
Pennsylvania	Historical Society of Pennsylvania, Philadelphia	1826	P	Pennsylvania, Colonial and Revolutionary
Puerto Rico	Institute of Puerto Rican Culture, University of Puerto Rico, San Juan	1955	A	Puerto Rico

State	Agency and Location	Established	Type	Significant Holdings
Rhode Island	Rhode Island Historical Society, Providence	1822	P	Rhode Island, Colonial
South Carolina	South Carolina Historical Society, Charleston	1855	P	South Carolina, Low Country
	Archives Department, Columbia	(1891) 1905	D	South Carolina, Upcountry
South Dakota	State Historical Society, Pierre	(1861) 1901	S	South Dakota
Tennessee	Division of Archives, State Library and Archives Building, Nashville	(1919) 1941	D	Tennessee
Texas	Texas State Historical Association, Austin	1897	A	Texas, Southwest
Utah	State Historical Society, State Capitol, Salt Lake City	1897	S	Utah, Mormons
Vermont	Vermont Historical Society, Montpelier	1838	P	Vermont
Virginia	Virginia Historical Society, Richmond	(1831) 1834	P	Virginia, Colonial and Revolutionary, Civil War
Washington	State Historical Society, Tacoma	1891	S	Pacific Northwest
West Virginia	Department of Archives and History, State Capitol, Charleston	1905	D	West Virginia
Wisconsin	State Historical Society, Madison	(1846) 1849	S	Wisconsin, Midwest, Mass Communications
Wyoming	State Archives and History Department, Cheyenne	1951	D	Wyoming
	Wyoming State Historical Society, Cheyenne	(1895) 1952	P	Wyoming

The extensive efforts at the state level to collect and preserve the manuscript sources of American history have resulted in a wealth of material at the expense of bibliographical disorder. Until the Union Catalog of Manuscripts is fully operable, locating the necessary manuscript documentation for any topic beyond the obviously national ones will be something of a hit-or-miss undertaking. It has been suggested many times that the federal government make more of a contribution to the support of manuscript documentation through the Manuscripts Division of the Library of Congress and through its contribution to the Union Catalog of Manuscripts. A bill to assure such support by direct federal subsidy was introduced in 1963 in the Eighty-eighth Congress. Basically, the bill provided for federal grants-in-aid (to a total of $500,000 a year) to state, local, and other manuscript agencies for the collection, reproduction, and publication of documentary sources significant to the history of the nation. In support of this bill, a stellar cast of witnesses appeared, including Bernard L. Boutin, Administrator of General Services; Julian P. Boyd, editor of the Jefferson Papers; Lyman H. Butterfield, editor of the Adams Papers; Wayne C. Grover, Archivist of the United States; Supreme Court Justice John M. Harlan (representing himself and Justice Felix Frankfurter) ; L. Quincy Mumford, Librarian of Congress; Professor Arthur M. Schlesinger, Sr.; and Boyd C. Shafer, secretary of the American Historical Association.[14]

The majority report in support of the bill forcibly argued the wisdom of a federal subsidy for a function previously left, if not reserved, to the states and localities. The report stressed the obvious need for additional financial support, the tax squeeze upon state and local governments, and the federal obligation for cultural advancement. In the initial phase of the project, the committee envisioned the use of federal grants to finance an intensive nationwide distribution through microfilm of the key documentation for American history. Such a program would specifically strengthen the ability of the newer graduate schools to produce adequately trained historians with a broad national outlook. Secondly, grants would be awarded for the completion of a number of existing programs of manuscript publication bearing upon the debates concerning and ratification of the Constitution, the Bill of Rights, and the transactions of the First Congress. The ultimate ends were generally praised, but a minority report questioned the necessity of extending the federal government into this virgin field, and the wisdom of injecting the federal bureaucracy into the "writing of history." Enactment of the bill (P. L. 88-383) and its approval on July 28, 1964, made

---

[14] U. S., 88 Congress, 1 session, *Hearings Before a Subcommittee of the Committee on Government Operations on H. R. 6237, June 18, 1963.*

available a yearly federal allocation of $500,000, to be dispensed upon recommendation of the National Historical Publications Commission as grants to federal agencies and co-operating manuscript institutions for "collecting, describing, preserving and compiling, and publishing (including microfilming and other forms of reproduction) of documentary sources of significance to the history of the United States."[15]

LOCAL MANUSCRIPT COLLECTIONS

IT IS the duty of every good citizen to use all the opportunities which occur to him, for preserving documents relating to the history of our country." So wrote Thomas Jefferson in the twilight of his life.[16] The Sage of Monticello practiced what he advocated for others, both as a historian and as a "good citizen," for he regularly collected and preserved manuscripts of his own and of others relating to the history of his own times.

On the other hand, the English historian, E. A. Freeman, boasted that he never consulted an original manuscript in his labors. The American historian John Fiske, while in England working on his history of the colonies, never went near the British Museum and quite probably never heard of the Public Record Office. In fact, Fiske once likened the painstaking investigation of manuscripts to a sleeping dog snapping at fleas. In a period of increasing emphasis upon scientific historiography, both Freeman and Fiske slighted the social, economic, and commercial aspects of their topics, with the result that Freeman has now been consigned to the second rank of historians, and Fiske falls several degrees lower on the scale.[17]

The historical society movement in America generally preceded the rise of the scientific and professional practice of history, and a full complement of historical societies at the state level was busily collecting manuscripts long before there was

---

[15] *Ibid.*

[16] Thomas Jefferson to Hugh P. Taylor, October 4, 1823, in Liscomb and Bergh, eds., *Writings of Jefferson*, XV:473, as quoted in Van Tassel, *Recording America's Past*, 105n.

[17] Charles McLean Andrews, "On the Preservation of Historical Manuscripts," in *William and Mary Quarterly*, 3rd series, 1:123–124 (April, 1944).

a body of American historians to use them. Yet, coolness marked the relations between the academic historians and the state societies, and relations with the local societies was even more chilly. The early scientific historians were generally critical of historical societies for the provinciality of their collections and publications. The Turner thesis, by which the national development was explained through its frontier experience, drew microcosmic attention to the locality, and the rise of economic history reinforced the historian's interest in the development of small communities. Local historical societies and their manuscript collections, once scorned as the province of genealogists and antiquarians, have thus become a legitimate field of research and interest for an increasing number of historians.[18]

At the 1904 meeting of the AHA in Chicago, a committee composed of Reuben Gold Thwaites, Benjamin F. Shambaugh, and Franklin L. Riley was directed to study and report upon the scholarly activities of state and local societies. Their report of 1905 discussed the great variety of types of organizations and attempted to establish some common plan of operation for the advancement of historical scholarship:

> In our judgment, an historical society, be it sectional, State, or local, should collect all manner of archaeological, anthropological, historical, and genealogical material bearing upon the particular territory which that society seeks to represent. The problem would be simplified were the ideal recognized that, whenever practicable, there should in each State be some one place where all manner of historical data relative to the Commonwealth at large may be placed for preservation and consultation, and in each community or county a similar treasure house for its purely local records and relics.[19]

Furthermore, the committee recommended that all manuscripts held by state and local societies be properly indexed or cataloged and comprehensive bibliographies be distributed. It was also pointed out that disclosure of holdings should lead to exchange and transfer of material grossly misplaced, and that state

[18] Boyd, "Historical Societies," 10–11.
[19] Reuben Gold Thwaites, "Report of the Committee on Methods of Organization and Work on the Part of State and Local Historical Societies," in American Historical Association, *Annual Report* (1905), 1:251–265.

agencies had a general responsibility to enforce all these minimum conditions upon local societies.[20]

Sixty-five local historical societies had been established in the
United States before 1860, primarily in New England and in
areas settled by pioneers from that same area. By 1961, however,
there were over 2,000 such local societies in the nation. At first
glance it would appear that the recommendations of the AHA
had been taken to heart, but only about one-third of the local
societies reported possession of library or research material, and
only 209 reported holdings in the *Guide to Archives and Manuscripts in the United States*. Most of this number were concentrated in the Northeast and the Midwest.[21]

The case for and against the collection of manuscripts by
local societies continues to be debated. Weary of chasing about
the country to out-of-the-way repositories, some scholars wish
local societies would forego the practice, but they also acknowledge the impracticality of stopping a practice long-established.[22]
Others welcome the active laissez-faire competition for manuscripts among local societies as a means of ensuring that the
resources are preserved *somewhere* and as an expression of interest by a local society in its own area's history.[23]

Still another proponent of local history has observed that a
local focus for professional history is as valid as a larger view-
point, that local history can be handled more intimately (hence
more interestingly) for the non-professional, that it is a proving
ground for hypotheses in general history, and that a local focus
is the means whereby history can regain its lost audience.[24]

Perhaps a more common sense and professionally acceptable
view has been expressed by Arthur Bestor, who observed that all
history perforce must be related to its local setting; hence, the
gathering of documents must be done locally. Beyond that, what

[20] "Report of the Conference of Historical Societies," in American Historical
Association, *Annual Report* (1907), 1:51–64.

[21] Whitehill, *Historical Societies*, 349; see also, Dixon Ryan Fox, "Local Historical
Societies," 263–267.

[22] Richard McCormick, in Clifford L. Lord, ed., *Ideas in Conflict, A Colloquium
on Certain Problems in Historical Society Work in the United States and Canada*
(Harrisburg, Pennsylvania, 1958), 62–64.

[23] Martin Schmitt, in *ibid.*, 63.

[24] K. Ross Toole, in *ibid.*, 152–153.

is local history? As Bestor expressed it, "We need history, not grassroots history, which is, to all intents and purposes, the worm's eye view of the world."[25]

If history looks to local societies for general documentation rather than for the development of a new kind of provincial discipline, there are a number of identifiable categories of local manuscripts likely to be of value to future researchers. The papers of political leaders, whatever their level of origin—national, state, or local—are obviously most important. Secondly, the papers of businessmen and industrialists are significant, for the efforts of these individuals have contributed to making America an economic entity. Similarly, the exchange of legal and cultural concepts is documented in the papers of jurists, lawyers, novelists, poets, dramatists, and writers of all kinds, however local their fame. Educators, journalists, labor leaders, and churchmen are the molders of public opinion and value systems, and their papers are frequently incisive in their grasp of complex social issues. The papers of farmers and physicians add another dimension to the understanding of the past as locally exemplified.[26]

It has been suggested that local historical societies are the democratic equivalent of family archives in an aristocratic society, for the convenience of deposit in them saves innumerable manuscripts from being irretrievably lost in the mobility of American society.[27] Yet, the very convenience which encourages the deposit of manuscripts also allows their dispersal, a case in point being the papers of Thomas Jefferson. The process of publishing that body of prime documentation has graphically demonstrated the difficulty of locating and using material scattered in various societies and libraries and has elicited the suggestion that the privilege of collecting manuscripts should carry with it a concomitant duty of publicizing their location.[28]

Lest the problems of maintaining institutionalized manuscript collections in local societies be regarded as outweighing the advantages, consider the status of manuscripts in the South, where

[25] Arthur Bestor, in *ibid.*, 160.

[26] Downs, "Collecting Manuscripts," 340–341.

[27] Bourne, "Historical Societies," 121.

[28] Harry C. Bauer, "Where Manuscripts Should Be," in *Oregon Historical Quarterly*, 51:163–167 (September, 1950).

there is a weak tradition of local historical societies and a strong institutionalization of the family. Since the southern hegemony of the colonial and post-Revolutionary eras, the changing fortunes of its history have produced a decreasing amount of significant documentation. Few manuscripts have been preserved from the Civil War and Reconstruction periods. Since then, the harsh years of sectional poverty, a preoccupation with industrialization, and the erection of defenses by a crouching, closed society have all combined to restrict the production of manuscripts of prime historical importance.[29] That documentation which has been produced is not preserved and collected in the South to the degree it is elsewhere in the nation. Southern brides and tidy housekeepers are the nemesis of historians, while maiden ladies are their best friends. In the absence of a maiden aunt to serve as family archivist or a family quarrel or litigation in the settlement of an estate, no papers are usually preserved from the average southern family. Only if its members leave footprints upon the sands of history at the county courthouse is there likely to be any documentary evidence of their having passed this way—and southern courthouses all too often burn.[30]

Southerners are not alone in having a low opinion of the historical importance of their "unimportant" manuscripts, yet it is frequently true that the most routine, the most mundane, the most common and ordinary documentation is the most historically valuable. How else can the social history of the common man be written? Of greatest significance are personal letters, account books, diaries, and the like,[31] and these are the materials from which manuscript collections of local societies should be built.

The collection of manuscripts by numerous local societies has and will continue to result in displacement of materials from their original locality. Assuming that publication of such local documentation normally is not justified and that institution-

[29] Hamilton, "Southern Records," 16–24.

[30] Thomas D. Clark, "Preservation of Southern Documents," in *American Archivist*, 16:28–29 (January, 1953).

[31] J. G. DeR. Hamilton, "On the Importance of Unimportant Documents," in *Library Quarterly*, 12:511–518 (July, 1942).

al pride will prevent an exchange, microfilm offers an effective means to send strayed manuscripts back to their home areas. Only when a local historical society with a manuscript collection can certify to a visiting scholar that it possesses or has bibliographical knowledge of all the known documentation for its region will it be fulfilling its true function in support of historical scholarship.[32]

Unrestricted and unproductive competition for manuscripts is probably the greatest problem of local historical societies. Conflicts smolder between manuscripts libraries and archival agencies, but more often they blaze between manuscript agencies themselves.[33] As long ago as 1912, Worthington C. Ford of the Massachusetts Historical Society attempted to alleviate the worst aspects of this competition by proposing that all societies practice a reciprocal exchange of all manuscripts not indigenous to their local areas. Many societies approved the idea, and some even applied for the return of manuscripts to them, but no society offered to transfer strayed materials to the Massachusetts society. Sadder but wiser in the ways of historical societies, Ford wistfully remarked, "The time has not come when one institution can act in that distribution. There must be reciprocity. Yet I am still of the opinion that the idea is a good one, and hope to live till it has come to be recognized practice."[34]

Competition for manuscripts continued and so did the idea of cooperation to alleviate it. After World War II, Sylvester K. Stevens took up the battle against unrestricted competition. He protested "the peculiar and utterly unintelligent way in which our local and state historical resources have been scattered to the four winds of the nation without any regard to logical locations where they would do the most good,"[35] but the protest has gone largely unheeded.

Numerous contemporary examples of the acquisition by dis-

---

[32] Stevens, "Present State," 21–31. See also, S. K. Stevens, in *Where Are the Historical Manuscripts, A Symposium* (*Bulletin of the American Association for State and Local History*, vol. II, no. 4, September, 1950), 115.

[33] David C. Duniway, "Conflicts in Collecting," in *American Archivist*, 24:55 (January, 1961).

[34] Ford, "Manuscripts," 84.

[35] Sylvester K. Stevens, "Cooperation for the National Societies," in *Autograph Collector's Journal*, 1:25 (April, 1949).

tant repositories of manuscripts of local or state significance can be cited, and the most frequent offender seems to be the Library of Congress.[36] It should be observed in justification of the position of the Library of Congress that the library feels a responsibility for the entire range of American history, especially after the rebuff in 1901 of Herbert Putnam's proposed division of collecting fields. Nevertheless, the library's official policy pledges it to "cooperate with other depositories of manuscript collection throughout the country, to the end that manuscripts of local interest may be placed in the depositories where they will be most useful." Reiterating an amendment to its collecting policy, the library further states that "materials of regional, State, or local, but not national interest, . . . belong in other repositories."[37] The library seems to be conscientiously implementing the policy of denying itself new acquisitions of local manuscripts, but it has not moved to divest itself of those it already possesses.

The alleged infringement upon the province of state and local manuscripts by the Library of Congress led the council of the American Association for State and Local History to lodge a formal protest in 1956. In reply, the Librarian of Congress attempted to smooth over the feelings ruffled by the incident, but he declared that the Library of Congress "is not prepared, however, to be disadvantaged or subordinated simply because it does not happen to be a State or local institution." For its part, the Library of Congress recognizes and welcomes competi-

---

[36] For example, in 1946 the Library of Congress acquired the papers of Colonel James G. Clark, which relate to social and economic affairs in South Carolina and Mississippi from 1832 to 1866; in 1947 it added the papers of William Medill, Civil War governor of Ohio, papers of the Blackman and Goodwin families of Georgia and Alabama, and church records of the Episcopal diocese of Maryland. Acquisitions in 1949 included papers of Maryland tobacco merchants of the eighteenth and nineteenth centuries. In 1953 came the papers of the Morris and Popham families (New Jersey, New York, and Pennsylvania) and Peyton Short (Kentucky). In 1954 the library acquired the papers of John Mitchel, reform mayor of New York, and in 1955, the papers of Nathan Hale, grandson of the Revolutionary patriot. See, Robert L. Brubaker, "The Library of Congress Versus the State Historical Societies: The Problem of Competitive Collecting" (Unpublished typescript in possession of the present author, 1962), 3–4.

[37] U. S., Library of Congress, *Departmental and Divisional Manual No. 17, Manuscript Division* (Washington, 1950), 16–18.

tion for manuscripts between itself and state and local agencies.[38]

Response to a 1962 questionnaire addressed to all state agencies regarding competition between themselves and the Library of Congress failed to substantiate the charges of the AASLH. Only the state society in Maryland flatly stated that such competition existed. All the other respondents hedged or denied competition from the Library of Congress at the state level or below, while recognizing it at the national level. There is reason to suppose that some of the responses were more conventional than candid. It is generally acknowledged that active competition exists between the national library and the larger state agencies, such as those in Wisconsin and Ohio, and it is possible that many smaller agencies, having been bested too often, have retired from the contest.[39]

Even if the problem of competition in collecting could be overcome, the local, relatively impermanent, and inexperienced societies would still be confronted with many other problems in the acquisition of manuscripts. The personal element in seeking manuscripts is so important that a bumbling failure on the part of one agency may well jeopardize the success of any other agency. There is a psychological moment for recruiting manuscripts, and an inexperienced recruiter often fouls himself in legal and ethical tangles relating to title, access, and usage of collections.[40]

Other problems of using manuscripts in local historical societies relate to the nonprofessional and often officious administration of the repositories. Many a researcher has had the experience of making a special trip to a local repository, only to find it closed except on rare occasions or at odd hours. If open at all, its collections may be available only to members. The catalog often exists in the librarian's head rather than on cards. Even more idiosyncrasies relate to the use or copying of manuscripts.[41]

---

[38] *History News*, 11:81–84 (September, 1956).

[39] Brubaker, "Problems of Competitive Collecting," 17.

[40] Jackson, "Manuscript Collections," 276; Downs, "Collecting Manuscripts," 341–342.

[41] "Report of the Conference of Historical Societies," in American Historical Association, *Annual Report* (1909), 302–307.

One of the most difficult problems in using local historical manuscripts continues to be bibliographical control. Under the urging of the AHA, a tentative list of manuscripts in the Midwestern historical societies was published by the State Historical Society of Wisconsin shortly after the turn of the century, and an extension of this approach was urged after World War I. Nothing came of the suggestion until after World War II.[42]

In the process of compiling the *Guide to Photocopied Historical Materials in the United States and Canada*, a great mass of local documentation was uncovered. Most of the material had been unused by scholars because of its location in relatively inaccessible or unknown repositories. If local pride refuses to release the papers in remote local societies, microphotography might permit their preservation and use elsewhere.[43]

Impatient for the family of manuscript repositories to put its own house in order, historians have proceeded to develop their own bibliographical guides to local manuscripts. In producing one of the most useful of such guides, one historian has declared: "The quantity of manuscript materials is so large and the holdings so widely dispersed in archival establishments, universities, research and public libraries, historical societies, and private collections, that a complete examination of all sources for any single problem, no matter how minute, would exhaust the energy and financial resources of the most diligent scholar."[44]

In 1948 the AHA consolidated its Committee of Manuscripts with a similar committee of the AASLH to form a Joint Committee on Historical Manuscripts. The group turned its attention first to the bibliographical problem of state and local manuscript collections. After consultation with the Library of Congress, the library proposed in 1951 a National Union Catalog of Manuscripts, to be created by adoption of uniform rules for cataloging manuscripts and by printing and distributing catalog cards for all collections so reported. After approval of the new rules by the American Library Association, the Union Catalog,

[42] Theodore C. Pease, "Historical Materials in the Depositories of the Middle West," in *Proceedings of the Seventeenth Annual Conference of Historical Societies, 1921*, 17–18.

[43] Robert B. Eckles, "The Importance of Photocopy Projects for Local and Regional History," in *American Archivist*, 25:159 (April, 1962).

[44] Billington, "Guides to American Manuscript Collections," 467.

as described elsewhere, was launched in 1952.[45] Hopefully it will contribute to the solution of the major problem regarding local manuscripts.

If historian Louis Hacker is correct in his observations, most of the problems of local history may be behind us, for the forces of centralization are destroying the historical significance of the locality. The importance and power of individual states undeniably is diminishing, and the significance of localities is similarly declining. Social mobility has seriously weakened the average American's attachment to place. The process of urbanization has produced localities too large to create or sustain a deep historical interest, while many suburban communities have no separate integrity, hence no basis for a distinct history. Other communities simply have no history at all. What, for example, is the heritage of Levittown—home for 80,000 people but built from nothing only a few years ago.[46]

Considering all the difficulties involved and the bleak prospects for the future, one is tempted to discard the "nub ends" of American historical documentation, those collections of manuscripts held by local societies. Without attempting to document the premise of utility, a few examples of local manuscript collections will illustrate the value of preserving local documentation despite its problems.

The Essex Institute at Salem, Massachusetts, unquestionably takes first place among local historical societies, surpassing many state agencies in prestige and in contribution to scholarship. With informal origins dating back to the 1620's, the institute was organized in 1848. No history of the Revolution, colonial New England, Massachusetts, or Boston should be written without reference to its collections.[47]

When Brooklyn still enjoyed an independent existence, the Long Island Historical Society, now somewhat lost in the shadow of the wealthy and powerful New-York Historical Society, was organized in 1863. Because of a very catholic collecting policy, the Long Island society once owned such treasures as a group

[45] Land, "Union Catalog," 196; Richard C. Berner, "Archivists, Librarians, and the National Union Catalog of Manuscripts," in *American Archivist,* 27:401–410 (July, 1964).
[46] Louis Hacker, in Lord, *Ideas in Conflict,* 154–156.
[47] Whitehill, *Historical Societies,* 352–356.

of Washington letters and a sizable collection of the papers of
Henry Laurens of South Carolina. Lately the focus of interest
of the society has shifted to genealogy, and a policy of selling
some manuscript collections has been adopted.[48]

Farther south, in Charlottesville, Virginia, the Albemarle
County Historical Society was formed in 1940. It has developed
as a happy marriage of the historical interests of town and gown.
All of its manuscripts have been deposited in the manuscripts
room of Alderman Library of the University of Virginia, where
they are available for public use.[49] Such a happy arrangement
obviously is restricted to those communities with a cooperative
academic or research library.

Even farther south, a local historical society flourishes in St.
Augustine, Florida, the oldest city in the United States. In this
fruitful and appropriate setting, in 1883 the St. Augustine Historical Society was formed for the primary purpose of caring
for and adding to the local manuscripts already held in the public library. This collection traces the city's history from its founding in 1565 by Pedro Mennéndez de Avilés to its racial demonstrations of 1964 led by Dr. Martin Luther King, Jr. Entrance
fees from Castillo de San Marcos (while on loan from the federal government) and from the "Oldest House" have supported
the collecting and publishing activities of the society in St. Augustine.[50]

On the Pacific Coast, the saga of Father Junipero Serra's work
in establishing a chain of California missions is the obvious basis
upon which to build a lively interest in local history. Of a number of local societies born of this interest, those at Santa Barbara and San Diego serve as leading examples.

Santa Barbara was the site of a presidio as early as 1782, and
the Franciscan mission dates from 1787. Cut off from most
avenues of commerce, it slept in its past through most of the
nineteenth century, its New England latecomers honoring and
perpetuating its Spanish heritage. In 1932 a Santa Barbara Historical Society was organized, and the society has largely been
responsible for the historical "boom" which has overtaken the

---

[48] *Ibid.*, 376–378.
[49] *Ibid.*, 325.
[50] *Ibid.*, 379–380.

city since World War II. In cooperation with the city government, the old Spanish center of the business district has been preserved and restored as an outdoor museum. The society has also pursued a program of collecting research material on the city and the county, housing its collection in the Old Mission. Included is a large amount of local genealogical material, census records, the papers of José Maria Corarrubias, secretary of state under Governor Pío Pico, the records of the pioneer trader Alphus Basil Thompson, and the papers of Colonel W. W. Hollister.[51]

In what was to become the southwestern corner of the United States, Father Serra established in 1769 a mission at San Diego. From these simple origins has grown a sprawling metropolis with layers of culture laid down by waves of subsequent settlers from New England, the Midwest, and the South. The more recent arrivals have been strongly impressed by their community's Spanish past, romanticizing and idealizing it. They have been influenced in part by the San Diego Historical Society, founded in 1928 by George White Marston. The founder built a handsome building, dramatically situated on Presidio Hill overlooking the harbor, as a memorial to Father Serra. This agency has developed a commendable body of material relating to the history of the city and of Upper California.[52]

The experience of several institutions demonstrates that local historical societies need not be antiquarian in their outlook and that local manuscript collections need not be marginal in their utility to history. The relationship of selected portions of local documentation to larger topics is well established, and a number of institutional histories of particular localities have staked their claim to importance within the larger historical context. As an example, consider the case study of the township of Newton in Manitowoc County, Wisconsin, written by Joseph Schafer, who limited himself to the local documentation available at the State Historical Society of Wisconsin.[53]

---

[51] *Ibid.*, 381–382.

[52] *Ibid.*, 383–384; Mary Gilman Marston, *George White Marston, A Family Chronicle* (Los Angeles, 1956), II: 140–166, 304.

[53] Joseph Schafer, "Documenting Local History," in *Wisconsin Magazine of History*, 5:142ff. (Spring, 1921).

The primary categories of documentation utilized by Schafer were plat books of the area in 1860, showing size and location of farms, 1860 census data on families and agricultural production, subsequent census figures and returns to show progressive changes, and manuscript and institutional histories to fill out the statistical outlines. From these meager sources, Schafer drew a remarkably detailed historical sketch of the township. He determined from the original surveyors' notes that the fertile area on the western shore of Lake Michigan originally was covered with a heavy oak forest with but few openings. These physical factors determined the location and the relatively small size of the farms in 1860. Most tillable land was given over to mixed farming, grain being the most significant single crop. As the township accumulated capital, these conditions produced a constant enlargement of average holdings and a decrease in total number of operating units. The beginning of cheese production in the area in 1885 produced a sharp rise in total farm income, a decline in grain production, and an increase in the supplemental income from timber as woodlands were cleared for pasture.

Newton became a distinctively German township, although the original entrymen, from 1836 to 1848, were all native-born Americans. There was an increase of foreign-born residents up to 1860, a decline thereafter, coupled with a steady decline of total population from 1880 to 1910. After considerable initial land speculation, the pattern of ownership was very stable once property had passed into the hands of resident owners, and a tightly-knit social and ethnic group of Lutheran Germans resulted. Schafer found here confirmation of his thesis that a heavy original forest cover makes for more permanent farmers than a prairie. Forest farmers, he believed, always conducted mixed operations with a greater investment and attachment to the land, while prairie farmers were single crop operators, who pushed on to a similar area when productivity began to decline. Politically, the homogeneous town voted overwhelmingly for Democratic candidates until 1860, when Lincoln carried the area. Thereafter, it switched back to the Democratic party until the election of 1896. Since then it has remained Republican. Schafer also noted a relatively high rate of professional and business success among the children of the original German settlers, and the constant emigration of that portion of the population has confirmed even more deeply Newton's cultural and social homogeneity.

Despite examples of the use of local documentation in producing interpretations and historical generalizations of a high order, a battle concerning the wisdom and necessity of collecting sources which are peculiarly applicable to local history continues to rage.

Simply stated, the case for local history and its documentation is a case of idealization, involving a commitment to the study and understanding of the whole of the past. Its supporters claim that local history is a necessary check upon the broader and often misleading assumptions made in national history, a more exact approach to history by virtue of the possibility of consulting more of the evidence. Projecting the contemporary trend of fragmentation of history into the future, partisans of local history assert that the future's demand for more minute data can be met only within the context of a locality. Local documentation is apt to be the newer material of which there is a great deal but of which relatively little is being intentionally preserved; hence, great care should be exercised in discouraging its collection. An emphasis on people rather than events, stemming from the assumption of the role of collector, makes local documentation an effective vehicle for the popularization of history and historical research.

The case against local history and its documentation proceeds from the premise that it is basically unimportant and that it tends to degenerate into mere antiquarianism. Moreover, its materials are bulky, they have been but little used, and there are no sound principles upon which safely to discriminate in preserving for future use. It has been charged that local history encourages documentation beyond historical utility. Some professional historians, viewing the matter in national context, ask what other than the rejects of other agencies will be left for local societies to collect. Among other scholars, popularization of history is synonymous with its prostitution, and local history, if it aids in the undertaking, is condemned by them. Finally, the collection of local documentation has generally involved the acquisition of material with a common geographical origin, and numerous scholars question whether this is a valid or sufficient basis upon which to write history.

The problem of local historical documentation has been debated since before the rise of scientific history and the professional historian, and it gives every indication of stimulating further discussion. Local history belongs to another tradition, to the gentleman scholar, to the amateur historian, and to the genealogist. Yet, the joint achievements which have come from cooperation between these groups and professional historians suggest that the historian may do well "to light a candle rather than curse the darkness."

VII

QUASI-PUBLIC
MANUSCRIPT COLLECTIONS

UNTIL THE OPENING of the twentieth century the preservation of the manuscript sources of American history
was almost exclusively the province of historical societies and
agencies at the state and local level. Their functions were conceived and the foundation of their splendid collections laid in
a period preceding the emergence of scholarly, scientific historiography in America. Under the guidance of professional historians, all of these agencies gradually moved in the same direction. Regardless of their origins, they all became more public
in character and more dedicated to historical scholarship in
its widest public context. Federal, state, and local governments
appropriated increasingly larger amounts for the collection and
preservation of historical manuscripts, and private societies gradually opened their collections to any qualified user. Historical
scholarship greatly profited from the liberalization of the policies of the older agencies, yet its insatiable appetite for original documentation outran the capacity or willingness of public
institutions to collect and preserve.

In the twentieth century the demand of scholars for the collection of manuscripts to support academic research has called
into being several categories of quasi-public manuscript repositories of no particular geographical distinction. The academic
historians, often discovering significant documentation in their
research, have for their own convenience sought to have such
manuscripts deposited in their institutional libraries. Their

effective use of such material has drawn manuscripts of like quality to the same academic libraries so that some of the newer repositories have far outdistanced older historical societies in the contest for possession of the literary remains of the past. The silent pressure and commanding prestige of historical scholarship have also coaxed several private manuscript collections into a quasi-public, institutional status. Scholarship has also worked upon the narrow interests of religious denominations, ethnic and cultural groups, and genealogists to encourage the creation of manuscript collections which transcend the supporting group and provide grist for the historian's mill.

The chase for historical manuscripts has also caught up a number of public libraries in America, mainly as passive rather than as active participants. The hesitancy of public librarians in accepting manuscripts, even when pressed upon them, stems from what the librarians regard as the special problems and limited appeal of the material.[1] The proliferation of the newer categories of manuscript repositories has been something of a mixed blessing. Certainly, the convenience and sympathetic administration of such collections is extremely conducive to scholarship, yet the very existence of additional major repositories has compounded the problem of bibliographical control and involved scholars in new questions of proprietary restrictions upon the research use of manuscripts. Furthermore, as scholars have become active participants in the warfare of competition for manuscripts, rather than observing the spirit of competitive scholarship they have at times stooped to guerrilla tactics.

RELIGIOUS, ETHNIC, AND GENEALOGICAL MANUSCRIPT COLLECTIONS

A NUMBER of major religious denominations in the United States have extended beyond the mere establishment of archival agencies to care for their own records their concern with and interest in the past. Some denominations have also

---

[1] Jackson, "Manuscript Collections in the General Library," 275–283; Herman Kahn, "Librarians and Archives—Some Aspects of the Partnership," in *American Archivist*, 7:244–251 (October, 1944).

established repositories for private manuscripts which have some bearing upon their denominational origin and development. Among these religious organizations are those which are historically-oriented and more hierarchical in organization—the Presbyterian, Moravian, Mormon, and Catholic churches.

In addition to archives, a significant collection of private manuscripts illuminating various aspects of the denominational history is held at the Presbyterian Historical Society in Philadelphia. Included are 250,000 pieces of correspondence from foreign missionaries and 50,000 pieces concerned with home missions. The latter group contains the papers of such domestic missionaries as Sheldon Jackson and part of the John D. Shane Collection (1716–1860) relating to the extension of Presbyterianism into the Mississippi Valley.[2]

The Moravian Church, founded in 1457 by the followers of John Huss, the Bohemian reformer, suffered great losses during the Thirty Years' War and failed to carve out for itself an area of Europe in which to predominate as the state religion. The fellowship was restored in 1722 by a group on the Saxon estate of Nicholas Louis Count Zinzendorf, who required the zealous missionaries who left for America to send back systematic accounts of their work in the new fields. The Moravian settlement made at Bethlehem, Pennsylvania, in 1741 has subsequently become the center of the Northern Province of the American Moravian Church. From its earliest years in America, the Moravian Church has been one which stressed records-keeping, and its archives are among the most complete of any denomination. The collection of material at Bethlehem, however, is much more than an archives of the church, for it contains numerous private diaries and letters from individuals as well as from congregations.[3]

Among the holdings at Bethlehem are 7,300 volumes and 58,000 pieces, 1457 to date, chiefly relating to the Moravian

---

[2] Presbyterian Historical Society, *Primary Source Material on Western Life at the Presbyterian Historical Society* (Philadelphia, 1948); Joseph B. Turner, "A Catalogue of Manuscript Records in the Possession of the Presbyterian Historical Society," in *Presbyterian Historical Society Journal*, 8:13–22 (March, 1915); Edward B. Shaw, "Calendar of the Shane Papers, A Preliminary Report," in *Presbyterian Historical Society Journal*, 19:183–192 (December, 1940).

[3] Whitehill, *Historical Societies*, 391–392.

Church in North America. Represented are the papers of John
Ettwein (1772–1797, North Carolina and Pennsylvania, missionary to the Indians), John Gottlieb Ernestus Heckewelder (1765–
1823, Pennsylvania and Ohio, author), Augustus Gottlieb Spangenberg (1744–1760, Pennsylvania and North Carolina, bishop
and missionary), and David Zeisberger (1745–1798, Pennsylvania
and Ohio, missionary and author). The mass of material is safely
housed in appropriate buildings and is lovingly cared for by
learned men, but the material needs extensive cataloging and
indexing for use by historians working on topics other than the
Moravian Church itself.[4]

The migration of Moravians southward from Pennsylvania
produced a second settlement called Wachovia, at Winston-
Salem, North Carolina. At the Wachovia Historical Society,
established by the Moravians as a southern regional archives
and manuscripts repository, there exists over 2,000 volumes
and over 10,000 individual manuscripts dating from 1752. In
addition to the daily diaries of the southern congregations, mem-
orabilia of the Moravian pioneers, minutes of church boards,
account books, church registers, and supporting archival records,
there are a number of significant manuscript collections and
individual diaries further illustrating the operation and evolution of this remarkable community. Until the 1850's the
material is written in German, thereafter in English.[5]

The most energetic and far-ranging activity in support of historical and genealogical research undertaken by any religious
organization is the international records-copying program of the
Church of Jesus Christ of Latter-Day Saints, through its Genealogical Society in Salt Lake City. Mormons believe in the
doctrine of the vicarious salvation of the dead, as derived from
the premise expressed in I Corinthians, 15:29, and enunciated
by the Prophet Joseph Smith in 1841:

> The doctrine presents in a clear light the wisdom and mer-
> cy of God in preparing an ordinance for the salvation of the

---

[4] Kenneth G. Hamilton, "The Resources of the Moravian Church Archives," in
Pennsylvania History, 27:263–272 (July, 1960); Paul A. W. Wallace, "The Moravian
Records," in *Indiana Magazine of History,* 48:141–160 (June, 1952).
[5] Robert B. Downs, *Resources of Southern Libraries* (Chicago, 1938), 53.

dead being baptized by proxy, their names recorded in heaven and they judged according to the deeds done in the body. This doctrine was the burden of the scriptures. Those saints who neglect it on behalf of their deceased relatives, do so at the peril of their own salvation.[6]

Mormons therefore are under obligation to trace their genealogies back as far as possible. To facilitate the work the Genealogical Society in 1938 began to collect by microfilm manuscripts throughout the older parts of the United States, offering a print of all records and manuscripts filmed within a given state to some central repository therein in appreciation for its cooperation in arranging access to the original materials. In 1941 the project spread to the British Isles, thence to the other areas of the world which furnished immigrants to the United States. This good work has been pursued with such diligence that by 1952, 77,861 rolls, or 4,422 miles of microfilm had been used. This is the rough equivalent of 112,000,000 pages or 372,139 bound volumes. Almost 70 per cent of this material was of European origin, the balance being from all parts of the United States. The film in Salt Lake City is kept in fireproof, air-conditioned vaults at optimum temperature and humidity, with regular mercuric chloride monitoring to insure against residual hypo.[7] This mass of microfilmed copies of otherwise scattered and inaccessible records and manuscripts is open to use by members of the public of "good moral standing," who will also find complementary collections of Mormon manuscripts in the Church Historian's Office in Salt Lake City.[8]

Another major microcopying project of considerable significance to American historical scholarship executed under religious auspices is the Knights of Columbus Vatican Microfilm Library at St. Louis University. The idea of filming part of the Vatican Library to create safety copies and to make the material available for scholarship in America originated in 1950. After Jesuit channels had opened the discussion, the Holy See authorized and approved the work in December, 1950. Selections were made

[6] As quoted in Whitehill, *Historical Societies,* 421.
[7] *Ibid.,* 424–426; Bennett, "Record Copying Program," 227–232.
[8] Powell, "Western Libraries," 272–273.

from the Vatican Manuscripts Library by Father L. J. Daly, and
the documentation related mainly to the Medieval, Renaissance,
and Modern periods. The principle of greatest research interests to scholars in the Western Hemisphere was followed in
selection of manuscripts.[9] The St. Louis microfilms are applicable most obviously to the era of exploration and discovery in
American history. The actual filming was done by technicians
from the Vatican Photograph Laboratory using American equipment and film. All told, over 11,000,000 pages from 30,400
codexes were copied.

In the network of Catholic chancery archives there have been
preserved collections of the private manuscripts of church officials and leaders, but it might be argued that such manuscripts
are but logical extensions of the principle of archives. An outstanding example is the collection of Father Junipero Serra at
the Santa Barbara Mission Archives, relating to the work of the
founding father of California and to the Franciscan frontier
outposts in the Far West.[10]

In the latter half of the nineteenth century, when the increasing numbers of foreign-born Americans became aware of the
process of their assimilation, historical societies devoted to the
study of particular ethnic groups began to emerge. Most of these
societies made their contributions through publications, and
few of them sought to collect manuscripts from the ethnic pioneers, but the very existence of such organizations has encouraged the collection and preservation of manuscripts in pre-exist-
ing repositories.

The earliest of the "racial" or ethnic historical societies in
America was the Deutscher Pioneer-verein of Cincinnati, which
was formed in the 1860's. Shortly afterward a similar organization with an identical name was formed in Philadelphia. In
1891 the Pennsylvania German Historical Society was founded
at Lebanon, but it soon moved to Philadelphia. In New York,
the German-American Historical Society was established in 1892,
and the German Society of New York followed in 1902. Chicago

[9] L. J. Daly and E. R. Vollmar, "The Knights of Columbus Vatican Microfilm
Library at Saint Louis University," in *Library Quarterly*, 28:165–171 (July, 1958).
[10] Powell, "Western Libraries," 276; Maynard J. Geiger, *Calendar of the Documents in the Santa Barbara Mission Archives* (Santa Barbara, 1947).

had a German-American History Society as early as 1900, and another German-American Historical Society was formed in Philadelphia in 1903.[11] The common goal of all these societies has been the recording of the process of acculturation and the preservation of records of the contributions of such German-Americans as Carl Schurz in the development of the republic, especially during the Civil War. Through the efforts of the German-American societies, many Union soldier letters have been preserved in appropriate manuscript repositories about the country.

Recording and publicizing the contributions of the Celts to the American experience was the purpose of the American Irish Historical Society, organized in Boston in 1897. An ethnic cousin was the Scotch-Irish Society of America, formed at Columbia, Tennessee, in 1889, with emphasis upon the pioneering propensities of persons of that ancestry.[12]

The Huguenot Society of America was organized in 1883 in New York City, and shortly thereafter associated societies were formed in the communities of substantial Huguenot settlement in New Rochelle, New York; Manakin, Virginia; Charleston, South Carolina; and various settlements in New Jersey and Pennsylvania. Following the pattern of most ethnic historical groups, the descendents of the French in America emphasized the publication of articles of French-American history. This effort culminated in the establishment in 1948 of the Institute Français de Washington.[13]

The history of Judaica and Hebraica in America is encouraged and supported by several Jewish historical organizations. The American Jewish Historical Society in Waltham, Massachusetts, organized in 1892 in New York, collects and preserves the manuscripts of Jewish scholars, philanthropists, merchants, and leaders. The Jewish Publication Society of America, formed in New York in 1893, correlates its activities with those of the historical society by encouraging the publication of research in Jewish history. More recently, the American Jewish Archives at Hebrew

---

[11] Charles H. Wesley, "Racial Historical Societies and the American Heritage," in *The Journal of Negro History*, 37:11 35 (January, 1952).

[12] *Ibid.*, 19–22.

[13] *Ibid.*, 22–24.

Union College was formed in 1948 in Cincinnati to collect and preserve the manuscripts of American Jews and the records of their commercial and cultural institutions.[14]

History's rape of the American Indian is compounded through the failure to provide even minimal means to collect and preserve the meager documentation produced by Indian cultures. The Creek Indian Memorial Association formed at Enid, Oklahoma, in 1921 was the first such effort, followed by the Cherokee Seminaries Student Association at Northeastern State College. The movement has failed to grow and prosper, and for the foreseeable future the Indian must be content to reconstruct his history from the bits and pieces of the white man's documentation.[15]

The American Negro reached institutional consciousness of his history with the formation of the American Negro Historical Society in Philadelphia in 1892. Emphasis was placed upon the collection of manuscripts of such leaders of Negro society and of the abolition movement as Frederick Douglass, and the papers of the society have been deposited with the Historical Society of Pennsylvania. The Negro Society for Historical Research was subsequently organized in Yonkers, New York, for the encouragement of the teaching of Negro history in American colleges. This program was reinforced in 1897 with the formation of the American Negro Academy in Washington. In 1915 Carter G. Woodson and his associates created the Association for the Study of Negro Life and History, which has become the prime mover in the collection and preservation of Negro manuscripts.[16]

In 1925, to mark the centennial of the arrival of the first shipload of Norwegian immigrants, the Norwegian-American Historical Association was founded at St. Olaf College, Northfield, Minnesota. Dedicated "to seek and gather information about the people in the United States of Norwegian birth and descent and to preserve the same in appropriate form as historic records," the association has collected and published under very high and critical standards and has built at St. Olaf a small

---

[14] *Ibid.*, 26–27; Isidore S. Meyer, "The American Jewish Historical Society," in *Journal of Jewish Bibliography*, vol. 4, nos. 1–2 (January–April, 1943).

[15] Wesley, "Racial Historical Societies," 25–26.

[16] *Ibid.*, 27–32.

but significant manuscript collection relating to Norwegian settlement in Minnesota and other states, the history of the Norwegian Lutheran Church in America, and the development of the College.[17]

The Norwegian-American Historical Association has been described as "a prototype for other groups who would search the past to gain understanding of themselves, and of the America they have helped to build." On this prototype a number of other northern European immigrant historical groups have been formed, including the Netherlands Pioneer and Historical Foundation (Holland, Michigan, 1937); the Swiss-American Historical Society of Madison, Wisconsin (1928); the American-Swedish Historical Museum of Philadelphia (1926); the Swedish-American Historical Society of Chicago, Illinois (1905); the Finnish-American Historical Society of Cokato, Minnesota; and the Scandinavian Historical Research Committee at the University of Washington (1942). Although most of these organizations emphasize publication, their very existence has stimulated collection of ethnic manuscript material.[18]

For all the carping between them, there has also developed a solid area of cooperation between genealogists and historians in the collection and preservation of manuscript material for their respective researches. The primary genealogical organization, the New England Historic Genealogical Society, was chartered in 1845 in Boston "to collect, preserve, and publish historical, biographical, and genealogical data, and . . . to make such records available to members and the public." The society publishes the oldest and most distinguished genealogical quarterly, national rather than local in scope, and numbers among its collection almost 200,000 individual manuscripts relating to genealogy and local history.[19]

Among the number of regional and local genealogical societies in America, two will suffice as examples. Boston's Prince Society, organized in 1858, grew up within the shadow both of the New England Historic Genealogical Society and the Mas-

---

[17] Whitehill, *Historical Societies*, 402–407.
[18] Wesley, "Racial Historical Societies," 24–25.
[19] Whitehill, *Historical Societies*, 421–424; William Carroll Hill, *A Century of Genealogical Progress Being a History of the New England Historic Genealogical Society, 1845–1945* (Boston, 1945).

sachusetts Historical Society, and its operations in collecting and publishing have been largely influenced by the precedents established by the older organizations.[20] In a more rural environment, at Big Laurel in southwestern Virginia, is a semi-public genealogical collection known as the James Taylor Adams Library. The collection includes about 10,000 early letters concerning the Adams family, mostly in Virginia and Kentucky, and notes on the pioneers of Wise County, in which the library is located.[21]

PROPRIETARY MANUSCRIPT REPOSITORIES

AN AMORPHOUS GROUP of quasi-public agencies involved in the collection and preservation of historical manuscripts consists of proprietary manuscript repositories. This group includes special libraries, historical museums which buttress their artifacts with manuscripts, a number of magnificent, formerly-private libraries which have been dedicated to scholarly use, and a few examples of enlightened business interests which have created manuscript repositories not only for their own records but for regional and topical documentation as well.

The Library of the American Philosophical Society in Philadelphia was begun in 1727 by Benjamin Franklin and his associates. In its formative years the society emphasized the collection of books and the publication of its transactions, yet it almost unwittingly became a nationally prominent manuscript repository through the deposit of some of Jefferson's letters in 1806 and, through the cooperation of Jared Sparks, the bulk of the papers of Benjamin Franklin in 1840. For the remainder of the nineteenth century, during the development of the public library movement, the society languished through what has been called the "Smithsonian Era," with almost exclusive emphasis upon the earth sciences. More recently, revived by rising interest in special libraries, it has expanded its interests and operations to approximate more closely its earlier scope as a

---

[20] George G. Wolkins, "The Prince Society," in Massachusetts Historical Society, *Proceedings,* 4th series, 46:223–254 (1936–1941).
[21] Downs, *Resources of Southern Libraries,* 68–69.

historical research library. In addition to its own archives, the society holds the papers of Benjamin Rush, Charles Willson Peale, and a number of other scientists and artists of the last century.[22]

Another venerable historical agency which has already celebrated its bicentennial is the Charleston Library Society, organized in 1748 and still dependent solely upon the subscription dues of its members. It possesses some manuscripts relating to the history of South Carolina and an excellent file of early Charleston newspapers.[23]

The Peabody Museum of Salem, Massachusetts, is the survivor of the Salem East India Marine Society, organized in 1799 in part for the collection and preservation of records illustrating the feats of Yankee shipmasters sailing beyond the Cape of Good Hope and Cape Horn. In its library today is a manuscript collection of over 2,000 pieces plus almost as many boxes of logbooks, journals, account books, and other papers relating to American maritime history and trade with Africa, the Far East, and the Pacific Islands.[24]

The Smithsonian Institution, founded in 1846 after extended debate regarding the execution of the bequest of James Smithson, has always found room for some manuscripts among its artifacts. Once the prime national repository for nonofficial manuscripts, most of its miscellaneous acquisitions were transferred to the Library of Congress when the library developed a special division and facilities to care for such material. Yet the Smithsonian still retains and occasionally acquires[25] material

[22] William E. Lingelbach, "The Library of the American Philosophical Society," in *William and Mary Quarterly*, 3rd series, 3:48–62 (January, 1946); Whitehill, *Historical Societies*, 113–117.

[23] Whitehill, *Historical Societies*, 457.

[24] *Ibid.*, 396–398; Walter Muir Whitehill, *The East India Marine Society and the Peabody Museum of Salem, A Sesquicentennial History* (Salem, 1949), 3–15, 131; Ernest S. Dodge and Charles H. P. Copeland, *Handbook to the Collections of the Peabody Museum of Salem* (Salem, 1949), 24–214.

[25] See, for example, *The Opening of the Adams-Clement Collection, Exercises Held in the Arts and Industries Building, Smithsonian Institution, on the Afternoon of April 18, 1951* (Washington, 1951); W. P. True, *The First Hundred Years of the Smithsonian Institution* (New York, 1946); Paul H. Ochser, *Sons of Science: The Story of the Smithsonian Institution and its Leaders* (New York, 1949).

relating chiefly to the scientific and cultural activities of the Institution and its subordinate units.[26] It is, therefore, of prime significance to scholars in the history of American scientific and cultural development.

The Newberry Library in Chicago was founded in 1887, twenty years after the death of Walter Loomis Newberry, based upon provisions of his will. The estate which had been amassed by the commission merchant, banker, and real estate speculator thus came to be expended by his trustees in building the "greatest reference library in the United States." Seven years later, the John Crerar Library also came into being in Chicago, and an agreement was negotiated establishing a division of fields. Under it, the Newberry restricted its area to the humanities, leaving science and the applied arts to the Crerar.[27]

The Newberry Library is unique among private, proprietary libraries in that it has been built, *ab ovo*, as an institution rather than evolving from a personal collection. It has grown to become one of the largest of its type through its policy of acquiring whole libraries such as the Ayer Collection, especially strong in the history of the American Indian and of early America. The papers and manuscripts of several Midwestern authors and publishers are in its collections, as are the bulky corporate archives of the Chicago, Burlington and Quincy Railroad and the Illinois Central Railroad.[28]

Within the fields of science and the applied arts, the John Crerar Library in Chicago has collected since 1894 only a small number of manuscripts relating to science, technology, and medicine,[29] but it is moving to improve its holdings with special reference to the development of science and technology in the Midwest.

[26] True, *Smithsonian Institution, passim.*

[27] Ruth Lapham Butler, "For the Study of American Colonial History [Newberry Library]," in *William and Mary Quarterly*, 3rd series, 2:286–295 (July, 1945); George B. Utley, "Walter Loomis Newberry," in *Dictionary of American Biography*, XIII: 447–448.

[28] Whitehill, *Historical Societies*, 455–456; E. C. Jackson and Carolyn Curtis, *Guide to the Burlington Archives in the Newberry Library, 1851–1901* (Chicago, 1949); C. C. Mohr, *Guide to the Illinois Central Archives in the Newberry Library* (Chicago, 1951).

[29] John Crerar Library, *The John Crerar Library, 1895–1944: An Historical Report* (Chicago, 1945), 1–28.

The record of American philanthropy in support of American historical scholarship is relatively scant,[30] but in the particular category of the dedication of private libraries to quasi-public, scholarly purposes the record shines brightest with the names of John Pierpont Morgan and Henry Edwards Huntington.

The elder Morgan (1837–1913) gathered works of art, books, and manuscripts in the manner of a Renaissance prince, housing his treasures in his private library at 33 East Thirty-sixth Street, next door to his New York residence. At the time of his death, the library was acknowledged as the finest collection in America of cuneiform tablets, papyri, drawings, and manuscripts from the sixteenth to the twentieth century. Although the principal emphasis of the library was upon the Ancient, Medieval, and Renaissance periods, through what Morgan termed "personal indulgence" a significant group of manuscripts relating to American history was also brought within the collection.[31]

In 1924 J. P. Morgan, Jr., created a board of trustees to which he conveyed his father's library, the building, and an endowment for its maintenance "freely dedicated . . . to the purposes of scholarship." Under the direction of Belle da Costa Green, the Morgan Library became a mecca for serious scholars, including historians interested in consulting its holdings on the Yorktown campaign, the domestic letters of Thomas Jefferson, letters from early Episcopal church leaders, and miscellaneous material relating to George Washington.[32]

The closest approximation in the West of the Morgan Library and the most important repository for many of the fields it serves is the Huntington Library, the princely gift to scholarship of Henry Edwards Huntington (1850–1927). A nephew of the railroad magnate Collis P. Huntington, the younger Huntington was established in San Francisco in 1891 to look after the family interests. After 1900 he moved to southern California and entered the real estate and transportation business in his

---

[30] Richard D. Younger, "Foundations and the Study of History," in Hesseltine and McNeil, eds., *Clio*, 107–126.

[31] Whitehill, *Historical Societies*, 441–444; see also, Francis Henry Taylor, *Pierpont Morgan as Collector and Patron, 1837–1913* (New York, 1957), 3–16.

[32] Dorothy Miner, ed., *Studies in Art and Literature for Belle da Costa Greene* (Princeton, 1954), 10–22.

own right. After a highly successful career he retired at sixty and devoted his remaining years to the collection of historical research material relating to Anglo-American civilization. To his 200-acre residence at San Marino, Huntington brought his treasures from all over the world, buying intact libraries whenever possible. His private library was institutionalized in 1919, and upon Huntington's death in 1927 control was vested in a board of trustees. It has since become a favorite workshop of scholars, with endowed research chairs, and every amenity to facilitate the labor of the scholar.[33]

Of the over one million manuscripts at the Huntington Library, the richest single field is the history of England from the introduction of printing to the Puritan Revolution. About one-fifth of the total collection is concerned with American history, particularly the period prior to the Civil War. Included are the papers of James T. Fields (Boston publisher), the Fourth Earl of Loudoun (for the French and Indian War), the Harbeck Collection on the United States Navy, and the Robert A. Brock Collection of Virginiana (which required an entire freight car when shipped to California from Richmond). Frederick Jackson Turner, who spent his last years at the Huntington Library as a research associate, accurately summarized its place among manuscript repositories when he observed: "The American historian can profitably engage in placer mining at the Huntington Library with the assurance that he will find rich nuggets. If he wants to follow an extensive vein of ore he can work better at the Library of Congress."[34]

A new category of business manuscript has been created by the Forest History Society and its subsidiary, the Forest History Foundation, both located at Yale University. Supported by commercial groups interested in the history of lumbering and re-

---

[33] Whitehill, *Historical Societies,* 444–445; Robert O. Schad, *Henry Edwards Huntington, The Founder and the Library* (San Marino, 1952), 27–32.

[34] Louis B. Wright, "For the Study of the American Colonial Heritage [Huntington Library]," in *William and Mary Quarterly,* 3rd series, 1:201–209 (July, 1944); Norma B. Cuthbert, *American Manuscript Collections in the Huntington Library for the History of the Seventeenth and Eighteenth Centuries* (San Marino, 1941), 1–79; John C. Parish, "California Books and Manuscripts in the Huntington Library," Huntington Library *Bulletin,* no. 7 (April, 1953); Powell, "Western Libraries," 265–275.

lated enterprises, the Forest History group has established its own small collection of materials and has sponsored the creation of collections in a number of repositories. Perhaps even more significantly, the Forest History group is engaged in compiling a bibliography of all known manuscripts in the United States and Canada which bear upon forest history and the conservation movement.[35]

Another example of enlightened and public-spirited generosity in support of historical scholarship is the pair of agencies established and maintained by the du Pont family in the vicinity of Wilmington, Delaware. One of these agencies is dedicated to early American cultural and social life, the other to early industrial development along the Brandywine River, site of the first du Pont powder mills.

Early in the twentieth century Henry Francis du Pont began to buy representative examples of American furniture for his home at Winterthur, near Wilmington. Through the creation of period rooms in the home, the establishment soon took on the attributes of a museum, and in 1951 du Pont dedicated the building and grounds as a teaching and research center in American architecture and the decorative arts. Since 1952 Winterthur has offered a Master of Arts program in Early American Culture in cooperation with the University of Delaware, with a growing collection of manuscripts to support research in the field.[36]

The du Pont institution paralleling Winterthur but dedicated to the industrial development of the du Pont companies and others along the Brandywine is the Eleutherian Mills-Hagley Foundation, Inc., at Greenville, Delaware. A combination industrial museum and manuscript repository, it houses the personal and business records of the du Pont family from their American establishment to the present. The institution serves

---

[35] Clodaugh M. Neiderheiser, comp., *Forest History Sources of the United States and Canada, A Compilation of the Manuscript Sources of Forest, Forest Industry, and Conservation History* (St. Paul, 1956), 1–140.

[36] Whitehill, *Historical Societies*, 447–449; Henry Francis du Pont, *Joseph Downs, An Appreciation and A Bibliography of His Publications* (Winterthur, Delaware [n.d.], reprinted from the 1954 Walpole Society Notebook); E. McClung Fleming, "The Winterthur Program in Early American Culture," in *American Studies*, 4:1–5 (July, 1959).

as the archives of the du Pont interests and a repository for documentation of the industrial development of the Brandywine, one of the cradles of the Industrial Revolution in America. At the same time, it serves as a model for other industrial philanthropists who may be moved to support and encourage historical research on a regional or topical basis.[37]

MANUSCRIPTS IN ACADEMIC INSTITUTIONS

IN THE TWENTIETH CENTURY the libraries of academic institutions, particularly those offering graduate instruction and training, have replaced the older private and public historical societies as the prime collectors of American historical manuscripts. The rise and growth of these quasi-public collections is directly attributable to the emergence of the professional historian within college faculties. The resulting manuscript collections are academically oriented, are not necessarily related to the area where located, but generally reflect the research interests of the faculty of the collecting institution.[38]

The development of campus manuscript collections can be regarded as an inevitable consequence of American historiographical development. The earlier avocational historian generally bought or generally secured his own research material. The newer breed of salaried professional historian can rarely afford such luxury. Through the accidents of historical geography, few academic institutions are located in close proximity to the traditional repositories of research materials, and convenience alone has become a compelling argument for bringing manuscripts to the campus. Then too, the size and diversity of the modern university's manuscript collection have become an important measure of the prestige and importance of its departmental faculties. In short, in the twentieth-century manuscript collec-

[37] Whitehill, *Historical Societies*, 449; *The Hagley Museum, A Story of Early Industry on the Brandywine* (Greenville, Delaware, 1957); John A. Monroe, "The Hagley Program," in *American Studies*, 4:5–6 (July, 1959); Paul C. Buck, "The Historian, the Librarian, and the Businessman," in *Eleutherian Mills Historical Library, A Record of its Dedication on 7 October, 1961* (Greenville, Delaware, 1961), 9–14.
[38] Whitehill, *Historical Societies*, 427.

tions have become both necessary tools and status symbols in the academic community in America, and the contemporary boom in higher education has carried along with it the development of a vast new system of repositories where none existed a century ago.[39]

In the last century the problem of manuscript collecting in American colleges and universities has been inverted from one of indifference to one of accommodating more and bulkier collections. On the scale pursued by leading university libraries, collecting and preserving manuscripts is a very expensive business, yet it goes on at an accelerated pace in all quarters of the nation. Not tied to an antiquarian or provincial outlook, the academic agencies collect broadly as to geographical areas. A few of them, such as Cornell, and the state universities of California, Texas, and Louisiana, emphasize the history of their own regions,[40] but most academic libraries approach the status of regional branches or small-scale copies of the manuscript collection at the Library of Congress. Even with their late start, the academic libraries generally are successful in collecting materials over a century old. They do less well in collecting more recent manuscripts, for librarians, even those under the reassuring influence of faculty members, are still uneasy when faced with the sheer bulk of modern collections.[41]

Academic libraries usually acquire manuscripts through purchase out of departmental funds or by bequests through a faculty intermediary, and it is generally accepted that a large and significant manuscript collection and a professionally distinguished department of history are mutually attracted one to another. In smaller libraries, manuscripts are often administered as a part of the rare-book division; in larger libraries, manuscripts are usually awarded a separate division. The ultimate use of any such collections by professional historians and students requires that the collections possess some integrated wholeness to reflect the economic, social, political, scientific, and philosophical aspects of the prospective research topics. In addition,

[39] Brubaker, "Problem of Competitive Collecting," 8.
[40] Handlin, *Harvard Guide*, 59–60.
[41] Roy P. Basler, "The Modern Collector," in Donald R. McNeil, ed., *The American Collector* (Madison, 1955).

manuscripts should have some substantial appeal for scholars outside the immediate campus community.[42]

Despite the highly selective policies of scholars and academic librarians, academic manuscript collections still do not all measure up to their own established standards. The single category of manuscript material which most often violates the criteria is that of diaries, not because of any inherent deficiency in that form of documentation, but because so few historically significant or perceptive individuals have kept diaries and because many accounts are so egocentric as to make them very poor documentation. When diaries, by whomever produced, record significant events in the world around the author, by all means they should be preserved. When they refer primarily to the real or imaginary state of the author's health, to his private thoughts and wishes, and to domestic crises, they might well be disposed of to make room for correspondence from the same author.[43]

In addition to traditional forms of manuscript material, most academic libraries have another form of material indigenous to such institutions, dissertations and theses. Most American graduate schools require deposit of bound typescript copies of dissertations, and approximately half require immediate or eventual publication, in whole or in abstract. The educational explosion since World War II has produced a formidable collection of such specialized manuscripts. They are generally cataloged only at the home library, but they are loaned in the original or on microfilm, subject to any restrictions which the degree-granting institution may impose for the protection of the author.[44]

A comprehensive catalog of the manuscript holdings of academic libraries or of libraries which hold manuscripts is not to be attempted here. Rather, a summary of such holdings and repositories is presented to support generalizations regarding the nature and extent of such collections, the circumstances un-

---

[42] Louis Round Wilson and Maurice F. Tauber, *The University Library: The Organization, Administration, and Function of Academic Libraries* (New York, 1956), 353–381.

[43] David C. Mearns, "Historical Manuscripts, Including Personal Papers," in *Library Trends,* 5:313–321 (January, 1957); Margaret Scriven, "They'd None of 'em be Miss'd," in *Manuscripts,* 7:114–116 (Winter, 1955).

[44] Wilson and Tauber, *The University Library,* 353–381.

der which they were built, and the projected course of their development.

In New England and among the Ivy League schools possessing manuscript collections, Harvard commands prime attention. The Harvard College Library, the oldest in the United States, dates from 1638 and is only a few years junior to the venerable Bodleian Library. This storehouse of scholarship was almost completely destroyed by fire on a cold night in January, 1764, but a new collection was built through the warm response of alumni and patrons. The great fire prompted the gift of books and manuscripts well into the nineteenth century from German-trained scholars like Christoph Daniel Ebeling, transitional figures such as Jared Sparks, and such influential alumni as Charles Sumner. In the period of building the second library at Harvard the collection also profited from the able leadership of librarians John Langdon Sibley and Justin Winsor.[45]

Sibley was the first librarian at Harvard actively to seek manuscript material for research purposes. In 1857 he urged the Alumni Committee on History to take a broader view of desirable library holdings and to make a place for unpublished manuscripts, pamphlets, and other types of "fugitive material." The following year the Visiting Committee approved the broader collecting policy, but with the understanding that it would mean no slackening of the main business of collecting books. Sibley immediately entered into a lively competition with New England junkmen for old paper of every variety, and by 1860 he reported the acquisition of over 50,000 pamphlets. The Civil War provided the impetus needed for the collection of maps, photographs, ephemera, and envelopes, the enclosed letters included almost as a bonus.[46]

In the latter half of the nineteenth century the prestige of the Harvard faculty and the literary prominence of many of its alumni brought to the campus a golden stream of manuscript treasures. In addition to an outstanding collection of Ancient

---

[45] "Harvard College Library, 1638–1938," in *Harvard Library Notes,* 29:207 (1939); John Eliot Alden, "Out of the Ashes, A Young Phoenix: Early Americana in the Harvard College Library," in *William and Mary Quarterly,* 3rd series, 3:487–498 (October, 1946).

[46] Kenneth J. Brough, *Scholar's Workshop: Evolving Conceptions of Library Service* (Urbana, Ill., 1953), 78–84.

and Medieval manuscripts, Harvard gathered a significant body of American materials, relating particularly to the careers of Nathaniel Hawthorne, Henry Wadsworth Longfellow, James Russell Lowell, Ralph Waldo Emerson, Oliver Wendell Holmes, and other literary lights of the last century. In the fields of political and intellectual history, there are papers of Arthur Lee, Daniel Webster, Charles Sumner, Jared Sparks, Theodore Roosevelt, William Cameron Forbes, and Joseph C. Grew. The special interest of Frederick Jackson Turner in the history of the West was reflected in the collecting policy after 1910, when he joined the faculty. There are also many photostats from European repositories collected by, or for the convenience of, Harvard's faculty.[47]

The establishment of the Graduate School of Business Administration of Harvard University early in the twentieth century gave another dimension to the collection of manuscripts at Harvard. To support the study of the evolution of the American business and industrial system, the Baker Library of the School of Business Administration actively collected business records and correspondence mostly from defunct firms in the New England area. This specialized manuscript collection, which borders upon a regional business archives, now involves some "4,000 boxes and 200 crates" of materials.[48]

The burning of the Harvard Library in 1764 and the destruction of the library of the College of William and Mary on several occasions have made possible Yale's claim of possessing the oldest collegiate library in the United States. The Yale Library is exceptionally strong in colonial American religious, social, and intellectual history, mostly in printed form. From the eighteenth and nineteenth centuries there are papers from Ezra Stiles (theologian and Yale president), Benjamin Trumbull (historian), Jedidiah and S. F. B. Morse (father and son, geographer and inventor of the telegraph), and a stellar list of New England pa-

---

[47] Alfred Claghorn Potter, *The Library of Harvard University* (Cambridge, 1934), 108–110; Whitehill, *Historical Societies*, 432; W. H. Bond, "The Cataloging of Manuscripts in the Houghton Library," in *Harvard Library Bulletin*, 4:392–396 (Autumn, 1950); Justin Winsor, *Calendar of the Jared Sparks Manuscripts in Harvard College Library* (Cambridge, 1889).

[48] Whitehill, *Historical Societies*, 435; M. R. Cusick, *List of Business Manuscripts in Baker Library* (Boston, 1932).

triots, literary figures, and cultural lights, most of such material being acquired in the late nineteenth century by the active solicitation of Librarian Addison Van Name.[49] The twentieth century is represented by the papers of such illustrious alumni as Henry L. Stimson, Robert A. Taft, and William L. Cross.

Of special interest at Yale is the William Robertson Coe Collection of Western Americana, established as a gift of Coe after a lifetime of cultivating and collecting the field. The collection is especially valuable for the history of California and the Pacific Northwest in the first half of the nineteenth century. It includes the papers of such frontiersmen as Meriwether Lewis Clark (U. S. army officer, son of William Clark), George Foster Emmons (U. S. naval officer), and Ambrose Bierce (California short-story author and journalist).[50]

The Providence merchant, John Carter Brown (1808–1874), began in 1846 to collect materials on American history from the era of discovery to 1800. After his death his family continued devotedly to care for the collection. In 1901 it was conveyed to Brown University, to be housed in a separate building and served by a staff independent of the university library. Because of its restricted field of interest, the John Carter Brown Library has continued to grow in depth rather than in size, primarily in the category of rare books, although manuscripts have always been acquired as they became available. The greatest emphasis of the collection is on the Spanish colonial period, but among the 325,000 pieces are pleasant surprises for the student of any part of the colonial period. In 1944 a group of "alumni" associates was formed for the dual purpose of supporting and promoting the wider use of this important specialized collection of research material.[51]

[49] James T. Babb, "The Yale University Library: Its Early American Collections," in *William and Mary Quarterly*, 3rd series, 2:397–401 (October, 1945); Brough, *Scholar's Workshop*, 78–84; Z. J. Powers, "American Historical Manuscripts in the Historical Manuscripts Room," in *Yale Library Gazette*, 14:1 (1939); Whitehill, *Historical Societies*, 433.

[50] Mary C. Withington, *A Catalogue of Manuscripts in the Collection of Western Americana founded by William Robertson Coe, Yale University Library* (New Haven, 1952).

[51] Lawrence C. Wroth, *The First Century of the John Carter Brown Library: A History with a Guide to the Collections* (Providence, 1946); *The John Carter Brown Library Conference, A Report of the Meeting Held in the Library of*

Cornell University's Collection of Regional History began un-wittingly with Cornell's foundation, the minutes of incorpora-tion being the first manuscript material received by the library for preservation. Ezra Cornell's papers were originally distributed among his descendents, but the placement in the library of those of Andrew White, the first president, shamed the Cornell heirs into re-collecting and depositing the founder's papers. Such manuscripts as had been acquired remained unprocessed and unpublicized until 1936, when Paul Wallace Gates joined the faculty. Professor Gates had previously worked on problems of land distribution in the West, and he turned his attention to the disposal of Cornell's pine lands in Wisconsin. In his studies he uncovered and acquired a large amount of records and manuscripts. Gates proposed that Cornell establish an up-state research center for New York for the collection and pres-ervation of regional historical material, including his own mate-rial. A Rockefeller grant in 1948 made possible the formal establishment of the center, the cataloging of manuscripts already on hand, and the active solicitation of other manuscript mate-rial. The collection now runs to several million pieces, largely from the nineteenth and twentieth centuries, and includes docu-mentation relating to Cornell University and western New York, business and industrial records of the Cornell timber interests, political correspondence, and papers relating to philanthropic and educational activities.[52]

In 1901 Columbia University's Librarian James Hulme Can-field proposed the establishment of a special research collection, including manuscripts to satisfy the rising demand for such mate-rial. Implementing that proposal has created at Columbia in ensuing years a very large collection of manuscripts, the founda-tion of which are the papers of many of the intellectual leaders of contemporary America who have served on the Columbia fac-

Brown University on the Early History of America (Providence, 1961), 7–13, 14–18; Whitehill, *Historical Societies*, 436–437; Damian Van den Eynde, "Calendar of Spanish Documents in the John Carter Brown Library," in *Hispanic American Historical Review*, 16:564–607 (November, 1936); Lawrence C. Wroth, "Source Materials of Florida History of Brown University," in *Florida Historical Quarterly*, 20:3–46 (July, 1941).

[52] Edith M. Fox, "The Genesis of Cornell University's Collection of Regional History," in *American Archivist*, 14:105–116 (April, 1951).

ulty. Examples of such individuals include Nicholas Murray Butler (president of Columbia), Melvil Dewey (librarian and originator of the Dewey Decimal classification system), and Allan Nevins (historian). Beginning in 1930, Columbia added another dimension of historical documentation through its Oral History Project, which has produced an increasing number of tapes and transcripts of interviews with individuals prominent on the national scene at mid-century.[53]

The manuscript collection at Princeton University, extending to over 270 file drawers and 4,200 feet of shelved manuscripts, has grown with the scope of the university's academic horizons, focused upon American and European literary history. In the field of American political and social history, there are a number of special, named collections, such as the Grenville Kane Early Americana Collection, Rollins Western Americana Collection, the Pierson Civil War Collection, and the Woodrow Wilson Collection (relating to his career at Princeton and in New Jersey). Twentieth-century manuscripts have generally been acquired by gift from prominent alumni, such as Secretary of Defense James V. Forrestal, Secretary of State John Foster Dulles, F. Scott Fitzgerald, and Eugene O'Neill.[54]

The Middle Atlantic and Upper South regions contain a number of academic libraries with significant manuscript collections. Most of these collections are of recent origin and have grown up under the shadow of the preeminent research collections in the national capital, notably those of the Library of Congress. That they have grown as they have is a tribute to the number of centers of graduate training which have emerged in the area in the twentieth century. In the capital itself are the manuscript collections relating to Catholic life and history at the two Catholic institutions of higher learning, Catholic University of America and Georgetown University.[55] Outside of Wash-

---

[53] Brough, *Scholar's Workshop*, 78–84; *Manuscript Collections in the Columbia University Libraries, A Descriptive List* (New York, 1959); [Columbia University], Oral History Research Office, *The Oral History Collection of Columbia University* (New York, 1960).

[54] Alexander P. Clark, *The Manuscript Collections of the Princeton University Library* (Princeton, 1958); Whitehill, *Historical Societies*, 433.

[55] Handlin, *Harvard Guide*, 60.

ington, major manuscript collections are to be found at most of the state universities of the area.

The development of the manuscript collection at the University of Virginia has provided a model for many other southern universities in this century. In the first academic session in 1819 Thomas Jefferson deposited some of his own manuscripts. Thereafter, for as long as he was active in the university's affairs, he insisted that the most meticulous care be taken in keeping the manuscript minutes of the board of trustees.

In the initial year of operations there also came to the university the papers of the Revolutionary hero, Richard Henry Lee. The Lee Papers, seldom used in the early years, were to become the leavening agent of the collection.[56] As the years passed, the Lee papers drew many inquiries and requests for examination, yet they remained virtually the only research manuscript material at the university. In 1881 a faculty member proposed that the Lee papers be sold to the federal government for deposit in the Library of Congress, the resulting funds being used to buy needed books for the library. By a majority vote the faculty recommended this course to the Visitors, but they demurred, stating that they regarded these manuscripts "to be especially appropriate and valuable to the archives of the University."[57]

At the turn of the twentieth century several small endowment funds (notably the Byrd Fund) dedicated to the purchase of research material centering on Virginia were received. These funds permitted for the first time the modest but direct acquisition of needed manuscripts. The national prestige of the university's law school attracted other manuscripts from John Bassett Moore, Justice James Clark McReynolds, and Judge John Monro Woolsey.[58]

Virginia, like the rest of the South, was at a distinct disadvantage in collecting manuscripts in the long period of recovery following the Civil War. The private collectors of the region were few and were men of only moderate means, and the tradi-

---

[56] Harry Clemons, *The University of Virginia Library* (Charlottesville, 1954), 23–24.
[57] *Ibid.*, 48–49.
[58] *Ibid.*, 67, 178.

tions of collection by academic libraries had to await the slow development of those institutions. In Virginia the systematic collection of manuscripts began in 1930 with the mailing of 20,000 copies of a broadside appeal written by Professor William Mynn Thornton. It called attention to the destruction visited upon the manuscripts of the South, "the devastations of war, the conflagrations of ancient houses, the besom of the tidy housewife, and the backyard bonfire," and announced that the University of Virginia was ready to offer its aid "in the preservation, the study, the interpretation, and the publication of memorials of Virginia's social, industrial, political, and intellectual life." The appointment of Dr. Lester J. Cappon as archivist, coupled with the creation of the Research Institute at the University, soon brought about the flow of manuscripts, primarily from the Piedmont and western sections, into the newly-completed Alderman Library. By mid-century the collections ran to about 5,000,000 pieces, the majority of which had been acquired since 1925. Individual collections from the Revolutionary and early national periods were those of Thomas Jefferson, the Lee family, Sabine Hall (the Carter family), the Berkeley family, and the Edgehill-Randolph papers (the grandchildren of Thomas Jefferson). Of more recent origin are the papers of Senators Carter Glass, Claude A. Swanson, and Miles Poindexter (a native of Virginia but elected to the Senate from Washington).[59]

The venerable College of William and Mary in Williamsburg, Virginia, took renewed interest in historical research with the restoration of its community. Since the 1930's, largely through the efforts of the former college librarian, Dr. Earl G. Swem, a significant manuscript collection of almost 500,000 pieces has been developed. The material principally relates to Tidewater Virginia and the South during the colonial period and closely complements the research interests and activity of Colonial Williamsburg. Dr. Swem was also single-handedly responsible for

---

[59] *Ibid.*, 155, 161; Lester J. Cappon and Patricia Holbert Menk, "The Evolution of Materials for Research in Early American History in the University of Virginia Library," in *William and Mary Quarterly*, 3rd series, 3:370–382 (July, 1946); Downs, *Resources of Southern Libraries*, 64–65; Whitehill, *Historical Societies*, 431.

the production of the *Virginia Historical Index*, an indispensable tool for work in Virginia history.[60]

A large collection of manuscripts, from literate frontiersmen to those of contemporary political leaders, is housed at the University of Kentucky in Lexington. Of particular significance to the history of trans-Appalachia is the university's collection of account books, ledgers, and other business records of early enterprises, and papers of such prominent Kentuckians as Henry Clay and Alben W. Barkley.[61]

The famed Southern Historical Collection at Chapel Hill is in reality the Manuscripts Division of the University of North Carolina Library. It was formally established in 1930, but its origins go back to 1833, when the North Carolina Historical Society was chartered, and to 1844, when the Historical Society of the University of North Carolina came into being and began to collect manuscripts. These predecessors provided the foundation upon which the Southern Historical Collection, embracing material from fourteen southern states, was developed by J. G. deR. Hamilton. At one time the collection of some of the material aroused local sentiment in a number of states, but that was before there were suitable repositories throughout the South. The collection, the largest gathering of manuscripts (over 3,200,000 pieces) relating to the South, is strongest in the antebellum period and is weakest in material for colonial history.[62]

Close by, at Duke University, is a manuscript collection much akin to that at Chapel Hill. The Duke Collection consists of about 2,700,000 items, chiefly on American history from the

[60] Whitehill, *Historical Societies*, 432; "Historical Manuscripts in the Library of the College of William and Mary," in *William and Mary Quarterly*, 2nd series, 20:388 (1940); Jane Carson, "Historical Manuscripts in Williamsburg," in *Manuscripts*, 5, no. 4:9–15 (Summer, 1953).

[61] Whitehill, *Historical Societies*, 433; Downs, *Resources of Southern Libraries*, 50; Jacqueline Bull, "The Samuel M. Wilson Library," in Kentucky Historical Society, *Register*, 47:52–54 (January, 1949).

[62] Charles E. Rush, ed., *Library Resources of the University of North Carolina* (Chapel Hill, 1945); U. S. Historical Records Survey, *Guide to the Manuscripts in the Southern Historical Collection of the University of North Carolina* (Chapel Hill, 1941); Whitehill, *Historical Societies*, 434. Carolyn Andrews Wallace, "The Southern Historical Collection," in *American Archivist*, 28:427–436 (July, 1965).

Revolution to the present, especially on the southern states and the Confederacy.[63]

South Carolina's state university holds a collection of over 1,000,000 pieces, principally relating to the state's up-country. The papers of such nationally-known figures as Wade Hampton, Hugh S. Legare, and the historian Samuel Chiles Mitchell are here. The voluminous papers of John C. Calhoun are distributed between the University of South Carolina and Clemson College.[64]

The educational institutions of Georgia possess a sizable number of manuscript sources for the history of the state. Emory University in Atlanta holds a small but cohesive collection on the history of Methodism and of the South, particularly during the Confederacy.[65] At the University of Georgia in Athens is a considerable body of uncataloged manuscripts relating primarily to the history of the state in the nineteenth century. Atlanta University has a small collection of manuscripts relating to Negro affairs following the Civil War.[66]

At the University of Alabama the manuscript collection extends to about 700,000 items, including the papers of the state's famous sons, Surgeon General William C. Gorgas, Senator James T. Heflin, and Representative Sam Hobbs.[67]

The library at the Louisiana State University at Baton Rouge has about 2,100,000 volumes of private manuscripts and state archives dating back to 1750 and chiefly relating to Louisiana, Texas, Mississippi, and the lower Mississippi Valley.[68] Comple-

[63] N. M. Tilley and M. L. Goodwin, *Guide to the Manuscript Collection in the Duke University Library* (Durham, North Carolina, 1947); Mattie Russell and Edward Graham Roberts, "The Processing Procedures of the Manuscript Department of Duke University Library," in *American Archivist*, 12:369–380 (October, 1949); Whitehill, *Historical Societies*, 434; Mattie Russell, "The Manuscript Department in the Duke University Library," in *American Archivist*, 28:437–444 (July, 1965).

[64] Downs, *Resources of Southern Libraries*, 57.

[65] *Ibid.*, 48; Robert B. Harwell, "A Brief Calendar of the Jefferson Davis Papers in the Emory University Library," in *Journal of Mississippi History*, 4:20–30 (January, 1942); and James H. Young, "Alexander H. Stephens Papers in the Emory University Library," in *Emory University Quarterly*, 2:30–37 (March, 1946).

[66] Downs, *Resources of Southern Libraries*, 48.

[67] Whitehill, *Historical Societies*, 433.

[68] Downs, *Resources of Southern Libraries*, 50–51; U. S., Historical Records

menting these materials is a collection, especially strong in business and literary manuscripts, of about 250,000 manuscripts in the library of Tulane University in New Orleans.

The University of Texas Library in Austin is the largest historical research center in the Southeast, housing 3,200,000 manuscripts on the history of Texas and Latin America. Included are about 250,000 pages of records relating to the Spanish administration of Texas, 200,000 documents from the period of Mexican rule, and a large number of manuscripts for the period since independence, represented principally by the papers of Moses and Stephen F. Austin.[69]

The great universities of the Midwest have each developed their own collections of manuscripts for historical research, and collectively their holdings represent one of the strongest groups of such resources in the nation. The most distinguished, if not the largest, of the midwestern university collections was not built by the university itself but was, instead, a gift of a devoted alumnus. As a gift to historical scholarship, the William L. Clements Library at the University of Michigan ranks with the Morgan and Huntington libraries.

The Clements Library grew out of the collecting activities of William L. Clements of Bay City, Michigan (1861–1934), a wealthy industrialist engaged in the manufacture of heavy cranes for railway use. Clements became a recognized connoisseur of Americana in the 1890's, pouring his fortune into the acquisition of books and manuscripts for the period up to 1800. Relying upon his close ties with bibliographers, rare book dealers, and the University of Michigan historian Claude H. Van Tyne for advice concerning availability and desirability of manuscripts, Clements stressed quality of academic usefulness rather than quantity or intrinsic value. Even so, when the collection was offered to the University of Michigan in 1922 it was both large

---

Survey, *Calendar of Manuscript Collections in Louisiana . . . Taber Collection* (Baton Rouge, 1938), and *Guide to the Manuscript Collections in Louisiana: The Department of Archives, Louisiana State University,* vol. I (Baton Rouge, 1940).

[69] Downs, *Resources of Southern Libraries,* 60–61; William A. Whatley, "The Historical Manuscript Collections of the University of Texas," in *Texas History Teachers' Bulletin,* 9:19–25 (November, 1920); "The Eugene C. Baker Texas History Center," in University of Texas, *Library Chronicle,* 4:3 (Fall, 1950).

and valuable. The collection subsequently became even more distinguished and useful through Clement's policy of purchasing British manuscripts of the Revolutionary period and adding them to the material in Ann Arbor.[70]

The Clements Library has saved many American historians the time and expense of a research trip to England and has perhaps saved the priceless manuscripts themselves from loss and destruction. The collection entries are a veritable index to the period of the Revolution. Among them are Admiral George Clinton (governor of New York, 1743–1753); Sir Peter Warren (naval commander at the Battle of Louisburg); John Wilkes; George, Marquis Townshend; Secretary of State Lord George Germain and his undersecretary, William Knox; and the military commanders, Lieutenant General Thomas Gage and Lieutenant General Sir Henry Clinton. The peace negotiations ending the war are extensively documented in the papers of the Earl of Shelburne and of Franklin's initial contact, Richard Oswald. More recent periods are represented by the papers of such figures as Brigadier Josiah Harmon, James G. Birney, and Russell A. Alger.[71]

In Bloomington at the Indiana University Library is a manuscript collection of almost 1,500,000 pieces, strongest in American literary and business history in the nineteenth century and represented by individuals primarily of regional and state significance. Among the larger collections of better-known individuals are papers of Vice President Charles Warren Fairbanks, Paul V. McNutt, Marquis de Lafayette, James Whitcomb Riley, and Upton Sinclair.[72]

[70] Whitehill, *Historical Societies*, 440–441; Randolph G. Adams, "William L. Clements," in *Dictionary of American Biography*, Supplement One, 179–181; *The William L. Clements Library of Americana at the University of Michigan* (Ann Arbor, 1923).

[71] Howard H. Peckham, *Guide to the Manuscript Collections in the William L. Clements Library* (Ann Arbor, 1942); Howard H. Peckham and Carlton Storm, "The Clements Library," in *William and Mary Quarterly*, 3rd series, 1:353–362 (October, 1944); W. S. Ewing, *Guide to the Manuscript Collections in the William L. Clements Library* (2d ed., Ann Arbor, 1953), preface; Peckham, "Clements Library," 215–229.

[72] "Manuscripts in the Indiana University Library," in *Indiana Magazine of History*, 49:191–196 (June, 1953); Dorris M. Reed, *Indiana University Library Manuscript Collections Relating to Business History* (Bloomington, 1951). For an

The University of Chicago's manuscript collection, like the university itself, is of recent origin (1929). The collection has been built primarily for historical and literary research and therefore has greater cohesiveness and less regional character than most manuscript collections in academic agencies of the same region. Included among the larger and more significant collections are the papers of Senator Stephen A. Douglas, Governor Frank O. Lowden, and philanthropist Julius Rosenwald. Within the university's archives are the official records of the institution plus a larger group of manuscripts of many of the distinguished faculty members who have served this unique educational institution.[73]

An even younger manuscript collection came into being on the campus of the University of Missouri at Columbia in January, 1943. The Western Historical Manuscripts Collection was conceived by Elmer Ellis of the history department as a cooperative project between the State Historical Society of Missouri and the state university, the two agencies having already had the experience of jointly developing a book collection. A grant of $15,000 from the Rockefeller Foundation defrayed the initial expenses of locating and processing the available manuscripts, and, despite a very small staff and a short period of time, the collection is already quite a respectable one. Strongest in the fields of midwestern politics, agriculture, and lumbering, the collection can be expected to develop in these areas, especially for the period since the turn of the century.[74]

The manuscript repositories of the Southwest, in New Mexico and Arizona, have the Spanish background, the Indian period, and the colorful history of the recent frontier as foci for their

---

interesting account of collecting Indiana business manuscripts in the field, see Thomas P. Martin, "A Manuscripts Collecting Venture in the Middle West: Indiana, 1950–1953," in *American Archivist*, 17:305–312 (October, 1954).

[73] Whitehill, *Historical Societies*, 434; Brough, *Scholar's Workshop*, 78–84; Paul M. Angle, *Survey of Manuscript Collections, University of Chicago Libraries* ([Chicago], 1944).

[74] Lewis E. Atherton, "Western Historical Manuscripts Collection—A Case Study of a Collecting Program," in *American Archivist*, 26:41–50 (January, 1963); University of Missouri, *Guide to the Western Historical Manuscripts Collection* (Columbia, 1952); "Western Historical Manuscripts Collection," in University of Missouri Library, *Bulletin, no. 5* (1949).

relatively new collections. At the University of New Mexico at Albuquerque is an extensive group of papers from the Spanish period, which is supplemented by material from such prominent citizens of the region as Interior Secretary Albert B. Fall, Territorial Governor Miguel Antonio Otero, and chiefs and agents of the Navajo and Apache tribes.[75] A parallel but somewhat smaller collection exists at the University of Arizona in Tucson.[76]

The earliest and most conspicuous example of the development of academic manuscript collections in the Far West was the purchase of the Bancroft Library by the University of California at Berkeley in 1905. Since that time it has been steadily strengthened under the guidance of Henry Morse Stephens, Hubert E. Bolton, Herbert I. Priestly, and George P. Hammond. The collection now extends to more than 3,500,000 manuscripts relating to western North America and especially to California and Mexico. The collection is nominally worth more than $1,500,000, but for historical research it is priceless.[77]

As was pointed out earlier, the fame and deserved repute of the Bancroft Library lie in the fact that the library consists of highly specialized collections accumulated at a very early period in the history of the West, when such material was still readily available. The treasure of the Bancroft Library is the papers of General Mariano Guadalupe Vallejo of Sonoma, to which has been added the papers of such men as Thomas O. Larkin (U. S. Consul at Monterey) and Benjamin Hayes (antiquarian and historian of southern California).[78]

In the Pacific Northwest, academic institutions in Oregon and Washington have developed small but rapidly-growing manuscript collections pertaining to the region and its participation in the national experience. At the University of Oregon is a small collection of material from a wide range of commercial,

[75] Albert James Diaz, *Manuscripts and Records in the University of New Mexico Library* (Albuquerque, 1957).

[76] Powell, "Western Libraries," 273–274.

[77] *Ibid.*, 265–266; Whitehill, *Historical Societies*, 430.

[78] Hammond, "Manuscript Collections in the Bancroft Library," 15–26; Davis Marion Wright, *A Guide to the Mariano Guadalupe Vallejo documentos para la historia de California, 1780–1875* (Berkeley, 1953).

professional, and religious organizations, including the records
of the International Association of the Congo and of Henry M.
Stanley, who was active in its affairs.[79] A larger collection of
manuscripts is to be found at the library of the University of
Washington. The impetus to the collection has been the continuing interest and active participation of the strong departments of history and English at the university. Their efforts
have resulted in the acquisition of a number of collections, the
creators of which were especially susceptible to scholarly en-
treaty and influence. Examples include the papers of Richard
A Ballinger (Secretary of the Interior during the Ballinger-
Pinchot Affair) and David Hunter Miller (international lawyer
and special assistant in the State Department). An imaginative
program of microfilming regional records of the Northwest
seeks to consolidate in Seattle at least copies of all significant
regional documentation.[80]

The comity which generally exists between American institutions of higher learning does not necessarily extend to their
collections of manuscripts, according to a recent survey.[81] It
appears that the larger academic libraries are the most competitive agents in the chase for manuscripts. However deplorable
the resulting dispersal of material, and however desirable the
concept of a central repository for each state or region, free
competition for the indefinite future seems to be the established
system among American manuscript collectors, public and private, institutional and individual. The worst effects of the system are mitigated by several regional arrangements for cooperation between agencies and an increasing emphasis upon the development of regional and national union catalogs of manuscript collections.[82] The guiding principle among academicians
who are concerned with manuscripts long has been "to bring
valuable manuscripts into a safe place where they will be most
available to the largest number of users."[83]

[79] John Van Male, *Resources of Pacific Northwest Libraries: A Survey of Facilities for Study and Research* (Seattle, 1943), 164.
[80] *Ibid.*, 161–162; Powell, "Western Libraries," 268–269; Whitehill, *Historical
Societies*, 430–431.
[81] Brubaker, "Problem of Competitive Collecting," 22.
[82] Bauer, "Where Manuscripts Should Be," 163–167.
[83] "Report of an *Ad Hoc* Committee on Manuscripts Set Up by the American
Historical Association in December, 1948," 233; Land, "Union Catalog," 195–207.

A few academic libraries have moved in the direction of ne-gotiating bilateral delineation agreements or imposing unilateral-ly upon themselves certain restrictions in deference to other agencies in their immediate area. An excellent example is the University of Virginia, which has reached informal understand-ings with most of the repositories in the state, in the national capital, and in the southeastern states for the mutual reference of donors and manuscripts to the agencies which might have a superior claim on the material. The authorities at Charlottes-ville are convinced that the policy pays material dividends, not through receipt of those items which reciprocity brings to them but through their being relieved of collecting inappropriate mate-rials. As they have put it:

> It seems wasteful, outmoded, and a bit silly to collect items that appear more suitable for (a) the *archives* of another in-stitution, or (b) the strictly local regional history of an area where another repository is located, or (c) actually form an integral part of a collection already existing in another re-pository, or (d) has close relationship to a collection or col-lections existing elsewhere.[84]

Similarly, Yale generally does not accept manuscripts when it feels they would be more useful elsewhere.[85]

USE OF MANUSCRIPTS IN QUASI-PUBLIC REPOSITORIES

THE HETEROGENEITY of the content of the quasi-public repositories is matched only by the variety in the conditions under which these collections have been built and made avail-able for public use. Like sociologically isolated communities, each of these manuscript repositories has its own traditions, mores, and practices. The repositories have developed in a variety of milieu, have grown erratically, and have reached their present status without much regard to age and position.

Of all historical research material, manuscripts get out of hand most easily, yet they are also the richest ore a library can

---

[84] F. L. Berkeley, Jr. (Curator of Manuscripts, University of Virginia) to David C. Mearns, May 29, 1956, as quoted in Mearns, "Historical Manuscripts," 315.

[85] R. F. Metzdorf (Librarian at Yale) to Mearns, May 21, 1956, as quoted in *ibid*.

store for the research scholar. The material is the more useful when concentrated in a limited field, even when its unit research value is low, yet it thereby becomes of interest to a smaller number of scholars. It has been suggested, therefore, that some form of mathematical formula for evaluating manuscripts may be necessary. Such an index would express the relative usefulness of a collection by dividing the aggregate research value by the number of pieces in the collection.[86]

Some librarians, on the premise that manuscripts in quasi-public repositories exist primarily for the use of scholars, believe they should treat scholars like the experts they profess to be, giving only minimal guidance to the material and permitting scholars to burrow for themselves. Taking as their primary duty the collection and preservation of research materials, such librarians hold that there is a reciprocal duty on the part of scholars to respect the implications of exclusive and nonpublic ownership of such material.[87]

A cooperative approach, best exemplified by the development of the National Union Catalog of Manuscripts, more nearly represents the current concept of the function of manuscript librarians in the service of scholarship. The most enthusiastic support for it has come from the larger and more prominent repositories, long accustomed to serving the needs of visiting scholars.[88]

The traditional forms of bibliographical service to scholars using manuscript material, such as calendars, indexes, and printed guides, have largely given way to a brief citation of the location of collections in a central union list. Nevertheless, even in this age of high publication costs, an occasional project recalls the golden age in American historiography when scholars expected, albeit in vain, the day when all of the significant documentation for their labors would be available in printed form. While dis-

[86] Neal Harlow, "Managing Manuscript Collections," in *Library Trends,* 4:203–309 (October, 1955); Sherrod East, "Describable Item Cataloging," in *American Archivist,* 16:301 (October, 1953).

[87] Howard H. Peckham, "Aiding the Scholar in Using Manuscript Collections," in *American Archivist,* 19:221 (July, 1956).

[88] Land, "Union Catalog," 195–207; Peckham, "Manuscript Repositories," 319; "Report of an *Ad Hoc* Committee on Manuscripts," 229–232.

claiming any intent to transcribe individual manuscripts, the spirit of the Carnegie Guides series certainly pervaded the Virginia Colonial Records Project, begun in 1955 as a part of the 350th Anniversary of the Jamestown settlement. The project grew out of a Fulbright grant made to F. L. Berkeley, Jr., in 1952–1953 to enable him to search for some of the remote British and Scottish documentation for Virginia colonial history. Encouraged by the results of Berkeley's initial survey, the University of Virginia, the Virginia State Library, and the Virginia Historical Society embarked on a cooperative project to support a full-time research agent in the various British repositories for two years. The completed report has been described as an indispensable tool for research in colonial history.[89]

The nature of the material in quasi-public repositories and the type of use such material is most often subject to place the librarians charged with its care under obligations which differ even from those of librarians in other manuscript repositories. The users of such material may be assumed to be a professional fraternity motivated by a deep respect for manuscripts. They may resent the officious intrusion of librarians enforcing arbitrary rules of access and use contrary to the best interests of scholarship, yet they demand that the same librarians take sufficient care to preserve the materials for future use.

Curators of the manuscripts used primarily by scholars have a responsibility to screen those persons who are not prepared to make the best use of manuscripts or who are merely curious as to their contents. Although manuscripts may be held for the exclusive use of a scholar for a reasonable time, no proprietary discrimination in the granting of access to papers should be permitted. Repositories frequented by scholars are centers of professional association and contact, and an institutional staff has an obligation to suggest to users possible conflicts and duplication between their projected studies and those of others who have used the same material. Quasi-public institutions should co-operate through photographic duplication as freely as possible in dealing with individual scholars, but individuals,

[89] Boyd, "Virginia History," 3–13.

on their part, should understand that copying certain material
is thought to impair the intrinsic value of the original, and that
any duplication of manuscript material borders upon publication.[90]

Based on the 1948 report of a committee of the American Historical Association, the Library of Congress has developed a set
of rules governing access and use of its manuscript holdings,
and these rules are gradually being accepted as standard throughout the system of repositories frequented mainly by scholars.
In the Library of Congress readers are not permitted the use
of ink in bottles and may use it in pens only with great care. No
marks may be made on manuscripts, and no notes may be made
on paper lying on top of manuscripts. Readers are required to
preserve the existing order, calling attention of the staff to any
apparent misfiling. Readers are also expected to obtain, before
publication, knowledge relating to the literary rights to the
material under common law, and of the applicable provisions
of the law of libel.[91]

Inasmuch as quasi-public manuscript repositories are not
truly public in character, they can and perhaps should be discriminating in making available their holdings to the public.
What the community of scholars wishes is not for such agencies
to conform to the practices of public libraries, but for them
to become full participants in the free exchange of ideas and
information upon the terms and conditions generally acceptable
among scholars everywhere.

[90] Peckham, "Policies," 363. See also, "Report of an *Ad Hoc* Committee on
Manuscripts," 233–240; Robert H. Land, "Defense of Archives against Human
Foes," in *American Archivist,* 19:121–131 (April, 1956).

[91] *Ibid.;* see also, [Association of Research Libraries], "Report of the Committee
on the Use of Manuscripts by Visiting Scholars Set Up by the Association of
Research Libraries," in *College and Research Libraries,* 13:58–60 (January, 1952).

VIII

PRIVATE MANUSCRIPT
COLLECTIONS AND COLLECTORS

COLLECTIONS OF MANUSCRIPTS are objects of a keen and fundamental historiographical interest; they can also be, and often are, items of lively commerce among collectors and scholarly agencies. The collection of historical manuscripts merely for the satisfaction of possession may strike the historian at best as a perversion of the past, at worst as an interference with his own legitimate interests. Yet, there has emerged between the antiquarian collector of manuscripts and the professional historian a fortuitous if unwilling partnership which mutually serves and preserves their respective purposes. This is certainly the case in the American historiographical tradition. It is not too sweeping a generalization to observe that the acquisition and collection of manuscripts in America was popularized by private collectors before the material took on significance to historians, and that the interest pursued by collectors and by their institutional projections—the historical societies—has ultimately benefitted scholarly historians. How much poorer would American history be without the funds and efforts spent in the collection of manuscripts by such men as J. P. Morgan, Henry Huntington, Julian Boyd Thacher, Jerome Kern, William Randolph Hearst, and William Cardinal Mundelein!

Since private collectors and professional historians are locked in a partnership springing from their common interests in manuscript materials, it behooves each group to be informed regarding its counterpart's motives, techniques, and ultimate in-

229

tentions. Particularly, it behooves the historian to be acquainted
with the tradition of manuscripts as marketable commodities and
with the process whereby they are bought and sold, that he may
take advantage of opportunities to channel such material into
repositories where general access may be assured. Furthermore,
rather than damn the collector as a rival, the historian may convert him into a friend by encouraging the collector to dedicate
his treasures to the purposes of scholarship, either voluntarily
or as a consequence of the operations of tax laws. Lastly, but
of recent import, historians need to become more familiar with
the law of literary property, with the rights and liabilities which
attach to the possession and use of manuscript source material.

If such a broadening of interests makes strange bedfellows of
historians, manuscript collectors and dealers, tax collectors, and
copyright lawyers, it is but the price of successful pursuit of the
sources of history. The diversified American society has evolved
a mixed economy of manuscript materials, in which private ownership and dedication to public use exist side by side in reasonable harmony. The success of the system in American historiography suggests that its special strengths and advantages outweigh
its weaknesses, and the system may be expected to continue its
functionally successful service to scholarship for the indefinite
future.

MANUSCRIPT COLLECTING

WHY do individual collectors engage in the acquisition of
the literary remains and momentoes of the American past?
The reasons, as varied as the collectors, may be reduced to a
few common ones. Like all collectors, those who specialize in
manuscripts enjoy the thrill of exclusiveness, of owning a unique
item, something coveted by other collectors. Manuscript material satisfies these collectors in an especially appropriate manner.
Moreover, manuscripts have an inherent aesthetic value; they
may often be displayed with great artistic effect. Manuscripts
are imbued with a very high degree of personal interest, which
may range from the low and secret delight of reading another's
mail to the high and professional analysis of personality and
historical research. The avocation may serve as the means of
intimate and vicarious contact with great people.[1]

[1] Storm and Peckham, *Book Collecting,* 115–116.

There are still other reasons for the popularity of manuscript collecting. The treasures of manuscripts are easily portable and relatively easy to care for. They lend themselves to a great variety of applicable subject matter, and they offer the possibility of satisfying an interest in the past at a relatively slight expense. Manuscripts are less subject to the tides of fashion and taste than most other objects of collection and provide an opportunity, based upon intelligent management rather than blind chance, for economic appreciation. Manuscript collectors profess to enjoy a warm camaraderie between themselves and their dealers, a common tie as wide as the past and as colorful as those who peopled it.[2]

The American tradition of manuscript collecting is traceable to the Victorian fad of collecting "autographs," or "signatures," either specially produced on cards or inscribed in an album, or cut from the body of a letter or document. Fortunately, the fad is now largely passed, having been replaced by logical and orderly collection of the whole body of a series of interrelated letters or other writings produced by the same individual.

It should be noted that the European and American definitions of "manuscript" differ. European practice equates "manuscript" with holographic writing, whereas American practice applies the term to any writing not reproduced in multiple copies by printing or some other mechanical process. In Europe, general practice confines the term "manuscript" to writing produced by hand before the invention of printing. Writings produced since 1450 are referred to as "documents" or "modern manuscripts," as the case may be. On the other hand, a contemporary American letter is still a "manuscript," be it entirely handwritten or produced on a typewriter, but a photocopy of it in any form is a "reproduction." American manuscripts of whatever age are further subdivided into the categories of "letters" and "documents," depending upon their original purpose as correspondence or as some form of evidential or official writing.[3]

Manuscript collecting came about as an offshoot of the collection of rare books, and both categories of materials attract the same kind of collectors. Originally more interested in the associative than the substantive values of manuscripts, manu-

[2] Lady Charnwood, *An Autograph Collection* (New York, 1932), 5–10. For an example of the appeal of one such collection, see Icko Iben, "The Literary Estate of Lorado Taft," in *American Archivist*, 26:493–496 (October, 1963).
[3] Storm and Peckham, *Book Collecting*, 127–129.

script collectors brought into the collecting of written materials the procedures and values of the collecting of rare books.[4] The extension of book collecting into the field of manuscripts has also meant the extension of the point of view and characterization of book collectors, as the historian Worthington C. Ford has pointed out with a slight tinge of sarcasm:

> In the cabinet of the rich its [a manuscript's] interest depends upon its cost; it becomes invested . . . with a golden aura which will in time be more important than the document itself. The next stage is where it is framed with the check. It has now become a bit of furniture, a possible asset, a gilt-edged curiosity, convenient for starting conversation after dinner. But one more stage remains, in which it is irrevocably buried in the columns of the local newspaper, in an article describing the house and choice possessions of our public-spirited citizen, etc. . . . . After that it is periodically resurrected for church fairs or in the dog days, when journalistic "copy" is wanted, and may in the end be fortunate enough to find a permanent abiding place in an historical society whose rules prohibit its being copied. Here it will vie with eternity in undisturbed rest.[5]

The art and the hobby of collecting American manuscripts today has many more devotees than when it was begun in the middle of the nineteenth century by T. A. Emmet, W. B. Sprague, J. B. Thacher, Simon Gratz, and Israel Tefft. These pioneer collectors established the great tradition which is still being followed. They also laid the foundation for the institutional collections of manuscript Americana, to which scholars are so deeply indebted.[6]

The founders of manuscript collecting in America were men of similar background and interest, for the most part middle-class professional men with sufficient wealth and time to indulge their love for the past. For example, Dr. Thomas A. Emmet of Washington and New York spent his adult life and over $200,000 in building four of the first sets of the "Signers" of

[4] A. Edward Newton, *The Amenities of Book-Collecting and Kindred Affections* (Boston, 1918), 107ff.; W. D. Orcutt, *In Quest of the Perfect Book: Remembrances and Reflections of a Bookman* (Boston, 1926), 273–300.

[5] Worthington C. Ford, "Archives and Manuscripts," in American Historical Association, *Report* (1913), 77.

[6] Simon Gratz, *A Book About Autographs* (Philadelphia, 1920), 82–89, 170–186.

the Declaration of Independence.[7] He also is credited with saving countless manuscripts from destruction and the waste paper mill during the dislocations and paper shortages of the Civil War.[8] In like manner, Dr. William E. Sprague of Albany, New York, amassed the largest single collection in America of miscellaneous autographs and manuscripts from the colonial and Revolutionary eras. The enthusiasm of Dr. Sprague infected, in turn, the Savannah merchant, Israel K. Tefft, who built a smaller but parallel collection of manuscripts of the colonial and Revolutionary South. Another merchant, Robert Gilmore of Baltimore, exhibited the greatest perception of future values of all of the early collectors, and a Cincinnati banker, Louis J. Cist, built a collection second only to that of Dr. Sprague in size and significance.[9]

The special appeal of the manuscripts of American men of letters has helped to balance the childish sense of values attached to such arbitrary collections as sets of the "Signers." As the substantial American literary tradition has lengthened, the autographs of its members have become more desirable. The papers of Edgar Allen Poe, for example, combine the elements of inherent and associative value, rarity, and market value. Manuscripts of such literati often reflect the eccentricities of their genius, such as Lafcadio Hearn's letters in purple ink on yellow paper, or Eugene Field's in India ink on Japanese paper, with illuminated initials, marginal notes, and text in a draftsman's hand. While not artistically beautiful, and rather commonly available, the letters of Mark Twain are valued for their saltiness of expression. Of a completely different taste but equally delightful in their own merit are the letters of the great American historians of the last century, W. H. Prescott, Francis Parkman, and John Fiske.[10]

The focus of all of the early collections was colonial and Revo-

[7] Approximately forty complete sets of "Signers" are in existence. The extreme scarcity of the autographs of some of the more obscure signers, such as those of Thomas Lynch, Jr., of South Carolina and Button Gwinnett of Georgia, has driven the price to the level of $25,000 to $50,000. See, Thomas F. Madigan, *Word Shadows of the Great* (New York, 1930), 104–128.

[8] Benjamin, *Autographs*, 222; Richard Maass, "Collecting Manuscripts: By Private Collectors," in *Library Trends*, 5:330–331 (January, 1957).

[9] Madigan, *Word Shadows of the Great*, 22–23.

[10] *Ibid.*, 177–202.

lutionary America, for, by the middle of the nineteenth century, the men of these periods represented at once the romance and the stabilizing influence of the nation's past. The Revolutionary political leaders were especially valued because they were so literate and wrote in such quantity. Some of the less literate military heroes, like General Israel Putman, Colonel Ethan Allen, and Captain John Paul Jones, wrote less, and the collection of their manuscripts merely added a filip of luxury to a sport of the wealthy. In contrast, the Civil War was fought by virtual unknowns, who generated no significant contemporary collecting interest in their manuscripts.[11]

The activity of the collectors of the nineteenth century led to the age of the super-collectors, J. Pierpont Morgan and Henry E. Huntington. The result of untold expenditures, the Morgan collection became one of the greatest in the world, and the magnificence of the Huntington collection can be approached only with reverence.

J. P. Morgan, who began to collect manuscripts as a boy of fourteen in 1851, was encouraged by his father, Junius, who also collected assorted literary curiosities. The younger Morgan pursued his interest while in school in Germany, becoming devoted to Medieval and Renaissance materials but devoting some space in his collection to American manuscripts as well. Included from an early stage was the inevitable set of the "Signers."[12]

By contrast, Huntington was a more impetuous collector who, determined to please himself and impress scholars, bought up entire collections of manuscripts in Europe and America. Huntington retired early to indulge his interest and converted most of his fortune into prime research material for the history of England and the United States. In all his collecting, Huntington's activity was marked by specialization, decisiveness, foresight, and a rugged independence.[13]

The leading contemporary collectors of manuscript Americana continue to follow—on a somewhat reduced scope and scale—in these giant footsteps. Men like A. C. Goodyear of Buffalo and

---

[11] *Ibid.*, 78–103.

[12] F. B. Adams, Jr., "The Morgans as Autograph Collectors," in *Autograph Collectors' Journal*, 2, no. 4:2–7 (July, 1950).

[13] Robert O. Schad, "Henry Edwards Huntington," in *Autograph Collector's Journal*, 2, no. 4:15–19 (July, 1950).

Lloyd W. Smith of New York, John W. Garrett of Baltimore, Frederick S. Peck of Providence, and Robert C. Norton of Cleveland carry on the tradition by specializing in the manuscripts of the Civil War, the Presidents, and the miltary and naval heroes since the Revolution.[14] The specialization of these collectors is a result of the rising prices of manuscripts, and their principal problem is the ultimate disposition of their collections. At this juncture, other collectors and dealers, historians, the Internal Revenue Service, and institutional repositories all wait upon the harried collector and influence his decision.

Some of the prize manuscript collections in America were offered for sale in the 1920's, when a rising market brought many a collection out of the vault into the auction room. The larger auctions included the William F. Gable sale in 1925 (representing over forty years of active collecting), the James H. Manning sale in Albany in 1926, and the Jerome Kern sale in 1928–1929. Since the 1920's, permanent preservation of collections intact through deposit or gift in a repository rather than dispersal through sale has been emphasized. Among the results of the constant removal of manuscripts from the market have been rising prices, increased competition, elimination of the general collector, and the rise of the specialist collector. Correspondingly, the dealer has become more selective in serving his discriminating clients.[15]

There are today about a dozen exclusive manuscript dealers in the United States, perhaps again as many as in the rest of the world. In addition, several hundred antiquarian bookdealers handle manuscripts as a sideline. American manuscripts obviously are most likely to be found in the stocks of domestic dealers, but British, Dutch, Danish, Austrian, French and German dealers also engage in an active commerce in American materials. Whether from domestic or foreign dealers, sales are advertised by catalog on a "first ordered, first served" basis. Quoted prices are not subject to negotiation; cash with the order is expected from new customers; credit may be extended to established customers. In any case, since full contents of the manuscripts are rarely given in catalog descriptions, sales are

[14] Madigan, *Word Shadows of the Great,* 29–30.
[15] *Ibid.,* 28–30.

always upon approval. Because only a fraction of a dealer's stock is listed in any given catalog, collectors are expected to register their particular interests with dealers.[16]

At times, collectors have the opportunity to purchase manuscripts directly or at auctions. Generally, however, they prefer to buy through a dealer, cheerfully paying his mark-up as compensation for the protection and services he offers. In direct purchases, collectors have found that they are likely to be asked to offer a price, which is then played off against other offers. At public auctions, generally conducted by firms specializing in old books, collectors usually prefer to engage the services of a dealer, who for 10 per cent of the bid price undertakes to secure the material at a fair price and to guarantee its authenticity.[17] Neophytes are well advised to purchase only from reputable dealers and to rely upon the guidance of a dealer in building a collection.[18]

The crucial and varied role played by manuscript dealers has given rise to some concern regarding conflicts of interests.[19] To minimize these conflicts, several efforts have been made to establish codes of fair practice relating to traffic in manuscripts. One such code now widely observed seeks to secure mutual and professional respect between dealers and purchasers of manuscripts, but historical considerations do not as yet play a major role in the determination of what constitutes fair practice.[20]

To facilitate communication between manuscript dealers and collectors, a code of abbreviations has been devised and is used in all American and British catalogs and manuscript descriptions. Under the code, "A" denotes "autograph," or a holograph writing, the whole being in the personal hand of the author. "L" means "letter" in the usual personal or business sense; "D" is a "document," a non-letter, a writing of some legal or commercial purpose. "N" means a "note," similar to but shorter than a full letter. "Ms" refers to a writing in manuscript form, of an unknown hand or some amanuensis other

[16] Maass, "Collecting Manuscripts," 330–336.
[17] *Ibid.*, 332–333.
[18] Benjamin, *Autographs*, 72–86; Charnwood, *Autograph Collection*, 27.
[19] Duniway, "Conflicts in Collecting," 55–63.
[20] American Library Association, "A Code of Fair Practice," in *Manuscripts*, 10:63–65 (Spring, 1958).

than the author of the writing; "S" refers to a writing in a hand other than that of the author but carrying the signature of the author attesting its genuineness and authenticity. "MOC" refers, of course, to a "Member of the Continental Congress." These abbreviations and similar ones in combination thus convey precise information as to the nature and category of individual manuscripts. An ALS is, therefore, an Autograph Letter Signed (an entire holograph in the hand of the author); LS is a Letter Signed (a typescript or transcribed letter, with only the signature in the hand of the author), and so forth.[21]

Establishment of price levels for manuscripts in the United States has proceeded according to its own rationale, and an acquaintance with it is necessary on the part of scholars who also have interests in such material. Although the scholar might prefer to take a hard-boiled approach to the commercial evaluation of manuscripts, relating commercial value to historical utility only,[22] such a simple formula has been found inadequate by those who invest in the literary remains of the past. More complex formulae take into account such factors as intrinsic value, dealer cost at wholesale, guarantee of authenticity, pleasure of ownership, and the operation of the principle of supply and demand. One subjective scheme for assigning market value to manuscripts places emphasis, in order of descending importance, upon the identity of the creator, condition of the material, intrinsic and associative interest of the contents, length of the writing, and date.[23]

Other theorists of the market value of manuscripts have suggested other formulae for evaluation. One such stresses the following factors in descending order: historical context or content; fame of the author of the writing; rarity of the writing; and physical condition.[24] It may be noted that such a formula emphasizes most heavily the factors subject to frequent and wide shifts in opinion. Another formula stresses the following factors

---

[21] Benjamin, *Autographs,* 16–28; Hamilton, *Collecting Autographs and Manuscripts,* 240–241.

[22] Paul M. Angle, "Evaluating Historical Manuscripts," in *Autograph Collectors' Journal,* 3, no. 4:27–29 (July, 1951).

[23] Mary A. Benjamin, "Price vs. Value: What the Collector Pays," in *The Collector,* 64:49–53 (March, 1951); Gratz, *Book About Autographs,* 21–25.

[24] Maass, "Collecting Manuscripts," 335–336.

in descending order: length of life of the author (as a rough gauge of his production of manuscripts) ; volume of production; inherent or associative interest in the person and the writing; and human interest in the writing.[25] Attempts to be more objective and statistical in constructing theories of manuscript values have produced formulae which assign to the function of demand 40 per cent of the value; to contents, 25 per cent; to rarity, 20 per cent; and to condition, 15 per cent.[26]

It would appear that all of the suggested formulae, subjective as well as objective, are rationales of the prevailing price levels rather than determinants of them. It appears also that manuscript prices are largely determined by the levels established at wholesale auctions and supported at retail by what buyers are willing to pay. The wide discrepancy between auction prices and reported retail prices may be explained by the unpredictability of auction prices and by the customary retail mark-up of 100 per cent. As in all free markets, competition determines value, and, to protect themselves from inequitable competition, institutional collectors generally prefer to buy only upon fixed prices.[27]

Manuscript collections are rarely evaluated as a lot but are cumulatively evaluated piece by piece, the key being the putative value of a single, representative ALS from the hand of a single author. Other categories of manuscripts from the same creator are scaled down proportionally to the value of the key ALS. For example, for an average collection originating prior to 1900, in the days before the typewriter and multiple reproduction of copies, an ALS of "average" supply and demand, rarity, contents, length, condition, date, and association might be worth about $4.00 at retail. On that basis, an ADS or ANS from the same source would be worth about 75 per cent, or $3.00. A manuscript designated an LS from the same source would be worth about 50 per cent that of an ALS, or about $2.00, while a DS would be evaluated at only 25 per cent, or about

[25] Charnwood, *Autograph Collection*, 38–53.

[26] Madigan, *Word Shadows of the Great*, 249–250.

[27] Mary A. Benjamin, "Price Versus Value: What the Dealer Pays," in *The Collector*, 64:97–100 (May, 1951), and 64:121–125 (June, 1951); Mary A. Benjamin, "The Manuscript Market and the Library," in *Manuscripts*, 8:30 (Fall, 1955).

$1.00.[28] Variation of any of the assumed circumstances or conditions could sharply influence the above examples.

As examples of how theory and principles of manuscript evaluation have been translated into specific market values, some cases of values of American presidential manuscripts may be enlightening.[29]

The first two Presidents were as unlike holographically as personally. George Washington's pen was prolific; from it flowed thousands of letters and documents in a characteristically unwavering, fluent, symmetrical, and prim style, invariably inscribed "Go. Washington." Such a single ALS is worth upwards of $350, and LS are priced from $200 up. A Washington DS sells from $150 up. John Adams' autographs, on the other hand, are rather scarce considering the forty years he spent in public life. His hand was plain, somewhat labored, and very legible. Representative ALS of Adams are quoted from $150 up, LS from $50 up, and DS from $50 up.

The autograph of Thomas Jefferson is common in all forms, witness to the active production of writings and the near complete preservation of them. Jefferson's small, very legible hand, which often eschewed punctuation and capitals but which conveyed sparkling gems of thought and expression, is very plentiful. ALS are valued at $75 up, LS at $35 up, and DS at $20.

James Madison has also left posterity many examples of his small, angular, easily-read hand. His handwriting, like the man, was not given to flourish or affectation. During his later years many of Madison's letters were written by his wife, Dolley. Madison's ALS are quoted from $35 up, LS from $20 up, and DS from $10, all fairly plentiful to common.

The manuscripts of James Monroe are also very common. Samples of his compact and rugged hand are available in ALS for $25, LS for $15, and DS for $10.

The small, round, regular, pre-Spencerian hand of John Quincy Adams is also plentiful in all forms. A charming idiosyncrasy of Adams was the incorporation of quoted poems in many of

---

[28] Benjamin, *Autographs*, 34–54.

[29] The following information and quotations are all derived from Madigan, *Word Shadows of the Great*, 271–290. The values are those of 1929, but they are not significantly out of date at this printing.

his letters for effect and to give point to his already facile expression. His ALS sell for $35 up, LS from $15, and DS from $10.

Andrew Jackson characterized himself in his crude, bold hand, his hasty yet legible scrawl spattered with irregular spellings but strong, masculine expression. Examples of his calligraphy are fairly plentiful and are further devaluated by his practice of delegating the power of signature to many clerks during his tenure in the White House. Jackson ALS are worth $35 up, LS $15 up, and DS from $10.

Jackson's protégé, Martin Van Buren, communicated in an unattractive, free-running scrawl, which never improved, and he had little felicity of expression. Van Buren's manuscripts, more voluminous after he retired from the Presidency, are common in all forms and are quoted at $20 for ALS, $10 for LS, and $10 for DS.

William Henry Harrison wrote infrequently and in a rough, virile hand much like Jackson's. His autograph is scarce in all forms and is worth about $100 in ALS, $75 in LS, and $50 in DS. His successor, John Tyler, was another sort of man, as revealed in his small, round, careful, prim hand. His manuscripts are scarce, but lack of popular interest has kept the price of his ALS to about $25, LS to $10, and DS also to $10.

For many years the letters and times of James K. Polk were relatively neglected, but a recent revival of interest in the doctrine of Manifest Destiny has made for a more active market in Polk materials. They appear in a small, scrupulous, almost decorative and embellished, somewhat artificial hand. Scarce in all forms, Polk ALS are worth about $50, LS about $25, and DS about $25.

The autograph of Zachary Taylor is among the rarest of the presidential series, largely because he wrote little and because few examples have survived. His manuscripts, characterized by a heavy hand, often spattered with excess ink, are valued in ALS at about $150, in LS from $75, and DS from $50. In contrast, the hand of Millard Fillmore is clear, straight-forward, legible, with no eccentricities, but his correspondence is generally without any special content interest. Plentiful in all forms, ALS are quoted at $15, LS from $10, and DS at about $10.

Franklin Pierce's handwriting, unlike the man, is characterized by flourish and ostentation, by prominent vertical strokes, rather than moderation and evenness. His ALS are available from $20, LS from $10, and DS from $10, all moderately plentiful.

The bachelor President, James Buchanan, had a most attractive script—legible, graceful, usually conveying interesting contents. However, Buchanan was so prolific that there hardly exists a market for his writings. ALS are worth $10, LS are available at $5, and DS at the same price.

Abraham Lincoln, who signed himself "A. Lincoln" on all save public documents, wrote in a rugged, virile, unpretentious hand which suggests his strength and simplicity. Prolific in writing, although terse in expression, Lincoln created a vast amount of paper, but an insatiable demand for even the least scrap associated with him has driven the price of Lincoln writing to inflated heights. ALS are quoted at $250, LS at $100, ADS at $150, and DS at $75. All forms are moderately plentiful, but they are snapped up by eager collectors whenever offered for sale.

Andrew Johnson, who learned to write after reaching manhood, was never completely comfortable with the pen and wrote little, in a labored and angular hand. His son, Andrew Johnson, Jr., who had a remarkably similar hand, served as his father's secretary and even today deludes uninitiated manuscript collectors. Johnson's ALS are worth about $150, his LS about $35 up, and his DS about $20. The first category is very rare, the second moderately plentiful, and the third plentiful.

Ulysses S. Grant has left few pre-war letters, and they are very rare today. The necessities of war caused Grant to write many letters and reports during those years, making the manuscripts less valuable than his earlier production, and the decline of epistolary efforts as President and in retirement again makes the latter more valuable. His free-flowing, angular hand is quite legible and void of ostentation and flourish. On the average, Grant's ALS are worth $35, his LS $15, and DS about $10. All forms are sufficiently plentiful to meet the demand of collectors.

Rutherford B. Hayes's small, scratchy, somewhat feminine hand is perhaps the most plentiful of all presidential autographs. He corresponded extensively; most of his letters have been preserved; and he has not been accorded widespread popular interest. Hence, all forms of Hayes's writing are very common. ALS are nominally worth about $10, LS about $5, and DS about $5.

President James A. Garfield was served by a secretary who was an expert at duplicating his employers's handwriting, even to the characteristic of running certain words together. Therefore, the identification of Garfield autographs is a task best left to experts. The genuine examples are moderately scarce and are worth $35 in ALS, $20 in LS, and $20 in DS.

A bold, open style, with strong shading and a delicate touch, characterizes the hand of Chester A. Arthur. He rarely wrote a long personal letter, but there are multiples of official documents bearing his signature as Port Collector of New York. Arthur's ALS, very scarce, are worth about $75. LS and DS, both plentiful, are worth $15 and $10, respectively.

Grover Cleveland, one of the most masculine of the Presidents, wrote in a small, delicate, almost feminine script—but the contents of his writings removed any doubt as to the sex of the author! Cleveland continued to write voluminously well into his old age, and all forms of his autograph are common. Cleveland's ALS sell for $25, LS for $10, and DS from $10.

The personal reserve of Benjamin Harrison is readily apparent in his letters, written in a script very similar to Cleveland's, but somewhat heavier. Harrison seldom wrote, and then only briefly and with great restraint. His ALS, somewhat scarce, is worth about $40, his LS, rather plentiful, is worth about $10, while his DS, moderately scarce, is worth $15.

William McKinley was the first President regularly to use the typewriter in his correspondence. When found, letters in his own hand are vigorous and forceful in appearance, and in ALS are worth about $100. More plentiful are McKinley's LS and DS, worth $10 and $15, respectively.

The typewriter did not intimidate Theodore Roosevelt; rather, he used it in his own inimical way. Although his letters are typewritten, they also carry so many hand corrections and marginal notes that they border upon holographs; the inscriptions are scrawled in a sprawling, immature style almost like shorthand. This very popular President left more than 150,000 letters, each of them an extension of his vibrant personality, just the sort of material which most attracts manuscript collectors. Roosevelt's ALS are worth about $50, LS about $10, and DS about $20.

The legacy of William Howard Taft is pale in comparison with Roosevelt's. Taft's neat, orderly hand produced but a few holograph letters. When available, they sell for $100 in ALS. More plentiful are LS and DS, available at $10 and $20, respectively.

First honors in presidential calligraphy go to Woodrow Wilson, who wrote in his own hand but few letters, but who personally typed thousands of them. Hence, a holograph Wilson letter is scarce, usually bringing over $150 in ALS. Typed LS and printed DS are much more common, usually selling for $15 to $20.

Warren G. Harding was never liberal with his pen, and when used, it produced hastily written, careless, and illegible screed. There are few Harding ALS, and they bring prices of over $250 when offered for sale. DS are also relatively rare, worth about $35. More plentiful are Harding's LS, valued at about $20.

A very fine pen, a scratchy, large scrawl filling a sheet with only a few words very difficult to decipher is the holographic hallmark of Calvin Coolidge. Never really attractive or legible, Coolidge's hand became even more difficult in his old age. His ALS are scarce and worth over $100, LS are more plentiful and worth about $20, and DS are relatively scarce, worth about $20.

The handwriting of Herbert Hoover is graceful and legible—and moderately plentiful. ALS sell for about $100, LS for about $20, DS for about the same amount. Franklin D. Roosevelt is instantly recognized by the bold, broad strokes of his stubby pen, but his famous signature was also skillfully duplicated by a number of personal secretaries, even on such items as personal checks. The number of Roosevelt letters is truly staggering, but the ALS are sufficiently rare to command prices in excess of $100. More plentiful LS and DS are available for $10 to $15.

It is very difficult to obtain a full holograph of Presidents Truman, Eisenhower, Kennedy, or Johnson, so that fair market values for such material can hardly be said to have been established as yet. Experience indicates that recipients of these contemporary letters hesitate to sell them, and it will probably be a generation before these autographs become articles of commerce.[30]

---

[30] Hamilton, *Collecting Autographs and Manuscripts*, 85.

American manuscript collectors and historians are less plagued by forged and spurious manuscripts than are collectors and students of older, European nations. The most famous of a handful of forgers was Robert Spring (1813–1876), an Englishman who opened a bookshop in Philadelphia about 1858. To fill the lively demand for autographs of Washington and Franklin, Spring slipped into the black art of copying original holographs, using paper and ink of the correct age and type, and selling the product outside the country as the genuine article. During the Civil War, Spring met the British interest in southern autographs by turning out scores of fake "Stonewall Jacksons." Only by overreaching himself was Spring finally exposed. His plausible forgeries are still available, and they are now collected in their own right.[31]

As recently as 1928–1929, the *Atlantic Monthly* and a number of Lincoln scholars were taken in by forged and supposedly recently-discovered love letters of Lincoln to Ann Rutledge. Paul M. Angle exposed the hoax in April, 1929, to the mortification of those who had been duped by the clever trick. Even more recently, Raymond Moley reported in 1939 the existence during the 1932 presidential campaign of two Roosevelt "letter-writing mills" in Albany and New York City, which produced letters of acknowledgement and forged the Democratic candidate's signature. The practice was supposed to have been curbed when Roosevelt entered the White House in 1933, but it is common knowledge that private secretaries continued to sign the President's name to a wide variety of manuscript material.[32] Signature by proxy apparently is a practice which future manuscript collectors and historians will have to accept as routine.

Other examples of forgery and duplication of manuscripts are more difficult to categorize according to authenticity. One such famous example is the letter written by Lincoln to Governor Michael Hahn of Louisiana after the state had been occupied.

[31] Madigan, *Word Shadows of the Great*, 63–66; Storm and Peckham, *Book Collecting*, 239; Wilfred Partington, *Forging Ahead: The True Story of the Upward Progress of Thomas James Wise, Prince of Book Collectors, Bibliographer Extraordinary and Otherwise* (New York, 1941), 1–7; Gratz, *Book About Autographs*, 64–68. For an interesting example of forged documents and their influence upon written history, see John C. Fitzpatrick, "The George Washington Scandals," in *Scribner's Magazine*, 81:389–395 (April, 1927).
[32] Storm and Peckham, *Book Collecting*, 239.

Hahn had the letter lithographed for distribution to his friends, and copies continue to turn up to this day. The reproductions are so skillfully done that an expert is required to distinguish the copies from the original. On other occasions, copies have been made of official documents, all of the copies presumably having equal authenticity and authority. For example, about a dozen original copies were made of General Order No. 9 from Lee to the Army of Northern Virginia. All of the copies are identical, and all were signed by the General. Who can say which is the original and which are the copies?[33]

TAX CONSIDERATIONS

A MANUSCRIPT COLLECTOR desiring to dispose of the treasures so lovingly brought together is faced essentially with only four alternatives, all of them admixtures of sentimental and thoroughly practical considerations. First, the collector may break up his collection and give his manuscripts to interested parties, up to a maximum of $3,000 of market valuation per year. But the translation of prize manuscripts into market values may wrench the soul of a sensitive collector, and the dispersal of a collection will surely sicken the soul of the historian. Second, the collector may will his manuscripts to an heir—who may well be indifferent to their values. Third, in discharge of the obligations of sentiment or in order to escape taxation, the collector may present his manuscripts to a scholarly institution. Fourth, the collector or his executor may order the material sold at auction in order to liquidate the estate.[34] One needs only to recall that the William L. Clements collection was evaluated at $265,000 prior to its presentation to the University of Michigan in 1935 to be reminded that such decisions can have serious economic as well as academic consequences.[35]

Manuscript collectors and prospective donors are not unmindful of the tax considerations involved in disposing of this cate-

[33] Madigan, *Word Shadows of the Great*, 72–77.
[34] Colton Storm, *et al.*, "What to Do With My Collection," in *Manuscripts*, 5:16–17 (Summer, 1953).
[35] Charles E. Goodspeed, *Yankee Bookseller* (Boston, 1937), 186.

gory of property. Manuscripts, like money and other valuables, can be donated in order to reduce federal income, estate, and gift taxes. The greatest advantages are to be had when the taxpayer gives property which has appreciated in value, such as manuscripts held for a considerable period, because the appreciation counts in the allowable deduction but is not subject to income taxation.[36]

Under existing federal internal revenue statutes and regulations, individuals may reduce their taxes by disposing of money or valuables of up to 20 per cent of their adjusted gross income, with an additional 10 per cent allowed for gifts to churches, schools, hospitals, and certain medical research organizations. For corporations, the maximum deductible gifts may not exceed 5 per cent of its gross income. Estates and trusts are under no limitations whatever as to the amount of money or valuables they many donate to allowable charities and educational organizations. Practically speaking, therefore, individuals may dispose of manuscripts worth up to 30 per cent of their gross income each year and thereby significantly reduce their income tax liability. They may dispose of even greater values by spreading the gift over a number of years.[37] The difficulty in taking advantage of this provision of the law is the necessity of placing equitable valuations upon a category of property which does not have a ready market and which may have potential and unrealized value far in excess of the nominal value the market may now assign. The intent of the law is not to support scholarly research but to discourage tax evasion.[38]

Even more troublesome than the general problem of evaluation of manuscripts for tax purposes is that of evaluating those of recent origin, which have greater research value than open market value. Whereas it is quite clear that the intent of the law is to make tax evaluation the same as market value, or what a "willing buyer and a willing seller" would agree to be fair price, scholars and manuscript repositories effectively argue that the general rule is not applicable to contemporary materials. For such material there is generally no willing buyer, but his-

[36] Charles L. B. Loundes, "Tax Advantages of Charitable Gifts," in *Virginia Law Review*, 46:409–412 (April, 1960).

[37] *Ibid.*, 394–408.

[38] Mearns, "Historical Manuscripts," 320.

torical considerations may make the material virtually priceless, albeit in the future. The Bureau of Internal Revenue operates on the basis of accepting the legitimacy of such nonmarket evaluations, but challenges those which it feels to be excessive.[39] The resulting uncertainty and the threat of challenge is relied upon to keep most donors honest, but repositories and donors also are the poorer. The donation of manuscripts as deductions against taxable income and the resulting tax savings have without doubt saved countless manuscripts from destruction, but only at the high cost of questioning the legal and ethical considerations involved.[40]

The Bureau of Internal Revenue is properly skeptical of high values placed on contemporary manuscripts with no or only nominal market values. In a recent case it accepted two anonymous expert evaluations characterizing a modern collection as "practically worthless," even though scholarly considerations placed a relatively high evaluation on the material.[41] When such a deduction is challenged, imputing the integrity of the scholars and the agency making the evaluation, donors are understandably wary thereafter in trusting scholarly evaluations. Tax collectors, recognizing that all such evaluations are necessarily highly subjective, seem inclined to place greater trust in those made by wholly disinterested third parties, an attitude

[39] For purposes of establishing fair market value for tax purposes, prior litigation or incontestable documentary evidence enjoys highest priority. Evidence of expert witnesses may be relied upon to establish objective facts, and the opinion of a panel of experts is accorded *prima facie* standing. However, in all cases where the government's *prima facie* case can be overturned, the taxpayer's own evaluation must be deemed conclusive. See Cullers v. Commissioner, 237 F (2d) 611 (8th Cir. 1956). Where both sides rely upon expert testimony, courts tend to establish a compromise value. See Emanuel L. Gordon, "Valuation Techniques," in *New York University Institute on Federal Taxation Proceedings*, 17:73–86 (1959).

[40] William C. Marten, "Hanging Together: The Problem of Evaluating Manuscript Collections for Tax Deductions," (unpublished research paper, 1961, in the possession of the present author), 1–3. Marten refers to an interview with Dr. Leslie H. Fishel, Director, The State Historical Society of Wisconsin, March 21, 1961; and William S. Dix, Librarian of Princeton University to Marten, March 29, 1961; and Verner W. Clapp, President, Council on Library Resources, Inc., to Marten, March 28, 1961.

[41] At least one scholar agrees that much contemporary documentation is without discernible historical value. He has observed that many personal diaries, especially, prove "only that their authors were semi-literate, people devoid of both imagination and the power of observation." Angle, "Evaluating Historical Manuscripts," 27–29.

which has encouraged a new and profitable sideline activity on the part of manuscript dealers.[42]

Manuscript repositories which stand to benefit from donations of contemporary materials have adopted various means of adjusting to the policy of the Internal Revenue Service. For example, the University of Southern California and Stanford University pay annual retainer fees to an autograph dealer for appraisals of prospective manuscript donations. Princeton, on the other hand, refers all prospective donors to a competent dealer of the donor's own choosing for an independent evaluation. Other agencies calculate the cost of repairing, restoring, cataloging, and processing material as the basis of value when a fair market value cannot be determined. Another library decided that its own staff could evaluate contemporary manuscripts just as accurately as the three "outside" experts who evaluated the same collection as $10,000, $20,000, and $37,500.[43]

The confusion surrounding the tax evaluation of modern manuscripts could be clarified by the bureau were it to extend the analogies of rare books and art objects to manuscripts,[44] but the bureau, in line with long-standing policy, does not issue general advisory rulings. Friendly law suits are discouraged by the federal courts, and few repositories wish to become involved in the legal process even if a suit could be framed. To end this game played between the bureau and the collectors, agencies, and scholars interested in manuscripts, Dr. Alice E. Smith, of the staff of the State Historical Society of Wisconsin, in 1959 proposed a conference of leading manuscript specialists to consider the adoption of uniform appraisal practices and the drafting of a code of policy for Internal Revenue Service approval. To date, the proposal has failed to bear fruit for lack of funds and support among the interested parties.[45]

The co-operative approach suggested by Dr. Smith has much merit, for even the traditional evaluation of contemporary manuscripts by a disinterested dealer may not be applicable or equitable. One such dealer has commented: "Such large accumula-

---

[42] Marten, "Hanging Together," 3–4.

[43] *Ibid.*, 4–5.

[44] Ad Hoc Committee, "A Library Policy for Gift Appraisal," in *Manuscripts*, 13:56–57 (Winter, 1961).

[45] Marten, "Hanging Together," 5–7.

tions [of contemporary manuscripts] may require a greater expenditure than the dealer wishes to undertake since they generally cover only one period in history and include large quantities of unimportant and duplicated items written by a small group of people." In addition, since dealers generally charge from 2 to 5 per cent of the assessment for the preparation of their appraisal, there is some temptation to push the evaluation as high as can be substantiated. Furthermore, there is some confusion between the "market value" and "retail value" of manuscripts, and scholars insist that dealers are not necessarily equipped to assign market values to manuscripts which do not have a ready retail market at any price.[46]

A co-operative approach to the problem of tax evaluation of manuscripts would assure that other factors beyond the actual market value would receive consideration, and there are some leading precedents for such consideration being accorded. It has been clearly recognized that the test of fair market value is not always applicable, that in rare and exceptional cases the property in question may have no fair market value yet have an allowable value to a significant degree. The rule in such cases is that the allowable or nominal value must reasonably approximate what the market would theoretically establish as its value if such a market existed. Obviously, in such cases the opinion of experts is crucial, and their reasoning for stating their conclusions must be adduced in order to guarantee reasonable objectivity.[47]

The principle and precedent of the tax evaluation of good will could perhaps offer another approach to the problem of evaluating contemporary manuscripts. Good will—the presumption that customers will continue to come back to the same place of business—can certainly be accorded a tangible value.

[46] *Ibid.*, 9; Robert F. Metzdorf, "Manuscript Collecting for Historical Societies," in *Manuscripts*, 9:56–61 (Winter, 1957); Walter R. Benjamin, "Appraisals," in *The Collector*, 55:59 (March, 1941).

[47] Thomas N. Tarleau, "Tax Problems in the Valuation of Property," in *Taxes*, 25:520–524 (June, 1947). See also, Sections 29.44–4 and 29.111-1, Regulations 111 of the IRS, and Helvering v. Waldbridge, 293 U. S. 594 and 70 F. (2d) 683 (2d Cir. 1934). For further discussion and cases on the substantive rule of fair market value applied to items for which there is no market, see Whitlow v. Comm'r., 82 F. (2d) 568 (8th Cr. 1936); First Seattle Dexter Horton Nat. Bank, 27 B. T. A. 1242 (1933), off'd., 77 F. (2d) 45 (9th Cir. 1935), and Emanuel L. Gordon, "What is Fair Market Value?" in *Tax Law Review*, 8:44 (November, 1952).

Hence, by extension, presumptive future value can be assessed for tax purposes even though the burden of proof is upon the donor. The test question in evaluating intangible good will is: "What would a buyer willing to buy at a fair price pay in cold, hard cash for it?"[48] Similarly, if the same principle were applied to modern manuscripts: "What would a buyer, if he existed, willing to buy at a fair price, pay in cold, hard cash for this collection of manuscripts?"

Yet another approach to the establishment of allowable evaluations of contemporary manuscripts may be made by analogy with the law of air rights above city property. In a gross simplification, it can be said that both contemporary manuscripts and air rights have no present market value, but they both have enormous potential future values, which must be partially anticipated as the basis of transfer and evaluation today. Thus, when the owners of a commercial lot and a two-storey building in downtown Tyler, Texas, donated to a charitable foundation the air rights for five stories above the building and claimed a $70,000 deduction, the claim was upheld, air rights being held to be property with a reasonably accurate ascertainable value.[49]

Whether the government would welcome and give credence to a uniform system of manuscript evaluation without an amendment in the existing law is a moot point. Under the existing Internal Revenue Code, whenever problems involving new applications of the law or questions of substance are raised, a taxpayer may request a Special Ruling from the Commissioner of Internal Revenue under Section 3760. No such ruling will be made if unnecessary in an individual case, if a ruling will affect any pending judicial determination of a related question, or if the ruling would seriously disadvantage the government.[50]

---

[48] Thomas M. Davies, "The Valuation of Good Will . . . ," in *Nebraska Law Review*, 31:560 (May, 1952).

[49] The case was Mattie Fair, 27 T. C. No. 106 (Feb. 27, 1957), quoted in an unsigned article, "Taxation—Charitable Deductions . . . Contribution of Right to Air Space . . . ," in *Virginia Law Review*, 43:738–740 (June, 1957). A chain of precedents support the recent tax decision: Piper v. Ekern, 180 Wis. 586, 194 N. W. 159 (1923); Pearson v. Matheson, 102 S. C. 377, 382, 86 S. E. 1063, 1065 (1915); and J. Morgan Wilson, 11 CCH Tax Ct. Mem. 159 (1952).

[50] David W. Richmond, "How and When to Obtain Bureau Rulings," in *Taxes*, 28:46 (January, 1950); Martine Lore, ed., "When Not to Apply for Advance Rulings From the Internal Revenue Service," in *Journal of Taxation*, 12:244 (April, 1960).

Until some workable and equitable formula is devised, those interested in the tax aspects of manuscripts evaluation will have to continue to play a game of blind man's bluff with the government.[51]

THE LAW OF LITERARY PROPERTY

THE IMPACT of the law upon the collection and disposition of manuscripts is of fairly recent development. More ancient and perhaps of greater significance is the bearing of the law of literary property upon the copying and use of manuscripts. The incidence of the law of literary property upon manuscripts can be observed in three distinct but closely related areas: the law of copyright under statute and common law; the distinction between the ownership of literary rights in the word patterns of a writing and the possession of the physical remains of that writing; and the distinction between private and public use under the law of copyright, whether at common or statute law.

Copyright law, or the legal and exclusive right to make copies of writings expressing an original concept or system of thought, goes back in the Anglo-American tradition to a tale of the sixth century. St. Columba is reputed to have made a copy of the Psalter loaned to him by his teacher, Abbot Finnian of Moville. The abbot protested, claiming that the copy of his property was likewise his own, and the matter was brought before the Irish King Diarmed. Judgment was rendered for the abbot on the principle, "To every cow her calf, and accordingly to every book its copy." Columba refused to accept the verdict, raised a band of followers to wage war on the king, was defeated, and was forced into exile. Following this putative tale of copyright infringement, almost 1,000 years were to elapse before the first authentic complaint was recorded of invasion of copyright in English law. In 1533 Wynkyn de Worde sued for the protection of his right to print a treatise on grammar against invasion by one Peter Trevers, who had issued an unauthorized edition of the same work in 1523.[52]

[51] Philip Zunet, ed., *The Law of Federal Income Taxation: Code Commentary* (Chicago, 1955, with supplements to 1960), Sub-chapter B, 204.
[52] Philip Wittenberg, *The Law of Literary Property* (Cleveland, 1957), 19, 22.

The same legal protection against unauthorized copying of manuscripts was extended to the scarce, printed books first imported from the Continent under Richard III. Under Henry VIII, in 1533, the privilege of importing printing was revoked in order to encourage domestic practice of the art. Thereafter, every pressrun was to be licensed, carrying with it the exclusive privilege to print the material so licensed, to be enforced by Stationer's Company of London. After the Reformation, enforcement of licensing and copyright was shifted to the Court of Star Chamber because of the obvious political connotations of the freedom of the press.

As literary property took on increased importance, English common law correspondingly recognized a number of its aspects. It became accepted that an author or his licensee enjoyed the exclusive right to publish or not to publish his own literary creations. If an author elected not to publish, his potential rights to exclusive publications were recognized to exist inviolate and in perpetuity. In addition, the meaning of publication was narrowly defined to exclude all distribution except the deliberate offering to the public of an original work. The net result of the early common law of literary property was probably greater protection for publishers than for authors. Authors were largely dependent upon the vigilance and political influence of their publishers for protection from infringement.[53]

The English law of copyright was further refined by an Act of Parliament of June, 1643, which prohibited publication of of any writing without the express consent of the author and, in effect, made the author responsible for policing the freedom of the press. When the Copyright Act expired in 1694, the Stationers vainly petitioned for reenactment and continued voluntarily to respect the right of copy in perpetuity. Continued agitation ultimately resulted in the new Statute of Anne of April 10, 1710. Under it, an author's ancient, common-law right of copy was recognized and coupled with the exclusive right of publication for a period of fourteen years, renewable for a second period of fourteen years.[54]

[53] Horace G. Ball, *The Law of Copyright and Literary Property* (Albany, 1944), 26–30.
[54] Wittenberg, *Law of Literary Property,* 23–49.

The conflict between common and statute law of copyright was compounded rather than resolved under the Statute of Anne, and the Stationers soon challenged the implied abolition of perpetual common-law right of copy by resort to the statutory law. In 1774, in Donaldson v. Beckett, the House of Lords decreed that authors had perpetual right of copy at common law, which was extinguished when appeal was made to the Statute of Anne. This was the English law of copyright which was imported into colonial America. By resolution of May 2, 1783, the Continental Congress recommended to the states that copyright protection be extended to literary property, and all of the states save Delaware adopted legislation modeled after the Statute of Anne.[55] A provision was inserted in the federal Constitution in 1787 which gave Congress the power "to promote the Progress of Science and useful Arts, by securing for limited Times to Authors and Inventors the exclusive Right to their respective Writings and Discoveries." (Art. I, Sec. 8). The first federal Congress passed a Copyright Act modeled after the Statute of Anne on May 3, 1790. The same question raised in Donaldson v. Beckett appeared again in the United States in 1834 in Wharton v. Peters, with the same result.[56]

Since 1790 the American law of copyright has been altered and amended by some fifty public acts. In 1802 it was extended to cover engravings, etchings, and prints; in 1831, to musical compositions. Also under the 1831 amendment the period of protection was extended to twenty-eight years, renewable for a like period. In 1856 the copyright law was extended to protect public performances of dramatic compositions, and in 1870 protection was extended to drawings, statues, models, and all other unspecified fine arts. Gaps in copyright coverage were still found to exist, and in 1882 the law was further amended to apply to such decorative articles as tiles, plaques, and the like. In 1891 American copyright protection was extended to any categories of literature and art produced by foreign nationals

---

[55] Ball, *Law of Copyright*, 30–37.

[56] Wittenberg, *Law of Literary Property*, 50–54; Ball, *Law of Copyright*, 470–472. For case law supporting the principle that common-law copyright is perpetual but statutory copyright is terminal, see Donaldson v. Beckett, 4 Burr 2408, 2 Bro PC 129; Wheaton v. Peters, 33 US 591, 8 L ed 1055; Palmer v. DeWitt, 47 NY 532; RCA Manufacturing Co. v. Whiteman, 114 F (2d) 86.

whose governments would extend the same protection to American art and literature on a reciprocal basis.[57]

Despite all of the modifications and refinements of American statute copyright law, the basic protection available and accorded to unpublished manuscripts remains that provided by the common law.[58] Under it, any creation of an author is regarded as property incorporeal and intangible, to whatever extent it is original. The exclusive right to the use and benefit of such property remains intact until the creator waives or claims his rights under the statute law. The property of the author does not exist in the physical paper but in the original pattern of expression. This principle gives rise to the vexing possibility of a given writing having two owners. Its creator, under the common law, continues to own the literary rights to the pattern of expression until he voluntarily extinguishes those rights. On the other hand, the physical remains of the writing, the paper and ink, may be owned by a second party, one who originally received the writing or who subsequently acquired it, but who literally owns nothing more than the paper on which the words are written.[59]

The distinction between common-law copyright protection and the corporeal property rights in unpublished manuscripts was perhaps most cogently expressed by a trial court in 1944:

[57] Wittenberg, *Law of Literary Property*, 55.

[58] Current regulations of the Copyright Office define an unpublished work as one eligible for registration under the Copyright Act but which, at the time of registration, "has not been printed or reproduced in copies for sale or been publicly distributed." See Ball, *Law of Copyright*, 129, 480–482.

[59] *Ibid.*, 474, 495–496, 497–498. Common-law copyright is purely incorporeal, distinct from the corporeal rights adhering to the paper upon which the copyrighted material is written or printed. See, Keene v. Wheatley, 14 Fed Cas 180; Dart v. Woodhouse, 40 Mich 399, 29 Am Rep 544; Paige v. Banks, 80 US 608, 20 L ed 709; Kartlander v. Bradford, 116 Misc 664, 190 NYS 311. Adverse possession of literary property, if continuously maintained for over thirty years, establishes a right of ownership: O'Neill v. General Film Co., 152 NYS 599; Hart v. Fox, 116 NYS 793. For at least two centuries courts in England and the United States have recognized and protected the right of authors of private and business letters, irrespective of literary merit, exclusively to publish or to prevent publication thereof, provided only that the letters do not serve some criminal ends: Thompson v. Stanhope, Ambler 337 (1774); Gee v. Pritchard, 2 Swanton 402; Rice v. Williams, 32 Fed 437; Knights of the Ku Klux Klan v. International Magazine Co., 294 Fed 661.

The property in the copy-right is regarded as a different
and distinct right, wholly detached from the manuscript,
or any other physical existence, and will not pass with the
manuscript unless included by express words in the transfer.[60]

Regarding manuscript property, a crucial question is: What
constitutes extinguishing a copyright under the common law?
The usual means of so doing is by publication, the deliberate
act of dedicating to public use a certain writing. To preclude
unintentional voiding of copyright, the courts have generally held
a rather strict rule of construction. In general, private circulation does not void a copyright. Rather, "to constitute publication there must be a dissemination of the work of art itself
among the public as to justify the belief that it took place with
the intention of rendering such work common property."[61]

One of the most celebrated of the American copyright cases
illustrates the application of the common law to unpublished
manuscript materials. In 1876 Samuel L. Clemens wrote and
offered to the *Atlantic Monthly* a manuscript called, "A Murder,
a Mystery and a Marriage." He proposed that other leading
authors of the day be enlisted to write variant concluding chapters, but nothing ever came of the scheme. The manuscript was
not among Clemens' papers at his death in 1910, but in 1945
it turned up at an auction sale in New York City and was purchased by a collector, Dr. Lew D. Feldman. Dr. Feldman requested permission from Mark Twain's estate to publish the
manuscript. When permission was refused, Dr. Feldman proceeded anyway on the basis of his ownership of the manuscript.
The Twain estate sued to restrain the publication, and the
trial court upheld its plea on the basis of common law.[62]

The copyright law which applied to the literary manuscripts
of Mark Twain would apply equally well to the ordinary letters
of Mark Twain or of an unknown citizen. Formerly, courts attempted to distinguish between ordinary letters and manuscripts
with some literary pretensions, but that practice has not been

---

[60] Brunner v. Stix, 181 SW 2: 643; see also Stephens v. Cody, Sp Ct. 530, 531
(1852); Ralph R. Shaw, *Literary Property in the United States* (Washington,
1950), 26–28.

[61] Wittenberg, *Law of Literary Property,* 59–70.

[62] *Ibid.,* 69–70.

attempted since 1848.[63] American practice recognizes only four occasions when the possession of a manuscript carries with it the right or duty to make public the contents without the consent of the author. First, the possessor of a writing other than his own may bring it into court voluntarily or in response to a summons and there offer it in evidence. Second, the government may publish letters received by it from authors, since the act of sending a writing to the corporate agent of society is tantamount to publication. Third, if a writing is produced for hire, the employer has full rights to publish the writing at will. Fourth, the recipient of a letter can publish it against the will of the author in vindication of character.[64] All other violations or infringements of the common-law copyright risk legal action by the creator or his heirs or assigns. The rule of descent of rights at common law in perpetuity has been explicitly stated a number of times in the Anglo-American legal tradition.[65]

It is well established that the receiver of a letter, by gift or by purchase, obtains ownership of every material thing connected with the writing—paper, ink, envelope, postage stamps, and postmark. Most of the usual attributes of ownership apply save that they may not be used to insinuate the right of publication and that they may not be sold in insolvency or bankruptcy proceedings. Conversely, the author of the letters has a legal right to secure copies of his writing, and the holder of the original or a copy is free to appropriate and use any ideas contained therein, short of publication.[66]

---

[63] Unsigned article, "Property Rights in Letters," in *Yale Law Journal*, 46:499–501 (January, 1937). For the cases, see, Wheaton v. Peters, 8 Pet. 591, 656 (U.S., 1834); Caliga v. Inter Ocean Newspaper Co., 215 US 182, 188 (1909).

[64] "Property Rights in Letters," 501–503. For the case law for category 1, see, Hopkinson v. Burghley, L. R. 2 Ch. 447 (1867). For category 2, see, Folsom v. Marsh, 9 Fed. Cas. No. 4901 at 347 (C.C. Mass., 1841). For category 3, see, Howard v. Gunn, 32 Beav. 462 (1863). For category 4, see, Wildemer v. Hubbard, 19 Phila. 263 (Common Pleas Pa. 1887); Roberts v. McKee, 29 Ga. 161, 164 (1859).

[65] "Property Rights in Letters," 504–505. See also, Baker v. Libbie, 210 Mass. 599, 97 N. E. 109 (1912); Thompson v. Stanhope, Amb. 337 (1774); Lytton v. Dewey, 54 L.J. [N. S.] Ch. 293 (1884); Philip v. Pennell, [1907] 2 Ch. 577; Cadell v. Stewart, 1 Bell's Com. 116n (Court Sessions Scotland, 1804).

[66] "Property Rights in Letters," 493–498; Ball, *Law of Copyright*, 497–498. For the case law on the rights of the recipient, see, Grigsby v. Breckinridge, 65 Ky. 480, 486, 493 (1867); Baker v. Libbie, 210 Mass. 599, 606, 97 N. E. 109, 112 (1912); Tefft v. Marsh, 1 W. Va. 38 (1864). For the rights of authors, see, Philip v.

On the other hand, it is equally well established that the author of a letter retains common-law copyright in the pattern of words, and that he may publish them at will, the receiver of the letter being powerless to prevent him. However, if the receiver of a letter is a government, it may interpose a bar to publication, but only for the protection of state secrets. The very act of general publication, whether or not done under the color of statute copyright law, extinguishes all common-law rights, and the literary property becomes "property of mankind."[67]

Most of the case law relating to common-law copyright in manuscripts has arisen from considerations of literary values inherent in them, but the similar considerations of legal and historical values justify the application of the same law to archival and manuscript materials. An early case involving an archival stray was adjudicated in 1863 when the collection of John Alden was sold. Among the items was an address from George Washington to the Mayor and Aldermen of the City of New York, dated May, 1785. The city sued to recover what it regarded as public property, and the Supreme Court of New York agreed:

> In the present action the letter was a particular and peculiar species of property. Its style, address and responsive character to a legislative act, should of itself be regarded as having imparted notice to all, that from the moment of its reception and sending it became the property of the corporation to whom it was addressed. . . . This letter, so written, in such terms, and so addressed, held Alden to constantly

---

Pennell [1907] 2 Ch. 577; Thompson v. Famous Players—Laski Corp., 3 F (2d) 707 (N. D. Ga. 1925). For editorial comment on Baker v. Libbie, see Goodspeed, *Yankee Bookseller*, 220–221. See also, Henry W. Rogers, "The Literary Property of Authors," in *Central Law Review*, 12:338. 17:268. Private or business letters are not taxable as personal or corporeal property: Leon Loan Abstract Co. v. Equilization Board, 86 Iowa 127, 53 NW 94; nor may letters be seized to satisfy creditors: Baker v. Libbie, 210 Mass. 599, 97 NE 109.

[67] "Property Rights in Letters," 498. For case law on authors' rights of publication, see, Palmer v. DeWitt, 47 N. Y. 532 (1872); Kartlander v. Bradford, 116 Misc. 664, 190 N. Y. Supp. 311 (Sup. Ct 1921). For receivers' incapacity to prevent publication, see, Folsom v. Marsh, 9 Fed Cas No. 4901 at 347 (C. C. Mass. 1841); Knights of Ku Klux Klan v. International Magazine Co., 294 Fed. 661 (C. C. A. 2d, 1923) For the rule of state secrecy, see, Folsom v. Marsh, *supra*. For extinguishing common-law copyright by invoking statutory protection, see, American Code Co. v. Bensinger, 282 Fed. 829 (C.C. A. 2d, 1922). See also, Melville Cane, "Who Owns Your Letters?" in *Autograph Collectors' Journal*, 2, no. 3:19–22 (April, 1950).

recurring notice of its ownership by the corporation. His
possession was wholly unexplained, . . . without title by any
alienation from the corporation who were originally and
rightfully its possessors and owners.[68]

About the same time as the Alden case, another set of circumstances was laying the foundation for another legal contest
regarding the right of ownership of an archival stray. During
the Civil War, Lieutenant Colonel David Thompson of the
Eighty-second Ohio Infantry was stationed for a time at Fair-
fax Courthouse in northern Virginia. While his men were
burning some old papers in order to keep warm, Colonel Thompson rescued from the flames the original will of Martha Washington and took it home with him after the war. His daughter
subsequently sold the document to J. P. Morgan. In 1914 the
Daughters of the American Revolution began to agitate for the
return of the will to Virginia. Morgan demurred, offering instead to supply a photographic copy. After direct negotiation
with the governor of Virginia, Morgan offered to return the
will if Virginia would donate the will of George Washington
to Mount Vernon or to the Library of Congress. The governor declined and filed suit to compel Morgan to return the paper,
whereupon Morgan complied and the suit was dropped.[69] Such
experiences moved a number of states to pass laws, modeled after
the Massachusetts Public Records Act of 1897, forbidding the
removal, defacement, or possession of any public record.[70]

Perhaps the most famous case involving the law of possession
of archival strays involves the Lewis and Clark manuscripts. The
case had its origins in December, 1952, upon the death of Mrs.
Sophia V. H. Foster, daughter of Civil War General John Henry Hammond. In the attic of the family home in St. Paul were
discovered two packets of old papers which were transferred to
the Minnesota Historical Society. One packet contained the papers of General Hammond; the other was the original notes of
the Lewis and Clark Expedition of 1805. When a suit was entered in the state courts of Minnesota to clear title to the Lewis
and Clark notes, the United States intervened to claim owner-

[68] Storm and Peckham, *Book Collecting*, 129.
[69] *Ibid.*, 130.
[70] Goodspeed, *Yankee Bookseller*, 221–222.

ship and moved the suit to the federal district court. The court rejected the federal government's claim, but it raised as many questions as it settled. The Lewis and Clark notes were held to be purely personal, not official records, even though they were the basis upon which the official report was written.[71] Had the court determined that the notes had been produced in an official capacity, they would thereby be considered part of the archives of the United States, hence public property to be returned to the National Archives.

Collectors and institutions were deeply disturbed by the implications of the Lewis and Clark case. Assurances from the federal government and the National Archives that no effort would be made to press for the wholesale return of archival strays failed to quiet fears. Instead, a Manuscripts Emergency Committee was created by the AHA to fight any extension of the principle of the case.[72]

The Lewis and Clark case is only the third recorded American suit regarding the physical possession of archives and historical manuscripts, but the concern of collectors and institutions stems from the fact that the statute of limitations does not run against the government in such cases. It is feared that manuscripts long settled in established hands may suddenly be claimed for return to a governmental archives. Some of the concerned interests have suggested that the Lewis and Clark case dramatized the need for new legislation to protect the legitimate interests of all the parties to the dispute. The government sought primarily to preserve an information right, not dependent upon the physical possession of the notes themselves. The two agents in their private capacities surely enjoyed some form of common-law rights to their notes, which descended to their heirs, and the Hammond estate's interest in the physical ownership of the paper was also due respect.[73]

It has been pointed out that the National Archives did not institute the suit in the matter of the Lewis and Clark papers,

---

[71] U. S., District Court of Minnesota, "In the Matter of the Lewis and Clark Papers," in *Manuscripts*, 9:1–18 (Winter, 1957).

[72] Robert F. Metzdorf, "Lewis and Clark I: A Librarian's Point of View," in *Manuscripts*, 9:226–230 (Fall, 1957).

[73] Burt Griffin, "Lewis and Clark II: A Legal Analysis," in *Manuscripts*, 10:64–67 (Winter, 1958).

and that the staff of the archives rejoiced with all scholars at the finding of the court. The United States was reserved as a potential party in the original suit, and it decided to intervene only for professional reasons and to insure the integrity of all federal records.[74] The rarity of cases involving archival strays suggests that the concern of the National Archives staff may have been justified.[75]

Although the paucity of litigation may suggest that the problem of common-law copyright in manuscript materials may be more apparent than real, the scholarly professions have become alarmed by even the theoretical prospect of restriction of access to virtually all of their traditional documentation. Legal recognition of the contextual intent of the authors of manuscript material or enlarging the concept of "fair use" could resolve the question. Another means of resolution lies through amending the United States Copyright Law, as was proposed in 1965, to provide for extinguishing the common-law protection of unpublished writings 50 years after the death of the author, or 100 years after the date of the writing, whichever came sooner. A committee of the AHA endorsed the proposal in principle, but some scholars have pointed out that the life-plus-50-years rule would induce collecting agencies to steer clear of current materials, while still other scholars have urged that a shorter term of life-plus-25-years comes closer to striking an equitable balance between the rights in literary property and the rights of scholarship to "fair use" of that property.[76]

[74] Robert H. Bahmer, "The Case of the Clark Papers," in *American Archivist*, 19:19–22 (January, 1956).

[75] Randolph G. Adams, "The Character and Extent of Fugitive Archival Material," in *American Archivist*, 2:90 (April, 1939). The cases cited are Morris' Appeal, 68 Pa. 16 (1871) (failure by a government to exercise due diligence to recapture archival strays impairs its claim at a subsequent date); De la O. v. The Pueblo of Acanra, 1 N. M. 226 (1957) (Spanish land grant which served as basis of modern title may be ordered to be returned to public custody); and Alden v. New York, 51 Barb. 19 (1868) ("Time runneth not against the king in the possession of a royal writ.").

[76] Connor, "Literary Property," 143–152; Henry Bartholomew Cox, "Private Letters and the Public Domain," in *American Archivist*, 28:384–385 (July, 1965); Henry Bartholomew Cox, "The Impact of the Proposed Copyright Law Upon Scholars and Custodians," in *American Archivist*, 29:225–227 (April, 1966); Walter Rundell, Jr., "The Recent American Past v. H. R. 4347: The Historians' Dilemma," in *American Archivist*, 29:209–215 (April, 1966). For a learned discussion of the

The English Copyright Act of 1911 and the Canadian act of 1921 both incorporate and explicitly provide the statutory defense of "fair use," that minimal interest and the right the public exacts as toll for extending to an author for his exclusive use, under the law of copyright, protection of original ideas and expression of them. The doctrine of "fair use" is not incorporated in American copyright law, but it is universally recognized by American courts. It does not apply in the slightest to common-law copyright, but rather to rights secured under the statute law alone. The principle of operation is that the law, while encouraging authors by insuring to them the fruit of their labors, ought never to bar progress in the arts and sciences by forbidding any "fair use." The key question in the determination of "fair use" is: How much was taken out of context, and to what use was it put?[77]

The law of use of manuscripts by possessors was further clarified in the case of the painter James Whistler and his biographer. The court which heard the case permitted fair use of the letters in the service of scholarship and learning, over the executor's objections. This case brought the law of manuscript property one step closer to its modern statement that the recipient or legal possessor of a manuscript owns only the material paper; that he may sell, keep, destroy, or otherwise dispose of the article; that the right of publication is reserved to the creator of the writing and descends in perpetuity to his estate and his heirs, subject only to the doctrine of fair use.[78]

One final point may be made regarding the application of the law of literary property to manuscript material, that is, the law of libel. Libel is the recognized exception to freedom of expression because it involves the use of "fighting words" which

---

problem and an excellent summary of the case law, see Louis Charles Smith, "The Copying of Literary Property in Library Collections," in *Law Library Journal*, 46:197–204 (August, 1953), and 47:193–197 (August, 1954). Other recent discussions of the problem are to be found in "Personal Letters in Need of a Law of Their Own," in *Iowa Law Review*, 44:705–715 (1959); and J. L. Wilson, "The Scholar and the Copyright Law," in *ASCAP Copyright Symposium No. 10* (New York, 1959), 104–121. See also, Philip Wittenberg, *The Protection and Marketing of Literary Property* (New York, 1937).

[77] Wittenberg, *Law of Literary Property*, 146–156; Ball, *Law of Copyright*, 260–269.

[78] Cane, "Who Owns Your Letters," 19–22.

may result in irreparable harm or in a breach of the peace. Libel may take the form of an attack upon property rights, the right to gainful employment, or injury to personality, and the degree of libel is determined by the mores of the society within which it takes place. Libel is the permanent, written form of slander, and it is a creature of the common law. It is variously defined in each of the American states, but a working definition finds libel to be a false utterance tending to impugn the honesty, virtue, or reputation, or the publication of the alleged or natural defects of a person, thereby exposing him to public hatred, contempt, or ridicule Honest error, natural mistake, or scholarly zeal do not excuse a libel, and its defense consists in adducing legally acceptable evidence proving the truth of the questioned statement. In effect, there are only two general exceptions to the law of libel, and both exceptions relate to the right of public criticism of public figures and of criticism of public judgment, when requested.[79] Beyond that, let the historian beware that the canons of his discipline may not always be adequate to protect him from the charge of libel brought by some zealous descendant of a figure who has come under historical judgment.[80]

A recent and highly publicized case precisely pitted the historian's freedom of judgment and expression against the descendant's right to protect an ancestor against statements considered to be libelous. In 1964 Dr. Sylvester K. Stevens published a general history entitled *Pennsylvania: Birthplace of a Nation*, in which he rather incidentally referred to the industrial magnate, Henry Clay Frick, as "brusque and autocratic." A daughter, Miss Helen Frick, entered suit in a Pennsylvania court to enjoin Dr. Stevens and his publisher from further circulation of the work containing the offensive reference to her late father. In the original hearing of the case the trial judge excluded all secondary materials and ordered the defendant historian to produce original source material as evidence in support of his characterization of Frick, producing the irony of the law opera-

[79] Wittenberg, *Law of Literary Property*, 183–190.
[80] For an excellent summary, see Philip Wittenberg, *Dangerous Words, A Guide to the Law of Libel* (New York, 1947).

ting to force publication of the very historical evidence a descendant was attempting to repress.[81]

The tenor of the case and its ramifications considerably alarmed the historical profession, and several scholarly organizations joined Dr. Stevens in defending the suit. Prior to a decision in the trial court an unsuccessful effort was made in federal courts to enjoin the suit on the grounds that it violated Dr. Stevens' constitutional rights of expression as guaranteed by the Civil Rights Act of 1871.[82] When the decision of Judge C. R. Weidner on the substantive merits of the case at length was filed, it vindicated the right of scholars to judge their subjects on the basis of reasonable research, upheld Stevens' conclusions upon Frick as milder than the facts warranted, dismissed the suit as "frivolous," and scolded Miss Frick for reading history out of context. In one of the more witty passages of the decision, Judge Weidner observed that, "By analogy, Miss Frick might as well try to enjoin publication of the Holy Bible because being a descendant of Eve, she does not believe that Eve gave Adam the forbidden fruit in the Garden of Eden and that her senses are offended by such a statement of an ancestor of hers." Referring to the controversy surrounding the publication of William Manchester's *The Death of a President,* Judge Weidner also speculated upon the future litigation which might arise from over-sensitive regard by kinsmen of the late President Kennedy. The trial judge concluded that such perpetual mediation between the public's right to information and the personal right of privacy would be an intolerable burden upon courts of law.[83] An editorial in the New York *Times* hailed the decision as a ringing defense of a right which ought never to have been called into question, and it concluded that "such an invasion of the domain of scholarship and historical literature would be intolerable in any free country."[84]

Considering the weight of precedent and public policy, the Frick case could hardly have been decided otherwise. But lest

---

[81] Frick v. Stevens (Court of Common Pleas, Cumberland County, Pennsylvania), interim trial report in New York *Times,* July 23, 1965.

[82] Stevens v. Frick, 259 F. Supp. 654 (1966), affirmed 372 F (2d) 378 (1967).

[83] Frick v. Stevens, report in New York *Times,* May 26, 1967.

[84] Editorial, New York *Times,* May 27, 1967.

it be relied upon too extensively to protect the unwary historian going about his duty of interpreting the past in the light of the best available evidence, it should be remembered that the decision was one rendered by a trial court, and Miss Frick has announced her intention to appeal.[85] While taking comfort in the precedents favoring free inquiry and publication of conclusions, historians should remember that, when called to the bar to defend themselves, they are judged according to the canons of the law and not those of their own discipline. An acquaintance with the law of libel, as with the law of literary property, would seem to be a requisite of producing historical scholars.

[85] *Ibid.*

vvvvvvvvvvvvvv vvvvvvvvvvvvvvvvvvvvvvvvvvvvvvvvvvvvvvvvv

IX

vvvvvvvvvvvvvv vvvvvvvvvvvvvvvvvvvvvvvvvvvvvvvvvvvvvvvvv

NEWSPAPERS AS
HISTORICAL EVIDENCE

WILLIAM MAKEPEACE THACKERAY, in one of his novels, has a vapid feminine character inquire, "Is there anything in the paper, Sir?"

"Anything in the paper!" is the masculine reply. "All the world is in the paper. Why, Madam, if you will but read what is written in the *Times* of this very day, it is enough for a year's history, and ten times as much meditation."[1]

This snippet of domestic conversation, however stilted, does suggest something of the tremendous significance of newspapers as historical evidence. Although printed in multiple copies and distributed widely, newspapers can be regarded as primary documentation in that the prior forms of information from which they are compiled are not generally available. To the contrary, newspapers are often not only not derived from prior forms, they are also the only sources for certain types of information. Furthermore, the contemporaneous nature of newspapers qualifies as good evidence under most heuristical tests. Even the inherent problem of editorial bias is partially self-correcting due to the public nature of newspapers.

American historians have been curiously reluctant and apologetic about using newspapers as primary documentation, preferring generally to cite archival or manuscript material. The historiographical mistrust of newspapers is an interesting phe-

---

[1] Lucy M. Salmon, *The Newspaper and the Historian* (New York, 1923), title page.

265

nomenon and requires some examination. Newspapers satisfy
many of the canons of historical evidence. As contemporary, written records produced without a knowledge of the outcome of
pending events and issues, they cannot long favor or advance
any particular cause without convicting themselves of their own
partiality. However prevalent newspaper bias may be, it is generally readily discernible, and historiographical compensation may
be made for it. Moreover, newspapers are social documents, mir-
rors of the society which they serve. To mix the metaphors of
St. Paul, if the glass be dark and the reflections imperfect, the
maturity of the observer will give him better vision.

James F. Rhodes once reminded his fellow historians that
newspapers have not always been regarded as such lowly forms
of documentation. When scientific history was in its infancy,
newspapers were relied upon very heavily. True, that reliance
may have been through necessity rather than virtue. Through a
curious exchange of values, it would appear that modern historians value documentary evidence more highly because it is
more difficult to come by, and overlook newspapers as evidence
because they are so readily available. As Herbert Spencer has
observed, "A modern newspaper statement, though probably
true, if quoted in a book as testimony, would be laughed at,
but the letter of a court gossip, if written some centuries ago,
is thought good historical evidence."[2]

NEWSPAPERS: EYE WITNESSES TO HISTORY

HISTORIANS have only recently begun to use newspapers
as evidence *per se* and not as a substitute for manuscripts,
and this development seems to be a manifestation of the growing sophistication of the profession. Historians have become
more adept at using newspapers as evidence and have learned
how to discount journalistic bias and inaccuracy. They have
learned that when newspapers in a free society misrepresent the
truth, they generally do it by suppression rather than by outright falsification. Historians have even learned to award news-

---

[2] James F. Rhodes, "Newspapers as Historical Sources," in *Historical Essays* (New
York, 1909), 83–86; J. W. Piercy, "The Newspaper as a Source of Historical Information," in *Indiana Historical Bulletin*, 10:387 (Fall, 1933).

papers, as private agencies serving the public, the right within acceptable bounds to select what they will report and emphasize. While newspapers as historical witnesses are no longer subject to peremptory challenge, they still display very human frailties, the chief being the uneven quality of their recall. Newspapers generally fail to give continuous coverage to the entire spectrum of historical events. Rather, they record only selectively, shifting to full reporting only in a period of crisis. The press is also hampered by the existence of previously established community sentiment and public opinion. The importance of newspapers in molding public opinion notwithstanding, newspapers are obliged to submit to community values if strongly held.[3]

So far, newspapers have been considered as historical evidence only as a total entity. Their evidentiary value, however, is obscured by efforts to judge the whole rather than its component parts. Modern newspapers are actually composites of many different kinds and forms of information, some inherently subject to greater bias than others. Certain types of statistical information, such as banking, financial, and weather reports, are generally acceptable at face value. On the other hand, the expression of editorial opinion may be taken conclusively only as proof that, for whatever reason, such opinion was in fact expressed. Without corroborating evidence, newspaper editorials may be relied upon as only inferential expressions of public opinion or special interest. Even what purports to be straight news reporting contains varying amounts of fact, half-truth, surmise, guess, rumor, and wishful thinking. If a historian requires information which a newspaper file is competent to supply, the evidence should be accepted and subjected to the appropriate heuristical tests.[4]

As reflections of the contemporary scene, newspapers are, so to speak, the first drafts of history, and they daily wrestle in their own way with the same historiographical problems of truth and accuracy which ultimately occupy the historian. In newspaper reporting, literal accuracy may be misleading and untruthful, as for example, a report of fragmentary election returns without reference to past trends and voting patterns. Moreover, a

[3] Salmon, *The Newspaper and the Historian,* 425–448.
[4] Spahr and Swenson, *Scientific Research,* 120–121.

specious accuracy, as in some editorial analysis, is perfectly compatible with a genuine and fundamental misconception of reality. By the same token, a wholly speculative report may well turn out to be fundamentally accurate. To overcome these perplexing contradictions, newspaper editors, like historians, seek to create an intellectual wholeness from which they may interpret objectively and fully the entire sweep of events, select what is significant, and construct an approximation of the human experience. The more closely a newspaper editor approaches the canons of a historian, the more valuable the newspaper is apt to be as general historical documentation.

Historiographical use has been made of all of the varied contents of modern newspapers, but the portions most used and perhaps most valuable to historians are editorials, illustrations, and advertisements. When journalism was a highly personal affair, editorials were indicative of not much beyond the prejudices of the editors. As newspapers have become more highly institutionalized, editorial comment has become depersonalized. Editorials are now an imperfect yet effective means for reconstructing and roughly gauging the opinion of the newspaper readers as well as of those men and agencies collectively engaged in publishing the newspaper. Editorial comment, then, is today the froth which rises when a society boils and not a sample of the soup itself, and it is the task of the historian correctly to infer the flavor of the soup. The historian is aided in his inference by illustrative and advertising matter which appears in modern newspapers in quantity. Newspaper illustrations range from photographic coverage to political cartoons, from graphical documentation of specific events to exaggerated characterization of complex trends and circumstances. Lastly, advertising is an index to commercial and folk activity and concerns. Because it is directed to those who buy, it is reflective of consumer interests and desires as well as of the availability of wares for sale.[5]

The evolution of newspapers as an increasingly significant, if difficult and complex, source of historical evidence imposes on the historian the particularly delicate task of critical and creative evaluation. The United States is embarrassed with the most extensive if not the most varied newspaper documentation of

[5] Salmon, *The Historian and the Newspaper*, 468–478.

any national state, and the nature and availability of that evidence has uniquely influenced America's historical image of itself.

A favorable intellectual climate, a heterogeneous society, and the heavy concentration of major commercial interests combined to create an active press in colonial America. However active, the papers of New England and elsewhere were also quite provincial in their politics and outlook and may well have helped to perpetuate the British and purely local loyalties. A spirit of Americanism was long delayed in part precisely because there was no distinctively American press until the Revolution. Moreover, with a few exceptions, the colonial newspapers were the uninspired and undistinguished products of job printers primarily seeking full employment for their presses rather than the development of a responsible means of public communication. Not until most of the colonial journalists were caught up in the emotion and the politics of the Revolution did many of them venture into public affairs other than an occasional defense of freedom of the press.

The colonial press was a slender reed upon which to rest major historical writings, but the Revolution was hardly over before the files of back issues were being riffled for evidence to justify the colonial position. Typical of the early historiographical use of American newspapers were John Eliot's *A Narrative of the Newspapers Printed in New England* (1798) and Dr. Samuel Miller's study of the role of editorials in promoting the policy of independence (1803). These early historical uses of journalistic sources suggested to Isiah Thomas the systematic collection of newspapers for purposes of research and to Hezekiah Niles the development of a newspaper deliberately conceived as a historical source for the future.[6]

Whatever else may be said of the journalism of early America, it did not lack color or personality. Choice epithets were indiscriminately hurled by editors with little regard for professional restraint or the law of libel. The depths of partisan animosity were reached in the Federalist and Jacksonian eras, when newsmen generally subscribed to a free-swinging right of insult. The influence of this brand of brawling journalism in

---

[6] Clarence Saunders Brigham, *Journals and Journeymen: A Contribution to the History of Early American Newspapers* (Philadelphia, 1950), 1–4.

shaping the form and style of American party politics has been extensively documented.[7]

The partisan newspaper, conceived in the euphoric glow of nationalism and democracy, was one of the connecting links between Jeffersonian Republicanism and Jacksonian Democracy, and it played a vital part in dramatizing the issues and personalities of that political transition. The Democratic press was one of the agencies through which national issues filtered down to the common man, galvanizing him into political consciousness and action. Circulating as a "penny-press" daily in the urban East or as a country weekly in the rural backlands, such papers were highly prolific but short-lived. For all their lack of continuity, political bias, and exaggeration, the newspaper of the 1830's and 1840's is still of great value as among the few available sources for the history of the conversion of a rural republic into an urban democracy. Here may be most graphically read the rise of class consciousness and the struggle between the divisive sectionalism and an inept traditionalism, resulting in the Civil War. In a real sense, the American newspaper was prominent in causing, delaying, and shaping the American Tragedy.[8]

The unprecedented demands made by the Civil War upon American newspapers inevitably changed them. Momentous and rapidly-developing events, press censorship, and a political supercharge made the public on both sides insatiable for details of the conflict. All too often what the public received was garbled fragments and incomplete accounts, further compounding the general confusion and demoralization. The circumstances necessitated a pooling of battle reports and their transmission by telegraph, innovations which were later to lead to wire press associations and syndicated feature columns. These developments came as a mixed blessing. Improving war reporting was bought at the heavy price of journalistic centralization, passivity, and standardization. Local journalism went into a decline during the Civil War from which it never completely recovered.

The postwar future of American journalism belonged to the

[7] For example, see W. G. Bleyer, *Main Currents in the History of American Journalism* (Boston, 1927), 100–120; Edwin Emery and Henry Ladd Smith, *The Press and America* (New York, 1954), 125–212.

[8] Bleyer, *American Journalism*, 100–153; Carl Weicht, "The Local Historian and the Newspaper," in *Minnesota History*, 13:45–54 (March, 1932).

big-city daily with sufficient capital and staff to adapt technological innovations to the increasingly impersonal needs and
tastes of urban subscribers. Joseph Pulitzer showed the way to
success in the Gilded Age by emphasizing the editorial concept
of continuous news coverage and exhorting his staff: "Never be
satisfied with printing the news." His spectacular success was
based upon combining a liberal domestic position, a titillating
obtrusion into the international scene, and a lurid appeal to
the frankly sensational—a combination which came to be known
as "Yellow Journalism." Pulitzer was the pioneer of the art,
but its perfector was his arch rival, William Randolph Hearst.[9]

The American press suffered an epidemic of Yellow Journalism during the Spanish-American War, but not all of the papers
succumbed to it. Perhaps the most notable exception was the
New York *Times,* which had enjoyed a precarious existence from
the 1850's until controlling interest was purchased by Adolph
Ochs. He remade the venerable paper in the image of the highly respected and influential London *Times,* and within a few
years Ochs's *Times* had become the American newspaper of record.[10] Other metropolitan dailies might develop more lively
personalities,[11] but by World War I the *Times* had no close
rival in utility as a prime source of historical documentation.

Rural America, particularly the New South, also developed
a characteristic press in the years between the Civil War and
the turn of the century. The common people of the country,
and especially those of the South, left little in the way of personal documentation. The story of their struggle against the
force of nature, oligopoly, and centralization must be read primarily in their county weeklies. Wholesomely informal and
given to an honest statement of position, the editors of such papers were happily spared many a libel suit. What sets the papers
of the New South apart from their Populist cousins of the Midwest is their ubiquitous treatment of the race problem, their
anachronistic adjustment to the one-party system, their making
a virtue out of the necessity of a single-crop economy, and their

[9] Emery and Smith, *The Press and America,* 369–446.

[10] Meyer Berger, *The Story of the New York Times* (New York, 1951) is a
recent and commendable treatment.

[11] Philip Kinsley, *The Chicago Tribune, Its First Hundred Years* (3 vols., New
York, 1943–1964), I:1–7.

mixed reaction to the impact of Reconstruction and industrialization. While the southern press was provincial in its outlook,
it was refreshingly frank and full in its reporting of local news.[12]

The latter half of the nineteenth century brought a number
of technological advances to the collecting and printing of news,
and these advances produced corresponding changes in the procedures and character of American journalism. The experience
of collective reporting and dissemination of battle reports by wire
was applied after the Civil War on a subscription basis to national and international reporting, and the concept was further
developed in 1900 with the organization of the Associated Press
of New York, tying its members into a copyright network. Subsequently, the United Press and the International News Service
(now United Press International) and the Scripps-McRae Press
Association have provided a measure of competition for the AP
in providing "canned news" for the nation's newspapers.[13]

An insatiable demand for more rapid printing of newspapers
has also produced a host of technological improvements which
have had major editorial ramifications. The invention in 1861
of stereotyped plates expanded the size of the typical newspaper
—but at the cost of filling it with "patent insides." After 1863
roll-fed cylinder presses further speeded press runs, and after
1870 the sulphite process for manufacture of wood-pulp paper
drastically lowered costs. This latter advance, however, has been
at the expense of historical permanence, as testified by thousands
of bound volumes of yellow, crumbling copies of newspapers of
the 1880's and 1890's which are inexorably destroying themselves
by their own excess residual acidity.

Other mechanical and technological advances of the industrial era contributed to American journalism. By 1877 the telephone had become sufficiently reliable to permit its regular
use for the instantaneous reporting of news. Soon thereafter a
Milwaukee newspaper editor, Christopher Sholes, devised the
first practical typewriter to facilitate the preparation of newspaper copy. In 1886 came the perfection of the Mergenthaler
linotype, which eliminated the tedious hand composition of

[12] Thomas D. Clark, *The Southern Country Editor* (Indianapolis, 1948), preface.
[13] Victor Rosewater, *History of Cooperative News-Gathering in the United
States* (New York, 1930).

type. In the 1890's color presses were perfected, and in 1914 the introduction of the Rotogravure process permitted illustrated supplements to become a hallmark of the metropolitan Sunday papers. In the 1920's the invention of radio was harnessed to the service of journalism both as an additional channel of news collection and as an additional means of dissemination, since the early radio stations were often owned by metropolitan newspapers.[14]

The development of the American magazine closely paralleled that of American newspapers, the period after the Civil War witnessing the flowering of the new form of journalism. A variety of factors combined to stimulate the launching of popular journals. The Civil War had destroyed virtually all of the antebellum literary and women's magazines; only *Atlantic Monthly* and *Harper's New Monthly Magazine* survived the ordeal. Moreover, the ready audience for war reminiscences and domestic fiction could not be served by book publishing alone, especially after the financial contractions following the Panic of 1873. A number of astute publishers appreciated the peculiarly southern taste for literature of the local-color genre, and they launched such popular magazines as Scribner's *Hours at Home* and Scott's *Monthly Magazine,* Atlanta's southern counterpart. The success of these new ventures encouraged a number of publishers to follow suit, and the pages of these new journals were filled by southerners and northerners alike, who established a new school of American literature based upon local color. The Reconstruction Era also saw the proliferation and growth of intellectually nationalizing critical-review journals modeled after the *North American Review.* Outstanding among the new reviews were the *National Quarterly Review* (1860) and the *Nation,* established in 1865 by E. L. Godkin. New weekly journals, such as *Chimney Corners* (1865) and Appleton's *Journal* (1869), applied the formula of the *Saturday Evening Post* (1821) to the provision of light reading for the entire family. The Reconstruction Era also witnessed the rise of specialized magazine journalism. By 1870 there were over 140 religious journals published in the United States, at least one for every major sect or denom-

---

[14] "Development of American Newspapers," in *Encyclopedia Americana,* XX: 283–287.

ination. This period also marked the beginning of a host of professional, trade, and commercial journals, juvenile and art magazines, and other special-interest publications.[15] Indeed, since the middle of the nineteenth century, the richness of American magazine publication has been matched only by its in-depth newspaper coverage, making the United States the best-endowed of all modern nations with journalistic documentation.

The wealth of newspaper and magazine files already available to the historians of the United States gives rise to the crucial need for bibliographic control. The standard guide to American newspapers grew out of a suggestion made in 1911 by Professor William MacDonald of Brown University. The work catalogs over 2,120 different newspapers which have appeared in all of the states and territories of the United States. Inventories of files of these newspapers indicate that the six leading depositories, in descending order, are the American Antiquarian Society, the Library of Congress, Harvard University Library, the New-York Historical Society, the New York Public Library, and the State Historical Society of Wisconsin.[16]

NEWSPAPERS AND THE WRITING OF HISTORY

NEWSPAPERS have become increasingly valuable as sources of American historical documentation in recognition and in consequence of the freedom of the press in the United States. This freedom may have been abused in the publication of all kinds of bias, but competition between free papers is at least partially self-correcting of the more gross abuses. As Bliss Perry has observed, "No one can watch the development of our current journalism without becoming aware that this sense of responsibility to the public is raising the whole level of the American press."[17] Thus, historians who must rely upon contempo-

[15] Frank L. Mott, *A History of American Magazines, 1865–1880* (Iowa City, 1928), 4 ff.
[16] Clarence Saunders Brigham, *History and Bibliography of American Newspapers, 1690–1820* (2 vols., Worcester, Mass., 1947), I:ix-xvi. See also, Herbert O. Brayer, "Preliminary Guide to Indexed Newspapers in the United States, 1950–1900," in *Mississippi Valley Historical Review*, 33:237–258 (September, 1946); and Winifred Gregory, *American Newspapers, 1821–1936* (New York, 1937).
[17] Salmon, *The Newspaper and the Historian*, 467.

rary newspapers have grounds for a cautious optimism regarding the reliability of this category of documentation.

In addition to supplying direct information, newspapers also provide the basis for inferences as to the context of information or even the negative confirmation of heuristical assumptions. For example, the tragic events in Kansas in 1856 were journalistically referred to by such impassioned phrases as "Potawatomi Massacre," and "Bleeding Kansas," and the newspaper publicity has been thought to have had a highly significant bearing upon the Frémont-Buchanan campaign of 1856. As Allan Nevins has demonstrated, however, a study of contemporary newspapers from various parts of the country proves that no significant reporting or political manipulation of the events in Kansas took place; hence, newspaper coverage of these events could not have been as politically significant as popularly supposed. On close examination the ante-bellum press does provide an excellent index to the shifting tides of public opinion on the question of slavery. In the decade before the Civil War, editorials in northern newspapers convinced the nation of the moral stigma of the institution. Conversely, the southern press in this period became increasingly defensive and militant, encouraging or reflecting the drift of secessionist sentiment. Newspaper reports are not needed to supplement and correct the official account of the Union's military effort, but press reports are vital to the story of the Confederacy in both civil and military affairs. Newspapers are likewise invaluable for charting public reaction, North and South, to the conduct of the war and Reconstruction.[18]

The influence which contemporary newspapers will have upon future historiography of our times is highly speculative, but some generalizations have been drawn by two students of the contemporary American press, Allan Nevins and Douglas Cater. Both men have observed that we have become so sophisticated in the art of public information that the federal government (and the forces of the lobby) regularly "use" the press for their own purposes through news releases, planned "leaks," private briefings, and personal relationships. The reporter's classical image of himself as a fearless and free agent of the truth may no longer hold true. Reporters may be in the employ of a private news

[18] Rhodes, "Newspapers as Historical Sources," 87–97.

media, but they often function as a part of the governmental
bureaucracy, or what Cater has called "the fourth branch of
government." Cater holds the wire services responsible for the
emasculation of the American reporter. No longer does the individual reporter make his personal contribution to shaping the
first draft of history. In trading the passive role of reporter for
the active one of commentator, he has lost a certain historical
perspective and objectivity. In becoming too intimately involved
in the scene he records, he may have forfeited his right to make
a first interpretation of it for posterity.

The ulterior "use" of the press in its contemporary form
dates from World War II, when editorial applications began
to catch up with the technological innovations of modern mass
communications and invested the mass media with unprecedented
influence. Most of President Truman's political difficulties can
be traced to a determined effort by a hostile Congress to catch
up with the executive branch in its use of the reporting process
for partisan purposes. The making and dissemination of images
became the business of politicians as well as hucksters. Within
the white light of publicity, many a contemporary public figure
has been forced to conform to his public image, such as Senator
John McClellan, the country judge in the McCarthy hearings,
or Senator Arthur Vandenberg, the tent-meeting convert in the
creation of the post-war, bipartisan internationalism.[19]

Walter Lippmann has observed that "nothing affects more
the balance of power between Congress and the President than
whether the one or the other is the principal source of news and
explanation and opinion," and both parties in this political power struggle are well aware of the truth of that observation. As
a continuing and integrated entity, the executive has a natural
advantage, but despite its diversity Congress is learning the
ways of publicity. Even if it wished to, Congress could never
really be out of the public view. Publicity has been the life-
blood of a Congressman's continued effectiveness throughout
American history. On the part of the press, there has been
an observable bias towards Congressmen and their activities;
the members of the legislative branch are forgiven indiscretions

---

[19] Nevins, *Gateway*, 200–209; Douglass Cater, *The Fourth Branch of Government*
(Boston, 1959), 1–21.

which members of the executive cannot expect. Congressional displeasure with the press can be and often is displayed on the floor without fear of retaliation, but members of the executive branch can rarely afford to engage in public controversy with the Fourth Estate. Congressional committees are ever ready, with the fullest cooperation of the press, to ferret out executive wrongdoing, but congressional incompetence and venality must assume crisis proportions before there is a disposition to turn the light of publicity upon it.[20]

The contemporary investigating committee has become the most potent weapon in the publicity warfare, for the executive has nothing in its armory effectively to cope with it. Carefully and elaborately staged for the convenience of the press, the participants in these proceedings are usually outnumbered and often overawed by the attending reporters. Members of committees don sunglasses for protection against the glare of television and movie lights, and they suffer heroically through the heat and clamor to build or preserve their public images. All this activity is ostensibly justified in the finding of fact upon which to base legislation, but both external and internal evidence casts grave doubt upon the efficacy or objectivity of congressional investigations in a field already supercharged with emotion. In earlier days, congressional investigators were generally supported by the executive and restrained by quasi-judicial procedures. In recent years the investigations of congressional committees have as often as otherwise been directed at the executive, and the committees have departed from judicial practices and safeguards in the search for publicity. That congressional hearings have not resulted in even greater excesses is to be explained by the diligence by which the executive has maintained its constitutional independence and by which the courts have insisted upon the proper respect of individual civil liberties.[21]

For a country whose founders were passionately devoted to the freedom of the press, America's newspapers have often failed to respond with judgment and responsibility, or with a readiness to champion the cause of the people against even their own elected representatives. Instances abound in which the press has

[20] Cater, *Fourth Branch of Government*, 47–56.
[21] *Ibid.*, 56–74.

failed in its simple duty, or in which it cravenly has submitted to official domination. For example, when the capital was moved to Washington in 1800, none of the newspapers of Philadelphia or New York felt obligated to report the event. More significantly, the government, perhaps without really intending to, kept the national press docile by the distribution of public printing contracts until the Government Printing Office was established in 1860. Only gradually did independent newspaper correspondents appear in Washington, and not until there was a national press corps, held together by camaraderie and barrels of whiskey, could an individual reporter hope to defend himself against of ficial displeasure and retribution. The imposition of military censorship during the Civil War did much to produce a more independent and responsible press in America. Among other things, it encouraged the use of by-lines for attribution of news reports. What began as a technique of censorship developed into the means of making reports more responsible to the reading public.

Professionalization of American political reporters continued to develop after the Civil War, but at a slow pace. Not until 1908 was the National Press Club established, balanced two years later by the appointment of the first paid press officers in government bureaus. Press releases prepared by the latter permitted some reporters to become glorified errand boys, walking from office to office to collect the pre-edited information which the government agencies wished to plant in the public press.[22]

The Great Depression and the New Deal ushered in a new era in Washington journalism. For the first time, the sheer volume of news threatened to overwhelm the correspondents, and reporters were forced to become specialists or syndicated columnists. These princes of the press were relieved of the urgency of collecting "hard" news. Rather they created a storehouse of background information and a well-developed *Weltanschauung* with which to interpret the stream of daily events. The success of such men as David Lawrence, Walter Lippmann, the Alsop brothers, James Reston, and Drew Pearson has firmly established the columnist as a distinctive feature of American journalism, further magnified the power of the press, and tempted its corruption.

[22] *Ibid.*, 75–93.

Photographic journalism has created a new sub-specialty within the ranks of the columnists, a new breed of reporters in the *Time-Life* tradition. With an expensive camera in one hand and an educated pen in the other, striving for impact rather than for impartiality, seeking involvement rather than perspective, the photographic reporter of the news magazines has tended to truncate the role of the traditional reporter. Caught up in the limitations of his medium, he exaggerates for effect, and seeks to resolve infinite shades of gray into black and white. By accident and by design, he evokes visceral response rather than reasoned reaction, and the trends which began with the picture-filled magazines have been accelerated with the advent of television.[23]

The concentration of power in the American nation and in its chief executive has also profoundly affected the manner in which the press reports upon them. No monarch ever had a retinue like that of the press corps which regularly follows every public activity of the President of the United States. Some twenty to thirty reporters are assigned exclusively to the White House, and this number swells to 150 or 200 for presidential news conferences. It is on such occasions that the chief of state of the most powerful nation and the leader of the free world is most fully exposed to public scrutiny and to the judgment of posterity. Why does the President subject himself to such an ordeal? Simply because he and the government he heads need the publicity and the opportunity to shape public opinion. Here he can speak to Congress in the confidence that the full weight of his prestige will be translated into political pressure upon Congress. He can speak to the world at large, backed by the full force of his nation's power. By anticipating questions and supplying ready and convincing answers, he can instill public confidence. On such occasions the President can also use the press as a weather vane to test public reaction to proposed action.

Although of recent origin, presidential news conferences have had a colorful and significant history. The growth of the Presidency in this century has brought increased intercourse between the chief executive and the press, but it has decreased the intimacy of the relationship. Theodore Roosevelt initiated the press conference, Woodrow Wilson institutionalized it, Warren G.

[23] *Ibid.*, 94 ff.

Harding was victimized by it, and Calvin Coolidge first learned to use it to its greatest advantage. Herbert Hoover's association with the press was largely sterile, but Franklin D. Roosevelt played upon the press conference with all the virtuosity of a concert pianist, however informally. President Truman injected a new formality into his dealings with the press, and although the conferences were marred by occasional outbursts of bad temper, in general they suggested a country schoolroom filled with bad boys on the verge of rebellion. President Truman enjoyed the wit of the deadly serious repartee with reporters he considered as enemies, although at times he was adversely used by them. President Eisenhower, on the other hand, never mastered the knack of submitting gracefully to public questioning, nor did he ever learn to state effectively his replies.[24] President Kennedy was a master of the press conference, his sparkling wit turning even hostile reporters into grudging admirers. The labored responses of President Johnson in his news conferences have been suggested as contributing to the "credibility gap" and the loss of image from which he appeared to suffer.

If it is true that the government and its officers have learned to use the press for their own purposes, it is also true that the press has learned effectively to protect not only its use but its management. Official suppression or selective release of information, or "managed news," is not a new area of controversy. It is as old as the conflict between the interests of national security and the right of a free citizenry to be informed, but this familiar conflict appears more critical in the context of the proliferation of intelligence activities. It has been argued that there is no valid conflict between a need for secrecy and the public's right to information, for until an event has occurred or until the government has definitely acted, nothing which the public is entitled to know has taken place. This reasoning may be begging the question. The press counters with its claim to access to news in the making, and it charges that government frequently takes advantage of the cloak of secrecy to hide its mistakes and to avoid public accounting. The conflicts inherent in the continuing security crisis of the Cold War have posed a constitutional problem which has not yet been fully resolved.

[24] *Ibid.*, 22 ff.; J. E. Pollard, *The Presidents and the Press* (New York, 1947).

Since September, 1951, federal agencies have operated under the provisions of Executive Order No. 10290 and subsequent legislation, which established procedures for handling information affecting the national security. These procedures theoretically insure that classified information comes into the hands only of those persons approved to receive it and then only on a "need-to-know" basis. How, then, does the press secure access to so much classified information? The answer is not an indictment of the federal security system but a testimony to the shrewdness and perseverance of the nation's newsmen. As one Washington reporter has described his method of penetrating the security curtain: "I shut my eyes and asked where I'd go if I were a blind horse: I went, and the horse was there." James Reston of the New York *Times* has few peers in the practice of out-guessing the security system. Reston understands that its weakness is the human frailty of public officials. The late James Forrestal sought to close that loophole by having the press assume the duty of policing its own violations of security, but the press has so far shown no inclination for self-policing. The uneven struggle between reporters and press officers continues.[25]

The problem of denial of access to news is further complicated by a policy of controlled access to it on an unattributed basis. At times, selected news is privately passed to a favored correspondent. On other occasions, background briefings, such as those sponsored during World War II by General George C. Marshall and Admiral Ernest J. King, are employed to condition the context of the leaks in the security system. On their own, reporters have sought to reverse the process by socially entertaining key officials for the purpose of casually eliciting information from them. Some of the techniques of the press in penetrating the veil of government secrecy have become so successful that Ernest K. Lindley and others have adopted the device of "anonymous plagiarism"—of telling all they know without revealing the source, and permitting at least one day's delay so that the source can get out of town or develop some plausible alibi.

Background briefings, anonymous attribution, and the like may sometimes pit various government officials at apparent cross

---

[25] Cater, *Fourth Branch of Government*, 112–127.

purposes, but even this appearance may be a part of a larger, deliberate scheme to test public opinion on various policy alternatives. All such Machiavellian devices which have crept into the reporting of the news raise some significant questions not only for the reading public but for the future historian as well. Are reporters still intelligence agents for the public, or have they become a part of the intelligence apparatus of modern government? The public as well as the historian relying upon a given newspaper and its reporters needs to know who is using whom.[26]

The questions regarding the evidentiary integrity of modern American newspapers are serious ones, and to alleviate the growing problem of "managed" news reporting some scholars have suggested the restructuring of the relations between the government and the press. Rather than leave the onus of serving as public watchdog on the press, some students have urged that the government become its own self-critic through instituting something like the House of Commons' Question Period. Even granting the effectiveness of the British system of public oversight, is there any guarantee that it can be transplanted to America? Who is to ask the penetrating questions in Congress, and how may Congress effectively correct wrongdoing short of impeachment? The seniority system and the relative balance between the two major parties precludes congressional committees from criticizing too sharply members of the opposition in the executive branch. Furthermore, the British seem to be better at conducting parliamentary post-mortems than members of the American Congress. The British characteristically seek to determine why a political catastrophe occurred; Americans generally are more interested in fixing personal responsibility.[27]

The stunning success of governmental control and manipulation of the mass communications media has opened new vistas for its future development. A classic example is the "Eisenhower-Nixon Research Service," created in the 1952 campaign to study and develop the most effective means of utilizing mass communications to promote the Republican candidates. After the election the fledgling organization was renamed Research Associ-

[26] *Ibid.*, 128–141.
[27] *Ibid.*, 142–155.

ates and launched into a general study and research in the applications of mass communications to popular control. The new
organization provided a focus for the efforts of agencies and individual scholars working in the emerging science of cyber-
netics.[28]

The governing insistence upon material profit and popular
acceptance in the big business of the gathering and reporting
of news has molded the character of such newer media as television, and it is having a powerful influence upon more traditional forms, such as newspapers. In mass communications, the
consumer is viewed as the median man, whose intelligence and
tastes do not increase or develop. He must have basic concepts
repeatedly explained and complex issues reduced to a few simple
ideas. With varying degrees of commitment and success, contemporary mass media thus seeks to sell a complex reality at
retail value. There are many public and private services, such
as the *Congressional Quarterly*, which do a commendable job
in the wholesale distribution of current intelligence, and the
success of their specialized appeal within a mass market raises
the hope that human curiosity and aspiration for excellence may
yet upgrade the system of mass distribution of information.[29]

For all its faults and shortcomings, the public press, as Homer
C. Hockett has reminded us, can approximate the acuity and
objectivity of a professional historian. At its best, it can therefore serve the historian as one of his best and most trustworthy
sources. It is unfair, however, to hold the reporter to such standards in his daily routine. He cannot afford the luxury of two
of the historian's most valuable assets, perspective and time, to
insure complete accuracy of detail. What is required of the historian is to apply the same tests to information found in newspapers as those used to evaluate evidence derived from other
sources. The question is not *whether* historians should use newspapers in their research, but *how*.[30]

If newspapers are to be preserved and used for historical research, it is agreed that they should be collected in full runs and
should be given every reasonable protection against loss or dam-

[28] *Ibid.*, 156–169.
[29] *Ibid.*, 170–177.
[30] Hockett, *Critical Method*, 47 ff.

age. The collecting agency must be prepared to cope with a voluminous category of material. Somewhat more than 1,900 daily newspapers in the United States are now producing over 12,000 bound volumes yearly, and 9,500 weekly papers add another 3,000 volumes. For each year the collection of the total productivity of the national press would run to about 15,000 volumes. The total number of existing bound volumes of newspapers in holding agencies is just over 150,000; hence, the coverage of the outpouring of the American press is admittedly sketchy. Even so, indexing of existing holdings rather than expansion of them seems to be the most critical need of scholars.[31]

[31] Icko Iben, "The Place of the Newspaper," in *Library Trends,* 4:140–155 (October, 1955).

vv

X

vvvvvvvvvvvvvvvvvvvvvvvvvvvvvvvvvvvvvvvvvvvvvvvvvvvvvvvv

RECORDS OF THE MASS CULTURE

WHEN ALEXIS DE TOCQUEVILLE visited the United States in the early years of the nineteenth century, he found many points upon which invidious comparisons with European society could be drawn. Among the objects of his stinging criticism of the raw democracy were its historical rootlessness, its carelessness about its past and its records. As de Tocqueville expressed it, "The instability of the administration has penetrated into the habits of the people; it even appears to suit the general taste, and no one cares for what happened before his time. No methodical system is pursued; no archives are formed; and no documents are brought together when it would be easy to do so. Where they exist, little store is set upon them. . . ."[1]

However insensitive Americans were in de Tocqueville's day to the creation and preservation of records, they have experienced a "paper revolution" since that time. From being perhaps the least-documented literate society in the western world a little over a century ago, the United States has become the most extensively documented nation. This embarrassment of riches has posed a problem for historians unaccustomed to dealing with records in the mass. This superabundance of records was created not for the benefit of the historian, but rather in spite of his anguish, and for the first time in the annals of historiography the problems of documentation have become those of selection, sampling, and control rather than those of searching, lacunae,

[1] de Tocqueville, *Democracy in America*, 213–214.

and total absence. Earlier generations of American historians could leisurely remain at comfortable centers of research such as the Boston Athenaeum or the Library of Congress, but more recent generations have been forced to adopt the habits of traveling salesmen, dashing about the country in pursuit of their sources.[2]

Paralleling the population explosion and the convolutions of society, the public records of American society have expanded enormously since about 1800. The population growth over the last 150 years has been largely the result of scientific and technological innovations. These innovations, in turn, have given rise to a proliferation of governmental activity and a consequent expansion of the records both of government and the components of the social order. Indeed, it can be said that the technological developments of the Industrial Revolution have both made necessary and made possible the modern expansion of records, and the process has been accelerated with the rise of the mass culture of the twentieth century. A case in point is the historical development of modern physical and medical science, the documentation for which exists in such quantity as to defy utilization by traditional historiographical means.[3]

Some statistics on the growth of federal records may suggest the scope of the explosion of paper which has occurred and which threatens to engulf modern society. From 1789 to 1861, a period of seventy-two years, the federal government produced about 100,000 cubic feet of records of all categories. From the Civil War to World War I, a period of some fifty years, the total was five times the previous accumulation, or approximately 500,000 cubic feet. The decade of the 1930's, in which governmental activities expanded on an unprecedented scale, witnessed the production of about 3,500,000 cubic feet of records; during World War II the annual rate of production was 2,000,000 cubic feet.[4] In 1940, it was estimated that the services of 340,000 em-

[2] Francis L. Berkeley, Jr., "History and Problems of Control of Manuscripts in the United States," in American Philosophical Society, *Proceedings*, 98:171–178 (June, 1954).

[3] W. James King, "The Project on the History of Recent Physics in the United States," in *American Archivist*, 27:237–244 (April, 1964); John B. Blake, "Medical Records and History," in *American Archivist*, 27:229–236 (April, 1964).

[4] Schellenberg, *Modern Archives*, 35–36.

ployees, costing $680,000,000 per year, were required to create and maintain the federal records. The accumulated total of such records ran to over 18,500,000 cubic feet, enough to fill six buildings the size of the Pentagon. Allowing $27,000,000 yearly amortization for that amount of space, plus the expenses for office materials and equipment, the estimated total annual expenditure on federal records making and keeping was $1,200,000,000.[5] By the 1960's, federal records scheduled for permanent retention as archives were accumulating at the rate of 200,000 cubic feet per year and exceeded 6,000,000 cubic feet. To translate these figures into more familiar units of measurement: one cubic foot of records consisting of 3,000 letter-size sheets of paper weighs approximately 30 pounds, and about 70 cubic feet equal one ton.[6]

While its records have been burgeoning, the federal government has also become more conscious of its records, a manifestation of its bureaucratic maturity. In 1954, the Hoover Commission reported that all departments of the government held in their possession a total of about 23,000,000 cubic feet of records. The government agencies of Great Britain held only 600,000 linear feet of papers in that same year. The difference in volume of records is obviously out of proportion to the size and age of the two governments and must be explained by the premise that American society has been built in the contemporary period upon a paper foundation.[7]

The complexity of American records is a reflection of the inherent complexity of the American government and the society it serves. The system of checks and balances, the political party system, and the demands for increasing and specialized services from the government have made hopelessly antiquated earlier methods of haphazard records-keeping. Governmental agencies and business firms struggled along, inventing and per-

[5] Emmett J. Leahy, *Records Management in the United States Government: A Report with Recommendations Prepared for the Commission on Organization of the Executive Branch of the Government* (Washington, 1949), 1–7.

[6] U. S., National Archives and Records Service, Records Management Division, *Federal Records Centers* (Washington, 1954), 2–7, 24; J. J. Hammitt, "Government Archives and Records Management," in *American Archivist*, 28:219–222 (April, 1965).

[7] Schellenberg, *Modern Archives*, 35–36.

fecting more efficient records procedures as circumstances required. The result was a confused and heterogeneous records system, but one which uniquely revealed the form and functions of the creating agencies. Even in filing systems, for example, eclecticism was the rule, and procedures ranged from application of the Dewey-decimal system, to the subject-numeric, to the duplex-numeric.[8]

A cruel fate has prepared a bitter irony for the historian who must rely upon contemporary mass documentation. Although bulkiness of the material has passed beyond the capacity of the individual historian using traditional methods, this same high-bulk documentation contains less and less of what traditionally the historian wishes to know. He has been primarily interested in the origin and formulation of policy; these functions now are often accomplished by telephone or in conference, without benefit of documentation. It is the routine applications of fixed policy which produce the rising mountain of paper. Paul Hasluck, Australian Minister for Territories, with great truth has called the telephone the "great robber of history."[9]

The Federal Records Act of 1950, the basic response of the federal government to the problem of high-bulk documentation, provides mainly for establishing a program of records management. Under it, the central archival agency of the United States was given the power of inspection over all federal records in order to formulate "standards, procedures, and techniques of management of records to facilitate retaining and disposal of records." Furthermore, the National Archives and Records Service was given the authority to regulate inter-agency transfers of records, to establish standards for the selective retention of records of continuing value, and to establish and operate records centers for material of intermediate record and evidentiary value, pending a determination of its final disposition. Inherent in the program was an analytical and promotional function aimed at curbing the production of records.[10] Similar programs of rec-

[8] *Ibid.*, 37–39; Oliver W. Holmes, "Archival Arrangement—Five Different Operations at Five Different Levels," in *American Archivist*, 27:23–41 (January, 1964).

[9] Schellenberg, *Modern Archives*, 37–39.

[10] *Ibid.*, 40–41. See also U. S., National Archives and Records Service, *Records Management Bibliography* (mimeographed, Washington, 1954), 1–41.

ords management have been adopted and applied in private industry wherever the mass of documentation has threatened to hamper the routine operations of an organization.

RECORDS MANAGEMENT AND HISTORICAL DOCUMENTATION

THE IMPOSITION of arbitrary management procedures upon the creation and preservation of records quite obviously has an immediate bearing upon the value and use of such materials for historical documentation. Historians quake at the prospect of coping with high-bulk documentation; they would very probably prefer that nature and documentary accidents take their course, they would leave to fire, water, carelessness, and rats the task of whittling down to manageable size the total documentation. The realization that normal attrition cannot contend with the mass production of records has led historians into an uneasy alliance with modern-day records managers, however.

If the analogy is not indelicate, contemporary records may be regarded somewhat in the same vein as the fruits of the population explosion. In twenty years, historians, like draft boards, will be engaged in selecting an unrepresentative sample of today's production to serve tommorrow's needs. Records managers, for their part, are perhaps analogous to the men of medicine or science, upon whose professional judgment may be based the production, classification, distribution, and ultimate disposition of the offspring of contemporary society.

Control of production, without interfering with the normal routine of society, is the first means of attacking proliferation, either of people or of records. The extent and complexity of a governmental operation is usually so firmly set by law or custom that it cannot be changed. However, the specific way in which a program is conceived and executed is subject to administrative simplification. Because the machinery of government tends to become ever more complicated, radical measures such as the Hoover Commission investigation may be required to cut through precedent and establish even the most elementary reforms in records management.[11]

[11] Schellenberg, *Modern Archives,* 44–45.

Simplification of the work process is the key to production control of records. Take, for example, the system of proving land titles. In the Anglo-Saxon tradition, title is usually proven by establishing a crown grant and linking it by chain of title to the present owner. Sir Robert Richard Torrens (1814–1884) proposed that the complex system be replaced by one of simple land title registration. Under the Torrens system, proof of ownership is represented by a certificate of title, the indefeasibility of which is guaranteed by the government. Once issued, the certificate itself carries all subsequent transactions by endorsement. The necessity of a title search upon each transaction is thus eliminated. The system was enacted in South Australia in 1857 and has been subsequently adopted in New Zealand, Canada, and some states of the American union.[12]

The records of a governmental or private agency which relate to routine or repetitive activity are usually suitable for standardization. In a very large agency, most records are of that character, and, because of the volume involved, some form of control of records production is imperative. Uncontrolled, records can multiply and develop into a cancerous growth upon the host organism. Realizing that some governmental and private agencies were already creating records beyond their means to care for them, the Hammermill Paper Company engaged the Business Trading Corporation of New York to do a pioneer study of standardizing and simplifying paper work in 1930. The resulting report by Ladson Butler and O. R. Johnson was published as *Management Control through Business Forms*. The authors advocated a logical and creative use of forms to facilitate work flow and to minimize the paper residue of routine operations. Scattered applications of these principles were made in American industry, but no large-scale application was made in the federal government until after World War II, when, in 1947, the Bureau of the Budget published a guide similar to the Hammermill project and entitled, *Simplifying Procedures through Forms Control*.[13]

Traditional procedures for records distribution and filing have

---

[12] *Ibid.*, 45–46.
[13] *Ibid.*, 46–48; Ollon D. McCool, "The Metes and Bounds of Records Management," in *American Archivist*, 27:87–94 (January, 1964).

an important bearing upon the quantity of material produced. When a new subject comes to the attention of a government office under the European registry system, a new file is opened for that subject. Thereafter, the file moves from office to office, single copies only of the relevant papers being added to it. Under the American system, each department or office concerned gets a duplicate copy for its files, and at times the multiplication of copies assumes frightening proportions. Records managers, therefore, must be particularly alert to the dangers of carbon paper in their war upon records production.[14]

From the experience of business and government in handling high-bulk records has emerged a standardized system in which production control is but the first step. To the records must also be applied the principles of effective handling in current use, of wise selection for retention and disposal, of retirement or transfer to intermediate storage, and of effective archival administration over what remains. The key to records management in all of these steps is prior planning of what records are to be controlled, how they are to be preserved for current use, when they are to be converted to archives, and when they are to be finally retired.[15]

Accumulations of high-bulk records are most immediately dependent upon the classification scheme employed to facilitate the prompt retrieval of specific pieces of paper and information from the body of the files. As applied to accumulations of records, classification means a consistent arrangement of records, usually by a registry or filing system. The action to which the records relate, the organizational structure of the agency producing the records, or the subject matter of the records may provide the basis upon which records may be classified. Beyond these primary elements, records may be further subdivided. Action reflected in records may be regarded in terms of functions, activities, and transactions. Functions are basically substantive and facilitative in character. Substantive functions have to do with the technical and professional work of an agency, which work

[14] Schellenberg, *Modern Archives*, 49–51.
[15] Philip C. Brooks, *Public Records Management* (Chicago, 1960), 1–4; Jesse Clark, "Current Paperwork Problems in American Industry," in *American Archivist*, 27:391–394 (July, 1964).

distinguishes it from all similar agencies. Facilitative functions relate to the internal operations and housekeeping details which are common to other agencies. Transactions may be regarded as those discrete events which link the agency in question to specific persons, corporate bodies, places, and topics. Finally, all activities, whether substantive or facilitative, are composed of transactions, either policy or operational in nature.[16]

When records are classified according to a functional scheme, they take on the form familiar in American practice, in which the smallest unit of the files consists of a folder on a person, event, place, or like category. The first grouping of folders is by activity, such as personnel, fiscal matters, supply, transportation, communications, and the like. At the next level, records may be further grouped by functional category.[17]

The second major element in the classification of records is to be found in the organization of the creating agency. Most governmental and many private agencies have adopted in recent years the line and staff basis of organization developed in the armed services in Western Europe and the United States. As a clue to finding one's way through the maze of records produced by such an organization, it should be remembered that, generally speaking, the staff of an agency handles significant policy papers as extensions of the will of the head of the agency, while line officers carry out the established policy.[18]

Organizational classification involves a grouping made by the classification scheme employed within an agency, or by the decentralization of records to parallel the geographical location of the component offices of an agency. American records practice carries the principle of decentralization to the ultimate degree, each subsection of an office retaining its own files. Thus, multiple series, separate from the main correspondence files and relating to fiscal, personnel, or transportation activities (all of which are facilitative), are established. So, too, are separate files of substantive records created by each subagency.[19]

Classification by subject is the exception to the rule of classi-

[16] Schellenberg, *Modern Archives,* 52–54.
[17] *Ibid.,* 57–61.
[18] *Ibid.,* 55.
[19] *Ibid.,* 57–61.

fication by either organizational lines or function, and the system is more applicable to classes of records created for reference and information than to those arising from governmental action. With this category of records, the best schemes of classification arise from the materials themselves rather than from application of some external system, such as the Dewey decimal.[20]

Once a classification scheme has been adopted for a series of records, it must be translated into a workable procedure both by a system of filing and by physical housing of the records. American filing systems are distinguished from their European counterparts by the absence of a register, relying instead upon a self-indexing arrangement. Current American practice undoubtedly sprang from loose application of British usage of an earlier day. For example, the filing system employed by the Continental Congress closely followed the records practices of the House of Commons except for the use of a register. The Revolutionary Congress established five classes of records according to function and to subject. First, a file for copies of all outgoing documents and letters on domestic matters was opened, paralleled by a file of copies of all outgoing correspondence on foreign affairs. A third series of records consisted of all incoming documents on foreign matters, including letters from American ministers abroad. A fourth series contained the "rough" journal of the Congress and all papers supporting the reported abstracts of its debates and transactions. Lastly, a class was created of all other "loose" and unrelated papers. Helen L. Chatfield has suggested that the "simple and primitive" filing system employed by the clerks of the Founding Fathers irrevocably set the pattern for handling the records of the future federal government. The underlying theme of classification has remained constant—in, out, and internal miscellaneous—in and out correspondence being indexed separately and bound or arranged in chronological order.[21]

The development of the modern vertical filing system had to await technological developments in the creation of records. Particularly, some simple means of duplicating letters sent to others was required for the interfiling of incoming and outgoing

[20] Brooks, *Public Records Management,* 5–8.
[21] Schellenberg, *Modern Archives,* 78.

letters, and the development of filing cabinets and associated folders was required for the arrangement of records on a self-indexing basis.

The first press-copying machine, invented by James Watt in 1780, employed the use of a glutinous ink and involved pressing a page of newly written material against a moistened sheet of thin paper. With the use of aniline dyes, press-copiers attained even wider use by mid-century. By 1887 the Cockrell Committee on Methods of Business in the Executive Departments recommended that the copying of letters by hand be discontinued and that the press-copy machine be adopted in all bureaus. The press copier was on the way to universal use when the perfection of the typewriter and carbon paper dealt it a mortal blow.[22]

The typewriter was a child of the industrial and commercial boom which followed the Civil War. Invented by Christopher Latham Sholes in 1868, it was first used by a government agency in 1874, when the War Department purchased a Sholes and Glydden machine for $125. By 1900 the typewriter had come into general use through design improvements which permitted the typist to view his work while operating the machine. Carbon papers, first developed in the 1880's, remained unsatisfactory until Brazilian carnauba wax was used to stabilize carbon ink in 1905. This technological breakthrough was followed in rapid order by the perfection of the mimeograph, the hectograph, and the photostat, enabling each office with a typewriter to duplicate anything produced on the machine.[23]

Once produced, records must be filed and housed in some systematic order, and that order largely governs their accessibility for future historical research. The early American filing scheme separated records from letter books and registers. Records were usually folded in thirds, tied in bundles, and placed on shelves or in chests, as in the Navy Department, until after the Civil War. In 1868 two new filing systems met with widespread acceptance. One system, perfected by E. W. Woodruff, consisted of standardized wooden boxes, 3½″ by 8″, in which folded documents were placed in sequential order. In competition, the vertical filing system, first offered by the Amberg File

[22] *Ibid.*, 81–82.
[23] *Ibid.*, 82–83.

and Index Company, involved the filing of unfolded sheets of documents in cardboard folders. Refinements and modifications made on the Amberg system by Dr. Nathaniel S. Rosenau of Buffalo permitted the vertical file to win government preference over the Woodruff system. In 1912 its adoption by the government was recommended by the Taft Commission on Economy and Efficiency.[24]

The only significant differences in application of the now widely-used vertical filing system are in the internal arrangement of records within file cabinets and drawers. Three basic types of arrangement have evolved. One places file units in numerical sequence in the order sent or received. Another arranges all records in one master alphabetical series, including entries by persons, subjects, and places. A third arrangement places records in a rational order according to an external and often arbitrary classification scheme.[25] Alphabetical organization is usually adopted for smaller files, numerical and external organization for more bulky and more complex files.[26]

Numerical filing systems were first adopted in federal agencies to provide a transition from the registry system in operation in some of the colonial administrations. In practice the numeric systems have not been successful because they tend to break down dossiers into very small units and to make more, rather than less, difficult the retrieval of a given piece of documentation. The system works better in handling bulky files or files relating to legal, regulatory, and investigatory activities of the government. The code in general use assumes the following primary classifications: 1 = Education; 2 = Communications; 3 = Accounts; 4 = Personnel; 5 = Supplies; 6 = Organization; 7 = Finance; 8 = Publications; 9 = Reports; 10 = Legislation. A further refinement of the scheme is the duplex-numeric system, whereby additional numbers are added to show subdivisions, as 2 = Communications; 2-1 = Mail; 2-1-1 = Postage.[27]

[24] *Ibid.*, 83–84.
[25] *Ibid.*, 84.
[26] Allen Chaffee, *How to File Business Papers and Records* (New York, 1938), 8–28. Adaptations of the three basic systems are sold in the United States by such trade names as Beehive, Direct Name, Skyline, Duplex Numeric, Dewey Decimal, Nual, Leader, Natural, Perpetual, Safeguard, and Tri-Guard. See *ibid.*, 19–107.
[27] Schellenberg, *Modern Archives*, 84–85.

Alphabetical filing was introduced into federal practice by General Fred C. Ainsworth through his carded Civil War records. The success of the system in facilitating the processing of pensions claims led the Cockrell Committee in 1887 to recommend the application of the principle to all appropriate federal records. The recommendation was supported by the American Library Bureau, which urged use of the then new vertical cases. For very large files the Soundex system, whereby material is arranged by homonymic sound rather than by orthographic spelling, was developed. The system has received its widest application in Census Bureau in the arrangement of 100,000,000 cards on which information on 100,000,000 persons has been abstracted from the censuses of 1880, 1900, and 1920.[28]

The inadequacies of the alphabetic and numeric systems of arranging files have led to repeated attempts to adopt some logical, external order, one usually modeled upon the Dewey-decimal system of library classification. A form of this scheme was first applied to high-bulk records in 1898 by the Baltimore and Ohio Railroad. Known as the "Railroad Classification File," the system was copyrighted in 1902 and was recommended for government use by the Taft Commission in 1912. The scheme has proven to be unsuited, however, to the practical needs of the government.[29]

The most difficult single problem facing the modern archivist, that of appraising the records entrusted to his care, is compounded by their contemporary nature and great bulk. Because the material is so new, historians cannot easily lay down the guidelines of value in use. On the other hand, the bulkiness of the material makes manifestly impossible the retention of the whole on the chance that it will be of future research value. Amid these conflicting interests, and largely without precedents derived from experience, the modern archivist must grope and fumble towards a correct appraisal of his records. By the application of logic and the projection of sound principles he can close the gap of error and ultimately arrive at an educated guess as to the research and reference values of his materials. Ap-

[28] *Ibid.*, 86; Margaret K. Odell and Early P. Strong, *Records Management and Filing Operations* (New York, 1947), 8–18.
[29] Schellenberg, *Modern Archives*, 90–93.

praisal of records is a continuous process, and, for the sake of consistency, one single authority, governed by all the viewpoints bearing upon any of the values inherent in records, should be given the responsibility.

The archivist proceeds first to distinguish between evidential and informational values, between primary and secondary justifications for retaining records. Evidential values are to be found in documentation illustrating the origins of policies and programs, the implementation and administration thereof, matters of public relations, and internal management or "housekeeping." On the other hand, informational values in documentation refer to uniqueness, to form as opposed to substance, to the historical importance which can be readily attributed to a given program, and to the records of persons, things, or phenomena of which the government may be only the records keeper.[30]

In order of descending importance, justification for the retention of records is based upon evidentiary usefulness to the creating agency beyond current need, evidence of fundamental importance to individual citizens (such as vital statistics and land titles), evidence supporting individual rights (such as pensions), and information supporting general research interests.[31]

Despite these guidelines, appraisal should still be undertaken seriously and with an open mind. None of the considerations can be reduced to exact standards, nor can standards be applied with absolute consistency. Appraisals should be based neither upon intuition nor on arbitrary supposition of values, but rather upon standards applied with moderation and common sense. If an archivist cannot adequately appraise a given body of records, he should seek the help of experts after he has done the basic work of analysis. Finally, the archivist should be aware of his role as moderator among the conflicting interests of various organizations and groups in his records and should seek to serve each to the fullest extent without infringing upon the legitimate interests of any.[32]

The appraisal of records is greatly simplified if the archivist

[30] *Ibid.*, 1–44, 233–276; U. S., National Archives, *How to Dispose of Records: A Manual for Federal Officials* (Washington, 1946), 5–20, 24–33.

[31] Brooks, *Public Records Management*, 8–11.

[32] Schellenberg, *Modern Archives*, 44–46.

is permitted to project his insight and experience backward to the creation of records, to participate in the process of records management. Such an arrangement not only comes closest to serving all of the various interests in records or archives, but subjects the entire process of records creation, preservation, and disposal to a master plan. As a bonus, proper records management increases the efficiency of the creating agency while reducing the cost of files maintenance.[33]

The concept of selective disposal of records as an aspect of archival responsibility made little headway in America during the first hundred years of independence. What little legislation there was enacted relating to records provided stiff penalties for their unauthorized destruction rather than authority for their orderly retirement. Frequent requests for relief from the burden of superfluous records all met with congressional indifference or with outright opposition.[34] Instead of giving rise to a program of records management, the problem of excess federal records in the last century was deflected to the support of the movement for a federal archives.

A critical paper shortage created by the manufacture of munitions in Great Britain during World War I led to the first objective appraisal in the Anglo-American tradition of old records. From that experience and from the discovery that a large percentage of old records could be disposed of without any serious loss of their supposed evidentiary or informational values has grown the science of records management.[35] The science has been rooted in a need for economy of business operation and for keeping the size of archives within manageable bounds, within the ability of the creating agency to support and care for that portion of its records of continuing or permanent value.[36]

The dislocations of World War II engendered a serious interest in records management in the United States. On the

[33] Chaffee, *How to File,* 49–60; Ladson Butler and O. R. Johnson, *Management Control Through Business Forms* (New York, 1930), 1–2, 29–30.

[34] Henry P. Beers, "Historical Development of the Records Disposal Policy of the Federal Government Prior to 1934," in *American Archivist,* 7:181–189 (July, 1944).

[35] Philip C. Brooks, "The Selection of Records for Preservation," in *American Archivist,* 3:221–234 (October, 1940).

[36] Emmett J. Leahy, "Modern Records Management," in *American Archivist,* 12:231–233 (July, 1949).

strength of a pilot project planned and executed by Emmett J. Leahy for the United States Navy and other parallel activities, the "father of American records management" suggested a number of principles and components of any program of records reduction. Practically speaking, any such program originates from within the organization; administrative officers must conscientiously wish to reduce the volume of their records before any efficient steps can be taken. The first such step is the employment of a trained archivist to design and implement a records program for that particular agency. After the scattered records have been accumulated and inventoried, the process of appraisal begins. Based upon the archival mediator's appraisal of conflicting opinions and values, a master program is devised specifying the permanent retention, intermediate storage, or prompt elimination of all existing records and the planned limitation of future records. An orderly transfer of records to archives and records centers frees valuable working space while improving the care given to those records which are retained. Meaningful samples are taken of all records destroyed, and grants or loans of records are considered as alternatives to destruction. Wherever indicated, microfilming is adopted to reduce the bulk of materials which have been designated for permanent or long-term preservation.[37]

Since World War II the functions of archivists and records managers have become virtually interchangeable, despite some charges that records managers are too pragmatic to be regarded as members of a "scholarly" profession.[38] Even if the pragmatic interests of the records manager have led him to sell his scholarly soul, a rising interest in business history has forced him at the same time to cater to the historical utility of the material he preserves. Businessmen have come to realize that their records are weapons in the contest for the good will of the public, and

[37] Emmett J. Leahy, "Reduction of Public Records," in *American Archivist*, 3:18–38 (January, 1940); Brooks, *Public Records Management*, 12; Odell and Strong, *Records Management*, 256–276; Brooks, "Archives in World War II," 263–280; Emmett J. Leahy and Robert E. Weil, "Planning the Records Storage Center," in *The Office*, 35, no. 6:64–70, 142–147 (June, 1952).

[38] LeRoy DePery, "Archivists and Records Managers—A Partnership," in *American Archivist*, 23:51 (January, 1960).

this realization has led to a number of advanced projects in records management within the American business community.[39]

The widest application by far of principles of records management has been in the myriad agencies of the federal government, particularly in the selective disposal of records of the lowest evidentiary and informational value. The Act of February 16, 1899, which provided authority for the selective disposal of records, was reenacted on June 19, 1934, as the basic law for the newly created National Archives.[40]

Prior to 1935 there had been no careful and systematic appraisal of the records of the federal government. File clerks and office managers usually indiscriminately disposed of their oldest and largest records series in order to make room for newer accumulations. In 1935, with the opening of the National Archives, the retirement and disposal of records in the federal government came under professional archival control. The quality and character of that control is revealed in the following statement issued for the guidance of government agencies by the staff of the National Archives:

> Documentation includes a knowledge of the manner in which an agency documents itself as a necessary consequence of its activities; the character and value of the resulting documents; the means by which they should be organized for use; the manner of their disposition through appraisal and evaluation; placement in appropriate custody throughout their life history, and disposal when their record value has diminished to the point of practical uselessness; and finally, the means by which the information in the material is made available to the users of the records.[41]

Various experiments in records management in selected agencies blazed the trail to general application throughout the federal establishment. One such experiment, undertaken in the TVA in 1943, required every writer and recipient in the authority to indicate upon the face of every letter his evaluation of it as a piece of permanent ("P") documentation, or merely temporary

---

[39] Robert A. Shiff, "The Archivist's Role in Records Management," in *American Archivist*, 19:111–120 (April, 1956).

[40] Schellenberg, *Modern Archives*, 97–103.

[41] Helen L. Chatfield, "Records and the Administrator," in *Public Administration Review*, 10:119–122 (Spring, 1950).

("T"). "T" papers were to be automatically destroyed two years after their creation. Lack of consistency in evaluating and the absence of authority for destruction of records without the concurrence of the National Archives and a congressional committee almost undermined the pre-classification experiment. The necessary modifications were hit upon by accident. In 1947 the operating supervisors within the TVA drafted a list of categories of unnecessary records suitable for destruction, and the list grew to embrace about half of the total volume of the authority's files. When the entire list was subsequently approved for destruction two years after creation, the way was cleared for a continuation of the pre-classification experiment. A continuing audit of the system confirms its effectiveness and suggests the possibility of application in other agencies.[42]

Reference has already been made to the records management project at the Navy Department. The project came into being as an emergency measure in 1943 when it was learned that the files of the department were expanding at the annual rate of one-third the total existing accumulation, or more than 5,000 additional file cabinets for 1943 alone.[43] The work proceeded in a routine manner. First came a survey to determine the exact nature and bulk of the proliferating records. Under the Disposal Acts of 1939 and 1940 transfer commitments were concluded in 1944. Non current personnel records were among the first categories to be subjected to general scheduling for transfer or destruction. In addition, routine inquiries, complaints, correspondence concerning distribution of publications, and "fan mail" were scheduled for disposal three months after receipt.[44]

The "paper explosion" of World War II precipitated a similar experience in records management in the War Department. In 1943 the Records Branch was created as a "necessary and essential" custodian facility in the Military District of Washington to relieve the National Archives of the obligation of acquiring

[42] Sidney R. Hall, "Retention and Disposal of Correspondence Files," in *American Archivist,* 15:5–14 (January, 1952). See also, U. S., Tennessee Valley Authority, *TVA Files Audit Handbook* (Washington, 1950).

[43] Robert H. Bahmer, "Scheduling the Disposal of Records," in *American Archivist,* 6:169–175 (July, 1943).

[44] Philip C. Brooks, "Archival Procedures for Planned Records Retirement," in *American Archivist,* 11:308 (October, 1948).

masses of military records of only temporary value. Out of this wartime necessity grew another line of experience which flowered into techniques applicable to high-bulk documentation of intermediate value. The Records Branch was expanded to serve the entire Department of Defense after 1947, and it survived the assimilation of such masses of additional material as that supporting the ninety-seven-volume official history of the Army during the war and the captured German military documents.

The additional documentation created by the Korean conflict and the creation of the North Atlantic Treaty Organization seriously strained the capacity of the Records Branch, and in 1954 the National Archives assumed responsibility with the reluctant agreement of the Department of Defense. An estimated total of 235,000 cubic feet of records and a staff of 102 were transferred to the Federal Records Center at Alexandria, Virginia, in January, 1958, and the material has subsequently become the nucleus of the World War II Records Division of the National Archives.[45]

The Records Disposal Act of 1943 permitted federal agencies to submit schedules for records disposal, but the anticipated flood of such schedules never materialized. Finally, the National Archives, bursting with material already admitted and anxious about the tremendous quantity of records which threatened to sweep down upon it like an avalanche, after the war drafted general schedules applicable to all agencies of a common type, and the Archives received limited statutory power to enforce these schedules in the Records Act of 1945. Originally, seven general schedules were drawn up, all relating to civilian personnel and housekeeping activities. Since then, additional instructions have been issued to facilitate records disposal when specified by the general schedule, to insure better care of records containing information of continuing value, to assure the maximum utilization of records centers, to limit the total number of retained copies of a document, to designate the master copy of a series of multiple character, and to facilitate the authorized and automatic disposal of scheduled records.[46]

---

[45] Sherrod East, "Archival Experience in a Prototype Intermediate Depository," in *American Archivist*, 27:43–56 (January, 1964).

[46] Isadore Perlman, "General Schedules and Federal Records," in *American Archivist*, 15:27 (January, 1952).

The pioneering efforts at records management were too feeble to stem the rising tide of paper, and the total continued to increase at an alarming rate. A preliminary report of the Hoover Commission, largely drafted by Emmett J. Leahy, pointed up some startling statistics. From 1930 to 1948 the total volume of federal records grew from about 4,000,000 cubic feet to almost 20,000,000 cubic feet. In 1948 some 18,000,000 square feet of office and storage space was occupied by federal records, and, on the basis of rental value alone, merely housing these records was costing more than $20,000,000 annually. Filing equipment worth $154,000,000 at current prices was tied up in serving non-current records. It was estimated, on a cost-accounting basis, that $29.00 per year is required to house and maintain but one file cabinet of records occupying six square feet of floor space. In contrast, the same material could be stored in a records center for about $2.15 per year, saving $26.85 for each file cabinet of records so transferred. It was calculated that up to 50 per cent of all federal records could be removed from their respective offices of creation without serious inconvenience to the government. Therefore, the commission recommended "the creation of a Records Management Bureau in the Office of General Services, to include the National Archives," "enactment of a new Federal Records Management Law to provide for the more effective preservation, management, and disposal of Government records," and "establishment of an adequate records management program in each department and agency.[47]

An immediate result of the preliminary Hoover Commission report on records management was the passage of the Federal Records Act of 1950. The act authorized the General Services Administration to survey the files of all federal agencies and to report under a number of standard and comprehensive headings.[48] When the massive inventory of federal records was completed, a summary dated June, 1960, revealed that the federal records had grown to a total of 24.5 million cubic feet, or roughly

[47] U. S., Commission on Organization of the Executive Branch of the Government [Hoover Commission], *Office of General Services: A Report to the Congress, February, 1949* (Washington, 1959), 6–7; Angel, "Federal Records Management," 13–26.

[48] Homer L. Calkin, "Inventorying Files," in *Public Administration Review*, 11:242–252 (Autumn, 1951).

seven times the capacity of the Pentagon. Of this total, some 18 million cubic feet of records were found to be still in the hands of operating agencies; 6.5 million cubic feet had been screened and transferred to archival custody. About 1,100,000 cubic feet of material was stored in the National Archives proper. The remaining 5,000,000 cubic feet of records were in storage in records centers. An obvious solution was the transferring of more records to archival custody, and an obvious alternative to erecting multiple copies of the National Archives building was a massive program of microfilming. It was suggested that if some 340,000 cubic feet of permanent archival materials were microfilmed each year and if a more selective accession program were established, the National Archives could continue to function as then constituted for about twenty-six years. The staff of the National Archives of course strongly objected to the proposal. Rather, it urged that stronger records management programs be instituted at once, together with a wider use of records centers, and that the National Archives be enlarged when it became necessary.[49] Otherwise, the citizens of the United States are faced with the geometric progression of a budget for creating and keeping records now estimated at $4,000,000,000 per year.[50]

While the federal government was struggling to contain its paper explosion, states, municipalities, and the corporate giants of American industry were waging a parallel war upon the proliferation of records.[51] Although business firms can theoretically afford to be more ruthless than government in the destruction of obsolete records, in practice they have tended to be more timid. In addition, those business firms which have seriously approached their paper problem tried selectively to dispose of their records on an *ad hoc* basis rather than by a master plan. Experience

---

[49] U. S., General Accounting Office, *Report to the Congress of the United States: Review of Certain Records Management Activities, National Archives and Records Services Administration, December, 1961* (Washington, 1962), 1–28. The National Archives reiterated its basic proposal incorporated earlier in its *How to Dispose of Records*, iii–22.

[50] Arnold Olsen, "The Federal Paperwork Jungle—The Natives are Becoming Restless," in *American Archivist*, 27:363–370 (July, 1964).

[51] Katsaros, "Managing the Records of the World's Greatest City," 175–180; I. MacLean, "Trends in Organizing Modern Public Records, with Special Reference to Classification Methods," in *Archives and Manuscripts*, 1, no. 3:1–17 (December, 1956).

indicates that a corporation can safely dispose of about 80 per cent of its non-current records. Since a typical, large, nationally-based American corporation may possess upwards of 800,000 cubic feet of records, a maximum reduction could bring the central archives down to about 150,000 to 200,000 cubic feet, with corresponding reductions in cost and advances in operating efficiency. Any such reduction should be carried out, however, under the direction of a trained archivist or records manager, who would require a staff of about twenty-five clerks to implement the program with optimum success.[52] Examination of several business records management programs will illustrate their operating formulas and the degree of success which they have enjoyed.

An early records management program was established in 1944 at the Ohio Oil Company following a records inventory and appraisal by a committee of company officers. This intermediate-size company established retention policies on managerial correspondence, purchase orders, requisitions and promotional material issued by the advertising department, cancelled checks, main office purchase orders, charge sale orders, and cash sale tickets. All other categories of routine records were found to be duplicated in more concentrated form elsewhere or to be expendable information.[53]

It is not exclusively the older established corporations whose records go back to the turn of the century or before which suffer from a surplus of records. For example, when an unnamed young company engaged principally in electronics research under government contract surveyed its records in 1952, it found them to be growing at an alarming rate, complicated by a large number of documents bearing a security classification. Widespread microfilming and destruction of the original records, obviously the most practical solution, was applied to about one-fourth of the corporation's files at an annual cash saving of about $1,000.[54]

In 1952 the Mutual Life Insurance Company of New York also surveyed its massive files for a possible reduction of bulk.

[52] Irving P. Schiller, "A Program for the Management of Business Records," in *Business History Society, Bulletin,* 21:47–48 (April, 1947).
[53] Jewel Moberly, *et al., Case Studies in Records Retention and Control* (New York, 1957), 15–60.
[54] *Ibid.,* 61–90.

The peculiar longer-term and documentary nature of the life insurance business precluded any sweeping disposal of records, but some reductions were effected. The archives of the corporate entity itself were separated from the policy-holder files, and seventy-five year retention schedules were adopted for sales commission warrants, policy payment warrants, policy registers, actuary registers, actuary dividend records, checks and drafts in settlement of surrender claims, abstracts, and disability claim payment cards. Disposal of all other categories of non-current records has resulted in an annual saving of about $15,000.[55]

The experience of the U. S. Rubber Company is probably more typical of the application of records management techniques to various types of corporate records. After making a survey early in the 1950's, the company decided to retain permanently the rules and regulations of the Board of [Personnel] Benefits and Awards, note and bond records, bonus and manager share plan rules, bylaws of the corporation, certificates of incorporation and organization, charters, correspondence on all-corporate matters, minutes of corporate meetings, mortgage records, real estate records, reports to stockholders, corporate seals, specimen copies of stock and bond certificates, and stock ledgers. Financial audit reports, applications to and correspondence of the Board of Benefits and Awards, correspondence relating to company policy, correspondence regarding real estate, legal matters, and correspondence regarding policies and procedures were scheduled for preservation on microfilm for fifty years. All other categories of records were to be preserved in their original form for only twenty-five years, then destroyed.[56]

One of the newer and more promising weapons in the arsenal of the records manager is the principle of creative design of records. Successful application of the principle accomplishes the multiple purposes of facilitating the current use of records, curbing their proliferation, and simplifying the segregation of permanent from purely temporary documentation. The principle seeks to control the character and bulk of records of a routine or repetitive nature by functionally designing the printed forms upon which they are created. In application, the existing forms

[55] *Ibid.*, 91–143.
[56] *Ibid.*, 339–369.

are analyzed as to their actual need, their ease of use and read-
ability, ease of filing, and ease of reference.[57] Existing forms and
all prospective ones are evaluated to insure maximum efficiency
in handling and filing in order to guarantee least bulk and effort and the greatest ease of disposal without the necessity of
weeding.[58]

Identification of records for automatic destruction remains
a matter of high priority for any records management program.
The decision to destroy records is irrevocable, but that consideration should not deter the decision when it is indicated. Once
made, the decision is usually carried out as quickly as possible.
If sold as waste paper, the contract covering the sale of records
usually includes a clause to prevent the resale of materials as
documents. In the case of confidential records, either macera-
tion or burning is acceptable as means of total destruction.[59]

At the other extreme on the scale of records utility, a selected
portion of modern, high-bulk materials remain admissible to archives. The traditional criteria of appraisal are still applicable.
To be transferred to archives, records should have not only continuing evidentiary value but also a high secondary value for
research and information. These records should be sufficiently
aged to avoid conflicts of use between the public and the creating agency. They should be transferred in complete and logical
units, regardless of bulk, to insure the integrity of the file. There
should be a free and equal access to such archives, automatically with the passage of time if not immediately. If any of these
criteria can not be met, the records at hand probably deserve
some disposition other than admission to archives.[60]

Although general debate concerning the feasibility, desirability, and proper application of microfilming as a technique in
records management continues, the advantages obviously outweigh the disadvantages on some occasions. Microfilming serves
the dual purposes of reducing bulk and insuring permanence,
but at the expense of high cost. The technique is ideally applied

---

[57] U. S., National Archives and Records Service, *Forms Analysis* (Washington, 1960), 1–62.

[58] U. S., National Archives and Records Service, *Forms Design* (Washington, 1960), 1–87.

[59] Schellenberg, *Modern Archives*, 104–105.

[60] *Ibid.*, 110.

to records of high bulk, in long series, in which each constituent document is an integral part of the series. Because microfilm involves a large labor cost, the use of only the finest quality film is justified. It frequently happens, therefore, that microfilming gives permanence to records created on short-life paper.[61]

The concept of records centers also has particular application to modern, high-bulk documentation. The idea in its modern form was first advanced in 1923 by the Belgian archivist, C. J. Cuvelier, who urged a form of intermediate storage for the overflow of contemporary records pending transfer to an archival institution. The concept was applied to the records of the United States Navy Department as a part of its emergency records management program during World War II. The Hoover Commission later endorsed the concept on the basis of both its functional utility and its economy.[62]

The economics of records centers are truly impressive. Storage of records in a records center costs about $0.55 per cubic foot per year as compared with about $2.30 per cubic foot for maintenance in an operating agency of the government. The saving on capital equipment is even more dramatic. About $0.77 for cardboard containers and $3.90 for shelving is required to contain the same material housed in a $50.00 filing cabinet in an office. Space is also better utilized in a records center than in an office file room. In a records center, one square foot of floor space will support up to three cubic feet of records, whereas only one cubic foot of records can be accommodated upon one square foot of office file space.[63]

In the years since World War II the federal government has become the world's largest single employer and has developed a corresponding accumulation of personnel records. By 1950 "dead" civilian personnel files ran to more than 485,000 cubic feet of bulk, required the services of 360 clerks, cost about $5,700,000 yearly to maintain, and were spread out in more than 22,950 locations. This category of records was regarded as particularly suitable for transfer to records centers, and in 1951

[61] *Ibid.*, 106–107.

[62] Wayne C. Grover, "A Note on the Development of Records Centers in the U. S.," in *Indian Archives*, 4:160 (July–December, 1950).

[63] U. S., National Archives and Records Service, *Records Centers*, 3–24.

the Army and Air Force began transferring to the General Services Administration all inactive civilian personnel records. The Navy followed suit a few weeks later, and by 1953 all federal agencies were required to comply. These records have been consolidated in the records center at St. Louis, Missouri. Included are service folders for over 40,000,000 individuals who have been employed by the federal government in a civilian or service capacity. These records are retained until the seventy-fifth birthday of the former employee, or until the sixtieth anniversary year of his first federal employment; thereafter, the records are destroyed. This mass of documentation is so arranged that it requires only 300,000 square feet of floor space and the services of only 260 persons.[64]

A network of ten federal records centers has been established at Boston, New York, and Philadelphia; Alexandria, Virginia; East Point, Georgia; Bedford Park, Illinois; Kansas City and St. Louis, Missouri; Fort Worth and New Orleans; Denver; South San Francisco and Wilington, California, and Honolulu; and Seattle and Portland.[65] All are operated under the Records Management Division of the General Services Administration.

Records center storage has been found to be a valuable aid in managing records of intermediate value. It is a safety valve through which large accumulations of records may be drawn out of the operating offices without destroying the records or admitting them to archives. Furthermore, records centers are the obvious custodians of the raw files of defunct organizations or of terminated activities, as well as excellent bases for the accumulation and sorting of material ultimately destined to become archives.[66]

However necessary records management may be regarded by archivists, it is viewed as a mixed blessing by most historians. The latter may sympathize with efforts of the former to curb the proliferation of copies and to integrate the creation and filing of records with their ultimate preservation as archives. Historians of the recent past who have confronted bulky govern-

---

[64] Everett O. Alldredge, "The Federal Records Center, St. Louis: Personnel Files and Fiscal Records," in *American Archivist*, 18:111–122 (April, 1955).

[65] U. S., National Archives and Records Service, *Records Centers*, 24.

[66] Schellenberg, *Modern Archives*, 107–108.

mental and corporate records may even be impressed with the necessity of appraising for preservation groups or samples of records, rather than attempting to preserve the whole of an archives or a subjective selection. As a profession, however, historians are as yet hesitant to give unqualified endorsement to the practice of records management. So do they mistrust their own ability to predict their future research interests that they are slow to approve the destruction of any prospective documentation, regardless of its bulk. If pressed to consider the staggering costs of maintaining modern, high-bulk records according to traditional archival practices, historians generally devise their own formulae for preserving what is significant, consistent with reasonable costs. One such effort suggests the possibility of a standard "information quotient," whereby the estimated aggregate research value of a record group is divided by a standard measure of its physical bulk. The lower the resulting quotient, presumably the better the prospect for safely destroying that record group.[67]

HISTORICAL RESEARCH IN MASS DOCUMENTATION

THE VAST ACCUMULATION of modern mass documentation is still *terra incognita* for most American historians, a shore only dimly seen beyond a sea of the more familiar types of material for historical research. Contemporary mass documentation poses a number of special problems for research scholars, for not only is it more extensive, but it is qualitatively different as well. While the new guidelines are not yet clear, it is obvious that traditional approaches of historians to less abundant quantities of research material may be entirely inadequate in coping with the new, mass materials. New concepts and techniques of research may well be indicated.

Even before the advent of mechanical data processing, scholars were falling behind in their ability to assimilate large collections of contemporary research material. With indifferent success, they have used rough and often unscientific sampling techniques, or employed research assistants who cannot be expected to be as

[67] Harlow, "Managing Manuscript Collections," 203–212.

alert as more mature scholars to the implications of evidence. Other scholars have merely narrowed their fields of research, working longer days and longer years to master the mounting documentation on ever smaller and less significant segments of the past. The difficulties of the traditional heuristical approach to modern sources has been further compounded by the tendency to apply archival principles to large manuscript collections, blurring the distinction between the two primary forms of historical evidence. Historians are thereby forced to accept less adequate bibliographical controls and more general subject headings, resulting in less efficient retrieval of information.[68]

The major obstacle to overcoming the problem of high-bulk documentation has been the facile but misleading idea that sampling techniques are the solution. Historians have long employed what they have been pleased to call sampling in an imprecise manner, as in using several divergent editorials from scattered geographical areas to reconstruct public opinion on a given issue. The publicity and admitted accuracy characterizing contemporary voter opinion and preference polls has further heightened the prestige of the sampling process upon which they are based. Unfortunately, most historians understand that process only imperfectly and are tempted to employ sophisticated research tools in a manner for which they were not intended.

In the first place, a random sample of information from even a large body of statistics has a margin of error too high for purposes of historical research. If generalizations are to be made upon the basis of a sample, that sample must be a guaranteed model of the larger mass it represents. Rather than drawing generalizations on a given society by selecting the raw census returns for every thousandth family unit, historians must instead draw upon designated returns to match the statistically-deter mined averages and norms within that given society. All of these principles can be summarized by the observation that sampling

[68] George L. Anderson, "Mechanical Aids in Historical Research," in Hesseltine and McNeil, eds., *Clio*, 78. For an early treatise on mechanical aids in support of historical research, see Robert C. Binkley, *Manual of Methods of Reproducing Research Materials* (Ann Arbor, 1936); Theodore R. Schellenberg, *The Management of Archives* (New York, 1965), *passim;* Robert L. Brubaker, "Archival Principles and the Curator of Manuscripts," in *American Archivist*, 29:505–514 (October, 1966).

is valuable as a means of understanding *form* in a large mass of information rather than as an effective approach to its *substance*.

If sampling is to be employed in historical research, it must take into account periodic fluctuations, in order that trends and historical shifts may be observed and documented. To be true to that which it represents, a sample must be complete for its category, by day, by type, or by any other meaningful classification. Intra-period sampling is also necessary to show any seasonable or nonperiodic variations. A series of statistical records to be sampled should have some substantive content not entirely susceptible to reduction by statistical summary.

The informational approach to sampling is particularly appropriate to contemporary, high-bulk governmental records. One application of sampling for information rather than evidence was the detailed analysis of the letter "C" of the general correspondence file of the main office of the Home Owners Loan Corporation for the period 1933–1936 for information on the origins of administrative practices followed by the agency. Another example of informational sampling was the review of correspondence of the Bureau of Indian Affairs of the last five working days of 1933 and 1934 for information on changes in procedures and policy.[69] However interesting the information derived from such samples, the evidential value is limited to those samples selected. It may reasonably be inferred that the administrative practices observed in the file of one letter of the alphabet or in one period of the year will be followed throughout the alphabet and the year, but any generalization based upon such inference must be qualified by the arbitrary nature of the sample.

In the rosy dawn of the Age of the Computer, extravagant claims were advanced for the ability of the machine to do all manner of research, including that of an historical nature. Skeptics, however, recalled Jonathan Swift's satirical sketch of the Grand Academy of Lagado, in which a group of professors constructed out of "bits of wood," "squares of paper," and "slender wires" a "machine" whereby "speculative knowledge" could be so improved by "practical and mechanical operations" that ignorant persons could "write books in philosophy, poetry, poli-

---

[69] Paul Lewinson, "Archival Sampling," in *American Archivist*, 20:291–312 (October, 1957).

tics, law, mathematics, and theology, without the least assistance from genius or study."[70]

Historians first became acquainted with mechanical data processing through its library applications, as in the Keysort system of the McBee Company. Utilizing a pattern of marginal holes and notchings and a needle to select cards similarly punched or notched, the system makes possible the coding of as many as 4,000 non-conflicting classifications along one edge of a standard filing card and the sorting of up to 90,000 cards per hour. These early mechanical data processing systems did have an immediate application to bibliographical, statistical, and correlative studies but have produced little savings in the processing of substantive historical data.[71]

The second generation of data processing systems employing punched cards and electronic manipulation increased the number of possible classifications of information bits to the near-infinite total of 100 trillion decillion decillions, and with computation time reduced to microseconds, such data processing systems became the easy masters of massive bibliographic, correlative, and statistical projects. One of the most successful applications of data processing of historical interest has developed since 1958 in the Presidential Papers program at the Library of Congress. Through a computer application of the old hand process of item indexing, addressee-author and chronological indexes to the massive presidential collections on microfilm are being prepared at a fraction of the former cost if, indeed, they could be prepared at all.[72]

Insofar as professionally competent abstracts of mass statistical information are available, historians are expected to make maximum use of them. For example, the Department of Commerce reduces census figures and other mass information to usable form in its publication, *The Statistical Abstract of the United States*. This service can provide the historian with tre-

---

[70] Jonathan Swift, *Gulliver's Travels* (London, 1919), 209–210, 216–217.

[71] Murray Lawson, "The Machine Age in Historical Research," in *American Archivist,* 11:142–144 (April, 1948).

[72] *Ibid.,* 144–149; Frank G. Burke, "The Application of Automatic Techniques in the Management and Control of Source Materials," in *American Archivist,* 30:255–278 (April, 1967); Russell M. Smith, "Item Indexing by Automated Processes," in *American Archivist,* 30:295–302 (April, 1967).

mendously valuable insights into population growth and migra
tion, economic development, and a wide range of commercial
interests. Comparable abstracts are being produced in a wide
variety of scholarly studies on society, economics, and related
fields.[73]

Since the beginning of the New Deal, federal expenditures
for the compilation of statistical information on American society have increased tenfold. Various social welfare projects have
propelled the government into accumulation of more and more
detailed information about a wide range of subjects. This body
of information is qualitatively and quantitatively different from
that traditionally compiled by governments. The new types of
social statistics in general serve the future purposes of planning
and involve the measurement of trends previously only estimated.[74]

The evolution of machine data processing has suggested its
possible application in historical research, and the poetic justice
of using an invention of the mass society to cope with its documentation appeals to many—mostly non-historians. Carl S. Wise
and James W. Perry, in their "Multiple Coding and the Rapid
Selector," have selected history to illustrate the possible uses of
machine data processing. If the historical dimensions of time,
person, organization, and action could be coded into punched
cards, then all of the permutations could be mechanically developed, relieving the historian of the drudgery of hand manipulation of information. Thus, if the entire body of historical facts
regarding the Civil War were to be put on punched cards, a
computer programmed to select references to "General U. S.
Grant" and "Negroes in South Carolina" presumably could do
most of the work of writing a monograph on the interrelationship between those two topics.[75] It should be remembered, however, that such a hypothetical historiographical function is largely

[73] Morris B. Ullman, "Contemporary Trends in the Production and Use of
Social Data," in *American Documentation*, 4:137–146 (October, 1953); Lewinson,
"Archival Sampling," 291–312.

[74] Ullman, "Contemporary Trends," 137–146.

[75] Anderson, "Mechanical Aids," in Hesseltine and McNeil, eds., *Clio*, 96–97.
See Howard F. McGraw, *Marginal Punched Cards in Colleges and Research Li-
braries* (New York, 1949), and Ralph H. Parker, *Library Applications of Punched
Cards* (New York, 1950). See also Lawson, "Machine Age," 141–149.

one of bibliographical recall; little manipulation of statistical information resulting in essentially new insights is provided for or required.

Perhaps a better illustration of the possibilities of mechanization of historical research is provided by a project suggested by George Anderson on the landholding pattern in Kansas. Previous studies of land tenure in the American West have been based upon sampling techniques, and the competitive analysis and the area included have been restricted by the human limitations of statistical manipulation. If *all* of the relevant data could be brought together from census returns, land entry records, land types and values, and resettlements, then meaningful correlations between origin of settlers, ages, economic success, and the like could be drawn.[76]

The tardiness of historians in mastering and applying mass-data techniques may appear at first blush to be a professional scandal, but sober reflection may lead to the conclusion that historians are merely exercising a sound if conservative professional judgment. Historiography is among the most conservative of the scholarly methodologies, and its strength may well lie in that fact. It is the archivist and records manager operating largely independently of the historian who have perfected the concepts of high-bulk documentation. That the historian should fail to succumb to the blandishment of archival theory is no more than to be expected. He is unmoved by whole journals filled with speculation on how best to contend with a rising tide of documentation. Rather, the historian waits for his own fellows to report their practical experience in writing history out of records which have been "managed," appraised, and sampled. Only after the techniques of mass documentation have been proven to provide the means for writing history of traditional quality will they have passed the critical examination historians have a right to make.

---

[76] Anderson, "Mechanical Aids," in Hesseltine and McNeil, eds., *Clio,* 97–100. For a recent experiment in advanced applications of machine-data processes to historical research see Elizabeth Ingerman Wood, *Report on Project History Retrieval; Tests and Demonstrations of an Optic-Coincidence System of Information Retrieval for Historical Materials* (Philadelphia, 1966).

vv

XI

vvvvvvvvvvvvvvvvvvvvvvvvvvvvvvvvvvvvvvvvvvvvvvvvvvvvvvvvvvvv

AURAL AND GRAPHICAL
DOCUMENTATION

WESTERN HISTORICAL SCHOLARSHIP from its founding has been decidedly idea-oriented, formulating and transmitting its concepts through the medium of the written word. Historians, therefore, have been among those scholars most at home in a library. Printed books have been the traditional tools of their trade, and they have been relatively slow to adopt or to employ the newer means of communication. Indeed, when the historian has strayed from familiar means of communication and documentation, he has generally sought what amounts to the preliminary forms of printed materials—archives, manuscripts, newspapers, and the like. He has displayed a marked resistance to nontraditional, nonverbal, irregular documentation, and only within the last twenty years has the rising tide of such sources begun to impress itself upon historians as the new documentation for contemporary history.

Because the collection, care, preservation, and use of aural and graphical documentation for historical scholarship is of recent development and is still in the process of evolution, an attempt at systematic discussion of such a complicated and fluid subject would be premature. Nevertheless, efforts towards categorization can be made, and tentative precepts regarding the integration of these newer forms of documentation with the more traditional ones can be advanced.

For the purposes of this study, aural and graphical documentation shall be considered to be all material, other than archives, manuscripts, and newspapers, of an original or largely underived nature and of possible utility as historical documentation. Included as major divisions are audiovisual materials of printed, mechanical, or electromagnetic character; graphics in the form of maps, prints, still photographs, and the like; fugitive ephemera of whatever form; and historical artifacts.

Although predecessor forms of audiovisual material existed prior to the development of electrical means of transmission and utilization, library science and historiography alike were slow to take cognizance of them. From 1876 to 1920 Cannon's *Bibliography of Library Economy* made no reference whatsoever to audio or visual aids as such, although evidence exists therein and elsewhere that librarians were becoming concerned with such non-book materials as pictures and slides. In *Library Literature* for 1921–1932 there were still no references to visual aids, but in 1933–1935 the heading "visual aids" appeared twice in the index, and in the period 1936–1939 the number of entries climbed to seventeen. The number of entries since that date has enjoyed a prodigious increase, and in 1940 the subject heading was changed to "audio-visual aids," signifiying a new concept of irregular documentation.[1]

As library recognition was being accorded audiovisual material, alarmists were direly, gloomily contemplating the downfall of the traditional book. For example, George Duhamel in 1939 observed: "The decadence of the book, the greatest instrument for the diffusion of knowledge, may be delayed a little longer. . . . For the man in the street, the book, defenseless, is henceforward to be supplanted by less laborious methods of information and recreation."[2] The proliferation of audiovisual material obviously was regarded within the circle of letters as more of a menace than as a modern adjunct to the traditional categories of documentation and communication.

Library and scholarly experience with non-book materials, especially nonverbal materials, developed at an accelerated pace after World War II, reflecting the voluminous production of

---

[1] Andrew H. Horn, "Introduction," in *Library Trends*, 4:119–122 (October, 1955).
[2] Louis Shores, "Audio-Visual Dimensions for an Academic Library," in *College and Research Libraries*, 15:393–397 (October, 1954).

such documentation and its insinuation into every phase of American life. In 1945 only three university libraries in the United States had separate departments of such special documentation; by 1954 the number of institutions having such material had grown to fifteen. The Department of Special Collections of the Library of the University of California at Los Angeles, while not typical, is perhaps the most comprehensive of all. Included in the collection and suggestive of the gamut of materials regarded as "special" are rare books, maps, manuscripts, pamphlets, posters, broadsides, newspapers, music, disc recordings, non-musical recordings, microfacsimiles, microfilms, university archives, subject collections, slides and films, bookplates, pictures and prints, paintings, graphic arts material, coins and currency, stamps, little magazines, scrapbooks, clipping files, blue-books, photoduplication services and laboratory, and the library's exhibition service.[3] The Committee on Audio-Visual Materials of the American Council on Library Resources surveyed in 1955 the extent of such collections in academic libraries. Of 1,726 libraries responding, 84 per cent had some such material, usually decentralized from the library proper.[4]

The process of integrating aural and graphical materials into book collections was and is attended by theoretical discussions concerning the proper procedures to be followed in acquisition, cataloging, and arranging. With the enthusiastic encouragement of leaders in the field of library science,[5] most academic librarians have advanced beyond their academic patrons and have at least admitted, albeit sometimes grudgingly, the necessity of acquiring special materials. However, the argument continues as to whether special materials should be integrated with the book collection to produce what in library circles is known as a "learning resources center," or whether special materials should be regarded as an appendage to the library proper.[6]

---

[3] Horn, "Introduction," 119.

[4] Fleming Bennett, "Audio-Visual Services in Colleges and Universities in the United States," in College and Research Libraries, 16:11–19 (January, 1955).

[5] See, for example, Edgar Dale, "The Challenge of Audio-Visual Media," in Louis Shores, ed., Challenge to Librarianship (Florida State University Studies, no. 12, Tallahassee, 1953), 93–106.

[6] For a sample of the literature, see C. W. Stone, "The Place of the Newer Media in the Undergraduate Program," in Library Quarterly, 24:358–373 (October,

AUDIOVISUAL MATERIAL

THE CATEGORY of material referred to as audiovisual is generally understood to include motion picture films, phonograph records, and tapes. By extension and for convenience, to these inventions of Thomas A. Edison will be added musical scores, which are usually associated in a library with their recorded performances, and the documentation produced by the recording process such as that of the oral history projects.

The federal government played a pioneering role in the creation and development of motion picture film as a form of historical documentation. Long before the development of motion pictures, the Navy began the use of still photography for its official record of ships and installations around 1850, and a photographer was detailed to the Perry Expedition to Japan in 1853. Photography was widely employed by the Union forces in the Civil War, and thereafter in several western territorial surveys. The first recorded federal motion picture filming was of a flight of the Wright airplane at Fort Myer, Virginia, in September, 1908. In the following year, the same Wright aircraft took a camera aloft in an early experiment in aerial photography. In 1912, following the success of the Department of Interior in making motion pictures in the national domain in 1910, a photographic laboratory was established in the Department of Agriculture. In 1914 the Navy Department contracted with a civilian photographer to produce a documentary film on the fleet, and the Army Signal Corps exposed considerable film footage of combat in France during World War I.[7]

The Great Depression provided an opportunity to establish the precedent of governmental recording on film the transformations overtaking the nation. The conditions were ripe. There was an intellectual and artistic sensitivity in the government which had never before existed. There was a readily-available army of unemployed photographic artists to be directed by alert

---

1954); R. L. Collison, *The Cataloguing, Arrangement and Filing of Special Materials in Special Libraries* (*Aslib Manuals*, vol. 2, London, 1950); and R. L. Collison, *Modern Storage Equipment and Methods for Special Materials in Libraries* (London, 1955).

[7] Hermine M. Baumhofer, "Motion Pictures Become Federal Records," in *American Archivist*, 15:18–22 (January, 1952).

students of the social and political scene. And there was a need for propaganda material to ease the way for the New Deal reforms. Full of political motivation but also high in artistic standards were the resulting productions, "The Plow That Broke the Plains," and "The River."[8]

Federal support for motion picture documentation was further manifested in 1935 with the establishment of the Division of Motion Pictures and Sound Recordings within the National Archives. This division enjoyed all of the support and prestige accorded the new archival agency. No federal bureau had previous experience with long-term preservation of film, and this problem was immediately appreciated as being of paramount importance. Indeed, the flammability of earlier types of film represented a danger not only to the film but to the existence of other material in the Archives as well. High priority was given to the design and construction of film vaults which would permit the escape of gases produced by the natural process of deterioration but would effectively block fire from the outside. Photographic film demanded more exacting care than had been anticipated, greater care than that accorded the most fragile of paper records, and the optimum conditions of storage at 70° Fahrenheit and 50 per cent humidity were arrived at by a process of trial and error.

Once adequate provision had been made for safe storage, a survey was made of all government film in Washington, and arrangements were made to acquire copies of it and of all private film of a significant national interest. All film, from whatever source, was categorized as factual *per se*, expository, reenactments, arts and crafts, and distinctively historical.[9] The staff of the National Archives found difficult the establishment of archival *fonds* in films, and there were few guides as to the proper arrangement of the material.[10] Fortunately, the hesitancy of historians in using the material allowed the custodians time to evolve proper procedures applicable to the material.

World War II brought an even more extensive governmental

---

[8] *Ibid.*

[9] Dorothy Arbough, "Motion Pictures and the Future Historian," in *American Archivist*, 2:106–109 (April, 1939).

[10] Hermine M. Baumhofer, "Film Records Management," in *American Archivist*, 19:235–236 (July, 1956).

interest in picture films both as instruments of public information and as documentation. A great many public information films, such as "The Fighting Lady," "Combat America," and "Desert Victory," were produced under contract by Hollywood studios. Hundreds of military training and indoctrination films such as "Why We Fight" were turned out for the armed forces. In addition, the thousands of air strike and combat films will make it possible for future historians to penetrate the fog of war by means of superb photographic documentation.[11] Following the war, little was done to plan the orderly retention or disposal of this enormous mass of war photography, and until it was cataloged and pilot studies were made to illustrate its value in historical research, its use was restricted to such highly successful documentary movies of the war as "The Longest Day."

While the federal government remains the largest single producer and collector of film documentation, other agencies have amassed significant collections. One such collection is the Film Library of the Museum of Modern Art, established in 1935 by a grant from the Rockefeller Foundation. From its inception the Film Library has used a catalog card system of bibliographical control which generally follows the Dewey Decimal system.[12]

It is generally accepted that World War II was responsible for bringing film material into American libraries. As early as 1924, however, the American Library Association had created the Visual Methods Committee, which in 1940 became the Audio Visual Committee. From these vague expressions of interest, or perhaps of apprehension, have grown the present thoroughgoing interest in films, in a form of communication produced at the rate of over 4,000,000 feet each year, largely in 16 mm format. A good deal of this production is of a promotional character, and careful selection is even more crucial than in selection of books.[13]

Films still occupy a minor place in the library, but their use

[11] Baumhofer, "Motion Pictures," 22.

[12] Evelyn Hensel, "Treatment of Nonbook Materials," in *Library Trends*, 2:192–193 (October, 1953). Perhaps the most extensive catalog of American films is to be found in the Museum of Modern Art Film Library, *The Film Index, A Bibliography* (New York, 1941).

[13] Dorothy L. Day, "Films in the Library," in *Library Trends*, 4:174 (October, 1955). See also W. A. Wittich, *Colleges and Universities: A Symposium, Sixty Years of 16mm Film, 1923–1983* (Evanston, Illinois, 1954), 56–76.

is growing steadily. When a collection has achieved considerable
size, it is generally recommended that films be segregated into
a separate section, where their inherent problems of cataloging
may be given specialized attention. Main entries of film catalogs should be by title, for films usually have memorable ones,
but additional entries should be provided for producer, director,
and writer. Description of films is most important to their effective use, and the information included should be standardized.[14] A significant step in the direction of bibliographic control of films was taken in 1951 when the Library of Congress
began to issue printed catalog cards for motion pictures and
filmstrips. Standards for cataloging were offered for international adoption by the United Kingdom National Commission
for UNESCO in 1953 and by corresponding sessions in Washington in the same year.[15]

The status of films in American libraries is reflected by the
fact that in 1955 over 250 public institutions held films, usually
for entertainment purposes or closely interrelated with public
school instructional programs. That more libraries did not hold
films has been attributed to the failure of the medium to live
up to its promise and to the difficulty, due to inadequate cataloging, of locating and using films.[16] Among the larger and more
significant collections of films are those of an educational nature
at Teachers College, Columbia, and a group of newsreels at
the University of Virginia.[17]

That films will eventually commend themselves as historical
documentation seems beyond question, but a number of associated problems will remain. Fortunately, the problem of storing and handling the newer safety film is minimal, and collecting agencies might well emphasize current production rather
than early examples. In view of the probable evidentiary use

[14] R. L. Collison, *The Treatment of Special Material in Libraries* (rev. ed.,
London, 1956), 59–71; Forrest Alter, "Films in Libraries—Problems and Possi-
bilities of Previewing," in American Library Association *Bulletin*, 50:217–220
(April, 1956).

[15] Hensel, "Nonbook Materials" 192–193.

[16] Grace T. Stevenson, "Films in Libraries—The Library Use of Films," in
American Library Association *Bulletin*, 50:211–214 (April, 1956).

[17] Wilson and Tauber, *University Library*, 376; Peter Baechlin and Maurice
Muller-Strauss, *Newsreels Across the World* (Paris, UNESCO, 1952).

of films, libraries would do well to acquire the unedited, the off-beat—the usual equivalent of raw documentation—rather than the finished product. The existing public collections at the National Archives and at the Library of Congress should be expanded and enriched against the time when scholars will develop the historiographical sophistication to demand full film documentation for research rather than merely for illustration of conclusions already reached from traditional material.[18]

Musical recordings are a line of materials collateral to motion pictures as library resources, and they have sprung from the more traditional form of printed or manuscript scores. Both the traditional form and the electromechanical forms of preserving and transmitting are newcomers, however, to American libraries. No formal allowance for the inclusion of music in any form in libraries was made until the early years of the twentieth century, when the volume of music accessions forced provision to be made in both the Cutter *Rules* and the ALA *Catalog Rules*. The Music Library Association Committee on Cataloging and Classifying in 1941 wrote a new code for music cataloging, which was published in 1949. In the American library experience, the Library of Congress has been the dominant force in the field of music. The culmination of this influence and leadership in indexing and cataloging musical scores is the *Inventory of Musical Sources*, which includes all printed and manuscript scores produced before 1800.[19] Outside of the Library of Congress, the largest academic collections of scores are at Harvard, Princeton, Chicago, Texas, Ohio State, Oregon, Yale, and Rochester universities, in that order. By far the heaviest use of such material has been by musicologists, but some promising cross-disciplinary use has been demonstrated by the efforts of anthropologists analyzing the collection of aboriginal music at the University of Pennsylvania.[20]

Even more promising for historical research is a contemporary ability to re-create the true sound of musical performances through the medium of phonograph recordings and their subsequent technical refinements. Such recordings can not be filed

[18] Arbough, "Motion Pictures," 111.
[19] Vincent H. Duckles, "Musical Scores and Recordings," in *Library Trends*, 4:164–166 (October, 1955); Jack B. Spear, "Films and Sound Recordings," in *Library Trends*, 5:406–416 (January, 1957).
[20] Wilson and Tauber, *University Library*, 365–367.

like books, nor can they be cataloged with the same speed, for
one disc often may carry two or more musical compositions with
no organic relationship. Record catalogs, therefore, must be carefully constructed with many cross references to composers, titles,
artists, issuing companies, record sizes and speeds, and method
of recording.[21]

To govern shelf arrangement of phonograph records, four
standard schemes have been employed—by composer, by form or
medium, by record number, or by local accession number. Considerable library experience has shown arrangement by accession
number to be the most satisfactory since the constant shifting
produced by the other methods is thereby eliminated. Cataloging of musical recordings in America has been governed since
1946 by the *Code for Cataloging Music,* drawn by a joint committee of the Music Library Association and the ALA Division
of Cataloging and Classification.[22]

Of greater potential interest to historians of American society are the collections on record and tape of folk songs. The
pioneer work in the field was done by John A. Lomax and his
associates on the staff of the Library of Congress. A project of
the Great Depression, the collection represents a cross-section
of American folk songs, but especially valuable are the so-called
"sinful" songs of the Negro, previously unknown to whites. An
example is "Dink's Song," recorded by a Negro woman in Texas:

> *When I wo' my ap'ns low,*
> *Couldn't keep you from my do'.*
> *Fare thee well, O Honey, fare thee well.*
>
> *Now I wears my ap'ns high,*
> *Sca'cely ever see you passin' by.*
> *Fare thee well, O Honey, fare thee well.*[23]

If the humanity and pathos of such social commentaries require
gilding, Carl Sandburg has pronounced "Dink's Song" compar-

---

[21] Collison, *Treatment of Special Material,* 34–44.

[22] Hensel, "Nonbook Materials," 193–194. A valuable guide to the care of
musical recordings is A. G. Pickett and M. M. Lemcoe, *Preservation and Storage
of Sound Recordings: A Study Supported by a Grant from the Rockefeller Foundation* (Washington, 1959).

[23] Donald Day, "John Lomax and His Ten Thousand Songs," in *The Saturday
Review of Literature,* 28: no. 38:5–7 (September 22, 1945).

able in eloquence and passion to anything written by Sappho.[24]

Oral history is another significant application of modern recording techniques to produce historical documentation, although it has been suggested that Lyman Draper was the real "Father of American Oral History" and that Draper anticipated the methods of the modern oral historian long before the modern technological refinements were dreamed of.[25] Whatever its origins, the idea of oral history has proven itself in practical usage by such historians as Allan Nevins, Merle Curti, A. M. Schlesinger, Jr., Frank Freidel, Oscar Handlin, James McGregor Burns, Matthew Josephson, and George Kennan, all of whom have been concerned with capturing contemporary documentation of a personal and confidential nature to substitute for that written documentation which modern society generally fails to produce. How else than through an oral history interview with Albert Lasker, one of the pioneers of modern American advertising, could one derive such a revealing insight as the suggestion that modern advertising was born in a Chicago office—the result of a crap game.[26]

Oral history interviews have been compared with the familiar newspaper interview techniques, but developed to a high form to anticipate the future needs of the historian. Although historians have not eagerly rushed to utilize the material so thoughtfully provided them, its utility has been adequately demonstrated. In the Allan Nevins' study of Henry Ford, the best example of the use of oral history documentation, 186 out of 1,449 footnotes, or 13 per cent, are references to oral reminiscences. By contrast, only 66 notes are references to contemporary manuscript letters. Oral history material supplied the basis for about 66 per cent of all documented factual statements, all other forms

[24] U. S., Library of Congress, Music Division, *A List of American Folksongs Currently Available on Records* (Washington, 1953). For a list of recommended recordings for building a basic library of folk songs, see Adrienne Claiborne, "Folk Recordings for the Library," in *Library Journal*, 74:470–473 (March 15, 1949).

[25] Charles William Conaway, "Lyman Copeland Draper, 'Father of American Oral History,'" in *The Journal of Library History*, 1:234–241 (October, 1966).

[26] "The Oral History Project of Columbia University," in *American Heritage*, 6:73–84 (December, 1954); and "Oral History: Columbia's Library on Tape," in *Library Journal*, 85:36–37 (January 1, 1960). Another more commercialized oral history project is that of Lou Blachly of Pioneer Foundation, Inc. This project involves taping interviews with old-time residents of the Far West to develop material for sale to Hollywood film writers. See Albert Rosenfeld, "The Wild West Lives Again," in *Colliers*, 134:48–56 (November, 1954).

supplying only 33 per cent of this category of information. In summary, more substantive information and less "color" was drawn from oral history sources in this pioneer study than might have been supposed.[27]

If oral history documentation of the calibre of that used by Nevins is to be produced, an orderly plan should be followed to prepare the interviewee and to insure high quality and objectivity in the resulting interview. Obviously, the interviewer should prepare himself by thorough study of the region, subject, and personalities to be covered in the interview. A leisurely approach during the initial exploratory interview will permit the interviewer to evaluate the interviewee as a potential source. If an actual recording session ensues, the transcript should carry full autobiographical information on the interviewee, reference to source materials used, the date, place, and time of the interview, and the identity and professional background of the interviewer.[28]

A code of conduct for the oral history interviewer has been suggested to protect the professional integrity of the documentation produced by the joint efforts of the interviewer and interviewee. Since the primary purpose of the process should be to develop material for the widest possible use, the interviewer should make clear from the outset the purposes of the interview and should strive to enlist the enthusiastic cooperation of the participant. It should always be understood that the interviewee has the right of review and correction over the final typescript, and he should have the option specifically to grant or to withhold the right of use of the final draft.[29]

GRAPHICS

G RAPHICS, in the sense of material capable of serving as historical documentation, is generally understood to include

[27] Vaughn D. Bornet, "Oral History *Can* Be Worthwhile," in *American Archivist,* 18:241–247 (July, 1955).

[28] Helen Mc. White, "Thoughts on Oral History," in *American Archivist,* 20:21–28 (January, 1957); Donald C. Swain, "Problems for Practitioners of Oral History," in *American Archivist,* 28:65–69 (January, 1965).

[29] White, "Oral History," 29–30.

any painting, drawing, engraving, picture, or other art form which expresses ideas by means of lines, marks, and characters of other than verbal nature. Furthermore, recognition of graphics as an art form implies that examples of materials of this category are generally prepared with care, that their creators are aware of their possible use as documentation, and that however fanciful or inaccurate their pretensions to reality, they convey a sense of the historical milieu in which they were produced. Among the more common forms of graphic documentation are maps and a wide variety of pictures, prints, and other two-dimensional art objects.

Manuscripts have been collected for over 4,000 years, but the making of maps, their dissemination and their collection have been restricted for centuries by political and military considerations. Maps are so closely related to military intelligence and political intrigue that an aura of furtiveness and secrecy surrounds their collection and their study. Maps did not come into vogue as historical documentation until late in the eighteenth century, and they are not yet as widely used as they might be. Despite all the vital and unique information which they can convey, maps are still relied upon to supplement verbally derived information rather than to serve as substantive sources. Nevertheless, the use of maps in historical studies, particularly those on the American Revolution, has proven the value of such material as documentation.[30]

The cartography of America is more eagerly collected than that of any other world area, both by Americans and by other nationals. The charm, appeal, and comparative availability of maps of the New World attract serious students and antiquarians alike. The oldest of American maps dates back to about 1500, to crude charts of the Caribbean coastline ascribed to Juan de la Cosa. More attractive but equally inaccurate were the fanciful maps generated by the Age of Discovery and produced by Matteo Giovanni Contarini (1506) and Martin Waldseemüller (1507). These early examples set the pattern for American cartography for the next several centuries and are the ex-

---

[30] Colton Storm, "Maps as Historical Documents," in *Publisher's Weekly*, 146: 2060–2065 (November 25, 1944). See also, Lloyd A. Brown, *The Story of Old Maps* (Boston, 1949).

pensive and rare foundations upon which have been built many collections of maps.[31]

Maps have always posed problems in collection because they have no proper author and often no real title, and they often lack dates. In addition, because no standard system of cataloging and filing exists, ultimately each map must be cataloged separately. Main entry is usually by primary geographical area covered. The catalog entry should also carry the formal title, place and agent of publication, edition, scale in fractions, collation, and other pertinent description. If maps play a major role in a library's function, they are usually included in the main catalog. Otherwise, they are separately cataloged.[32]

As in the case of film documentation, the creation of maps in America has been dominated by the United States government. Since 1783 consistent policy has ensured the thorough mapping of each successive addition to the national territory, and the myriad governmental programs dependent upon precise location of points and geographic features have stimulated and sustained a most comprehensive mapping program. Today more than twenty United States agencies publish a varied assortment of maps, most of which are available to the public and to institutions.[33] These officially-produced maps have accumulated in government offices without much attention being paid to their conversion into archival material.[34]

Although the institutional collection of maps in America began in 1852 with the creation of the Map Department of the American Geographical Society,[35] until the end of World War

[31] R. V. Tooley, *Maps and Map-Makers* (London, 1952), 110–114; Storm and Peckham, *Book Collecting,* 144–164.

[32] Collison, *Treatment of Special Material,* 51–58.

[33] Herman R. Friis, "Cartographic and Related Records: What Are They, How Have They Been Produced, and What Are Problems of Their Administration?" in *American Archivist,* 13:137 (April, 1950); Walter Thiele, *Official Map Publications* (Chicago, 1938), chapters VII–IX.

[34] Price List 53, from the Superintendent of Documents, includes a selected list of official maps for sale by the federal government. Because most government-issued maps are sold directly by the publishing agency, see Nellie M. Bowman, "Publications, Maps, and Charts Sold by U. S. Government Agencies Other than the Superintendent of Documents," in *Special Libraries,* 44:53–65 (February, 1953).

[35] Eva L. Yonge, "The Map Department of the American Geographical Society," in *The Professional Geographer,* 7:2–5 (March, 1955).

II libraries generally regarded maps as unwanted and unruly stepchildren. Little agreement could be reached concerning the processing, filing, and servicing of this category of library material. Some librarians even denied that it belonged within their domain. The *Bulletin* of the Geography and Map Division of the Special Library Association, launched in 1948, has given focus to the new popular and scholarly interest in maps and map study engendered by World War II, the Cold War, Korea, and the other rude shocks to the familiar world of provincial America. Furthermore, over 50,000 surplus war maps distributed to educational institutions by the Army Map Service during the years after the war provided the leaven which enabled many of these institutions to create map collections within their libraries. As a result, a survey of map collections in the United States revealed the existence in 1954 of 497 institutional collections, 25 having over 100,000 sheets each. Especially noteworthy were the collections at California, Chicago, Columbia, Dartmouth, Harvard, Illinois, Northwestern, Princeton, Stanford, Yale, and Wisconsin.[36] Public libraries with large map collections in separate departments are located in Baltimore (Enoch Pratt), Birmingham, Boston, Buffalo, Chicago, Cincinnati, Cleveland, Detroit, Los Angeles, Milwaukee, Newark, New York, Oakland, Philadelphia, and St. Louis.[37]

The Library of Congress remains the leader among American institutional collectors of maps by virtue of the size and significance of its collection and of its pioneering work in descriptive cataloging of maps. The disparity characteristic of map production remains the greatest single obstacle to collecting the media, and bibliographical control is the greatest need. Here, again, the Library of Congress has been of great value.[38] The

---

[36] Walter W. Ristow, "What About Maps," in *Library Trends,* 4:123–125 (October, 1955); Wilson and Tauber, *University Library,* 363–365; and Hensel, "Nonbook Materials," 194. For valuable guides, see, U. S., Army Map Service, *A Researcher's Guide to the Army Map Service Library* (A. M. S. Technical Manual no. 46, Washington, 1951); Walter W. Ristow, *The Services and Collection of the Map Division* [Library of Congress] (Washington, 1951); and Charlotte M. Ashby, "The Cartographic Records Branch in the National Archives," in Geographic and Map Division *Bulletin,* 16:6–10 (April, 1954).

[37] Ristow, "What About Maps," 125.

[38] Lloyd A. Brown, *Notes on the Care and Cataloging of Old Maps* (Windham, Connecticut, 1941); Brown, "Special Reference Problems in Map Collections," in

library and, more recently, the United Nations have made the initial contributions towards securing world co-operation in the bibliographical control of maps.[39]

Before striking out into the jungle of graphic documentation, it might be well to establish a few definitions as guides. Paintings and other original works of art constitute a category which is self-evident. Prints, on the other hand, are copies or reproductions of paintings, engravings, sketches, or other original works of art produced by printing or some other mechanical process. Pictures may include all of the materials just defined as prints, plus printed reproductions of photographs. Photographs proper refer only to unpublished positive prints of a photographic negative. The basis for grouping all of these graphic art forms is their similarity of shape and format rather than their subject matter. The resulting collections may be categorized as those formed for artistic or other specific purpose within a museum or other agency, those of significant national focus such as exist at the Library of Congress and the New York Public Library, and those of local focus found in local libraries and historical societies.[40]

American painting has been used even less as historical documentation than American literature, yet it has some of the same

P. Butler, ed., *The Reference Function of the Library* (Chicago, 1943), 144–162; Ristow, "What About Maps," 128–129; Clara Egli LeGear, *Maps: Their Care, Repair and Preservation in Libraries* (Washington, 1949), 1–75; and LeGear, in Special Libraries Association, Geography and Map Division, *Keys to Map Evaluation* (multilith, Washington, 1953).

[39] An early check list which is still useful is P. L. Phillips, *A List of Maps of America in the Library of Congress* (Washington, 1901). The Library of Congress Map Division annual reports are an excellent source of descriptions of current acquisitions, and the *Catalog of Copyright Entries, Part 6*, lists all maps and related material published under American copyright since 1947. Current cartography can be reviewed through *Surveying and Mapping;* Geography and Map Division *Bulletin;* and *The Professional Geographer.* At the international level, *Bibliographie Cartographique Internationale* (Paris) lists over 30,000 official and private map publications in more than twenty countries, and *World Cartography,* a United Nations journal, covers map making in some of the more remote corners of the world. Two standard works by Lloyd A. Brown, *The Story of Old Maps* (Boston, 1949), and *Map-Making: The Art That Became a Science* (Boston, 1960), will be of value.

[40] May D. Hill, "Prints, Pictures, and Photographs," in *Library Trends,* 4:156–158 (October, 1955). See also the September, 1954, issue of *Special Libraries,* which is devoted to a description of twelve leading graphics collections in the United States.

qualities of hard, colloquial vividness that are found in the works of Mark Twain, Edgar Allan Poe, Herman Melville, and Nathaniel Hawthorne. While drawing its strength and inspiration from the roots of western culture, American painting also reveals the distinctive influence of the American scene and American society. Where is there a better insight into the colonial character and personality than in its portraiture and ivory miniatures? Originally self-indulgent, American portraiture learned to be more honest, finding in Gilbert Stuart the first great technical master of American painting, an expert in handling masses through light and shadow. Not only is such material valuable for conventional illustrations of verbal history, but there is also raw documentation in such masterpieces as Stuart's familiar portrait of Washington.[41]

A largely untapped but rich vein of documentation for the social historian is to be found in American folk art, a form transmitted from its European origins primarily through the Puritans and Quakers. As the work of plain people little trained in the techniques of art and little schooled in its theoretical appreciation, sentiment and direct expression of thought shine through without complication. In the colonial period, a simple yet often rollicking love of life and family are coupled with a decent respect for the Biblical God. In the nineteenth century materialism and naturalism, glossed over by a maudlin sentimentality, become the dominant themes in American painting.[42] A more accurate summary of the transformation of American character would be hard to devise.

For the period since 1880, the Museum of Modern Art in New York towers above all others as the preeminent collector of contemporary American art. Founded in 1929, the museum has remained remarkably active in collecting and interpreting the contemporary scene. A mecca for historians of art, the promise of its treasures can also be appreciated by the social historian

[41] John Walker and MacGill James, eds., *Great American Paintings from Smibert to Bellows, 1729–1924* (London, 1943), 1–20; H. B. Wehle, *American Miniatures, 1730–1850* (Garden City, 1927), 12–28; H. L. and W. L. Ehrichs, eds., *One Hundred Early American Paintings* (New York, 1918).

[42] Holger Cahill, ed., *American Folk Art, The Art of the Common Man, 1750–1900* (New York, [1932]), 3–28; Elizabeth B. Wood, "Pots and Pans History: Relating Manuscripts and Printed Sources to the Study of Domestic Art Objects," in *American Archivist*, 30:431–442 (July, 1967).

through some of the remarkable documentary collections prepared for use during World War II.[43]

Of particular interest to historians is the Library of Congress collection of battle art, which encompasses the French and Indian Wars through World War I. What has been published is but a sample of the rich store which is available. Although most of the items in the collection were rendered after the time of the actual military engagement, they are remarkably vivid and convey a dimension unobtainable through the written word.[44]

In the category of prints, the American collector can have a field day. The natural grandeur of the American scene has inspired many an artist, and numerous historical ceremonies and natural and accidental catastrophes have served as subjects for a long list of print makers.[45]

An interesting case study in the proliferation of historical prints and their impact upon historiography is found in the various renderings of the Boston Massacre of March 5, 1770. The first print was executed in 1770 by one Henry Pelham, and it has remained unique. The most celebrated version, prepared by Paul Revere in 1772, was widely circulated in Boston and elsewhere as an adornment of *The Massachusetts Calendar* for that year. A few years later Jonathan Mulliken copied Revere, but he executed the work poorly. In 1832 the Revere work was again engraved by William F. Stratton, and in 1911 a new engraving, derived from Revere, was prepared by Sidney L. Smith. All of the prints illustrate the older interpretation of the patriot martyrs, but newer historical research views the incident more as a street brawl than as a precursor of the Revolution. These prints, however, have helped to establish in the public mind a patriotic image of the incident. In fact, the entire progress of the Revolution was engraved in great detail, and these prints have played an enormously significant role in fixing the concept of the struggle between liberty and tyranny.[46] The same observations hold true in varying degree for the numerous prints

[43] J. T. Soby, *The Museum of Modern Art* (New York, 1946), 1–16.
[44] U. S., Library of Congress, *An Album of American Battle Art, 1755–1918* (Washington, 1947), especially xii–xvi.
[45] Storm and Peckham, *Book Collecting*, 134–143.
[46] Goodspeed, *Yankee Bookseller*, 107–143.

made of all manner of events before photography brought a degree of mechanical accuracy and perspective to the graphic recording of public events.[47]

A more crude but highly revealing commentary upon American life and manners is to be found in the well-nigh unique American institution, the political cartoon. Examples are very numerous, and several excellent anthologies are available.[48]

The ease and comparative inexpensiveness of taking still photographs during the past century have created a file of potential documentation so vast as to almost defy systematic analysis and discussion. Again, the American government has pioneered both in creation and preservation of this category of documentation. The report of Commodore Matthew Perry's visit to Japan in 1853 was the first United States government document to be illustrated with photographs. A daguerreotype artist had been attached to the fleet, and he went ashore at the first opportunity to practice his art. Some forty illustrations in the final report bear the credit line, "E. Brown." The government has continued to produce photographic coverage ever since in a constantly expanding volume. The practice of making identification photographs of all officers was begun during the Civil War, and extensive photographic coverage was made of the Spanish-American War and World War I. In sheer number of exposures, however, government photography came into its own during World War II. The Air Force alone exposed over 8,000,000 aerial negatives and over 1,250,000 shots of ground installations and activities.[49]

It is the influence of the Turner frontier thesis upon American historiography which has called forth an increasingly active demand for photographic documentation of the common, the everyday routine, and the commonplace out of which social

[47] An extensive bibliography of American print collections is available. See, among others, C. W. Dreppard, *Early American Prints* (New York, 1930); I. N. P. Stokes and D. C. Haskell, comps., *American Historical Prints, Early Views of American Cities, Etc.* (New York, 1932); and John Robinson and G. F. Dow, eds., *The Sailing Ships of New England, 1607-1907* (3 vols., Salem, Massachusetts, 1922-1928).

[48] Allan Nevins, ed., *A Century of Political Cartoons* (New York, 1944); William A. Murrell, *A History of American Graphic Humor* (2 vols., New York, 1933-1938).

[49] Joe D. Thomas, "Photographic Archives," in *American Archivist*, 21:419-420 (October, 1958).

history is constructed. It may be more than coincidental that the suggestion of the frontier thesis and the rise of photography were close contemporaries. With photographic coverage, history has been given a new cast of players. Pre-photographic history was peopled with idealized heroes; contemporary history is more often than not peopled with ordinary mortals caught off guard by the camera.[50]

The heterogenous and catchall class of documentation known as picture collections raises extremely difficult problems of collection and cataloging. Here is the exact antithesis of book collecting and cataloging. The significance and forms of a book are immediately apparent, giving purpose to the collection and form to the cataloging process. In collections of picture documentation, neither the form nor the purpose is apparent, and both must be externally imposed so that the picture may receive some functional use by a future researcher. For example, an early illustration of a horizontal steam engine will be important for its subject, not its draftsman. It is valuable as documentation according to its accuracy and detail rather than to its artistic appeal. Thus the most commonplace of illustrations may be among the most valuable, its contribution as evidence arising from inference rather than from direct observation. Hence, cataloging and accurate information concerning origin assume great importance as guarantees of relative integrity.[51]

Practices in cataloging picture collections vary widely in degree and extent. Arrangement is usually by subject according to the anticipated pattern of use. The Library of Congress has introduced a useful feature in cataloging loose pictures by mounting a microfacsimile of the picture upon the catalog card itself. The innovation facilitates the search for material and often makes unnecessary reference to the original.[52] The library has also

[50] Hermine M. Baumhofer, "A New Tool for a New History," in *Minnesota History*, 28:345 (December, 1947). Albums of published photographs have enjoyed popularity from time to time, and they illustrate the quality of that which is on file in collecting institutions. Hirst D. Milhollen and Milton Kaplan, eds., *Presidents on Parade* (New York, 1948), is a collection of photographs and popular art on the Presidents, a sample of the genre. At the lower end of the social spectrum, see Agnes Rogers and F. L. Ellen, eds., *The American Procession: American Life since 1860 in Photographs* (New York, 1933).

[51] Collison, *Treatment of Special Material*, 5.

[52] Hensel, "Nonbook Materials," 195–196.

pioneered in the creation of special collections of photographs and in their cataloging.[53]

Anthologies of picture collections have enjoyed great popularity as publication forms since the turn of the century, and numerous editions of widely varying merit are available.[54]

EPHEMERA

IN MANY RESPECTS the bane of a book-oriented librarian's professional life is printed ephemera. The principal difficulty in dealing with this class of material is the conferring of long life on essentially short-lived objects. For the most part, ephemera comes into being in consequence of some routine commercial or political activity; it does not have even secondary research value when created, yet the very act of creation often invests such material with a unique documentary value. Among the materials generally considered to be ephemera are newspaper clippings, broadsides, and pamphlets. Whenever a research library embarks on the collection of any or all of these categories, the collection should be kept within bounds by constant review and evaluation by all groups with an interest in the material.[55]

The disemboweled snippings of the daily press can be a valuable tool for historical research, especially when prepared by professional librarians from local papers which otherwise have few indexes to the location of obscure bits of documentation. When a clipping file comes to hand already prepared by a nonprofessional, it is likely to be of questionable value. When pre-

[53] Paul Vanderbilt, comp., *Guide to the Special Collections of Prints and Photographs in the Library of Congress* (Washington, 1955).

[54] For guides to collections of illustrations, see, E. V. Corbett, *The Illustration Collection; Its Formation, Classification, and Exploitation* (London, 1941), 79ff.; Norma O. Ireland, *The Picture File in School, College, and Public Libraries* (rev. ed., Boston, 1952), 50–132; J. C. Dana, ed., *The Picture Collection* (5th ed., Boston, 1943), 43–86. Examples of the genre will indicate the range of quality. G. W. Bonté and S. E. Forman, eds., *America Marches Past* (New York, 1936), is an unimaginative, scissors and paste job, an example of how not to do it. A. C. Collins, ed., *The Story of America in Pictures* (Garden City, 1940), achieves archival quality in a selection of illustrations of the usual and the routine in American life. M. B. Davidson, ed., *Life in America* (2 vols., Boston, 1951), is excellently done by a museum man with an eye for social history.

[55] John Cook Wyllie, "Pamphlets, Broadsides, Clippings and Posters," in *Library Trends*, 4:195–196 (October, 1955).

pared from well-indexed papers such as the New York *Times,* it may be regarded as wasted effort and disposed of.[56]

Broadsides and posters, usually produced for some passing political or commercial purpose, are of great value for purposes of research or illustration. The color and inherent interest of broadsides have brought about their collection in an earlier day before the material was appreciated as historical documentation, and these collections now await discovery and use by historians.[57]

Pamphlets, the mini-books which are non-books, are difficult to catalog into a book collection, but they often contain valuable information for research purposes. Unless they are treated as books, singly, they are usually "packed like sardines without scaling" and bound together in a folder of common heading.[58]

Trade catalogs are also a very valuable source for research into the commercial and social aspects of American life. These printed pieces are designed to sell specific wares without consideration of comparative merits and prices of other vendors, and the result is something which generally offends the librarian's love of order. Until trade associations standardize the catalogs in their fields, the frustrated librarian dealing with such material has no alternative but to file the catalogs alphabetically by name of manufacturer or wholesaler, with a corresponding card catalog by subject and cross heads. The ephemeral nature of the material suggests that cataloging be reduced to the barest essentials.[59]

Special-interest libraries are usually among the first to collect ephemera relating to their special fields, and the most significant collections have been assembled under such auspices. One such collection of broadsides and other ephemera of World War II has been assembled at the War Documentation Center by the Bibliographical Planning Committee of Philadelphia. Another

[56] M. F. Tauber, ed., *Technical Services in Libraries* (New York, 1954), 335–336.

[57] C. P. Horning, ed., *Handbook of Early American Advertising Art* (New York, 1947). Other guides to examples of the genre include Sol Bloom, *Broadsides Relating to the Ratification of the Constitution and the Formation of the Government of the United States from Historical Societies and Libraries* (Washington, 1939); D. C. McMurtrie, *Massachusetts Broadsides, 1699–1711* (Chicago, 1939); and E. L. Rudolph, *Confederate Broadside Verse* . . . (New Braunfels, Texas, 1950).

[58] Tauber, *Technical Services,* 334–335; A. F. Kuhlman, "The Preparation of Guides for the Collection, Care, Organization and Preservation of Fugitive Materials," in *Public Documentation* (1935), 236–247.

[59] Collison, *Treatment of Special Material,* 45–50.

significant collection of such material is at the Hoover Library at Stanford University.[60]

ARTIFACTS AND MUSEUM OBJECTS

THAT COMMENTARY upon artifacts and museum objects as historical documentation should be called for at all will strike some historians as somewhat extreme, yet other students of the past will regard the necessity as entirely obvious. Unfortunately, there has grown up a dichotomy between the "idea-oriented" and "object-oriented" students of the past, and the traditional, "idea" historian is apt to dismiss the "object" colleague as an inferior being. Thereby, he displays an unbecoming academic snobbery and reveals an ignorance of the priority of different forms of historical scholarship. Actually, verbal scholarship is much junior to object scholarship. The distinction arose in modern times because manuscripts have been collected for the use of scholars while objects have been collected primarily for public display. The collection of political paraphernalia in the Smithsonian Institution comes close to bridging the gap between research and display purposes and sets a standard for others to emulate.[61]

It is the field of military history which perhaps most often demands that historians go beyond verbal documentation and come to grips with physical remains and gross objects, to examine site and terrain as a part of historical research. The federal government again has led the way in preserving and utilizing this type of documentation. Its efforts go back to the Antiquities Act of 1906 which granted to the President the authority to establish national historical monuments on federal property, mainly in the Far West. The Historic Sites Act of 1935 placed all such national historic sites under the professional administration of the National Park Service, whose quality of research and interpretation has been high.[62]

---

[60] Wilson and Tauber, *University Library*, 367–370.

[61] Wilcomb E. Washburn, "Manuscripts and Manufacts," in *American Achivist*, 27:247–250 (April, 1964); Washburn, "The Great Autumnal Madness: Political Symbolism in Mid-Nineteenth Century America," in *Quarterly Journal of Speech*, 49:417–431 (December, 1963).

[62] A. P. Stauffer and C. W. Porter, "The National Park Service Program of Conservation for Areas and Structures of National Historic Significance," in *Mississippi Valley Historical Review*, 30:25–30 (June, 1943).

The high calibre of the historical work of the National Park Service has been in large measure dictated by a need to fix the exact location of sites for popular interpretation. The traditional historical scholar may err a few miles in locating precise points without invalidating his conclusions. Sites historians, on the other hand, must be exact in their placements, and they are forced habitually to rely upon other than verbal documentation. Official pronouncements, sworn statements, and popular traditions notwithstanding, surveyors' plats and physical remains must be given first priority in such research. Nor can historical sites work be protected by the imprecise and indefinite form of such expressions as "it would appear that. . . ."[63] The public expects the exact spot of such historic events as Stonewall Jackson's amputation to be marked with a clear and unequivocal statement of unimpeachable accuracy.

The quality and accuracy of historic sites research and documentation also obtain in the best of the more than 1,500 historical museums in the United States and Canada.[64] For the purposes of a traditional historian, the museums of perhaps greatest significance are those operated in conjunction with an academic institution. These ventures represent a movement to give greater emphasis in college teaching and research to museum collections. Examples include the Stephen Collins Foster Memorial collection at the University of Pittsburgh, the Edgar Fohs Smith Memorial collection on the work of chemists at the University of Pennsylvania, the Brander Matthews Dramatic Museum at Columbia University, the Jewish Theological Seminary Museum in New York, and the Historical Museum of Louisiana State University.[65]

An atypical but illustrative example of the use of nonverbal museum collections for traditional historical research is furnished by the Lincoln Museum in Washington, D. C. The

---

[63] Charles W. Porter, "Documentary Research Methods Applied to Historic Sites and Buildings," in *American Archivist*, 14:201–202 (July, 1951). See also, L. V. Coleman, *Historic House Museums* (Washington, 1933), 3–24.

[64] L. V. Coleman, *The Museum in America* (3 vols., Washington, 1939), I:59–78. For a listing of historical museums, see the American Association of Museums, *Handbook of Historical Museums* (Washington, 1932).

[65] L. V. Coleman, *College and University Museums* (Washington, 1942), 57–59; A. C. Parker, *A Manual for History Museums* (New York, 1935), 83–90. See also, L. V. Coleman, *Company Museums* (Washington, 1943).

antecedents of the institution lie in the deep interest and de-
votion to the memory of the martyred President displayed by
Osborn H. Oldroyd of Ohio. Discharged from the Grand Army
in 1865, Oldroyd began collecting pictures, speeches, books, furniture, and other Lincoln mementos, a task he continued for
over sixty-six years. In 1883 this professional collector of Lin-
colniana moved with his treasures into Lincoln's former home
in Springfield, Illinois. Ten years later he removed with his
expanding collection to the government-owned Petersen House
(where Lincoln died) at 516 Tenth Street, NW, Washington.
In 1926 Oldroyd's collection was purchased by the government
for $50,000 and was integrated with the smaller collection of the
Lincoln Museum. The collection and museum have subsequently
been placed under the direction of the National Park Service,
and its documents, sheet music, magazine articles, broadsides,
and photographs of and relating to Lincoln have been of value
to scholars of the Civil War and of the wartime President.[66]

Traditional historical scholarship has rested for so long upon
the comfortable alliance between research in manuscript sources
and publication by way of the printed page that any innovation
has been resisted by the historical profession. Such snobbishness
of form could be tolerated so long as historians were dealing
with societies which left their most significant documentation
in the form of manuscripts and learned of their past through
books. However, the pervasiveness of books and manuscripts is
passing. The book may not yet be decadent, but new forms of
mass communication offer sharp competition as effective means
of scholarly communication. Furthermore, some of these same
media of communication, in supplanting verbal correspondence
and record-keeping, are creating new forms of historical documentation which cannot be ignored. Pouring new wine into
old bottles is disastrous, but old wine in new bottles is pointless. Books and manuscripts need not be supplanted, but supplemented, by every applicable aspect of the new technology of
communication. In its form as well as its substance, historiography is called to make a transition from a doctrinaire exclusiveness to a pragmatic pluralism.

[66] Josephine D. Allen, "Documenting the Lincoln Museum Collection," in
American Archivist, 26:463–365 (October, 1963).

PRESERVATION AND DISSEMINATION
OF HISTORICAL EVIDENCE

ALTHOUGH ENGLAND is indeed a "profoundly historically minded country" compared with the United States, historiography in England has been termed a "minor matter, a hobby, a respectable activity but not big business, not one of the pillars of the State."[1] The area in which American historiography far overshadows British activity is in the publication and dissemination of documentary materials by state historical societies, scholarly agencies, and the federal government. While the British can point with justifiable pride to such historical projects as the *Dictionary of National Biography* and the *Complete Peerage*, they admit to having nothing comparable to the contemporary compilation and publication of the papers of Washington, Jefferson, and Hamilton.[2] On the other hand, until quite recently European practices in the preservation of original documents far outstripped American standards.

The publication or other dissemination of historical documentation is not an exclusively American genius. Rather, the motivation appears to derive from the same forces which led to the documania in both England and America in the nineteenth century, but now compounded and intensified in twentieth-century America by the simultaneous professionalization of historiography and the rise of popular interest in history. The process of historical editing, the process whereby documents are

---

[1] *London Times* Literary Supplement, special number, September 17, 1954.
[2] *Ibid.*

prepared for publication, is basically a British science. What is distinctly American is the scale, extent, and universality with which the principles has been applied. According to the American historiographical creed, the more significant parts of the mountain of primary documentation are to be brought to the historian; the historian need not go to the mountain. More often than not, this moving of mountains is done at public expense. Therefore, producing historical documentation in America has become big business. It has also become a means of enlisting history as a servant of the state.

Within the last generation and especially within the federal system, the dissemination of documentation has become so widely accepted and so highly institutionalized that multiple copies of the printed edition have completely obscured the original, non-published source. The original copy has thus become a vestigial remnant and an object of antiquarian interest, the printed copy serving all normal historiographical and legal purposes. Moreover, the zealous federal support of historical research has often included publication of edited and printed selections from larger masses of archives and dissemination by microfilm copies of primary documentation which may not have been created by the federal government but which happens to be under the control of federal agencies. Even when direct federal subsidy is not involved, the dissemination of documentary materials has always been regarded as such a worthwhile public service that it has been supported and encouraged by other governmental agencies. The result is a mass of copied documentation more extensive than that of any other nation and a range of editorial experience unsurpassed anywhere.

THE EDITORIAL PROCESS
IN DOCUMENTARY DISSEMINATION

THE SPECIFIC editorial process applied to each documentary publication project is dependent, of course, upon the nature and extent of the materials involved; the high degree of institutionalization nevertheless has resulted in a surprising amount of uniformity in concept and execution. The process is usually viewed in two phases—selection and editing proper.

Selection of materials for inclusion in a documentary publication project begins with a systematic search for relevant papers and ends with the application of a governing rule of inclusion. American projects generally have been based upon one of four plans. In the first, or totally inclusive plan, all of the papers from, by, to, or about a central theme or person are collected from whatever locations for inclusion in the compilation. In the second, or selectively inclusive, a selection is made from the total mass of documentation compiled from all sources. In the third plan, which might be called topical, all papers relevant to a limited period, topic, or area are compiled, and a selection is made from the total mass. In the fourth plan, institutional in focus, papers relating to a given topic, period, or area are selected from a given agency, without regard for known collections of similar or parallel material available in other agencies. In determining which of these four basic plans of inclusion to adopt, the factors of fiscal limitations, previous publication, triviality, routine nature, duplication, and value to research are all given consideration in a priority based upon the anticipated use of the collection.[3]

Once a basic choice has been made of materials to be included in the documentary collection, consideration moves on to the steps of textual criticism, transcription, arrangement, annotation, collation, preparation of the completed copy for duplication, and final editorial review prior to dissemination.[4]

The basic rules and concepts of documentary editing were noted in 1857 by the Master of the Rolls in planning the "Chronicles and Memorials of Great Britain and Ireland from the Invasion of the Romans to the Reign of Henry VIII." The rules of procedures required that each document considered for inclusion be collated with the original manuscript or the best copy available, and that a brief description of the original be attached to each document to facilitate positive identification. These rules were not the first statement of modern editorial usage, but they have been so universally adopted as to constitute a landmark. The most frequent single point of difficulty

[3] Clarence E. Carter, "Historical Editing," in U. S., National Archives, *Bulletin* No. 7 (1952), 8–15.
[4] *Ibid.*, 7–8.

comes with the deciphering of illegible handwriting.[5] Fortunately, this problem has not been so acute in American materials as to require a special study of American calligraphy.[6]

The editorial standards applicable to the dissemination of historical documentation have been implicitly observed in American practice since the turn of the twentieth century, and they have recently been explicitly codified by a leading historical editor.[7] In American practice, the traditional rules of external criticism are applied to a document; rarely is internal criticism invoked, however, the editor usually refraining from interpretation. Accuracy of transcription is the chief goal of the American editor, and his most exacting injunctions relate to literal copying, correct dating, inclusion of end material and endorsements, treatment of variant spellings, punctuation, deleted words, and signatures,[8] These rules are perhaps best illustrated in contemporary projects for publishing the papers of Thomas Jefferson, Benjamin Franklin, and the Adams Family.[9]

THE CONTEXT OF DOCUMENTARY PUBLICATION

THE AMERICAN EXPERIENCE in documentary publication can be most conveniently summarized by citing the

[5] Clarence E. Carter, "The Territorial Papers of the United States," in *American Archivist*, 8:131–135 (April, 1945).

[6] For a short article on the subject, see C. K. Bolton, "Colonial Handwriting," in *Essex Antiquarian*, I:175–176 (November, 1897). Guides to the older calligraphy of Europe, which must on occasion be consulted by students of the European antecedents of the American past, include: Andrew Wright, *Court-Hand Restored, or the Student's Assistant in Reading Old Deeds, Charters, Records, Etc. . . . .* (10th ed., corrected by C. T. Martin, London, 1912); Hilary Jenkinson, *The Later Court Hands in England, from the Fifteenth to the Seventeenth Centuries* (Cambridge, England, 1927); J. J. Bond, *Handy-Book of Rules and Tables for Verifying Dates* (London, 1889); Maurice Prov, *Manuel de paléographie latine et francaise* (4th ed., Paris, 1924); Jesus Muñoz y Rivero, *Manual de paleografiá diplomática española de los siglos XVI al XVII* (2d ed., Madrid, 1917).

[7] Carter, "Historical Editing." Carter relied heavily upon British precedents, conveniently stated in R. L. Poole, *et al.*, "Report on Editing Historical Documents," in University of London Institute of Historical Research, *Bulletin*, I:6–28 (June, 1923).

[8] Carter, "Historical Editing," 25–37; James C. Olson, "The Scholar and Documentary Publication," in *American Archivist*, 28:187–193 (April, 1965).

[9] Walter M. Whitehill, ed., "Publishing the Papers of Great Men," in *Daedalus*, Academy of Arts and Sciences, *Proceedings*, 86:47–79 (1955).

contextual categories of sponsorship rather than chronological sequence, and by describing the mechanical process of reproduction involved. The historiographical significance of the various documentary publication projects lies in the scholarly goals they sought to serve. It so happens that the purpose of publication has changed, over the years, to correspond very closely to the agency of publication. Projects involving the dissemination of documents can thus be treated as proprietary, academic and scholarly, governmental, and special projects, in roughly chronological order.

Early documentary publication projects in America were all proprietary in character, and the earliest of these reflected the efforts of Ebenezer Hazard to issue his collection of archives and personal manuscripts. Born in Boston in 1744, Hazard grew up in the same history-conscious culture which produced Thomas Prince and Jeremy Belknap. Hazard's documentary project was an outgrowth of his collection of English trade laws and was proposed in 1772 or 1773. He solicited and received subscriptions from about 250 persons, including John Adams and Thomas Jefferson, but the project was deferred by the Revolution, during which Hazard served successively as Surveyor of Post Roads and as Postmaster General. In 1778 Hazard sought to capitalize upon his political position to advance his documents project, and a committee of the Continental Congress was induced to endorse the project and to recommend a public subsidy of $1,000.[10] There is no record that the subsidy was ever paid, but for the next three years Congress indirectly supported the project. Hazard continued to draw his salary as Postmaster General while spending most of his time copying letters and records, mainly those of the New England Confederation at Plymouth. "I wish to be the means," he declared, "of saving from oblivion many important papers which without something like this collection will infallibly be lost. . . ."

Hazard made an abortive attempt at publication after the war. When he was unceremoniously removed as Postmaster General upon the organization of the new federal government in 1789, Hazard redoubled his efforts to fulfill obligations to publish two

---

[10] Fred Shelley, "Ebenezer Hazard: America's First Historical Editor," in *William and Mary Quarterly*, 3rd series, 12:44–49 (January, 1955).

already subscribed volumes of American documents. He moved to Philadelphia and formed a partnership with the printer Thomas Dobson. The first volume, which finally appeared in January, 1792, under the title *Historical Collections: Consisting of State Papers and Other Authentic Documents; Intended as Material for an History of the United States of America,* included material from Columbus' first commission in 1492 to colonial papers of 1656. Hazard himself deemed the project too extensive, dissolved his partnership, and accepted a position as secretary of the Insurance Company of North America.[11]

Spurred to renew the task by his own deep interest and by his obligations to his subscribers, Hazard in February, 1793, began to set type on his second volume, which was distributed in 1794. This volume consisted mainly of previously unpublished manuscripts relating to the United Colonies of New England, 1656–1664. Having discharged his obligations, but at considerable financial loss, Hazard sadly gave up the idea of continuing the project "for want of taste in the age."[12]

Although Hazard's pioneer project was a commercial failure, it is regarded a historical success. His *Historical Collections* were used effectively by Abiel Holmes, Timothy Pitkin, James Grahame, George Bancroft, James Savage, John G. Palfrey, and Herbert L. Osgood. Hazard set the pattern of documentary publication for the next century. Peter Force alluded to the project in his proposal to Congress for the *American Archives,* and genealogists still delight in the full texts which include names of subscribers of documents.[13]

Hazard's dream approached realization in the wave of intense nationalism which followed the War of 1812. To this period belongs the uncompleted *State Papers* series of Thomas Waite and the abortive efforts of Peter Force to publish his *American Archives.* The project which came nearest the ideal of comprehensive publication of the documentary sources of the republic was the *American State Papers* of Gales and Seaton. Their thirty folio volumes, covering the period of 1789 to 1832, were for nearly a century the most complete edition of American archival material. They were further enhanced in value by the

---

[11] *Ibid.,* 68–70.
[12] *Ibid.,* 70–71.
[13] *Ibid.,* 71–72.

subsequent disappearance of many of the original documents. This great documents series, the last to be issued as a proprietary project, was abruptly terminated in 1861, a victim of the Civil War.[14]

The documania which overcame Americans in the first half of the nineteenth century was a commentary upon the shallow historical roots of their infant nation. In a time of rapid expansion and perilous sectionalism, there was comfort and security to be found in the documents of an earlier and simpler age. For a generation caught up in the giddy whirl of the generalized present, and confronted by an indefinite future, there was a kind of compulsive need to identify with the historical particular. The publication of historical documentation came close to being a panacea for the ills of the American society and intellect. At once it conjoined the heritage of philosophic inquiry left from the eighteenth century, the spirit of scientific investigation contributed by the nineteenth, and the romanticism of the Victorian Era.[15]

The Age of Romanticism in American history meant a love of the specific as well as a veneration of the grand, and it produced page upon page of documentation in such journals as the *North American Review* and the *Saturday Review of Literature*. Historical societies vied with one another in publishing their "Collections," and states garnered prestige by gathering and publishing their archives. *Niles' Register* confidently declared that "an enlightened legislature will always regard these things as important," while the *North American Review* editorialized that there was "no expenditure of the public money more creditable."[16]

In these halcyon days, before professional historians entered the Garden of History, documentary history was regarded, as John Spencer Bassett has observed, as "the only real way in which it was to be written." These earlier students of the past believed that posterity, if not themselves, "would while away its hours of ease poring over collections of laws, state papers, and political

[14] Carter, "Territorial Papers," 123.
[15] George H. Callcott, "Antiquarianism and Documents in the Age of Literary History," in *American Archivist*, 21:25 (January, 1958).
[16] *Ibid.*, 17–20.

correspondence."[17] Spurred by this kind of popular interest and enthusiasm, up to 1861 Congress supported at least eighteen major documentation projects, embracing at least 322 volumes, at an estimated cost of about $7,000,000![18]

The decades following the Civil War brought some basic changes in the documentation of American history and in its dissemination. The rise of a professional class of historical scholars and students made inevitable the development of standards of selection and editing approximating the best European tradition. Collections of documents were no longer grudgingly bought by the well-to-do as a charity to scholarship; the community of scholars now eagerly conceived and executed its own collections of documents to serve its own interests. Moreover, a resurgent scholarly interest in the colonial and Revolutionary periods resulted in significant editions of documents of those periods. Finally, an incessant desire to search beyond formal documentation and to approximate total recall of the historical past shifted the field of documentary publication from governmental archives to private manuscripts, usually the personal papers of national leaders.

However conscientiously edited, the early compilations of personal papers were not inclusive, and they soon needed revisions or supplements. For example, the collected works of Washington, Jefferson, and Madison which were published about the turn of the century did not include all of the then incomplete holdings of manuscripts in repositories. The collections generally stressed the obvious contributions of the Founding Fathers but supplied little of the material upon which the revisionary historiography was to be based. True to their origins and purposes, virtually all of these projects were conceived, supported, and executed wholly within the academic community—but it is safe to say that commercial publishers did not mourn the loss of this particular field of publishing.

The rising costs of printing, the supposed inability to match the thoroughness with which earlier volumes of personal papers were edited, and the development of less expensive means of

---

[17] *Ibid.*, 23–24.

[18] An excellent bibliography of the early documentary projects issued at federal expense may be found in *ibid.*, 20–21.

dissemination of documentary material led early in the twentieth century to dire predictions of the impending obsolescence of all printed editions of personal papers. The renaissance of that genre of scholarship following World War II has belied that prophecy and has witnessed an improvement in the quality of editorial workmanship, as exhibited in such projects as the publication of the papers of Jefferson, Franklin, and the Adams Family.

The Jefferson project well illustrates the inclusive and comprehensive scope of a modern edition of personal papers, one which includes all known documents wherever located and many classes and types of material not previously included.[19] The Franklin papers are perhaps even more widely scattered than the Jefferson material, and their collection and publication has been an exercise in co-operation between members of an international scholarly fraternity.[20] The Adams Family papers present even greater problems of bulk over a longer time span. Overcoming these obstacles has required a commercial subsidy.[21]

Documentary publication as an official function of the federal government is as old as the Republic itself, but involvement on the scale of the *Monumenta Germania Historia* or of the British *Rolls Series* is a twentieth-century development in the United States. In the earliest days of the nation, the government printed documents for its own use rather than for the use of historians. In those days historians were expected to search out their own documentation or to subscribe to editions of documentary proprietors.[22]

The federal government did not become its own printer until 1861, after which date the scholar's demand for printed documentation could easily be indulged by integrating it with the routine production of the multiple copies of government documents needed for administrative purposes. Bibliographical control proved to be a serious problem until Dr. John G. Ames devised a scheme for the identification and cataloging of congressional documents. Since the Fiftieth Congress (1889–1891) con-

---

[19] Whitehill, "Publishing Papers," 49–56; Carter, "Territorial Papers," 123.

[20] Quoting Leonard W. Larabee, in Whitehill, "Publishing Papers," 57–62.

[21] Views of L. H. Butterfield, in *ibid.*, 62–71.

[22] Julia H. Powell, *The Books of a New Nation, U. S. Government Publications* (Philadelphia, 1957), 17–137.

gressional documents have been assigned to and serially numbered within one of six series—Senate Journals, House Journals, Senate Reports, House Reports, Senate Documents, and House Documents. They have been distributed under this system to some 500 selected repository libraries throughout the country.[23]

The bewildering variety of extra-congressional publications can be fitted into a number of broad classifications, which include directives and registers; administrative rules, regulations, orders, and manuals; judicial opinions; compilations of laws; executive reports and compilations; maps and charts; bibliographies; and miscellaneous materials. Most of this outpouring of documents comes in series, often without a formal author, and it is generally understood to include anything printed at public expense.[24] The material is also regarded as the *bête noire* of librarians for its inherent difficulty of cataloging.

The number of the publications of the United States government exceeds that of every other government and publisher. These publications span the whole range of human knowledge and have a considerable impact upon scholarship and scholarly communication. Many government documents are transcripts of original records, and their publication constitutes merely a facilitation of access to source material. Others are annual reports or summaries of a statistical nature which are intended to eliminate duplicate effort. Increasing numbers of government documents result from extensive research in the physical and social sciences and are in competition, so to speak, with the production of the academic community and the commercial and scholarly presses. In any case, a government document derives no special sanctity from its official character but must be judged on its own merit. Often partisan and politically motivated, government documents sometimes resort to deliberate misstatement of fact. In matters that do not have a political bearing, they are generally accurate and excellent.[25]

[23] Anne Morris Boyd (rev. Rae Elizabeth Rips), *United States Government Publications* (New York, 1952), 36–53; Eric J. Dingwall, *How to Use a Large Library* (Cambridge, England, 1933), 56–60.

[24] Boyd, *U. S. Government Publications*, 27–32; A. F. Kuhlman, ed., *Public Documents, Their Selection, Distribution, Cataloging, Reproduction, and Preservation* (Chicago, 1935).

[25] Lawrence Frederick Schmeckebier, ed., *Government Publications and Their Use* (2d ed., Washington, 1939), 1–4.

The documentary foundation of the federal and state governments and thus the bedrock of historical documentation is their respective constitutions and organic laws. Primarily for the purposes of the law but secondarily as a service to historical scholarship, this material was collected, annotated, and published under federal auspices in 1907. From that base, amendments are periodically reported. This series constitutes the basis for constitutional and legal scholarship of the most fundamental variety.[26]

Research requiring reference to the published text of federal laws may turn to a number of documentary compilations. Prior to 1938, the series entitled *Sessional Laws of the United States* included the legislation approved by each biennial session of Congress. Since 1938 the series has been replaced by *U. S. Statutes at Large*, which incorporates essentially the same material. At irregular intervals, general indexes to federal legislation and general codifications such as the *U. S. Code* have appeared. On occasion, limited codifications of federal legislation on special subjects, such as bankruptcy, are issued.[27]

The transactions of the Congress of the United States, indispensable documentation for a wide range of historical subjects, have been faithfully recorded and published since the establishment of the federal government in 1789. From that year until 1824 the reports in journal form were published under the title *Annals of Congress.* Abridged reports of congressional debates were made available in the volumes of two serial publications, the *Register of Debates* (1824–1837) and the *Congressional Globe* (1833–1873). Since 1873, full verbatim reports of the public debates and proceedings of Congress have been published as the *Congressional Record.*[28]

Most judicial decisions in the United States, as in Great Britain, lie in a documentary no man's land, somewhere between what is officially and publicly disseminated and what is known only by interested members of the legal profession. Although

[26] *Ibid.,* 185–196; see F. N. Thorpe, ed., *The Federal and State Constitutions, Colonial Charters, and Other Organic Law* (Washington, 1907).

[27] Schmeckebier, *Government Publications,* 197–247; Everett Somerville Brown, *Manual of Government Publications, United States and Foreign* (New York, 1950), 10–14.

[28] Brown, *Government Publications,* 16–22.

these decisions are promulgated largely through professional service organizations, proprietary in nature, their volumes of reports are invested with a quasi-official character. Within the federal system, only since 1922 have the *U. S. Reports* of Supreme Court decisions been official publications of the federal government, replacing such familiar series of proprietary reports as Dallas, Cranch, Peters, and Wheaton. Also reported now as official publications are the decisions of the Court of Claims, the Court of Customs and Patent Appeals, the Customs Court, and the Commerce Court.[29] The reports of all other federal and state courts are still issued by quasi-public proprietors.

Attention has been called elsewhere to the special immunity conferred upon the records and papers of the Chief Executive by the constitutional division of powers. From the inception of the federal system, the principle that the bulk of the presidential papers is of a private character and is not subject to publication or dissemination by any other branch of the government has been well established. On the other hand, any formal and public pronouncement of a President, such as the annual State of the Union Message to Congress, is in the constitutional sense the property of the nation and may be widely disseminated as constituting a public document. Although the concept of presentation might result in all of a President's public addresses being scattered in public documents, for convenience it has seemed desirable that they be collected in one printed series and issued as an official publication entitled *Messages and Papers of the Presidents.*[30]

Another category of federal records in which public and scholarly interest has justified the costs of publication is the diplomatic correspondence of the Department of State. These records consist primarily of the dispatches and instructions exchanged by the Department and American diplomats abroad, and the similar, parallel exchange between the Department and foreign diplomats in Washington. Couched in the studied and ritualistic language of diplomacy and often deliberately concealing more

[29] Schmeckebier, *Government Publications,* 258–278; Brown, *Government Publications,* 32–34; Seymour W. Connor, "Legal Materials as Sources of History," in *American Archivist,* 23:159–165 (April, 1960).

[30] Schmeckebier, *Government Publications,* 310–328; Brown, *Government Publications,* 35–37.

than is revealed, this material is the obvious basis for the history of American diplomacy, and it is among the most intensively used of all groups of federal records. In the earlier days of the Republic, portions of the diplomatic correspondence were occasionally published by Congress or by the Department itself, generally to vindicate the American position in an international dispute or to provide background when a foreign issue became involved in American domestic politics. Following the Civil War, however, the publication of diplomatic correspondence, with the inauguration of the series entitled *Foreign Relations of the United States,* was placed on a regular basis. Each year the staff of the Department of State selects from its files that portion of the correspondence which seems to be most significant, publication of which will not be diplomatically embarrassing to the United States in its continuing relations with any friendly nation.[31]

As liberal as the federal government has been in the publication of the more significant of its records, its liberality has not kept pace with the growing expectations and demands of the historical profession. It is largely the concerted pressure of the profession which has been responsible for the creation of the National Archives and the evolution of the current National Historical Publications Commission. Both plans were conceived, however, in the fertile mind of J. F. Jameson.

Jameson spent most of his professional years promoting the collection, preservation, and wider dissemination of the primary sources for American history. He began the task in 1886 by urging Ainsworth Spofford and the Library of Congress to collect and edit the records of the Virginia Company. He also succeeded in having inserted in the Civil Appropriations Act of March 3, 1887, a proviso for a documents commission. The commission was to consist of the Secretary of State, the Librarian of Congress, and the Secretary of the Smithsonian Institution and was to be charged with recommending a plan for the systematic publication of the manuscript records in the possession of the federal government. Because the commission failed to receive a supporting appropriation, it died aborning. Jameson,

---

[31] Schmeckebier, *Government Publications,* 329–359; Brown, *Government Publications,* 38–44.

however, was undaunted. In 1890 he wrote and published a pamphlet entitled *The Expenditures of Foreign Governments in Behalf of History*, pointing out that little had been done in America beyond the publication of the *Official Records of the War of the Rebellion*, a publication he cited as an example of the documentary project he had in mind. Despite the continuing efforts of the American Historical Association and the Carnegie Institution of Washington, however, nothing similar was undertaken for the next forty-four years, until 1934.[32]

Official inaction notwithstanding, Jameson pressed his plan for the federal government to assume the responsibility of extensive publication of its own documents. Largely through his efforts, the AHA established in 1895 a Historical Manuscripts Commission, consisting of Douglas Brymner of Ottawa, Talcott Williams of Philadelphia, William F. Trent of Sewanee, Frederick Jackson Turner of the University of Wisconsin, and Jameson, of Brown University, as chairman. The commission recommended an extensive publicly-supported documentary publication program, which was duly endorsed by the parent organization—and ignored by Congress. Meanwhile, as editor of the *American Historical Review*, Jameson opened the journal to the publication of documents in the style of many of the state historical society organs. Jameson was also instrumental in creating the Public Archives Commission in 1899 and in forming the Conference of Archivists in 1909, both of which organizations helped to secure publication of archival material at federal expense. Simultaneously, the AHA appointed Charles Francis Adams, Andrew C. McLaughlin, and Jameson to constitute a records committee to study the feasibility of operating a study institution in Washington for advanced historical scholarship. This committee was ultimately incorporated into the Carnegie Institution of Washington and was responsible for the publication of the Carnegie Guides to archival materials in the United States and abroad. The guides were in part intended to stimulate the publication of the original materials, but they failed to achieve this goal despite the interest of President Theodore Roosevelt and Secretary of State Elihu Root.[33]

[32] Waldo G. Leland, "The Prehistory and Origins of the National Historical Publications Commission," in *American Archivist*, 27:187–190 (April, 1964).

[33] *Ibid.*, 190–193.

The AHA records committee continued to recommend a publicly-supported, American approximation of the *Monumenta Germaniae Historia,* but through lack of public interest the project died in committee. Until it could secure its larger vision, the AHA under Jameson's leadership continued to support such specific federal documentary publication projects as the State Department's *Foreign Relations* volumes, Hunter Miller's *Treaties and Other International Acts of the United States,* and the *Territorial Papers* project, a proposal of the Mississippi Valley Historical Association.[34]

The mobilization of public interest which finally secured the creation of the National Archives also led in 1934 to the establishment by Congress of the National Historical Publications Commission. Purely advisory in character, the commission was expected to recommend a program of documentary publication, but it failed even in this function for want of a permanent secretariat. After three ineffectual meetings it lapsed into inactivity and was not revived until 1950 in the Truman Administration. The new commission was attached to the National Archives and was given the same basic task of serving as a clearing house for information and as an instrument for voluntary cooperation and coordination between all agencies, governmental and academic, engaged in the publication or dissemination of documentary materials for American historical research.[35]

The preliminary report (1951) and the *National Program* (1954) of the commission both called for the selective dissemination, in a variety of formats, of nationally-important source materials originating from some 361 individuals, including 112 on a priority list. In addition, the commission urged the publication of the records of the Continental Congress, ratification of the Constitution and the first ten amendments, and the First Congress. While the Commission's *Program* anticipated that most of the actual editorial work would be done by the usual "historical and other learned societies, libraries, archival institutions, and colleges and universities," it also recognized the inevitable need for subsidies from "both governmental and

---

[34] Carter, "Territorial Papers," 124.

[35] Leland, "Publication Commission," 194; Schellenberg, *Modern Archives,* 215–224; Robert L. Brubaker, "The Publication of Historical Sources: Recent Projects in the United States," in *The Library Quarterly,* 37:195–199 (April, 1967).

nongovernmental sources," and it sought to commit the federal government to the principle of providing such financial support for projects of such transcendent scholarly importance.

The National Historical Publications Commission (NHPC) in 1963 projected a new and more active role for itself and the federal government in support of documentary publication by recommending that it directly support with a federal endowment the five primary publication projects already under way—the Adams, Franklin, Hamilton, Jefferson, and Madison papers—to assure their completion, and that it inaugurate a program of matching grants-in-aid to support other projects previously identified in its 1954 *Program*. Congressional debate on the proposals brought forth misgivings from several Republican opponents that public support might lead to politically-inspired tampering with the fundamental sources of the nation's history. By a generally partisan vote, the Congress finally appropriated $350,000 to be expended during the fiscal year ending June 30, 1965. This expression of public support moved the Ford Foundation to channel through the commission a grant of $2,000,000 designated to assure the continuation of the five priority projects for the next decade. During the first year of the grants-in-aid program the NHPC made grants to twelve projects for printed editions and to ten agencies for microfilm editions of documents. By mid-1966 grants had been made to support the publication of the papers of Henry Clay, John C. Calhoun, Andrew Johnson, Henry Laurens, James K. Polk, Daniel Webster, Jefferson Davis, Ulysses S. Grant, Henry R. Schoolcraft, Isaac Backus, John C. Frémont, John Marshall, and the Susquehannah Company. Some of the other publication projects which have been announced in filling parts of the *National Program* but which have as yet received no financial support from the NHPC are the papers of John Jay, John Dickinson, Rutherford B. Hayes, Franklin D. Roosevelt, Woodrow Wilson, Bishop Francis Asbury, Archbishop John Carroll, Theodore Roosevelt, and Abraham Lincoln.[36]

While ultimately subject to the political whims of Congress and the generosity of foundations, for the present the funding

[36] U. S., National Historical Publication Commission, *A National Program for the Publication of Historical Documents: A Report to the President* (Washington, 1954); Brubaker, "Publication of Historical Sources," 221–225.

of editorial expenses of the growing number of documentary projects seems reasonably assured. That being the case, the expanding corps of scholars and editors involved are free to devote their energies to the task of making their editions meet the high standards set in 1950 with the publication of the first volume of *The Papers of Thomas Jefferson*.

The proposal to publish the papers of Thomas Jefferson was first advanced in 1809 by a Petersburg, Virginia, bookseller, John W. Campbell. That idea was partially implemented, with indifferent success, in the several editions of Jefferson's writings issued in the nineteenth century. Now 150 years later, the proposal is in the process of definitive implementation, in a projected fifty-volume edition. Because no other President, save the second Roosevelt, had a stronger archival instinct, Jefferson is at once the joy and the nemesis of the documentary editor. Jefferson wrote prolifically, and he seldom destroyed any of his correspondence. The collection and publication of the whole body of his papers therefore had to await the modern development of microfilm, although the project has been materially aided by Jefferson's own Epistolary Record, neatly indexed. With such help, the search to date has netted over 50,000 separate documents from over 400 different sources. The project goes forward at Princeton University under the exemplary direction and thoroughness of Julian Boyd. The high standards which have marked the Jefferson project from its inception have made it the model for other contemporary efforts at documentary publication.[37]

The papers of James Madison have had a publication history remarkably similar to those of Jefferson. Madison bequeathed the bulk of his papers to his wife, Dolley, who intended to publish them. Failing that, in 1837 she sold one group of the documents to the federal government. This material was subsequently edited by Henry D. Gilpin and published in 1840 in three volumes. A second set of Madison's papers, bought by the government in 1845, appeared in 1865 in four volumes. A third group came to light in the 1890's and was transferred to the

[37] Lyman H. Butterfield, "The Papers of Thomas Jefferson: Progress and Procedures in the Enterprise at Princeton," in *American Archivist*, 12:131–145 (April, 1949).

Library of Congress in 1910. A revised and presumably inclusive edition of Madison papers was prepared in 1900 by Gaillard Hunt, but it suffered from the usual faults of the nineteenth-century editing. The need for a modern and complete edition was suggested in 1952 by Philip M. Hamer. In 1954 the University of Chicago joined forces with the Virginia Historical Society and the University of Virginia, with support from the Ford and Rockefeller foundations and the General Assembly of Virginia, to project an edition of upwards of fifty volumes, similar in format to the Jefferson Papers. Since 1956 the work has been moving forward at a scheduled pace.[38]

The University of Kentucky has assumed the burden of editing and publishing the papers of that commonwealth's most distinguished son, Henry Clay. The popular image of Clay has been that of a gambler, a philanderer, and a person deeply involved in political intrigue. Clay's letters, so the editors report, reveal him to have been an astute lawyer, a politician who had earnest opinions about most prominent men and issues of his day, a gentleman farmer with a genuine interest in things of the soil, and an affectionate husband and father—all traits revealed in a striking felicity of expression.[39] To date, the greatest problem has been locating the scattered products of Clay's pen.

Federally-supported documentary publication projects have inclined towards selectivity, illuminating a particular phase of the national development in which the federal government has played a dominant role. A typical example is the series of *Territorial Papers of the United States*. Because the western territories had the same relationship to the United States as the colonies once bore to Great Britain, the publication of the territorial documentation is roughly analogous to the collection and publication of colonial documentation by the various original states in the early years of the nineteenth century. The essential differences are that the parent government itself undertook the project and that the principal task was one of selection

[38] William H. Runge, "The Madison Papers," in *American Archivist*, 20:313–318 (October, 1957).

[39] James F. Hopkins, "Editing the Henry Clay Papers," in *American Archivist*, 20:231–238 (July, 1957).

rather than collection. The documentation of the American territories was already concentrated in the Department of State, which had administered the territories until 1873.[40]

The movement for the publication of selected portions of the territorial documentation began in 1911 with the publication of the Carnegie guide by David W. Parker, *A Calendar of Papers in Washington Archives Relating to the Territories of the United States to 1873*. As a response to the pressure from the states of the Middle West exerted through the Mississippi Valley Historical Association, in 1925 Congress passed an act for the collection of the territorial records included in Parker's guide, and the actual work was placed in the hands first of Newton D. Mereness and subsequently of Clarence E. Carter. Publication of the material was provided for by an act of 1929, and the work was begun in 1931.[41]

The impossibility of publishing the territorial documentation *in extenso* was soon evident, so bulky was the material. The scope of the project ultimately was determined by fiscal limitations. Publication was limited to materials located in the various governmental agencies in Washington, or to material which should have been in the capital but for some reason was elsewhere. To save funds, it was decided to omit all previously published documents, but to completely cite all omissions. All administrative and policy decisions affecting the government of the territories were included, as were letters of the territorial governors, records of the extension of the postal service, and all popular petitions. Also included were the records of all land sales, titles, and surveys. Little emphasis was placed on the documentation of Indian affairs, because such documentation often transcended territorial boundaries. Records of the defense of territories were included, as was material on any extra-territorial involvement.[42]

A fourth agency of documentary publication, in addition to those of proprietary, academic, and governmental, is that which can be called "special," involving institutions which do not fall precisely into any of the previous categories. Within this group

---

[40] Carter, "Territorial Papers," 123.
[41] *Ibid.*
[42] *Ibid.*, 124–131.

are such agencies as state historical societies and latter-day commercial publishers who occasionally and almost accidentally publish documents incident to their interests in American history.

Among state historical agencies, the usual pattern of documentary publication has involved the collection and printing of every available piece of documentation from whatever sources relating to a given geographical or political area. The series of the *Illinois Historical Collections, Indiana Historical Collections,* and the *New-York Historical Society Collections* are typical of ventures conceived in the nineteenth century and extended into the twentieth, although not always with a real appreciation of the costs or scholarly utility involved.[43]

Contemporary commercial publishers of historical documentation are generally not interested in documentation for its own sake, but rather in catering to popular interest in history, as is done in the pages of the magazine *American Heritage*. Its excursions into documentary publication are inspired by such items as a letter of Theodore Roosevelt regarding the funeral of King Edward VII, a long-suppressed manuscript account of the hanging of John Brown, General William Howe's orderly book covering the occupation of New York and including a reference to the hanging of Nathan Hale, Douglas Southall Freeman's letters regarding his research and writing on the Civil War, and the unpublished pictorial records of the Brewster Carriage Company. Such documentation is of a nature calculated to avoid didactic boredom to the 175,000 subscribers of *American Heritage*.[44]

While far removed from the tastes and interests of professional historians, the readers of *American Heritage* are distinguished in their educational level, over 27 per cent holding post-graduate degrees. A survey of reader preferences in original historical documentation revealed that the following topics had greatest appeal, in descending order: explorers, pioneers, old customs, colonists, battles, old houses, politics, ships, Indians, inventors, religion, antiques, industries, genealogy, and trains. Periods of history from which occasional documentation would be most welcome were: Revolutionary War and Civil War, opening of

---

[43] *Ibid.,* 123.
[44] James Parton, "Popularizing History and Documentary Sources," in *American Archivist,* 20:106–107 (April, 1957).

the West, pre-Revolution, and Indian Wars. Armed with this guide to the tastes of its readers, the editors of *American Heritage* frankly admit that they operate upon the basis of one of the fundamental rules of salesmanship: "Don't sell the steak; sell the sizzle."[45]

In the face of the varied and even discordant aims of contemporary documentary publication enterprises, the master plan developed by the National Historical Publication Commission does offer some hope of minimizing competition and duplicated effort and of channeling available effort into a more systematic coverage of the needs of scholarship.[46]

FORMS AND METHODS
OF DOCUMENTARY REPRODUCTION

UNTIL THE TURN of the twentieth century, any consideration of publishing historical documents in forms other than printed volumes would have been largely academic. A few projects of facsimile reproductions, such as those undertaken by B. F. Stevens, catered more to the amateur collector of documents than to the scholarly user of them. The standard, inflexible format for scholarly publication of historical documentation was letterpress printing from type set by hand or by machine. This method largely limited the type of documentation to be disseminated, even in earlier years of far less expensive unit costs. Since the turn of the century, however, with the advent of planographic printing, typewriters, photographic reproduction, and data processing machines (used singly or in various combinations), a new world of alternative forms and methods has been opened for documentary creation and reproduction. Despite rising unit costs, the new duplication processes have enabled an ever-growing torrent of documentation, reaching deeper and deeper into levels of specialization and scholarly interests, to be published. In truth, the largest remaining obstacle in documentary publication is the scholarly prejudice against any but the most traditional and prestigious form of

[45] *Ibid.*
[46] Hamer, "Authentic Documents," 3–13; U. S., National Historical Publication Commission, *National Program,* 11–35.

documentary publication—standard letterpress printing and hard-cover binding.

One pioneer and leading exponent of the newer forms of publication, especially as applied to historical documentation, has compared them to the types of highways crossing the American landscape. Traditional printed editions of documents are comparable to the broad, concrete highways which link points of major interest and carry the heaviest scholarly traffic. Mimeograph and planograph editions suggest the less expensive secondary road network, a necessity for getting to points off the main line of interest, but only lightly travelled. Photostats and microfilm are the dirt roads, foot paths, and trails which go everywhere and are of interest only to the occasional traveller. Thus, form of documentary reproduction should be determined by the anticipated degree of use, the least expensive, adequate form always being selected.[47]

In 1936 Robert C. Binkley published a classic guide to the various means of documentary reproduction, statistically indicating costs of publication under various conditions. Although Binkley's conclusions were based upon manufacturing costs of 1936, they are still valuable for illustrating the wide range of unit costs under varying conditions. The keys to Binkley's calculations were the cost of preparing the first copy and the number of copies over which this high fixed cost could be spread. According to Binkley, the minimum efficiency points at which the cost of creating multiple copies equaled the fixed cost of the first copy ranged from printing 2,000 copies from machine-set type to making microfilm reproductions of existing material, one copy at a time. Photo-offset, mimeograph, and hectograph processes could most efficiently reproduce material composed on a typewriter in minimum runs in the intermediate range of 1,000 down to about 100 copies.[48] Through choosing the most efficient mode of publication indicated by the minimum press runs, the reproduction costs could be held to the range of about 50¢ to 75¢ per 1,000 words per copy, exclusive of binding costs.[49]

---

[47] Robert C. Binkley, "Techniques and Policies of Documentary Reproduction," in International Conference on Documentation, 14th, Oxford and London, 1938, *Transactions,* 1:121–124 (1938).

[48] Derived from Binkley, *Reproducing Research Materials,* Table L, 185.

[49] Compiled from *ibid.,* 187.

In 1936 a maximum acceptable cost for reproducing documentary material was held to be approximately $1.50 per 100,000 words of text, exclusive of binding. Therefore, the minimum editions possible under the maximum acceptable costs ranged from 550 copies in letterpress, to 250 copies in photo-offset, to about 100 copies in mimeograph or hectograph, to a single copy in microfilm.[50] Fluctuations since 1936 in reproduction costs have widened the gap between letterpress printing and the various forms of near-printing and microfilm publication.[51] As scholars continually remind those who make decisions affecting the format of documentary publication, however, cost alone should not be the determining factor.

The traditional form of documentary publication, letterpress printing from machine composition, is still the most prestigious and the most expensive. Because printed editions of historical documentation under normal circumstances cannot hope to recoup their costs, this form of publication must be selected only for overriding, nonfinancial reasons and must be subsidized. This form of publication is therefore reserved for material of the greatest importance relating to the origins of institutions of national significance, such as the *Territorial Papers*, or relating to outstanding events or episodes in the nation's development, such as the *Official Records of the War of the Rebellion*. Printed publication is also appropriate for material which requires extensive editorial preparation and/or which relates to a wide range of topics, such as personal papers projects.[52]

The printing press has not given to professional authors the same freedom it has conferred upon the professional and commercial class of readers. The printing press restricts the author to material which can be readily sold at a profit in efficient press runs, substantive merit notwithstanding. Material of limited appeal, such as most documentary projects, simply cannot be accommodated by the publishing process without outside subsidy. An historian's decision to print limits the collection of documentation to that for which a subsidy can be found, either

[50] From *ibid.*, 188.
[51] Duyvis F. Donker, *et al.*, *Manual on Document Reproduction and Selection*, FID Publication No. 264 (2 vols., The Hague, 1954); Chester Kerr, *A Report on American University Presses* (Washington, 1949).
[52] Schellenberg, *Modern Archives*, 215–224.

directly or through the pages of a professional journal. Among other results, this situation has produced a decline in the publication of collections of letters, hence a decline in the art of letter writing, of poetry writing, and of conducting humane conversation in print. But scholars need not despair; the typewriter has come to their rescue. The machine has been much maligned for contributing to the literary decline of correspondence and for devaluating the prestige of publication. Such criticism is as unfair as it is foolish. Just as the use of the typewriter, carbon paper, and office reproduction machines has freed modern correspondence from the time-consuming labors of the clerk at a copying desk, so have these same instruments released scholarship from the arbitrary fetters of the printing press. The use in combination of the typewriter, office reproduction machines, and the offset printing press to produce which is called "near print" now accounts for more than a third of the total documentation produced by the federal government, and the percentage is probably higher in the dissemination of business documentation.[53]

An early application of near-print to documentary publication was made in the early days of the New Deal, in 1933 and 1934. The hearings of the NRA and the AAA preparatory to the issuance of their codes and regulations produced some 286,000 pages of unclassified material, dissemination of which was required by law. Printing that mass of material would have cost over $500,000. It was decided therefore to disseminate the material by hectograph and mimeograph, at a cost of about 2¢ per page per copy. A full file of the hearings was priced at about $5,000, but no library bought a complete set. Instead, selected portions were purchased at the somewhat higher price of 10¢ per page. Then, in an early application of microfilming, copies of the entire file were offered at $421, or at about 20¢ per hundred pages, a figure well below the printed cost in editions above 2,000 copies.[54]

Comparable savings apply to other documentation published by microfilm, but scholars have failed to respond unreservedly to the concept of near-print and microphotographic publication.

[53] Robert C. Binkley, "New Tools for Men of Letters," in *Yale Review*, 24:526–528 (Fall, 1937).

[54] *Ibid.*, 523–526.

Binkley has attributed the cool response to the institutional prejudices under which scholars labor. Even though most historical documentation closely resembles the "internal documentation" of business and government offices, near-print is regarded as not quite respectable among scholars. As Binkley expressed it, "The system by which professional research workers draw their livelihood from institutions of learning has had a curious repercussion upon their system of communicating, resulting in a kind of fetishism in the printed page."[55]

Just as printing once transferred the monopoly of scholarship from the medieval church to the modern university, so near-print may in the future break the present scholarly monopoly of large universities and make room for a wider democracy of scholarship. Scholars in small colleges are presently at a distinct disadvantage, and below the college level teachers do little research. As a format both for documentation and for original publication, near-print may offer a solution to the problem of centralization of research materials. As Binkley has movingly suggested, "When the programme for America is laid down and the high strategy of American policies defined, let there be included among our objectives not only a bathroom in every house and a car in every garage, but a scholar in every school house and a man of letters in every town."[56]

Technical improvements in printing and the development of newer mechanical and electromagnetic forms of mass communications have tended to concentrate the control of culture and contributed to its professionalization. In the process of such concentration and professionalization, mass media have lost their ability to produce cohesive documentation. What the contemporary historical scholar needs is not so much a copy of what everybody else is reading or watching, but access to the unique which underlies the creation of the mass product. He needs to study what no one else would think of reading. The dissemination of unique documentation in limited quantities is the distinct

[55] Ibid., 528–530.

[56] Ibid., 531–537. Other suggestions for the utilization of near-print in documentary dissemination will be found in Irvin A. Herrman, Manual of Office Reproduction: Processes, Systems Duplicating, and Imprinting Methods (New York, 1956); and Harry M. Silver, "The Publication of Original Research Materials," in American Documentation, 1:13–23 (Winter, 1950).

province of the various means of photographic reproduction.[57]

The photographic process has been extensively used in the reproduction of documents since its invention in 1839. As the original wet plate process was replaced by the dry plate process, the photographing of documents became easier. With the perfection in 1906 of the "Photostat" process, photographic copying of documents came into its own. Photostat cameras produce negative copies directly upon inexpensive photographic paper, but because the unit costs do not significantly decrease as the edition increases, the process is feasible only in the production of a very limited number of sheets and copies. The relative speed and ease of reproduction are the principal advantages of the process.[58]

In the twentieth century the basic principle underlying the Photostat process has been developed in a half dozen directions, revolutionizing the creation and reproduction of the records of business and government and providing multiple alternatives for the reproduction of limited copies of historical documentation. A lively competition exists between the various copying methods and machines, and the characteristics, advantages, and disadvantages of each determine their various applications.[59]

The most advanced systems of documentary copying, such as Xerox and Electrofax, convert the original into a pattern of electrostatic charges on a revolving metal plate, from which are printed dry copies in a matter of seconds. Such copies are permanent and may be produced on regular paper at a cost of 5¢ per page, but the equipment is rather expensive to purchase or rent and is economically feasible only where there is a high level of use.

A variation of the electrostatic, dry-copy process is facsimile reproduction by wire over distances, as provided in systems de-

---

[57] Binkley, "New Tools," 519–520.

[58] Vernon D. Tate, "Microphotography as an Aid to Research," in American Library Association *Public Documents* (New York, 1935), 210; Tauber, *Technical Services*, 389–402. For suggestions concerning reproduction of documents with graphic cameras, see Vernon D. Tate, "Documentary Reproduction," in Williard Detering Morgan and Henry M. Lester, *Graphic Graflex Photography: The Master Book for the Larger Camera* (New York, 1942), 129–147.

[59] Information on the equipment described in the following paragraphs is derived from Peter Scott, "Developments in Rapid-Copying Machines," in *American Archivist*, 20:239–251 (July, 1957).

veloped by Western Union, Times Facsimile Corporation, Air Associates, Inc., and Alden Impulse Recording Company. Again, the equipment is rather expensive, although the unit reproduction costs approximate 5¢ per page. The possibility of opening the national research collections of documentation by facsimile reproduction to any location served by telephone lines holds the tremendous promise of decentralizing and democratizing historical research.

A simpler process of office copying is that based upon the principle of diazo, or the bleaching action of light upon certain dyes. Copying machines employing this method of duplication are marketed by the Ozalid Company and Charles Bruning Company. The equipment is relatively expensive, but it produces copies for only 1¢ to 2¢ per sheet. The process is restricted, however, to reproduction of single sides of translucent originals, and the copies fade after five to twenty-five years.

Another and even larger family of office copying machines in current use employs the transfer, wet process, involving the making of a negative master from which multiple positive copies can be made. One group of machines—including Apeco, Copease, Contura-Constat, Cormoc, Duplomatultra, Dristat, Exact Photocopy, Heccokwik, Transcopy, Photorapid, and Copy Cat—employs a light-sensitive negative, with diffusion transfer to the positive copy by some means other than light. Another group—Eastman Kodak's Verifax and the Photostat Instant Copier—employs a negative coated with gelatin containing a dye-forming compound and a hardening agent. Both diffusion- and gelatin-transfer equipment produce copies with a life of five to twenty-five years, at a unit cost of 10¢ or less per copy, depending upon the number of copies made from a single master.

A unique process of copying by thermography is employed by the Thermofax system marketed by Minnesota Mining and Manufacturing Company. These copiers are transmission printers using heat-sensitive paper, and they are limited to the reproduction of originals produced in metallic inks (colors do not reproduce well). The manufacturer claims the copies to be permanent, but since the paper used is inherently heat-sensitive, archival permanence would not seem to be possible. Perhaps the principal advantages of the process are its simplicity and its low cost of operation (less than 4¢ per copy).

By far the most extensive application of photography to the reproduction of documents has been through microphotography. The process traces its development to about 1859, when Joseph Sidebotham, a cloth printer of Bowdon, England, began to apply to documents the earlier efforts of John Benjamin Dancer to combine a microscope and a camera. Soon the possibility of creating micro-archives on photographic film excited the imaginations of many amateur scientists, including George Shadbolt, who first successfully reduced documents to microfilm in the 1880's.[60]

Documentary reproduction by microfilming came into its own in the twentieth century as the cheapest of the inexpensive forms of reproduction. While there is no theoretical limit to the degree of reduction except clarity of the original document, in practice the effective limit of reduction is about 1:60—the micro image is one-sixtieth of the original. Microphotography therefore can inexpensively reproduce documents, in a form more permanent than many of the paper originals, and with up to 98 per cent reduction.[61] Microfilm has come to be so widely adopted as a form of documentary reproduction, especially for long series of documents, that its technique has become well established, even to the point of the creation of a National Microfilm Association in 1943 to promote high standards of microphotography.[62]

An alternate form of microphotographic reproduction which has been applied to printed material is the microcard. The microscopic image, mechanically or photographically printed upon opaque cards, is read with the aid of an enlarger. The process is a cheaper and adequate form of publishing infrequently used titles. Publication by microcard has come into fairly

---

[60] Frederick Luther, *Microfilm: A History, 1839–1900* (Annapolis, Maryland, 1959), 12–30.

[61] Chester M. Lewis and William H. Offenhauser, Jr., *Microrecording: Industrial and Library Applications* (New York, 1956), 29–63; Vernon D. Tate, "An Appraisal of Microfilm," in *American Documentation*, 1:91–99 (Spring, 1950); Vernon D. Tate, "Microphotography in Archives," in U. S., National Archives, *Staff Information Circular* No. 8 (Washington, 1940), 1–4. For an earlier treatment of the subject, see Llewellyn M. Raney, ed., *Microphotography for Libraries* (Chicago, 1936).

[62] Luther, *Microfilm,* 184–186.

common use within the last fifteen years as a means of duplicating books and magazines particularly.[63]

The linear sequence of microphotographic filming with the consequent difficulty of locating specific exposures and the limitation of resolution of the reproduction combine to impose some rather specific criteria upon the selection of documents to be microfilmed. Microphotography as a form of publication is generally restricted to bulky materials of high research value, to cases in which the ratio of research value to total volume is rather high and in which the material is otherwise unobtainable in more legible form. Reasonably good prospects for the sale of at least five copies of the material within a period of ten years should exist. Records to be published by microphotography should be serial in nature, and they should be reasonably complete and not subject to further accretion. Microphotography is recommended as a means of publication when the originals may be easily filmed and read and when no extensive rehabilitation is necessary.[64]

Microphotographic publication eliminates most of the editing associated with printed or near-printed documentary publication, but a minimal amount of arranging which can be considered to be editorial in nature remains. A few rules of arrangement are almost universally respected. Indexes, registers, and similar finding aids are generally filmed in front of the main body of the material, just as endorsements precede the main body of the document. Enclosures are filmed immediately following a letter of transmittal. Alphabetical or chronological files not in strict order should be refiled before filming and duplicate papers should not be filmed. Items of no apparent research value may be omitted, as may printed material likely to be available in most libraries.[65]

At the rate of two pages of letter or legal paper per exposure, a single 100-foot roll of 35mm film generally will yield about 1,600 pages of material, for a unit cost of $2\frac{1}{2}\not c$ to $2\frac{7}{8}\not c$ per ex-

---

[63] Tauber, *Technical Services*, 389–402; Lewis and Offenhauser, *Microrecording*, 29–63; and Hubbard W. Ballou and John Rather, "Microfilm and Microfacsimile Publication," in *Library Trends*, 4:182–191 (October, 1955).

[64] U. S., National Archives, *The Preparation of Records for Publication on Microfilm* (Staff Information Papers, no. 19, 1951), 2–4.

[65] U. S., National Archives, *Publication on Microfilm*, 5–6.

posure, or from 19¢ to 68¢ per hundred sheets of paper copied. Positive prints, up to 100 copies, may be easily and quickly made from the master negative.[66] Microphotography is therefore uniquely applicable to a number of categories of historical documentation for a number of different reasons. Newspapers are particularly susceptible to microfilming because of their fragile condition and their inherent sequential character. Public archives lend themselves very easily to microphotography because of their high bulk and their sequential character, and business records are excellent candidates for filming because of the high cost of maintenance in their original form. Ephemeral matter can profit from filming because it will disintegrate in its original form. Lastly, personal papers may be filmed for the ease of distribution of a category of documentation which would otherwise remain unknown.[67]

The nagging question of the legal status of microphotographic copies of original documentation has plagued many who would otherwise wholeheartedly embrace the convenience of the form. The question has been commented upon in what would appear to be a conclusive manner by the United States Circuit Court of Appeals for the Second Circuit in 1939.[68] As yet, however, there is no uniformity of legal acceptance of the rule that filmed copies or records produced in a routine course of business, followed by the routine destruction of the originals, succeed to the full force of the original records.

The widespread adoption of microfilm has elicited some protests from scholars who find the copies more difficult to read than the original documents. Even sharper protests have been registered by some records managers who feel that microphotography has been oversold and misapplied. One such critic has pointed particularly to the difficulties encountered in filming

[66] Margaret C. Norton, "Photography for State Records," in *Illinois Libraries,* 28:151–155 (February, 1946), and 28:180–187 (March, 1946); U. S., War Department, *Records Administration: Microfilming of Records* (Technical Manual, 12–257, Washington, 1946), 1–91; Tate, "Microphotography in Archives," 6–7.

[67] Binkley, *Reproducing Research Materials,* 198–202; Schellenberg, *Modern Archives,* 215–224.

[68] U. S. v. Martin T. Mantan and George M. Spector [102 N. Y. Law Journal 1,959–1,960], as reported in Tate, "Microphotography in Archives," 5–6. See also, Leon deValinger, Jr., "A Microfilmer Replies," in *American Archivist,* 21:305–310 (July, 1958).

engineering records, drawings, and heterogeneous types of material. He is also critical of the proprietors of what he calls "holes in the ground," who have capitalized upon the fear of atomic destruction in selling programs of microfilming of records for safe storage underground.[69] The proponents of microfilm answer such arguments by observing that most objections can be minimized or eliminated by high standards of workmanship and intelligent application of the process.[70]

It is a commentary upon the relative currency of historical scholarship that the most advanced and sophisticated means of disseminating documentation is through microphotography, a process developed a half century ago and publicized by Robert C. Binkley a generation ago. Dr. Vannevar Bush recently expressed concern over the inability of the means of the dissemination of information to match the rate of explosion of knowledge. When it is recalled that the holdings of research libraries are doubling in bulk approximately every sixteen years, some kind of radical solution to the problem of dissemination is indicated. Historical scholarship seems to be lagging about twenty to thirty years in the utilization of modern conveniences. Must we wait so many years, however, before some application of computer technology is made to the field of dissemination of historical documentation?[71]

CARE AND PRESERVATION OF ORIGINAL DOCUMENTS

THE PREDECESSORS of modern archivists and manuscript librarians were, to be sure, more "records keepers" than "keepers of records." Theirs was a ministerial function which combined the care and preservation of documents of the past with the creation of the continuing series in the present. The establishment of modern archives and manuscript collections

---

[69] Jerry McDonald, "The Case Against Microfilming," in *American Archivist*, 20:346 (October, 1957).

[70] Margaret M. Weis, "The Case For Microfilming," in *American Archivist*, 22:15–24 (January, 1959).

[71] Vernon D. Tate, "From Binkley to Bush," in *American Archivist*, 10:250 (July, 1947); Tate, "The Use of Microphotography in Manuscript and Archival Work," in American Library Association, *Archives and Libraries* (New York, 1939), 103–108.

has brought a separation of the functions of creation and preservation, undoubtedly to the advancement of scholarship.

The rise of the archival profession in the United States has been marked by a departure from its European antecedents both as to the connection with scholarship and the administrative routine of the bureaus which created the archives. American archivists have sought to develop their own rationales, their own reasons for being, their own procedures and value judgments sufficient unto their emerging profession. Technical questions of care, repair, and preservation of historical materials, and considerations of archival building design have largely replaced earlier emphasis on facilitating and encouraging scholarly use of such materials. Furthermore, these new concerns have come to influence the nature of archival training and dominate discussion within the profession. These trends are most easily illustrated in the areas of abbreviated description and cataloging of archival materials, and the integration of records management practices into archival science.[72]

Despite the relative quantity and youthfulness of the paper entrusted to their care, American archivists have been uncommonly concerned for the preservation and restoring of their trust. This conscientiousness has led the new profession at an early stage into the technicalities of paper aging and deterioration.

Simply stated, cotton rag paper is one of the purest and most stable forms of alpha cellulose. Paper made of any other fiber is subject to comparatively more rapid deterioration as a result of slow oxidation by exposure to air and moisture, slow internal breakdown due to atmospheric and residual acids, and slow breakdown due to ultraviolet light or microorganisms. By far the greatest single enemy of paper is acid, the intensity of which is expressed in the hydrogen-ion concentration, pH 7 being neutral. The acidity of the purest form of cellulose available is about pH5, that of ordinary newsprint is about pH4. Hence, all paper is inherently the carrier of some quantity of the principal agent of its own destruction. Paper can be preserved from

---

[72] Lovett, "Non-Government Archives," 385–386; Robert E. Burke, "Modern Manuscript Collections and What to Do with Them," in *Manuscripts*, 7:232–236 (Summer, 1955); Charles W. David, "The Conservation of Historical Source Material," in *American Documentation*, 7:76–82 (April, 1956).

excess acidity by the removal of impurities during the process
of manufacture, the addition of alkaline sufficient to neutralize
much of the residual acid, the sealing, coating, or laminating of
the paper against atmospheric moisture, the addition of inhibi-
tors to curb the chemical activity of metallic impurities, and
the storage of paper in atmospheres free from sulphur dioxide
and other acid-producing agents.[73]

In addition to paper, the principal material constituents in
collections of records are inks and adhesives, and an understanding of their chemical properties is important in the evolution
of the technical aspects of modern archival science.

The earliest inks, suspensions of carbon (soot) in gum, resulted in writing of relative permanence. The pigment in such
ink became entrapped between the fibers of the writing surface.
Iron-gall inks capable of "biting into" the greasy surface of vellum replaced the simpler carbon inks in the eleventh century,
and iron-gall inks were used thereafter until about 1860, when
aniline dyes were introduced to the manufacture of writing ink.
Modern writing inks are generally water-soluble to some degree,
rarely react chemically with the writing surface, and need special
protection from abrasion and the eradicative effects of alcohol
and other solvents. On the other hand, pencil marks resist solvents very well but may be easily erased. Typewriter ribbon ink
is an oil-soluble dye in an oily base and, after slow penetration
for several days, is relatively permanent. The variety of copying
inks produces a wide range of permanence. Hectograph ink
gradually fades into illegibility, and carbon paper produces
only surface marks which are easily removed or smudged. Mimeograph inks, on the other hand, are absorbed by the paper to
produce records at least as permanent as the paper, and offset
lithography produces the same degree of permanence. On un-
coated paper, printing inks are entirely permanent, but they
may not be relied upon on coated stock.[74]

The variety of adhesives used on records are another source
of professional concern for the new archival science. Starch
paste has been found to disintegrate under moisture and to at-

---

[73] William Herbert Langwell, *The Conservation of Books and Documents* (London, 1957), 12–33.
[74] *Ibid.*, 46–57.

tract vermin. Otherwise, it is relatively stable and permanent. Albumen adhesives manufactured from blood are highly susceptible to moisture, and casein glues made from milk are little used on paper because they host molds and other destructive microorganisms. Gum arabic is very sensitive to moisture, hence its use on paper records is limited. Rubber-based adhesives, while quite effective temporarily, are little used when permanence is desired. Because of their difficulty of application, synthetic glues are little used on paper. All pressure-sensitive tapes undergo chemical changes which also influence the paper to which they are attached, and they should be removed from archival material with carbon tetrachloride.[75]

The first American efforts to apply scientific principles of document preservation and restoration, adaptations of the privately-developed processes of the documentarian Henry Stevens, were made in the State Department's Bureau of Rolls and Library in 1882. Between 1889 and 1892 the sum of $14,000 was appropriated for restoring and binding the priceless treasures held by the bureau, the papers of the Continental Congress and the manuscripts of Washington, Madison, and Monroe. The work consisted of protecting the papers from dust and mishandling by mounting them upon heavy ledger paper by a linen hinge and binding the pages together in oversize volumes.[76]

Processes of documentary preservation other than mounting in volumes were soon developed. In 1894 Francis W. R. Emery of Holyoke, Massachusetts, first sandwiched documents between white, transparent, paraffin-coated silk fabric, and the process was patented two years later. First applied to the early archives of Massachusetts, the paraffin-silk method of mounting soon spread to Connecticut and to New York. A third method was developed in the early years of the twentieth century by the Government Printing Office for the Manuscripts Division of the Library of Congress. This latter method involved sandwiching with crepeline or mausseline, but without paraffin.[77]

Under Gaillard Hunt, the Library of Congress about 1900

---

[75] *Ibid.,* 62–81.
[76] James L. Gear, "The Repair of Documents—American Beginnings," in *American Archivist,* 26:469–473 (October, 1963).
[77] *Ibid.*

began experimenting with repairing documents, appropriating German and Italian methods. The German method, developed by Edwin Pussey of Dresden, involved the immersion of the document in a clear, protective liquid known as Zapone, which dried to a wax-like coating. In the Italian method, devised by Fr. Franz Ehrle, librarian at the Vatican, protective sheets of gauze were pasted over the document to be restored or preserved. The relative merits of the two systems were discussed at a meeting of archivists at St. Gall, Switzerland, in 1900, whence knowledge of the systems made its way to the United States.[78]

In actual practice the German Zapone method was found by the experiments at the Library of Congress excessively to stiffen the document, and the process was soon abandoned. Instead, the crepeline process, utilizing a gauze of cotton and silk and a paste of rice flour, water, and salicylic acid or pulverized alum, was adopted. By 1903 the process had proven its worth, and its use began to spread to other American repositories.[79]

More recent European practices of fabric lamination and liquid coating have been evolved by American archivists into the practice of laminating documents between two sheets of cellulose acetate. European archivists have made dire predictions that the volatile plasticizers will eventually exude from the film, leaving it hard and brittle to the detriment of the paper it supposedly protects. Some evidence to support this view was advanced at an archival conference in Nashville, Tennessee, in 1955, but the question has not yet been resolved.

Two competing methods of acetate lamination are now in general use by American archivists. The older process, developed at the National Archives and involving highly variable heating, pressure, and time factors, results in incomplete melting and adhesion, but hermetically seals the document from the atmosphere. A second method, developed at the Virginia State Library by William Barrow, involves initial preparation by chemical neutralization followed by lamination between polished metal plates at very high and constant pressures and heat. The latter process results in more complete melting and fusion

[78] Ibid., 473–475.
[79] Ibid.

of the paper and the acetate film, and the method is said to be capable of improvement whenever thinner acetate film becomes available. An investigation made possible by a recent grant of $5,000,000 from the Ford Foundation to the Council on Library Resources hopefully may resolve the relative merits of the two competing processes and witness the development of even better methods of preserving records.[80]

The National Archives of India in 1951 began to develop a simple, inexpensive, yet effective method of documentary rehabilitation based on the American methods of lamination but without employing either heat or high pressure. The Indian system of hand lamination uses acetone as an adhesive to join the document to a tissue sheet and the acetate foil. Tests have proven the documents so treated to have longevity superior to the American methods, and the Indian process has been adopted experimentally at the National Archives. The process promises to have particular application in small archival institutions which cannot afford large and expensive equipment.[81]

Until the remaning questions of acetate lamination are resolved, the principal archival concern relating to the physical care of records will continue to be protection from the most injurious effects of moisture, light, and heat by proper storage and housing, and elimination of the hazards of fire, insects, and rodents by proper archival design and housekeeping.

In addition to insuring the longevity of individual pieces of documentation, modern archivists are also concerned with the conditions of filing accumulations of them. Vertical storage is generally favored among American archivists, except in the case of maps and oversize documents. Sharply creased paper from the last half of the nineteenth century generally produces special problems in that folding the inherently unstable paper has produced breaks and weakened fibers. Such documents are usually

[80] Robert W. S. Turner, "To Repair or Despair?" in *American Archivist*, 20: 320–325 (October, 1957); William K. Wilson and B. W. Forshee, "Preservation of Documents by Lamination," National Bureau of Standards *Monograph 5* (Washington, 1959), 1–16; U. S., National Archives, "The Rehabilitation of Paper Records," *Staff Information Papers*, no. 16 (Washington, 1950), 1–7; William J. Barrow, "Restoration Methods," in *American Archivist*, 6:151–154 (July, 1943).

[81] Y. P. Kathpalia, "Hand Lamination with Cellulose Acetate," in *American Archivist*, 21:271–274 (July, 1958).

strengthened by the application of linen hinges at the folds. Multiple breaks or gross weakness along folds usually requires mounting on a cloth backing of approximately equal weight or acetate lamination. Once the records have been repaired or restored, containers of cardboard or paper consisting of the least possible residual acidity or other impurities detrimental to the paper of the records themselves should be provided for permanent storage.[82]

Beyond the paper containers in immediate contact with the archival materials, the general environment of records is also a matter of concern to archivists. The National Archives is considered as the example of optimum control of the total environment. There the recirculating air is passed over an alkaline solution to neutralize acidic contamination. A relative humidity of 55 per cent is maintained in the storage spaces, 45 per cent in the work areas. Constant temperature of 70° F. is maintained in winter, 80° F. in summer. Daylight is completely excluded from the stack spaces, lighting being provided by small incandescent lamps as needed. Glazed tile walls are used throughout to eliminate abrasive dust, and coated or nonferrous metals have been used to minimize the need for frequent painting. Fumigation is routinely applied to each batch of accessioned records so as to eliminate the possibility of insect infestation.[83]

The catastrophes of fire and water damage to archives present special challenges to the archivist. Documents with charred edges and weakened by fire, but otherwise intact and legible, may be laminated routinely. Documents completely burned but physically intact should be photographed with infrared film, and documents in iron-gall ink which have been damaged by water may be recaptured by photographing in ultraviolet light.[84]

---

[82] Adelaide E. Minogue, "Physical Care, Repair, and Protection of Manuscripts," in *Library Trends*, 5:347 (January, 1957); Adelaide E. Minogue, *The Repair and Preservation of Records* (U. S., National Archives, Bulletin No. 5) (Washington, 1943), 10–42; Victor Gondos, Jr., "A Note on Record Containers," in *American Archivist*, 17:237–241 (July, 1954).

[83] A. E. Kimberly and B. W. Scribner, "Summary Report of National Bureau of Standards Research on Preservation of Records," (National Bureau of Standards, *Miscellaneous Publication*, M 154, Washington, [1937]), 27ff.; Haselden, *Scientific Aids*, 27–33; Charles Johnson, *The Care of Documents and Management of Archives* (Helps for Students of History, no. 5, London, 1919), 1–57.

[84] Minogue, 'Physical Care of Manuscripts," 347.

The disastrous fire in the Administration Building at Colgate University on October 27, 1963, provided an unwelcome opportunity to develop and apply several new procedures for records salvage. The building had burned for almost nine hours and had smoldered for two days before salvage work could be begun. Tons of water had been sprayed upon the fire. Fortunately, most of the permanent records were housed in a vault, where they were found to be damaged, but salvageable. Thus, the greatest problem was the drying of large quantities of wet, soggy paper.[85]

Another area of concern for American archivists has been the designing of archival buildings to insure maximum utility and protection to the records housed in them. Projecting the scientific and technical knowledge now available produces archives buildings which are intentionally overdesigned, and American archivists consider it their duty to insure this engineering exaggeration.[86] The modern equipment for archival storage is bulky and requires heavy-duty electrical and utility connections, and archival buildings must be so designed as to accommodate them and future innovations.[87]

In addition to overdesign, other considerations play a part in determining the character of archives buildings in the United States. Contrary to European practice, American archives are located near the agencies which produced the records, near cultural and research institutions, near major centers of public life, yet distant from fire-threatening establishments. American doctrine also holds that an archives building should be designed from the inside out, in conformity with the principles of functional utility. Corridors, public areas, and other nonfunctional areas are thereby drastically reduced. Whereas most libraries devote only about 20 per cent of their total area to book stacks, in modern archives the storage areas occupy about 60 per cent of

---

[85] Howard D. Williams, "Records Salvage After the Fire at Colgate University," in *American Archivist*, 27:375–379 (July, 1964); Adelaide E. Minogue, "Treatment of Fire and Water Damaged Records," in *American Archivist*, 9:18 (January, 1946).

[86] Victor Gondos, Jr., "Collaboration Between Archivists and Architects in Planning Archives Buildings," in U. S., National Archives, *Bulletins*, No. 6, 157–169.

[87] William J. Van Schreeven, "Equipment Needs to be Considered in Constructing Post-War Archival Depositories," in U. S., National Archives, *Bulletins*, No. 6, 170–180.

the total space, and in records centers the figure reaches about 90 per cent.[88]

In 1899, Charles Francis Adams gloomily looked into the twentieth century and observed: "We are to be bankrupted by our possessions. . . . The progression has been, and is, geometric. At the same rate the accumulation of the twentieth century defies computation in advance—it will altogether defy any nice classification or exhaustive cataloging. . . . The question of the future, so far as the material of history is concerned, relates to getting at what has been accumulated—the ready extraction of the mal row." While Adams may not have been primarily concerned with the plight of the contemporary archivist, his observation, if somewhat overdrawn, is a poetic suggestion of the function of the profession—to facilitate the marrowing of mountainous possessions without being bankrupted by them.[89]

[88] Victor Gondos, Jr., "Archival Buildings—Programming and Planning," in *American Archivist*, 27:467–483 (October, 1964); Gondos, "Collaboration," 170–180; Gondos, "American Archival Architecture," in American Institute of Architects, *Bulletin*, I, no. 4:27–32 (September, 1947).

[89] T. R. Schellenberg, "The Future of the Archival Profession," in *American Archivist*, 22:49 (January, 1959).

BIBLIOGRAPHY

The following bibliography cites the works which were found most useful in preparing this study; it is not a definitive listing of bibliographies, guides, and articles—which are being published constantly—but it should prove a useful starting point for pursuing the trends discussed in the text.

BIBLIOGRAPHIES AND GUIDES TO MATERIALS

Alderson, William T., comp. *Directory of State and Provincial Archivists and Records Administrators, 1963.* Nashville, 1063

Allison, W. H., comp. *Inventory of Unpublished Material for American Religious History in Protestant Church Archives and Other Repositories.* Washington, 1910.

American Association for State and Local History. *Directory of Historical Societies and Agencies in the United States and Canada.* Madison, 1961.

Andrews, Charles M. *Guide to the Materials for American History, to 1783, in the Public Record Office of Great Britain: Volume I, The State Papers.* Washington, 1912.

———. *Guide to the Materials for American History, to 1783, . . . Volume II, Departmental and Miscellaneous Papers.* Washington, 1914.

Andrews, Charles M., and Davenport, Frances G. *Guide to the Manuscript Material for the History of the United States, in the British Museum, in Minor London Archives, and in Libraries of Oxford and Cambridge.* Washington, 1908.

Angle, Paul M. *Survey of Manuscript Collections, University of Chicago Libraries.* [Chicago] 1944.

———. *The Lincoln Collection of the Illinois State Historical Library.* Springfield, 1940.

Beers, Henry P. *The French in North America: A Bibliographical Guide to French Archives, Reproductions, and Research Missions.* Baton Rouge, 1959.

Bell, Herbert C., *et al. Guide to British West Indian Archive Material in London and the Islands for the History of the United States.* Washington, 1926.

Bemis, Samuel F., and Griffin, G. G. *Guide to the Diplomatic History of the United States, 1775–1921.* Washington, 1935.

Berthong, Donald J. *The Civil War Collection of the Illinois State Historical Library.* Springfield, 1949.

Billington, R. A., comp. "Guides to American History Manuscript Collections in Libraries of the United States." *Mississippi Valley Historical Review,* 38:467–496 (December, 1951).

Bleyden, Paul. *Guide to the Manuscript Collections of the Historical Society of Pennsylvania.* Philadelphia, 1940.

Brayer, Herbert O. "Preliminary Guide to Indexed Newspapers in the United States, 1850–1900." *Mississippi Valley Historical Review,* 33:237–258 (September, 1946).

Brigham, Clarence Saunders. *History and Bibliography of American Newspapers, 1690–1820.* 2 vols. Worcester, Massachusetts, 1947.

Carson, Jane. "Historical Manuscripts in Williamsburg." *Manuscripts,* 5, no. 4:9–15 (Summer, 1953).

Clark, Alexander P. *The Manuscript Collections of the Princeton University Library.* Princeton, 1958.

Cuthbert, Norma B. *American Manuscript Collections in the Huntington Library for the History of the Seventeenth and Eighteenth Centuries.* San Marino, 1941.

Delgado, David J., comp. *Guide to the Wisconsin State Archives.* Madison, 1966.

Diaz, Albert James. *Manuscripts and Records in the University of New Mexico Library.* Albuquerque, 1957.

Dodge, Ernest S., and Copeland, Charles H. P. *Handbook to the Collections of the Peabody Museum of Salem.* Salem, 1949.

Downs, Robert B. *Resources of Southern Libraries.* Chicago, 1938.

Eaton, Dorothy S., and Eaton, Vincent L. "Manuscripts Relating to Early America." *Library of Congress Quarterly Journal of Acquisitions,* 8:17–28 (November, 1950).

Ewing, W. S. *Guide to the Manuscript Collections in the William L. Clements Library.* 2d ed. Ann Arbor, 1953.

Faust, Albert B. *Guide to the Materials for American History in Swiss and Austrian Archives.* Washington, 1916.

Fish, Carl Russell. *Guide to the Materials for American History in Roman and Other Italian Archives.* Washington, 1911.

Ford, F. H. *Bibliography of Books and Annotated Articles on the History of Journalism in the United States.* Minneapolis, 1939.

Garrison, Curtis Wiswell. "List of Manuscript Collections in the Library of Congress, July, 1931." American Historical Association, *Annual Report* (1930), I:123–249.

Geiger, Maynard J. *Calendar of the Documents in the Santa Barbara Mission Archives.* Santa Barbara, 1947.

Golden, Frank A. *Guide to Materials for American History in Russian Archives.* 2 vols. Washington, 1917, 1937.

Greene, Evarts Boutell, and Morris, Richard Brandon. *A Guide to the Principal Sources for Early American History (1600–1800) in the City of New York.* New York, 1953.

Gregory, Winifred. *American Newspapers, 1821–1936.* New York, 1937.

Griffin, Grace Gardner. *A Guide to Manuscripts Relating to American History in British Repositories Reproduced for the Division of Manuscripts of the Library of Congress.* Washington, 1946.

Ham, F. Gerald, comp., *Labor Manuscripts in the State Historical Society of Wisconsin.* Madison, 1967.

Hamer, Philip M., ed. *A Guide to Archives and Manuscripts in the United States.* New Haven, 1961.

Hammond, George P. "Manuscript Collections in the Bancroft Library." *American Archivist,* 13:15–26 (January, 1950).

Handlin, Oscar, et al., comps. *Harvard Guide to American History.* Cambridge, 1960.

Harper, Josephine L. *Guide to the Manuscripts of the State Historical Society of Wisconsin, Supplement Number Two.* Madison, 1966.

Harper, Josephine L., and Smith, Sharon C., eds. *Guide to Manuscripts of the State Historical Society of Wisconsin, Supplement Number One.* Madison, 1957.

Hill, Roscoe R. *Descriptive Catalog of the Documents Relating to the History of the United States in the Peoples Procendentes de Cuba deposited in the Archive General de Indies at Seville.* Washington, 1916.

[Historical Society of Pennsylvania]. *Guide to the Manuscript Collections of the Historical Society of Pennsylvania.* 2d ed. Philadelphia, 1949.

Jackson, E. C., and Curtis, Carolyn. *Guide to the Burlington Archives in the Newberry Library, 1851–1901.* Chicago, 1949.

Jenkins, William Sumner, and Hamick, Lillian A. *A Guide to Microfilm Collections of Early State Records.* Washington, 1950.

Kaplin, Louis et al., comps. *A Bibliography of American Autobiographies.* Madison, 1961.

Learned, Marian Dexter. *Manuscript Materials Relating to American History in German State Archives.* Washington, 1912.

Leland, Waldo G., ed. *Guide to Materials for American History in the Libraries and Archives of France.* 2 vols. Washington, 1932, 1943. Vol. I.

———. *Guide to Materials for American History in Libraries and Archives of Paris: Volume I, Libraries.* Washington, 1932.

Leland, Waldo G., Meng, John J., and Daysie, Abel. *Guide to Materials for American History in Libraries and Archives of Paris: Volume II, Archives.* Washington, 1943.

Manigaulte, John W. "Sources for American History in Three Italian Archives." *American Archivist,* 27:57–62 (January, 1964).

Manuscript Collections in the Columbia University Libraries, A Descriptive List. New York, 1959.

Matteson, David M. *List of Manuscripts Concerning American History Preserved in European Libraries and Noted in their Published Catalogs and Similar Printed Lists.* Washington, 1926.

Mohr, C. C. *Guide to the Illinois Central Archives in the Newberry Library.* Chicago, 1951.

Museum of Modern Art Film Library. *The Film Index: A Bibliography.* New York, 1941.

Neiderheiser, Clodaugh M., comp. *Forest History Sources of the United States and Canada: A Compilation of the Manuscript Sources of Forestry, Forest Industry, and Conservation History.* St. Paul, 1956.

North Carolina Historical Commission. *Guide to the Manuscript Collections in the Archives of the North Carolina Historical Commission.* Raleigh, 1942.

Ohio State Archaeological and Historical Society. *An Index and List of the Letters and Papers of Rutherford Birchard Hayes.* Columbus [1933].

Parker, David W. *Guide to the Materials for United States History in Canadian Archives.* Washington, 1913.

Peckham, Howard H. *Guide to the Manuscript Collections in the William L. Clements Library.* Ann Arbor, 1942.

Phillips, P. L. *A List of Maps of America in the Library of Congress.* Washington, 1901.

Presbyterian Historical Society. *Primary Source Material on Western Life at the Presbyterian Historical Society*. Philadelphia, 1948.

Reed, Dorris M. *Indiana University Library Manuscript Collections Relating to Business History*. Bloomington, 1951.

Robertson, James A. *List of Documents in Spanish Archives Relating to the History of the United States*. Washington, 1910.

Rush, Charles E., ed. *Library Resources of the University of North Carolina*. Chapel Hill, 1945.

Shelley, Fred H., comp. *A Guide to the Manuscripts Collection of the New Jersey Historical Society*. Newark, 1957.

Shepherd, William R. *Guide to the Materials for the History of the United States in Spanish Archives*. Washington, 1907.

Smith, Alice E., ed. *Guide to the Manuscripts of the Wisconsin Historical Society*. Madison, 1944.

Surrey, N. M. M. *Calendar of Manuscripts in Paris Archives and Libraries Relating to the History of the Mississippi Valley to 1803*. 2 vols. Washington, 1926, 1928.

Thomas, David H. and Case, L. M. *Guide to the Diplomatic Archives of Western Europe*. Philadelphia, 1959.

Tilley, N. M., and Goodwin, N. L. *Guide to the Manuscript Collection in the Duke University Library*. Durham, North Carolina, 1947.

Twitchell, Ralph E. *The Spanish Archives of New Mexico*. 2 vols. Cedar Rapids, Iowa, 1913.

U. S., Army Map Service. *A Researcher's Guide to the Army Map Service Library*. (A.M.S. Technical Manual No. 46.) Washington, 1951.

U. S., Library of Congress. *Manuscripts in Public and Private Collections in the U. S.* Washington, 1924.

———. *National Union Catalog of Manuscript Collections*. 7 vols. Ann Arbor and Washington, 1962 –.

U. S., Library of Congress, Music Division. *A List of American Folksongs Currently Available on Records.* Washington, 1953.

University of Missouri. *Guide to the Western Historical Manuscript Collection.* Columbia, 1952.

Vanderbilt, Paul, comp. *Guide to the Special Collections of Prints and Photographs in the Library of Congress.* Washington, 1955.

Van Male, John. *Resources of Pacific Northwest Libraries: A Survey of Facilities for Study and Research.* Seattle, 1943.

Van Tyne, C. H., and Leland, Waldo G. *Guide to the Archives of the Government of the United States in Washington.* Washington, 1904.

Withington, Mary C. *A Catalogue of Manuscripts in the Collection of Western Americana founded by William Robertson Coe Yale University Library.* New Haven, 1952.

LEGAL CASES

Alden v. New York. 51 Barb. 19 (1868).

American Code v. Bensinger. 282 Fed. 829 (C.C.A. 2d, 1922).

Baker v. Libbie. 210 Mass. 599, 97 N.E. 109 (1912).

Brunner v. Stix. 181 SW 2:643.

Cadell v. Stewart. 1 Bell's Com. 116n (Court Sessions Scotland, 1804).

Caliga v. Inter Ocean Newspaper Co. 215 US 182, 188 (1909).

Cullers v. Commissioner. 237 F (2d) 611 (8th Cir., 1956).

Dart v. Woodhouse. 40 Mich 399, 29 Am Rep 544.

De La O. v. The Pueblo of Acanra. 1 N. M. 226 (1957).

Donaldson v. Beckett. 4 Burr 2408, 2 Bro PC 129.

First Seattle Dexter Horton National Bank. 27 B. T. A. 1242 (1933), off'd., 77 F. (2d) 45 (9th Cir., 1935).

Folsom v. Marsh. 9 Fed. Cas. No. 4901 at 347 (C. C. Mass., 1841).

Frick v. Stevens. Reported in New York *Times,* May 26, 1967.

Gee v. Pritchard. 2 Swanton 402.

Gordon's Case. 50 N.J. Eq. 397, 26 ATl. 268 (1893).

Grigsby v. Breckinridge. 65 Ky. 480, 486, 493 (1867).

Hart v. Fox. 116 NYS 793.

Helvering v. Wuldhridge. 290 U.S. 594 and 70 F. (2d) 683 (2d Cir., 1934).

Hopkinson v. Burghley. L. R. 2 Ch. 447 (1867).

Howard v. Gunn. 32 Beau. 462 (1863).

J. Morgan Wilson. 11 CCH Tax Ct. Mem. 159 (1952).

Kartlander v. Bradford. 116 Misc 664, 190 NYS 311 (Sup. Ct., 1921).

Keene v. Wheatley. 14 Fed Cas 180.

Knights of the Ku Klux Klan v. International Magazine Co. 294 Fed 661 (C. C. A. 2d, 1923).

Leon Loan Abstract Co. v. Equalization Board. 86 Iowa 127, 53 NW 94.

Lytton v. Dewey. 54 L. J. [N. S.]. Ch. 293 (1884).

Mattie Fair. 27 T. C. No. 106 (Feb. 27, 1957).

Morris' Appeal. 68 Pa. 16 (1871).

O'Neill v. General Film Co. 152 NYS 599.

Paige v. Banks. 80 US 608, 20 Led 709.

Palmer v. DeWitt. 47 NY 532 (1872).

Pearson v. Matheson. 102 S.C. 377, 382, 86 S.E. 1063, 1065 (1913).

Philip v. Pennell. 2 Ch. 577 [1907].

Piper v. Ekern. 180 Wis. 586, 194 N.W. 159 (1923).

RCA Manufacturing Co. v. Whiteman. 114 F (2d) 86.

Rice v. Williams. 32 Fed 437.

Roberts v. McKee. 29 Ga. 161, 164 (1859).

Stephens v. Cody. Sp. Ct. 530. 531 (1852).

Stevens v. Frick. 259 F. Supp. 654 (1966), 372 F. (2d) 378 (1967).

Tefft v. Marsh. 1 W. Va. 38 (1864).

Thompson v. Stanhope. Ambler 337 (1774).

Thompson v. Famous Player—Laski Corp. 3 F (2d) 707 (N. D. Ga., 1925).

U. S. v. Martin T. Mantan and George M. Spector. [102 N. Y. *Law Journal* 1959–1960], as reported in Vernon D. Tate, "Microphotography in Archives," in U. S., National Archives, *Staff Information Circular,* No. 8, pp. 5–6.

Wheaton v. Peters. 33 US 591, 8 Led 1055.

Whitlow v. Commissioner. 82 F. (2d) 568 (8th Cir., 1936).

Wildemer v. Hubbard. 19 Phila. 263 (Common Pleas Pa., 1887).

GOVERNMENT DOCUMENTS

U. S., Commission on Organization of the Executive Branch of the Government [Hoover Commission]. *Office of General Services: A Report to the Congress, February, 1949.* Washington, 1949.

U. S., 88 Congress, 1 Session. *Hearings Before a Subcommittee of the Committee on Government Operations on H. R. 6237, June 18, 1963.*

U. S., General Accounting Office. *Report to the Congress of the United States: Review of Certain Records Management Activities, National Archives and Records Services Administration, December, 1961.* Washington, 1962.

U. S., Historical Records Survey. *Calendar of Manuscript Collections in Louisiana . . . Taber Collection.* Baton Rouge, 1938.

————. *Guide to the Manuscript Collections in Louisiana: The Department of Archives, Louisiana State University.* Baton Rouge, 1940. Vol. I.

————. *Guide to the Manuscripts in the Southern Historical Collection of the University of North Carolina.* Chapel Hill, 1941.

U. S., Internal Revenue Service. Regulation 111, Sections 29. 44–4 and 29. 111–1.

U. S., Library of Congress. *Departmental and Divisional Manual No. 17, Manuscript Division.* Washington, 1950.

U. S., National Historical Publications Commission. *A National Program for the Publication of Historical Documents: A Report to the President.* Washington, 1954.

U. S., Statutes at Large. 69 (695).

U. S., Tennessee Valley Authority. *TVA Files Audit Handbook.* Washington, 1950.

U. S., War Department. *Records Administration: Microfilming of Records.* (*Technical Manual,* 12–257.) Washington, 1946, pp. 1–91.

U. S., Works Progress Administration. *Technical Series, Research and Records Bibliography, No. 7.* Revised, April, 1943.

SECONDARY WORKS

American Association for State and Local History. *Church Archives and History.* (*Bulletin,* Vol. I, No. 10, April, 1946.) Pp. 259–272, 272–286, 287–295.

————. *Where Are the Historical Manuscripts? A Symposium.* (*Bulletin,* Vol. II, No. 4, September, 1950.)

American Association of Museums. *Handbook of Historical Museums.* Washington, 1932.

American Library Association. *Archives and Libraries.* New York, 1939. Pp. 103–108.

American Library Association, Committee on Public Documents. *Public Documents . . . with Archives and Libraries.* Chicago, 1934–1938.

[American Society of Composers, Authors and Publishers]. *Copyright Symposium No. 10.* New York, 1959.

Angle, Paul M. *The Chicago Historical Society, 1855–1956: An Unconventional Chronicle.* Chicago, 1956.

———. *The Library of Congress: An Account, Historical and Descriptive.* Kingsport, Tennessee, 1958.

Baechlin, Peter, and Muller-Strauss, Maurice. *Newsreels Across the World.* Paris, UNESCO, 1952

Ball, Horace G. *The Law of Copyright and Literary Property.* Albany, 1944.

Barzun, Jacques, and Graff, Henry F. *The Modern Researcher.* New York, 1957.

Bauer, G. Philip. *The Appraisal of Current and Recent Records.* (National Archives Staff Information Circular No. 13, June, 1946.) Washington, 1946.

Beale, Howard K. *The Critical Year.* New York, 1930.

Benjamin, Mary A. *Autographs: A Key to Collecting.* New York, 1946.

Berger, Meyer. *The Story of the New York Times.* New York, 1951.

Berle, A. A. *American Corporations.* New York, 1946.

Bernheim, Ernst. *Lehrbuch der Historischen Methode und der Geschichtsphilosophie.* 6 ed. Leipzig, 1908.

Binkley, Robert C. *Manual of Methods of Reproducing Research Materials.* Ann Arbor, 1936.

Blegen, Theodore C. *A Report on the Public Archives.* Madison, 1918.

Bleyer, W. G. *Main Currents in the History of American Journalism.* Boston, 1927.

Bloom, Sol. *Broadsides Relating to the Ratification of the Constitution and the Formation of the Government of the United States from Historical Societies and Libraries.* Washington, 1939.

Bond, J. J. *Handy-Book of Rules and Tables for Verifying Dates.* London, 1889.

Bonté, G. W. and Forman, S. E., eds. *America Marches Past.* New York, 1936.

Bourne, Edward Gaylord. *Essays in Historical Evidence.* New York, 1901.

Boyd, Anne Morris (Rev. Rae Elizabeth Rips). *United States Government Publications.* New York, 1952.

Brigham, Clarence S. *Fifty Years of Collecting Americana for the Library of the American Antiquarian Society.* Worcester, Massachusetts, 1958.

——. *Journals and Journeymen: A Contribution to the History of Early American Newspapers.* Philadelphia, 1950.

Brooks, Philip C. *Public Records Management.* Chicago, 1960.

Brough, Kenneth J. *Scholar's Workshop: Evolving Conceptions of Library Service.* Urbana, Illinois, 1953.

Brown, Everett Somerville. *Manual of Government Publications, United States and Foreign.* New York, 1950.

Brown, Lloyd A. *Map-Making: The Art That Became A Science.* Boston, 1960.

——. *Notes on the Care and Cataloging of Old Maps.* Windham, Connecticut, 1941.

——. *The Story of Old Maps.* Boston, 1949.

Bullard, F. Lauriston. *Abraham Lincoln and the Widow Bixby.* New Brunswick, 1946.

Busch, Moritz. *Bismarck.* English translation. 3 vols. New York, 1898. Vol. I.

Butler, Ladson, and Johnson, O. R. *Management Control Through Business Forms.* New York, 1930.

Butler, P., ed. *The Reference Function of the Library.* Chicago, 1943.

Cahill, Holger, ed. *American Folk Art: The Art of the Common Man, 1750–1900.* New York, [1932]. Pp. [3–28].

Cannon, Carl. *American Book Collectors.* New York, 1941.

Carson, Hampton L. *A History of the Historical Society of Pennsylvania.* 2 vols. Philadelphia, 1940.

Cater, Douglass. *The Fourth Branch of Government.* Boston, 1959.

Caughey, John W. *Hubert Howe Bancroft: Historian of the West.* Berkeley, 1946.

Chaffee, Allen. *How to File Business Papers and Records.* New York, 1938.

Charnwood, Lady. *An Autograph Collection.* New York, 1932.

Cheney, C. R. *English Bishop's Chanceries, 1100–1250.* Manchester, England, 1950.

Christian, C. M., ed. *Two Hundred Years with The Maryland Gazette, 1727–1927.* Annapolis, 1927.

Christopher, Henry G. T. *Paleontology and Archives.* London, 1938.

Clark, A. C. *The Descent of Manuscripts.* Oxford, 1918.

Clark, Thomas D. *The Southern Country Editor.* Indianapolis, 1948.

Clemons, Harry. *The University of Virginia Library.* Charlottesville, 1954.

Coleman, L. V. *College and University Museums.* Washington, 1942.

———. *Company Museums.* Washington, 1943.

———. *Historic House Museums.* Washington, 1933.

————. *The Museum in America.* 3 vols. Washington, 1939. Vol. I.

Coleman, Peter J. *The Transformation of Rhode Island, 1790–1860.* Providence, 1963.

Collins, A. C., ed. *The Story of America in Pictures.* Garden City, 1940.

Collison, R. L. *Modern Storage Equipment and Methods for Special Materials in Libraries.* London, 1955.

————. *The Cataloguing, Arrangement and Filing of Special Materials in Special Libraries.* (Aslib Manuals, Vol. 2.) London, 1950.

————. *The Treatment of Special Material in Libraries.* Rev. ed. London, 1956.

[Columbia University], Oral History Research Office. *The Oral History Collection of Columbia University.* New York, 1960.

[Connor, R. D. W.] *The North Carolina Historical Commission, Forty Years of Public Service, 1903–1943.* Raleigh, 1943.

Corbett, E. V. *The Illustration Collection: Its Formation, Classification, and Exploitation.* London, 1941.

Craigie, Sir William A., and Hulbert, James R. *A Dictionary of American English on Historical Principles.* 4 vols. Chicago, 1938–1944.

Crick, B. R., and Alman, Miriam. *A Guide to Manuscripts Relating to America in Great Britain and Ireland.* London, 1961.

Crittenden, Charles. *North Carolina Newspapers before 1790, (The James Sprunt Historical Studies,* Vol. xx, No. 1.) Chapel Hill, 1928.

Cross, Harold L. *The People's Right to Know: Legal Access to Public Records and Proceedings.* New York, 1953.

Crump, C. G. *History and Historical Research.* London, 1928.

Cusick, M. R. *List of Business Manuscripts in Baker Library.* Boston, 1932.

Dabney, T. E. *One Hundred Great Years* [New Orleans *Times-Picayune*]. Baton Rouge, 1944.

Dana, J. C., ed. *The Picture Collection.* 5th ed. Boston, 1943.

Davidson, M. B., ed. *Life in America.* 2 vols. Boston, 1951.

Davies, James Conway, ed. *Studies Presented to Sir Hilary Jenkinson.* London, 1957.

de Tocqueville, Alexis. *Democracy in America.* 2 vols. New York, 1945. Vol. I.

Dingwall, Eric J. *How to Use a Large Library.* Cambridge, England, 1933.

Doane, Gilbert H. *Searching for Your Ancestors.* New York, 1937.

Donker, Duyvis F., *et al. Manual on Document Reproduction and Selection.* (FID Publication No. 264.) 2 vols. The Hague, 1954.

Dreppard, C. W. *Early American Prints.* New York, 1930.

Dunlap, Leslie W. *American Historical Societies, 1790–1860.* Madison, 1944.

Du Pont, Henry Francis. *Joseph Downs: An Appreciation and A Bibliography of His Publications.* Winterthur, Delaware [n.d.], reprinted from The 1954 Walpole Society Notebook.

Easterby, J. H. *The Study of South Carolina History.* Columbia, 1951.

Ehrichs, H. L. and W. L., eds. *One Hundred Early American Paintings.* New York, 1918.

Emery, Edwin, and Smith, Henry Ladd. *The Press and America.* New York, 1954.

Fay, Sidney Bradshaw. *Origins of the World War.* 2 vols. New York, 1928. Vol. I.

Fish, Carl R. *The Rise of the Common Man, 1830–1850.* New York, 1927.

Fling, Fred Morrow. *Outline of Historical Method.* Lincoln, Nebraska, 1899.

Galbraith, Vivian H. *An Introduction to the Use of Public Records.* London, 1935.

Garraghan, Gilbert J. *A Guide to Historical Method.* New York, 1957.

George, H. B. *Historical Evidence.* Oxford, 1909.

Giles, G. A., ed. *Old English Chronicles.* London, 1912.

Gooch, G. P. *Recent Revelations of European Diplomacy.* 4th impression, London, 1930.

Goodspeed, Charles E. *Yankee Bookseller.* Boston, 1937.

Gottschalk, Louis. *Understanding History: A Primer of Historical Method.* New York, 1950.

Grambling, Oliver. *AP: The Story of News.* New York 1940.

Grant, Julius. *Books and Documents: Dating, Permanence, and Preservation.* London, 1937.

Gratz, Simon. *A Book About Autographs.* Philadelphia, 1920.

Hagley Museum: A Story of Early Industry On the Brandywine. Greenville, Delaware, 1957.

Hall, Hubert. *British Archives and the Sources for the History of the World War.* London and New Haven, 1925.

Hamilton, Charles. *Collecting Autographs and Manuscripts.* Norman, Oklahoma, 1961.

[Harlow, Thompson R.] *125 Years of the Connecticut Historical Society, 1825–1950.* Hartford, 1951.

Harry S. Truman Library. *Acquisition Policy of the Harry S. Truman Library.* Independence, Missouri, 1958.

Haselden, R. B. *Scientific Aids for the Study of Manuscripts.* Oxford, England, 1935.

Herrman, Irvin A. *Manual of Office Reproduction: Reproduction Processes, Systems Duplicating, and Imprinting Methods.* New York, 1956.

Hesseltine, William B. *Pioneer's Mission: The Story of Lyman Copeland Draper.* Madison, 1954.

Hesseltine, William B., and McNeil, Donald R., eds. *In Support of Clio: Essays in Memory of Herbert A. Kellar.* Madison, 1958.

Hill, Roscoe R. *American Missions in European Archives.* Mexico, Distrito Federal, 1951.

Hill, William Carroll. *A Century of Genealogical Progress Being a History of the New England Historic Genealogical Society, 1845–1945.* Boston, 1945.

Hockett, Homer Carey. *The Critical Method in Historical Research and Writing.* New York, 1955.

Holand, H. R. *The Kensington Stone: A Study in Pre-Columbian American History.* Minneapolis, 1938.

Horning, C. P., ed. *Handbook of Early American Advertising Art.* New York, 1947.

Hower, Ralph M. *The Preservation of Business Records.* Boston, 1941.

Ireland, Norma O. *The Picture File in School, College, and Public Libraries.* Rev. ed. Boston, 1952.

James, M. R. *The Wanderings and Homes of Manuscripts.* London, 1928.

Jameson, J. Franklin. *The American Historian's Raw Material* . . . . Ann Arbor, 1923.

Jenkinson, Sir Hilary. *A Manual of Archive Administration.* London, 1937.

———. *The English Archivist: A New Profession: Being an Inaugural Lecture in Archive Administration Delivered at University College.* London, 1948.

———. *The Later Court Hands in England, From the Fifteenth to the Seventeenth Centuries.* Cambridge, England, 1927.

John Carter Brown Library Conference: A Report of the Meeting Held in the Library of Brown University on the Early History of America. Providence, 1961.

John Crerar Library. *The John Crerar Library, 1895–1944: An Historical Report.* Chicago, 1945.

Johnson, Allen. *The Historian and Historical Evidence.* New York, 1926.

Johnson, Charles. *The Care of Documents and Management of Archives* (Helps for Students of History, No. 5.) London, 1919.

——. *The Public Record Office.* (Helps for Students of History, No. 4.) London, 1918.

Jones, Louis C. *Cooperstown.* Cooperstown, New York, 1949.

Kane, Lucile M. *A Guide to the Care and Administration of Manuscripts.* (American Association for State and Local History, Bulletin No. 11.) Madison, 1960.

Keep, Austin Baxter. *History of the New York Society Library.* New York, 1908.

Kent, Sherman. *Writing History.* New York, 1941.

Kerr, Chester. *A Report on American University Presses.* Washington, 1949.

Kimberly, Arthur E., and Hicks, J. F. G., Jr. *A Survey of Storage Conditions in Libraries Relative to the Preservation of Records.* (National Bureau of Standards, Miscellaneous Publication No. 128.) Washington, 1939.

Kimberly, A. E., and Scribner, B. W. *Summary Report of National Bureau of Standards Research on Preservation of Records.* (National Bureau of Standards, *Miscellaneous Publication*, M145.) Washington, [1937].

Kinsley, Philip. *The Chicago Tribune, Its First Hundred Years.* 3 vols. New York, 1943–1964. Vol. I.

Kobre, Sidney. *The Development of the Colonial Newspaper.* Pittsburgh, 1944.

Kuhlman, A. F., ed. *Archives and Libraries.* Chicago, 1940.

——. *Public Documents: Their Selection, Distribution, Cataloging, Reproduction, and Preservation.* Chicago, 1935.

Langlois, C. V., and Seignobos, Charles. *Introduction aux études historiques.* Paris, 1898. Translated by G. G. Berry. New York, 1925.

Langwell, William Herbert. *The Conservation of Books and Documents.* London, 1957.

Larson, Henrietta. *Guide to Business History: Materials for Their Use.* Cambridge, 1948.

Lauay, Jerome B. *Disputed Handwriting: With Illustrations and Expositions for the Detection and Study of Forgery by Handwriting of all Kinds.* Chicago, 1909.

Leahy, Emmett J. *Records Management in the United States Government: A Report with Recommendations Prepared for the Commission on Organization of The Executive Branch of the Government.* Washington, 1949.

LeGear, Clara Egli. *Maps: Their Care, Repair and Preservation in Libraries.* Washington, 1949.

Lewis, Chester M., and Offenhauser, William H., Jr. *Microreading: Industrial and Library Applications.* New York, 1956.

Lord, Clifford L., ed. *Ideas in Conflict: A Colloquium on Certain Problems in Historical Society Work in the United States and Canada.* Harrisburg, Pennsylvania, 1958.

Lord, Clifford, and Ubbelohde, Carl. *Clio's Servant: The State Historical Society of Wisconsin, 1846–1954.* Madison, 1967.

Luther, Frederick. *Microfilm: A History, 1839–1900.* Annapolis, Maryland, 1959.

McGraw, Howard F. *Marginal Punched Cards in Colleges and Research Libraries.* New York, 1949.

McMurtrie, D. C. *Massachusetts Broadsides, 1699–1711.* Chicago, 1939.

McNeil, Donald R., ed. *The American Collector.* Madison, 1955.

Maden, Falconer. *Books in Manuscript: A Short Introduction to Their Study and Use, With A Chapter on Records.* London, 1893.

Madigan, Thomas F. *Word Shadows of the Great.* New York, 1930.

Marston, Mary Gilman. *George White Marston: A Family Chronicle.* 2 vols. Los Angeles, 1956. Vol. II.

Mearns, David C. *The Story Up to Now: The Library of Congress, 1800–1946.* Washington, 1947.

Mencken, Henry L. *The American Language.* 4th ed. New York, 1936.

———. *The American Language, Supplement I.* New York, 1945.

Milhollen, Hirst D., and Kaplan, Milton, eds. *Presidents on Parade.* New York, 1948.

Miner, Dorothy, ed. *Studies in Art and Literature for Belle da Costa Greene.* Princeton, 1954.

Minnesota Historical Society, Manuscripts Division. *The Care and Cataloging of Manuscripts.* St. Paul, 1936.

Minogue, Adelaide E. *The Repair and Preservation of Records.* (National Archives, Bulletin No. 5.) Washington, 1943.

Mitchell, Charles A. *Documents and Their Scientific Examination.* Philadelphia, 1922.

Moberly, Jewel, *et al. Case Studies in Records Retention and Control.* New York, 1957.

Morgan, Willard Detering, and Lester, Henry M. *Graphic Graflex Photography: The Master Book for the Larger Camera.* New York, 1942.

Mott, Frank L. *A History of American Magazines, 1865–1880.* Iowa City, 1928.

———. *American Journalism: A History, 1690–1960.* 3d ed. New York, 1962.

Muller, Feith, Fruin. *Manual for the Arrangement and Description of Archives.* Translated by Arthur H. Leavitt. New York, 1940.

Muñoz y Rivero, Jesús. *Manual de paleografía diplomática española de los siglos xvi al xvii.* 2d ed. Madrid, 1917.

Murrell, William A. *A History of American Graphic Humor.* 2 vols. New York, 1933–1938.

Nevins, Allan, ed. *A Century of Political Cartoons.* New York, 1944.

———. *The Gateway to History.* Boston, 1938.

Newton, A. Edward. *The Amenities of Book-Collecting and Kindred Affections.* Boston, 1918.

[New-York Historical Society]. *Survey of the Manuscript Collections in the New-York Historical Society.* New York, 1941.

Odell, Margaret K., and Strong, Early P. *Records Management and Filing Operations.* New York, 1947.

Oehser, Paul H. *Sons of Science: The Story of the Smithsonian Institution and its Leaders.* New York, 1949.

Oman, Sir Charles. *On the Writing of History.* New York, 1939.

Opening of the Adams-Clement Collection, Exercises Held in the Arts and Industries Building, Smithsonian Institution, on the Afternoon of April 18, 1951. Washington, 1951.

Orcutt, W. D. *In Quest of the Perfect Book: Remembrances and Reflections of a Bookman.* Boston, 1926.

Osborn, Albert S. *Questioned Documents with Citations of Discussions of the Facts and the Law of Questioned Documents from Many Sources.* 2d ed. Albany, 1929.

Oswald, J. C. *Printing in the Americas.* New York, 1937.

Parker, A. C. *A Manual for History Museums.* New York, 1935.

Parker, Donald Dean. *Local History.* New York, 1944.

Parker, Ralph H. *Library Applications of Punched Cards.* New York, 1950.

Partington, Wilfred. *Forging Ahead: The True Story of the Upward Progress of Thomas James Wise, Prince of Book Collectors, Bibliographer Extraordinary and Otherwise.* New York, 1941.

Pickett, A. G., and Lemcoe, M. M. *Preservation and Storage of Sound Recordings: A Study Supported by a Grant from the Rockefeller Foundation.* Washington, 1959.

Pollard, J. E. *The Presidents and the Press.* New York, 1947.

Poole, Reginald L. *Chronicles and Annals: An Outline of Their Origin and Growth.* Oxford, 1926.

Posner, Ernst. *American State Archives.* Chicago, 1964.

Potter, Alfred Claghorn. *The Library of Harvard University.* Cambridge, 1934.

Powell, Julia H. *The Books of a New Nation: U. S. Government Publications.* Philadelphia, 1957.

Prov, Maurice. *Manuel de paléographie latine et française.* 4th ed. Paris, 1924.

Raney, M. Llewellyn, ed. *Microphotography for Libraries.* Chicago, 1936.

Rhodes, James F. *Historical Essays.* New York, 1909.

Ricci, Seymour De. *English Collectors of Books and Manuscripts.* Cambridge, England, 1930.

Riley, Stephen T. *The Massachusetts Historical Society, 1791–1959.* Boston, 1959.

Ristow, Walter W. *The Services and Collection of the Map Division* [Library of Congress]. Washington, 1951.

Robinson, John, and Dow, G. F., eds. *The Sailing Ships of New England, 1607–1907.* 3 vols. Salem, Massachusetts, 1922–1928.

Rodabaugh, James H., ed. *The Present World of History: A Conference on Certain Problems in Historical Agency Work in the United States.* Madison, 1958.

Rogers, Agnes, and Allen, F. L., eds. *The American Procession: American Life Since 1860 in Photographs.* New York, 1933.

Rosewater, Victor. *History of Cooperative News-Gathering in the United States.* New York, 1930.

Rudolph, E. L. *Confederate Broadside Verse. . . .* New Braunfels, Texas, 1950.

Salmon, Lucy M. *The Newspaper and the Historian.* New York, 1923.

Schad, Robert O. *Henry Edwards Huntington: The Founder and the Library.* San Marino, 1952.

Schellenberg, T. R. *Modern Archives: Principles and Techniques.* Chicago, 1956.

——. *The Management of Archives.* New York, 1965.

Schmeckebier, Lawrence Frederick, ed. *Government Publications and Their Use.* 2 ed. Washington, 1939.

Shaw, Ralph R. *Literary Property in the United States.* Washington, 1950.

Shipton, Clifford K. *Isaiah Thomas: Printer, Patriot and Philanthropist, 1749–1831.* Rochester, New York, 1948.

Shores, Louis, ed. *Challenge to Librarianship.* (Florida State University Studies, No. 12.) Tallahassee, 1953.

Sinks, Perry W. *The Reign of the Manuscript.* Boston, 1917.

Smith, Bradford. *Captain John Smith: His Life and Legend.* Philadelphia, 1953.

Soby, J. T. *The Museum of Modern Art.* New York, 1946.

Social Science Research Council. *The Use of Personal Documents in History, Anthropology, and Sociology.* (Bulletin No. 53.) New York [1945].

Spahr, Walter, and Swenson, Rinehart J. *Methods and Status of Scientific Research: With Particular Application to the Social Sciences.* New York, 1930.

Spence, Thomas H., Jr. *Historical Foundation of the Presbyterian and Reformed Churches.* Montreat, North Carolina, 1956.

[State Historical Society of Missouri]. *Twenty-ninth Biennial Report of the Executive Committee of the State Historical Society of Missouri.* Columbia, 1959.

Stokes, I. N. P., and Haskell, D. C., comps. *American Historical Prints: Early Views of American Cities, Etc.* New York, 1932.

Storm, Colton and Peckham, Howard. *Invitation to Book Collecting: Its Pleasures and Practices, With Kindred Discussions of Manuscripts, Maps, and Prints.* New York, 1947.

Tauber, M. F., ed. *Technical Services in Libraries.* New York, 1954.

Taylor, Francis Henry. *Pierpont Morgan as Collector and Patron, 1837–1913.* New York, 1957.

Thiele, Walter. *Official Map Publications.* Chicago, 1938.

Thorpe, F. N., ed. *The Federal and State Constitutions, Colonial Charters, and Other Organic Law.* Washington, 1907.

Thoyts, E. E. *How to Decipher and Study Old Documents: A Guide to the Reading of Ancient Manuscripts.* London, 1893.

Tooley, R. V. *Maps and Map-Makers.* London, 1952.

True, W. P. *The First Hundred Years of the Smithsonian Institution.* New York, 1946.

U. S., Library of Congress. *An Album of American Battle Art, 1755–1918.* Washington, 1947.

———. *Herbert Putnam, 1861–1955: A Memorial Tribute.* Washington, 1956.

U. S., Library of Congress, Descriptive Cataloging Division. *Rules for Descriptive Cataloging in the Library of Congress: Manuscripts.* Washington, 1954.

U. S., Library of Congress, Division of Manuscripts. *Notes on the Care, Cataloging, Calendaring, and Arranging of Manuscripts.* 3d ed. Washington, 1934.

U. S., National Archives. *How to Dispose of Records: A Manual for Federal Officials.* Washington, 1946.

————. *The Disposition of Federal Records: How to Develop an Effective Program for the Preservation and Disposal of Federal Records.* (National Archives Publication No. 50–3.) Washington, 1949.

————. *The Preparation of Records for Publication on Microfilm. (Staff Information Papers,* No. 19.) Washington, 1951.

————. *Your Government's Records in the National Archives.* (National Archives Publication 51–4.) Washington, 1950.

U. S., National Archives and Records Service. *Forms Analysis.* Washington, 1960.

————. *Forms Design.* Washington, 1960.

U. S., National Archives and Records Service, Records Management Division. *Federal Records Centers.* Washington, 1954.

[Utah State Historical Society]. *Utah State Historical Society, Sixty Years of Organized History.* Salt Lake City, 1957. Reprinted from *Utah Historical Quarterly,* 25 (July, 1957).

Vail, R. W. G. *Knickerbocker Birthday: A Sesqui-Centennial History of the New-York Historical Society, 1804–1954.* New York, 1954.

Van Schreeven, William J. *Equipment Needs to be Considered in Constructing Post-War Archival Depositories.* (National Archives, *Bulletins,* No. 6.) Pp. 170–180.

Van Tassel, David D. *Recording America's Past.* Chicago, 1960.

Vincent, John Martin. *Historical Research: An Outline of Theory and Practice.* New York, 1929.

Walker, John, and James, MacGill, eds. *Great American Paintings from Smibert to Bellows, 1729–1924.* London, 1943.

Wehle, H. B. *American Miniatures, 1730–1850.* Garden City, 1927.

Whitehill, Walter Muir. *Independent Historical Societies: An Enquiry into their Research and Publication Functions and their Financial Future.* Boston, 1962.

————. *The East India Marine Society and the Peabody Museum of Salem: A Sesquicentennial History.* Salem, 1949.

Wigmore, John Henry. *A Treatise on the Anglo-American System of Evidence in Trials at Common Law.* 10 vols. Boston, 1940.

———. *Student's Textbook of the Law of Evidence.* Chicago, 1935.

William L. Clements Library of Americana at the University of Michigan. Ann Arbor, 1923.

Williams, L. F. Rushbrook. *Four Lectures on the Handling of Historical Material.* London, 1917.

Wilson, Louis Round, and Tauber, Maurice F. *The University Library: The Organization, Administration, and Function of Academic Libraries.* New York, 1956.

Winsor, Justin. *Calendar of the Jared Sparks Manuscripts in Harvard College Library.* Cambridge, 1889.

Wittenberg, Philip. *Dangerous Words: A Guide to the Law of Libel.* New York, 1947.

———. *The Law of Literary Property.* Cleveland, 1957.

———. *The Protection and Marketing of Literary Property.* New York, 1937.

Wittich, W. A. *Colleges and Universities: A Symposium, Sixty Years of 16mm Film, 1923–1983.* Evanston, Illinois, 1954.

Wood, Elizabeth Ingerman. *Report on Project History Retrieval: Tests and Demonstrations of an Optic-Coincidence System of Information Retrieval for Historical Materials.* Philadelphia, 1966.

Wood, Richard G. *The Vermont Historical Society: A Status Report.* Reprinted from *The New England Social Studies Bulletin* (October, 1957).

Wright, Andrew. *Court-Hand Restored, or The Student's Assistant in Reading Old Deeds, Charters, Records, Etc. . . .* Corrected by C. T. Martin. 10th ed. London, 1912.

Wright, Davis Marion. *A Guide to the Mariano Guadalupe Vallejo documentos para la historia de California, 1780–1875.* Berkeley, 1953.

Wroth, Lawrence C. *The First Century of the John Carter Brown Library: A History with a Guide to its Collections.* Providence, 1946.

Zunet, Philip, ed. *The Law of Federal Income Taxation: Code Commentary.* Chicago, 1955, with supplements to 1960. Subchapter B, 204.

ARTICLES IN JOURNALS AND COLLECTED WORKS

Ad Hoc Committee. "A Library Policy for Gift Appraisal." *Manuscripts,* 13:56–57 (Winter, 1961).

Adams, F. B., Jr. "The Morgans as Autograph Collectors." *Autograph Collectors' Journal,* 2, no. 4:2–7 (July, 1950).

Adams, Randolph G. "The Character and Extent of Fugitive Archival Material." *American Archivist,* 2:85–96 (April, 1939).

———. "William L. Clements." *Dictionary of American Biography,* Supplement One, 179–181.

Aeschbacher, William D. "The Nebraska State Historical Society." *Museum News,* 38:10–11 (September, 1959).

Alden, John Eliot. "Out of the Ashes, A Young Phoenix: Early Americana in the Harvard College Library." *William and Mary Quarterly,* 3rd series, 3:487–498 (October, 1946).

Alldredge, Everett O. "Archival Training in a Record Center." *American Archivist,* 21:401–407 (October, 1958).

———. "Still to be Done." *American Archivist,* 28:3–16 (January, 1965).

———. "The Federal Records Center, St. Louis: Personnel Files and Fiscal Records." *American Archivist,* 18:111–122 (April, 1955).

Allen, Josephine D. "Documenting the Lincoln Museum Collection." *American Archivist,* 26:463–468 (October, 1963).

Alter, Forrest. "Films in Libraries—Problems and Possibilities of Previewing." American Library Association *Bulletin,* 50:217–220 (April, 1956).

American Association for State and Local History. *History News,* 11:81–84 (September, 1956).

American Historical Association, *Ad Hoc* Committee on Manuscripts. "Report." *American Archivist,* 14:229–240 (July, 1951).

American Historical Association. *Annual Report* (1897), 53–59.

———. *Annual Report* (1901), I:115–120.

———. *Annual Report* (1904), 237–257.

———. *Annual Report* (1912), 269–273.

———. *Annual Report* (1913), 77, 78–79, 262–263.

———. *Annual Report* (1922), I:157.

[American Historical Association, Committee on Cooperation of Historical Societies and Departments]. "Report . . . of the Conference of State and Local Historical Societies of the American Historical Association." American Historical Association, *Annual Report* (1908), I:149–153.

[American Historical Association, Conference of Historical Societies]. "Report." American Historical Association, *Annual Report* (1907), 51–64.

———. "Report." American Historical Association, *Annual Report* (1909), 302–307.

[American Historical Association, Historical Manuscripts Commission]. "Report." American Historical Association, *Annual Report* (1896), I:467–480.

American Library Association. "A Code of Fair Practice." *Manuscripts,* 10:63–65 (Spring, 1958).

Andrews, Charles McLean. "On the Preservation of Historical Manuscripts." *William and Mary Quarterly,* 3rd series, 1:123–137 (April, 1944).

Angel, Herbert E. "Federal Records Management since the Hoover Commission Report." *American Archivist,* 16:13–26 (January, 1953).

Angle, Paul M. "Evaluating Historical Manuscripts." *Autograph Collectors' Journal,* 3, no. 4:27–29 (July, 1951).

Arbough, Dorothy. "Motion Pictures and the Future Historian." *American Archivist,* 2:106–109 (April, 1939).

"Archival Chart, 1957." *American Archivist,* 21:37–42 (January, 1958).

Ashby, Charlotte M. "The Cartographic Records Branch in the National Archives." Geographic and Map Division *Bulletin,* 16:6–10 (April, 1954).

[Association of Research Libraries]. "Report of the Committee on the Use of Manuscripts by Visiting Scholars Set Up by the Association of Research Libraries." *College and Research Libraries,* 13:58–60 (January, 1952).

Atherton, Lewis E. "Western Historical Manuscripts Collection—A Case Study of a Collecting Program." *American Archivist,* 26:41–50 (January, 1963).

Babb, James T. "The Yale University Library: Its Early American Collections." *William and Mary Quarterly,* 3rd series, 2:397–401 (October, 1945).

Bahmer, Robert H. "Scheduling the Disposal of Records." *American Archivist,* 6:169–175 (July, 1943).

———. "The Case of the Clark Papers." *American Archivist,* 19:19–22 (January, 1956).

———. "The Management of Archival Institutions." *American Archivist,* 26:3–10 (January, 1963).

———. "The National Archives after Twenty Years." *American Archivist,* 18:195–205 (July, 1955).

Ballou, Hubbard W., and Rather, John. "Microfilm and Microfacsimile Publication." *Library Trends,* 4:182–191 (October, 1955).

Barrow, William J. "Restoration Methods." *American Archivist,* 6:151–154 (July, 1943).

Bauer, G. Philip. "Recruitment, Training, and Promotion in the National Archives." *American Archivist,* 18:291–296 (October, 1955).

Bauer, Harry C. "Where Manuscripts Should Be." *Oregon Historical Quarterly,* 51:163–167 (September, 1950).

Baumhofer, Hermine M. "A New Tool for a New History." *Minnesota History,* 28:345–352 (December, 1947).

———. "Film Records Management." *American Archivist,* 19:235–248 (July, 1956).

——— "Motion Pictures Become Federal Records." *American Archivist,* 15:18–22 (January, 1952).

Beers, Henry P. "Historical Development of the Records Disposal Policy of the Federal Government Prior to 1934." *American Archivist,* 7:181–201 (July, 1944).

Bellot, H. Hale. "Some Aspects of the Recent History of American Historiography." Royal Historical Society, *Transactions,* 4th series, 28:121–148 (1946).

Bemis, Samuel Flagg. "The Training of Archivists in the United States." *American Archivist,* 2:154–158 (July, 1939).

Benjamin, Mary A. "Appraisals." *The Collector,* 63: 1–5 (January, 1950) and 63:215–228 (February, 1950).

———. "Price Versus Value: What the Collector Pays." *The Collector,* 64:49–53 (March, 1951).

———. "Price Versus Value: What the Dealer Pays." *The Collector,* 64:97–100 (May, 1951), and 64:121–125 (June, 1951).

———. "The Manuscript Market and the Library." *Manuscripts,* 8:30–36 (Fall, 1955).

Benjamin, Walter R. "Appraisals." *The Collector,* 55:59 (March, 1941).

Bennett, Archibald F. "The Record Copying Program of the Utah Genealogical Society." *American Archivist,* 16:227–232 (July, 1953).

Bennett, Felming. "Audio-Visual Services in Colleges and Universities in the United States." *College and Research Libraries,* 16:11–19 (January, 1955).

Berkeley, Francis L., Jr. "History and Problems of Control of Manuscripts in the United States." American Philosophical Society, *Proceedings,* 98:171–178 (June, 1954).

Berner, Richard C. "Archivists, Librarians, and the National Union Catalog of Manuscripts." *American Archivist,* 27:401–410 (July, 1964).

———. "The Arrangement and Description of Archives." *American Archivist,* 23:395–406 (October, 1960).

Berthel, Mary Wheelhouse, and Cater, Harold Dean. "The Minnesota Historical Society, Highlights of a Century." *Minnesota History,* 30:293–330 (June, 1949).

Binkley, Robert C. "New Tools for Men of Letters." *Yale Review,* 24:519–537 (Fall, 1937).

———. "Techniques and Policies of Documentary Reproduction." International Conference on Documentation, 14th, Oxford and London, 1938, *Transactions,* 1:121–125 (1938).

Binsfeld, Edmund L., C.PP.S. "Church Archives in the United States and Canada: A Bibliography." *American Archivist,* 21:311–332 (July, 1958).

Bischoff, William N. "Tracing Manuscript Sources." *Oregon Historical Quarterly,* 51:156–163 (September, 1950).

Blake, John B. "Medical Records and History." *American Archivist,* 27:229–236 (April, 1964).

Blegen, Theodore C. "State Historical Agencies and the Public." *Minnesota History,* 9:123–134 (June, 1928).

Bolton, C. K. "Colonial Handwriting." *Essex Antiquarian,* I:175–176 (November, 1897).

Bond, W. H. "The Cataloging of Manuscripts in the Houghton Library." *Harvard Library Bulletin,* 4:392–396 (Autumn, 1950).

Bordin, Ruth B. "Cataloging Manuscripts—A Simple Scheme." *American Archivist,* 27:81–86 (January, 1964).

Bornet, Vaughn D. "Oral History *Can* Be Worthwhile." *American Archivist*, 18:241–247 (July, 1955).

——. "The New Labor History: A Challenge for American Historians." *The Historian*, 18:1–24 (Autumn, 1955).

Bourne, Henry E. "The Work of American Historical Societies." American Historical Association, *Annual Report* (1904), 117–118.

Bowman, Nellie M. "Publications, Maps, and Charts Sold by U. S. Government Agencies Other than the Superintendent of Documents." *Special Libraries*, 44:53–65 (February, 1953).

Boyd, Julian P. "A New Guide to the Indispensable Sources of Virginia History." *William and Mary Quarterly*, 3rd series, 15:3–13 (January, 1958).

——. "State and Local Historical Societies in the United States." *American Historical Review*, 40:10–37 (October, 1934).

Brand, Katherine E. "Developments in the Handling of Recent Manuscripts in the Library of Congress." *American Archivist*, 16:99–104 (April, 1953).

——. "The Place of the Register in the Manuscripts Division of the Library of Congress." *American Archivist*, 18:59–68 (January, 1955).

Brannon, Peter A. "The Alabama Department of Archives and History." *Alabama Historical Quarterly*, 24:1–15 (Spring, 1962).

Brinton, Ellen Starr. "Archives of Causes and Movements: Difficulties and Some Solutions Illustrated by the Swarthmore College Peace Collection." *American Archivist*, 14:147–154 (April, 1951).

"British Museum." *Encyclopaedia Britannica*, XV: 997.

Brooks, Philip C. "Archival Procedures for Planned Records Retirement." *American Archivist*, 11:308–315 (October, 1948).

——. "Archives in the United States during World War II, 1939–1945." *Library Quarterly*, 17:263–280 (October, 1947).

———. "Archivists and Their Colleagues: Common Denominators." *American Archivist,* 14:33–45 (January, 1951).

———. "The Harry S. Truman Library." *American Archivist,* 25:25–38 (January, 1962).

———. "The Selection of Records for Preservation." *American Archivist,* 3:221–234 (October, 1940).

Brown, Henry J. "Raiding Labor's Records." *American Archivist,* 17:262–264 (July, 1954).

———. "The American Catholic Archival Tradition." *American Archivist,* 14:127–140 (April, 1951).

Brubaker, Robert L. "The Publication of Historical Sources: Recent Projects in the United States." *The Library Quarterly,* 37:193–225 (April, 1967).

———. "Archival Principles and the Curator of Manuscripts." *American Archivist,* 29:505–514 (October, 1966).

Bryan, Mary G. "Trends of Organization in State Archives." *American Archivist,* 21:31–42 (January, 1958).

Buck, Elizabeth. "General Legislation for Presidential Libraries." *American Archivist,* 18:337–341 (October, 1955).

Buck, Paul C. "The Historian, The Librarian and The Businessman." *Eleutherian Mills Historical Library, A Record of its Dedication on 7 October 1961.* Greenville, Delaware, 1961.

Bull, Jacqueline. "The Samuel M. Wilson Library." Kentucky Historical Society, *Register,* 27:52–54 (January, 1949).

Burke, Frank G. "The Application of Automatic Techniques in the Management and Control of Source Materials." *American Archivist,* 30:255–278 (April, 1967).

Burke, Robert E. "Modern Manuscript Collections and What to Do with Them." *Manuscripts,* 7:232–236 (Summer, 1955).

Butler, Ruth Lapham. "For the Study of American Colonial History [Newberry Library]." *William and Mary Quarterly,* 3rd series, 2:286–295 (July, 1945).

Butterfield, Lyman H. "Archival and Editorial Enterprise in

1850 and 1950: Some Comparisons and Contrasts." *American Philosophical Society, Proceedings,* 98:160 (June 15, 1954).

———. "Bostonians and Their Neighbors as Pack Rats." *American Archivist,* 24:141–159 (April, 1961).

———. "The Papers of Thomas Jefferson: Progress and Procedures in the Enterprise at Princeton." *American Archivist,* 12:131–145 (April, 1949).

Calkin, Homer L. "Inventorying Files." *Public Administration Review,* 11:242–252 (Autumn, 1951).

Callcott, George H. "Antiquarianism and Documents in the Age of Literary History." *American Archivist,* 21:17–30 (January, 1958).

Cane, Melville. "Who Owns Your Letters?" *Autograph Collectors' Journal,* 2, no. 3:19–22 (April, 1950).

Cappon, Lester J. "Historical Manuscripts as Archives: Some Definitions and Their Applications." *American Archivist,* 19:101–110 (April, 1956).

———. "Reference Works and Historical Texts." *Library Trends,* 5:369–379 (January, 1957).

———. "Tardy Scholars Among the Archivists." *American Archivist,* 21:3–16 (January, 1958).

———. "The Archival Profession and the Society of American Archivists." *American Archivist,* 15:196–202 (July, 1952).

Cappon, Lester, J., and Menk, Patricia Holbert. "The Evolution of Materials for Research in Early American History in the University of Virginia Library." *William and Mary Quarterly,* 3rd series, 3:370–382 (July, 1946).

Carroll, H. Bailey. "A Half-Century of the Texas State Historical Association." *Southwestern Historical Quarterly,* extra number (1 February 1947), 9–17.

Carter, Clarence E. "The Territorial Papers of the United States." *American Archivist,* 8:122–135 (April, 1945).

Case, Frank H. "The Corporate Secretary Looks at Records Management." *American Archivist,* 23:419–425 (October, 1960).

Caswell, John Edwards. "Archives for Tomorrow's Historians." *American Archivist,* 21:409–418 (October, 1958).

Chatfield, Helen L. "Records and the Administrator." *Public Administration Review,* 10:119–122 (Spring, 1950).

Child, Sargent B. "What is Past is Prologue." *American Archivist,* 5:217–227 (October, 1942).

Claiborne, Adrienne. "Folk Recordings for the Library." *Library Journal,* 74:470–473 (March 15, 1949).

Clark, Jesse. "Current Paperwork Problems in American Industry." *American Archivist,* 27:391–394 (July, 1964).

Clark, Thomas D. "Preservation of Southern Documents." *American Archivist,* 16:27–38 (January, 1953).

———. "The Archives of Small Business." *American Archivist,* 12:27–35 (January, 1949).

Cole, Arthur H. "Business Manuscripts: Collecting, Handling, and Cataloging." *Library Quarterly,* 8:93–114 (January, 1938).

Collier, Clyde M. "The Archivist and Weather Records." *American Archivist,* 26:477–486 (October, 1963).

Conaway, Charles William. "Lyman Copeland Draper, 'Father of American Oral History.'" *The Journal of Library History,* 1:234–241 (October, 1966).

Connor, R. D. W. "Our National Archives." *Minnesota History,* 17:1–19 (March, 1936).

———. "The Story of the Franklin D. Roosevelt Library." *American Archivist,* 3:81–92 (April, 1940).

Connor, Seymour W. "Legal Materials as Sources of History." *American Archivist,* 23:157–165 (April, 1960).

———. "The Problem of Literary Property in Archival Depositories." *American Archivist,* 21:143–152 (April, 1958).

Cox, Henry Bartholomew. "Private Letters and the Public Domain." *American Archivist,* 28:381–388 (July, 1965).

———. "The Impact of the Proposed Copyright Law Upon Scholars and Custodians." *American Archivist,* 29:217–227 (April, 1966).

Crittenden, Christopher, and Hines, Nell. "The Disposal of Useless State Archives." *American Archivist*, 7:165–173 (April, 1944).

Daly, L. J., and Vollmar, E. R. "The Knights of Columbus Vatican Microfilm Library at Saint Louis University." *Library Quarterly*, 28:165–171 (July, 1958).

David, Charles W. "The Conservation of Historical Source Material." *American Documentation*, 7:76–82 (April, 1956).

Davies, Thomas M. "The Valuation of Good Will . . ." *Nebraska Law Review*, 31:560 (May, 1952).

Day, Donald. "John Lomax and His Ten Thousand Songs." *The Saturday Review of Literature*, 28, no. 38:5–7 (September 22, 1945).

Day, Dorothy L. "Films in the Library." *Library Trends* 4:174–181 (October, 1955).

DePery, LeRoy. "Archivists and Records Managers—A Partnership." *American Archivist*, 23:49–56 (January, 1960).

De Valinger, Leon, Jr. "A Microfilmer Replies." *American Archivist*, 21:305–310 (July, 1958).

———. "Horizons Unlimited." *American Archivist*, 27:3–14 (January, 1964).

Deutrich, Mabel E. "American Church Archives—An Overview." *American Archivist*, 24:387–402 (October, 1961).

———. "Archival Developments in Lutheran Churches in the United States." *American Archivist*, 15:127–138 (April, 1952).

———. "Fred C. Ainsworth: The Story of a Vermont Archivist." *Vermont History*, 27:22–33 (January, 1959).

Dewing, C. E. "The Wheeler Survey Records: A Study in Archival Anomaly." *American Archivist*, 27:219–227 (April, 1964).

"Development of American Newspapers." *Encyclopedia Americana*, XX:283–287.

"Diplomatic." *Encyclopaedia Britannica*, VII:408–411.

"Directory of State and Territorial Archival Agencies." *American Archivist,* 17:209–219 (July, 1954).

Downs, Robert B. "Collecting Manuscripts: By Libraries." *Library Trends,* 5:337–343 (January, 1957).

Duckles, Vincent H. "Musical Scores and Recordings." *Library Trends,* 4:164–173 (October, 1955).

Duniway, David C. "Conflicts in Collecting." *American Archivist,* 24:55–64 (January, 1961).

Dunkin, Paul S. "Arrangement and Cataloging of Manuscripts." *Library Trends,* 5:352–360 (January, 1957).

Dunning, William A. "A Little More Light on Andrew Johnson." Massachusetts Historical Society, *Proceedings,* second series, 19:395–405 (November, 1905).

East, Sherrod. "Archival Experience in a Prototype Intermediate Depository." *American Archivist,* 27:43–56 (January, 1964).

———. "Describable Item Cataloging." *American Archivist,* 16:291–304 (October, 1953).

Eckert, Leone W. "The Anatomy of Industrial Records." *American Archivist,* 26:185–190 (April, 1963).

Eckles, Robert B. "The Importance of Photocopy Projects for Local and Regional History." *American Archivist,* 25:159–164 (April, 1962).

Edmunds, Henry E. "The Ford Motor Company Archives." *American Archivist,* 15:99–104 (April, 1952).

Edwards, Nina L. "The Stevens Mill Records—Triumph Over Chaos." *American Archivist,* 26:59–62 (January, 1963).

Erney, Richard A. "Wisconsin's Area Research Centers." *American Archivist,* 29:11–22 (January, 1966).

"Eugene C. Barker Texas History Center." University of Texas, *Library Chronicle,* 4:3 (Fall, 1950).

Evans, Frank B. "The State Archivist and the Academic Researcher—'Stable Companionship.'" *American Archivist,* 26:319–322 (July, 1963).

Farley, A. E. "Cataloging Special Collection Materials." *Journal of Cataloging and Classification*, 12:11–14 (January, 1956).

Finneran, Helen T. "Records of the National Grange in Its Washington Office." *American Archivist*, 27:103–112 (January, 1964).

Fitzpatrick, John C. "The George Washington Scandals." *Scribner's Magazine*, 81:389–395 (April, 1927).

Fleming, E. McClung. "The Winterthur Program in Early American Culture." *American Studies*, 4:1–5 (July, 1959)

Ford, Frederick W. "Some Legal Problems in Preserving Records for Public Use." *American Archivist*, 20:43–47 (January, 1957).

Ford, Worthington C. "Dr. S. Millington Miller and the Mecklenburg Declaration." *American Historical Review*, 11:548–558 (April, 1906).

———. "The Massachusetts Historical Society." American Historical Association, *Annual Report* (1912), 217–223.

Fox, Dixon Ryan. "Local Historical Societies in the United States." *Canadian Historical Review*, 13:263–267 (September, 1952).

Fox, Edith M. "The Genesis of Cornell University's Collection of Regional History." *American Archivist*, 14:105–116 (April, 1951).

Friis, Herman R. "Cartographic and Related Records: What Are They, How Have They Been Produced, and What Are Problems of Their Administration." *American Archivist*, 13:135–155 (April, 1950).

Gear, James L. "The Repair of Documents—American Beginnings." *American Archivist*, 26:469–476 (October, 1963).

Gingerich, Melvin. "A Manual for Church Archivists." *American Archivist*, 24:445–450 (October, 1961).

Glenn, Bess. "The Taft Commission and the Government's Record Practices." *American Archivist*, 21:277–303 (July, 1958).

Going, Allen J. "Historical Societies in Alabama." *Alabama Review,* 1:39–49 (January, 1948).

Gondos, Victor, Jr. "American Archival Architecture." American Institute of Architects, *Bulletin,* I, no. 4:27–32 (September, 1947).

———. "A Note on Record Containers." *American Archivist,* 17:237–241 (July, 1954).

———. "Archival Buildings—Programming and Planning." *American Archivist,* 27:467–484 (October, 1964).

———. "Collaboration Between Archivists and Architects in Planning Archives Buildings." (National Archives, *Bulletins,* No. 6.) Pp. 157–169.

Gordon, Emanuel L. "Valuation Techniques." *New York University Institute on Federal Taxation Proceedings,* 17:73–86 (1959).

———. "What is Fair Market Value?" *Tax Law Review,* 8:44 (November, 1952).

Gordon, Robert S. "Suggestions for Organization and Description of Archival Holdings of Local Historical Societies." *American Archivist,* 26:19–40 (January, 1963).

Griffin, Burt. "Lewis and Clark II: A Legal Analysis." *Manuscripts,* 10:64–67 (Winter, 1958).

Grover, Wayne C. "A Note on the Development of Record Centers in the U. S." *Indian Archives,* 4:160–163 (July-December, 1950).

———. "Federal Government Archives." *Library Trends,* 5:390–401 (January, 1957).

———. "The National Archives at Age 20." *American Archivist,* 17:99–107 (April, 1954).

Hafen, LeRoy R. "History of the State Historical Society of Colorado." *Colorado Magazine,* 30:161–185, 283–310 (1953) and 31:36–68 (1954).

Hall, Sidney R. "Retention and Disposal of Correspondence Files." *American Archivist,* 15:5–14 (January, 1952).

Hall, Virginius C. "Historical and Philosophical Society of Ohio: A Short History." *Bulletin of the Historical and Philosophical Society of Ohio*, 14:2–16 (April, 1956).

Hamer, Philip M. ". . .Authentic Documents tending to elucidate our History." *American Archivist*, 25:3–13 (January, 1962).

———. "The Records of Southern History." *Journal of Southern History*, 5:3–17 (February, 1939).

Hamilton, J. G. De R. "On the Importance of Unimportant Documents." *Library Quarterly*, 12:511–518 (July, 1942).

———. "Three Centuries of Southern Records, 1607–1907." *Journal of Southern History*, 10:9 (February, 1944).

Hamilton, Kenneth G. "The Moravian Archives at Bethlehem, Pennsylvania." *American Archivist*, 24:415–423 (October, 1961).

———. "The Resources of the Moravian Church Archives." *Pennsylvania History*, 27:263–272 (July, 1960).

Hammitt, J. J. "Government Archives and Records Management." *American Archivist*, 28:219–222 (April, 1965).

Harlow, Neal. "Managing Manuscript Collections." *Library Trends*, 4:203–212 (October, 1955).

"Harvard College Library, 1638–1939." *Harvard Library Notes*, 29:207 (1939).

Harwell, Robert B. "A Brief Calendar of the Jefferson Davis Papers in the Emory University Library." *Journal of Mississippi History*, 4:20–30 (January, 1942).

Hawes, Lillia M. "A Profile of the Georgia Historical Society." *Georgia Historical Quarterly*, 36:132–136 (March, 1952).

Hays, Samuel P. "Archival Sources for American Political History." *American Archivist*, 28:17–30 (January, 1965).

Hemphill, W. Edwin. "James Harold Easterby, 1898–1960." *American Archivist*, 24:160–161 (April, 1961).

Hensel, Evelyn. "Treatment of Nonbook Materials." *Library Trends,* 2:187–198 (October, 1953).

Hill, May D. "Prints, Pictures, and Photographs." *Library Trends,* 4:156–158 (October, 1955).

Hill, Richard H., Cullen, Dorothy, and Weeks, Mabel Clare. "The Filson Club's Seventy-fifth Anniversary." *The Filson Club History Quarterly,* 33:187–256 (Spring, 1959).

"Historical Manuscripts in the Library of the College of William and Mary." *William and Mary Quarterly,* 2nd series, 20:388 (1940).

Holmes, Oliver Wendell. "Archival Arrangement—Five Different Operations at Five Different Levels." *American Archivist,* 27:23–41 (January, 1964).

———. "Some Reflections on Business Archives in the United States." *American Archivist,* 17:291–304 (July, 1950).

———. "The Evaluation and Preservation of Business Archives." *American Archivist,* 1:171–185 (October, 1938).

Hopkins, James F. "Editing the Henry Clay Papers." *American Archivist,* 20:231–238 (July, 1957).

Horn, Andrew H. "Introduction." *Library Trends,* 4:119–122 (October, 1955).

———. "The University Archivist and the Thesis Problem." *American Archivist,* 15:321–331 (October, 1952).

Horn, Jason. "Municipal Archives and Records Center of the City of New York." *American Archivist,* 16:311–320 (October, 1953).

———. "Seventh Day Adventist Archives." *American Archivist,* 17:221–224 (July, 1954).

Hughes, Charles E., Jr. "The Philadelphia Program." *American Archivist,* 21:131–142 (April, 1958).

Iben, Icko. "The Literary Estate of Lorado Taft." *American Archivist,* 26:493–496 (October, 1963).

———. "The Place of the Newspaper." *Library Trends,* 4:140–155 (October, 1955).

Irvine, Dallas. "The Archives Office of the War Department, Repository of Captured Confederate Archives, 1868–1881." *Military Affairs,* 10:93–111 (Spring, 1946).

Jackson, Ellen. "Manuscript Collections in the General Library." *Library Quarterly,* 12:275–283 (April, 1942).

Jenkinson, Sir Hilary. "Archives." *Encyclopedia of Social Sciences,* II:176.

Jennings, John Melville. "Archival Activity in American Universities and Colleges." *American Archivist,* 12:155–163 (April, 1949).

Kahn, Herman. "Libraries and Archives—Some Aspects of the Partnership." *American Archivist,* 7:243–251 (October, 1944).

———. "The Presidential Library—A New Institution." *Special Libraries,* 50:106–113 (March, 1959).

———. "World War II and Its Background: Research Materials at the Franklin D. Roosevelt Library." *American Archivist,* 17:149–161 (April, 1954).

Kane, Lucile M. "Collecting Policies of the Minnesota Historical Society, 1849–1952." *American Archivist,* 16:127–136 (April, 1953).

Kathpalia, Y. P. "Hand Lamination With Cellulose Acetate." *American Archivist,* 21:271–274 (July, 1958).

Katsaros, James. "Managing the Records of the World's Greatest City." *American Archivist,* 23:175–180 (April, 1960).

King, Cyrus B. "The Archivist and 'Ancient Documents' as Evidence." *American Archivist,* 26:487–492 (October, 1963).

King, Jack. "Collecting Business Records." *American Archivist,* 27:387–390 (July, 1964).

King, W. James. "The Project on the History of Recent Physics in the United States." *American Archivist,* 27:237–244 (April, 1964).

Kirkendall, Richard S. "A Second Look at Presidential Libraries." *American Archivist,* 29:371–386 (July, 1966).

———. "Presidential Libraries—One Researcher's Point of View." *American Archivist,* 25:441–448 (October, 1962).

Knowlton, John D. " 'Properly Arranged and So Correctly Recorded.' " *American Archivist,* 27:371–374 (July, 1964).

Krauskopf, Robert W. "The Hoover Commission and Federal Record Keeping." *American Archivist,* 21:371–400 (October, 1959).

Kuhlman, A. F. "The Preparation of Guides for the Collection, Care, Organization and Preservation of Fugitive Materials." *Public Documentation* (1935), 236–247.

Kyte, E. C. "Archives of the United Church of Canada." *American Archivist,* 13:229–232 (July, 1950).

Lacey, George J. "Questioned Documents." *American Archivist,* 9:267–275 (October, 1946).

Lamb, W. Kaye. "The Archivist and the Historian." *American Historical Review,* 68:385–391 (January, 1963).

Land, Robert H. "Defense of Archives against Human Foes." *American Archivist,* 19:121–131 (April, 1956).

———. "The National Union Catalog of Manuscript Collections." *American Archivist,* 17:195–208 (July, 1954).

Larkin, Harold. "Retention of Life Insurance Records." *American Archivist,* 5:96–97 (April, 1952).

Larson, L. M. "The Kensington Stone." *Minnesota History,* 17:14ff. (March, 1936).

Lawson, Murray G. "The Machine Age in Historical Research." *American Archivist,* 11:141–149 (April, 1948).

Leahy, Emmett J. "Modern Records Management." *American Archivist,* 12:231–242 (July, 1949).

———. "Reduction of Public Records." *American Archivist,* 3:13–38 (January, 1940).

Leahy, Emmett J., and Weil, Robert E. "Planning the Records Storage Center." *The Office,* 35, no. 6:64–70, 142–147 (June, 1952).

Leland, Waldo Gifford. "John Franklin Jameson." *American Archivist,* 19:195–202 (July, 1956).

————. "R. D. W. Connor: First Archivist of the United States." *American Archivist,* 16:45–54 (January, 1953).

————. "The Creation of the Franklin D. Roosevelt Library: A Personal Narrative." *American Archivist,* 18:11–29 (January, 1955).

————. "The First Conference of Archivists, December, 1909: The Beginnings of a Profession." *American Archivist,* 13:109–120 (April, 1950).

————. "The Prehistory and Origins of the National Historical Publications Commission." *American Archivist,* 27:187–194 (April, 1964).

LeRoy, Bruce. "Washington State Historical Society Acquisitions." *Pacific Northwest Quarterly,* 50:172–180 (April, 1959).

Lewinson, Paul. "Archival Sampling." *American Archivist,* 20:291–312 (October, 1957).

————. "The Archives of Labor." *American Archivist,* 17:19–24 (January, 1954).

Lind, William E. "Methodist Archives in the United States." *American Archivist,* 24:435–440 (October, 1961).

Lingelbach, William E. "The Library of the American Philosophical Society." *William and Mary Quarterly,* 3rd series, 3:48–62 (January, 1946).

Lloyd, David D. "The Harry S. Truman Library." *American Archivist,* 18:99–110 (April, 1955).

Lokke, Carl L. "The Captured Confederate Records under Francis Leiber." *American Archivist,* 10:277–319 (October, 1946).

London Times Literary Supplement, special number, September 17, 1954.

Lore, Martin M., ed. "When Not to Apply for Advance Rulings From the Internal Revenue Service." *Journal of Taxation,* 12:244 (April, 1960).

Loundes, Charles L. B. "Tax Advantages of Charitable Gifts." *Virginia Law Review,* 46:409–412 (April, 1960).

Lovett, Robert W. "Business Records in Libraries." *American Archivist,* 20:255–266 (July, 1957).

———. "Care and Handling of Non-Government Archives." *Library Trends,* 5:380 389 (January, 1957).

———. "Property Rights and Business Records." *American Archivist,* 21:259–270 (July, 1958).

———. "Some Changes in the Handling of Business Records at Baker Library." *American Archivist,* 19:39–44 (October, 1956).

———. "The Appraisal of Older Business Records." *American Archivist,* 15:231 (July, 1952).

Maass, Richard. "Collecting Manuscripts: By Private Collectors." *Library Trends,* 5:330–336 (January, 1957).

McAvoy, Thomas T. "Catholic Archives and Manuscript Collections." *American Archivist,* 24:409–414 (October, 1961).

McCool, Ollon D. "The Metes and Bounds of Records Management." *American Archivist,* 27:87–94 (January, 1964).

McCormick, Richard P. "The Future of Historical Activities in New Jersey." New Jersey Historical Society, *Proceedings,* 69:230–234 (July, 1951).

McCoy, Donald R. "The Records of the Democratic and Republican National Committees." *American Archivist,* 14:313–322 (October, 1951).

McCrary, George W. "The Literary Property of Authors." *Central Law Journal,* 17:268–271 (October 5, 1883).

MacDermot, Anne. "University Archives in the Boston Area." *American Archivist,* 23:407–417 (October, 1960).

McDonald, Jerry. "The Case Against Microfilming." *American Archivist,* 20:345–356 (October, 1957).

MacLean, I. "Trends in Organizing Modern Public Records with Special Reference to Classification Methods," *Archives and Manuscripts*, 1, no. 3:1–17 (December, 1956).

McLellan, Peter M. "The Boeing Archival Program." *American Archivist*, 29:37–48 (January, 1966).

"Manuscripts in the Indiana University Library." *Indiana Magazine of History*, 49:191–196 (June, 1953).

Marchman, Watt P. "The Rutheford B. Hayes Memorial Library." *College and Research Libraries*, 17:224–227 (May, 1956).

Marcus, Jacob R. "The American Jewish Archives." *American Archivist*, 23:57–61 (January, 1960).

Martin, Dorothy V. "Use of Cataloging Techniques in Work with Records and Manuscripts." *American Archivist*, 18:317–336 (October, 1955).

Martin, Thomas P. "A Manuscripts Collecting Venture in the Middle West: Indiana, 1950–1953." *American Archivist*, 17:305–312 (October, 1954).

Mason, Philip P. "College and University Archives, 1962." *American Archivist*, 26:161–166 (April, 1963).

———. "Economic Status of the Archival Profession, 1965–1966." *American Archivist*, 30:105–122 (January, 1967).

Mearns, David C. "Historical Manuscripts, Including Personal Papers." *Library Trends*, 5:313–321 (January, 1957).

Menkus, Belden. "The Baptist Sunday School Board and Its Records." *American Archivist*, 24:441–444 (October, 1961).

Metzdorf, Robert F. "Lewis and Clark I: A Librarian's Point of View." *Manuscripts*, 9:226–230 (Fall, 1957).

———. "Manuscript Collecting for Historical Societies." *Manuscripts*, 9:56–61 (Winter, 1957).

Meyer, Isidore S. "The American Jewish Historical Society." *Journal of Jewish Bibliography*, 4, nos. 1–2 (January–April, 1943).

Minogue, Adelaide E. "Physical Care, Repair, and Protection of Manuscripts." *Library Trends,* 5:344–351 (January, 1957).

———. "Treatment of Fire and Water Damaged Records." *American Archivist,* 9:17–25 (January, 1946).

Mitchell, Thorton W. "Municipal Archival Programs." *American Archivist,* 23:181–183 (April, 1960).

Monroe, John A. "The Hagley Program." *American Studies,* 4:5–6 (July, 1959).

Moore, John H. "Jared Sparks in Georgia—April 1826." *Georgia Historical Quarterly,* 47:425–435 (December, 1963).

———. "Jared Sparks in North Carolina." *North Carolina Historical Review,* 40:285–294 (July, 1963).

Morrison, Samuel Eliot. "Jared Sparks." *Dictionary of American Biography,* XVII:430–434.

Mugridge, Donald H. "The Adams Papers." *American Archivist,* 25:449–454 (October, 1962).

Mullett, Charles F. "The 'Better Reception, Preservation, and More Convenient Use' of Public Records of Eighteenth-Century England." *American Archivist,* 27:195–218 (April, 1964).

Munroe, John A. "A Brave Man—or a Foolish One." *American Archivist,* 26:151–160 (April, 1963).

Newsome, A. R. "Objectives of the Study of American Archivists." *American Archivist,* 26:299–304 (July, 1963).

———. "The Archivist in American Scholarship." *American Archivist,* 2:218–220 (October, 1939).

———. "Uniform State Archival Legislation." *American Archivist,* 2:1–16 (January, 1939).

Norton, Margaret C. "Photography for State Records." *Illinois Libraries,* 28:151–155 (February, 1946), and 28:180–187 (March, 1946).

———. "Scope and Function of a State Archives Department." Society of American Archivists, *Proceedings,* 1936–1937. Pp. 73–76.

Notestein, Wallace. "History and the Biographer." *Yale Review*, 22:549–558 (Spring, 1933).

Olsen, Arnold. "The Federal Paperwork Jungle—The Natives are Becoming Restless." *American Archivist*, 27:363–370 (July, 1964).

Olson, James C. "The Nebraska State Historical Society in 1953 (With a Glance Backward to 1878)." *Nebraska History*, 34:289–310 (October, 1953).

——. "The Scholar and Documentary Publication." *American Archivist*, 28:187–199 (April, 1965).

"Oral History: Columbia's Library on Tape." *Library Journal*, 85:36–37 (January 1, 1960).

"Oral History Project of Columbia University." *American Heritage*, 6:73–84 (December, 1954).

Overman, William D. "The Firestone Archives and Library." *American Archivist*, 16:305–309 (October, 1953).

Paladin, Vivian A. "The Historical Society of Montana." *The People's Voice* [Helena], 21:34 (July 29, 1960), and 21:35 (August 5, 1960).

Parish, John C. "California Books and Manuscripts in the Huntington Library." Huntington Library *Bulletin*, No. 7 (April, 1953).

Parton, James. "Popularizing History and Documentary Sources." *American Archivist*, 20:99–109 (April, 1957).

Patterson, A. M. "State Archival Agencies' Services to Other State Agencies." *American Archivist*, 26:315–318 (July, 1963).

Paullin, Charles O. "History of the Movement for a National Archives Building in Washington, D. C." U. S. 62 Cong., 2 *sess., Senate Documents*, vol. XXVI, no. 297. Also printed as *Congressional Record*, vol. 53, part 14 (appendix), 1116–1119 (1916).

Pease, Theodore C. "Historical Materials in the Depositories of the Middle West." *Proceedings of the Seventeenth Annual Conference of Historical Societies, 1921*, 17–18.

Peckham, Howard H. "Aiding the Scholar in Using Manuscript Collections." *American Archivist,* 19:221–228 (July, 1956).

———. "Arranging and Cataloging Manuscripts in the William L. Clements Library." *American Archivist,* 1:215–229 (October, 1938).

———. "Manuscript Repositories and the National Register." *American Archivist,* 17:319–324 (July, 1954).

———. "Policies Regarding the Use of Manuscripts." *Library Trends,* 5:361–368 (January, 1957).

Peckham, Howard H., and Storm, Carlton. "The Clements Library." *William and Mary Quarterly,* 3rd series, 1:353–362 (October, 1944).

Perlman, Isadore. "General Schedules and Federal Records." *American Archivist,* 15:27–38 (January, 1952).

"Personal Letters in Need of a Law of Their Own." *Iowa Law Review,* 44:705–715 (1959).

Piercy, J. W. "The Newspaper as a Source of Historical Information." *Indiana Historical Bulletin,* 10:387 (Fall, 1933).

Pierson, Roscoe M. "Denomination Collections in Theological Seminary and Church Historical Society Libraries." *Library Trends,* 9:213–230 (October, 1960).

Pinkett, Harold T. "Investigations of Federal Record Keeping, 1882–1906." *American Archivist,* 21:163–192 (April, 1958).

Porter, Charles W. "Documentary Research Methods Applied to Historic Sites and Buildings." *American Archivist,* 14:201–212 (July, 1951).

Posner, Ernst. "Archival Training in the United States." *Archeion,* 4:35–47 (1955).

———. "Max Lehmann and the Genesis of the Principle of Provenance." *The Indian Archives,* 4:133–141 (July–December, 1950).

———. "Some Aspects of Archival Development Since the French Revolution." *American Archivist,* 3:159–172 (July, 1940).

——. "The College and University Archives in the United States." *Miscellanea Mercati*. Vatican City, 1952. Pp. 363–374.

——. "The National Archives and the Archival Theorist." *Amercian Archivist*, 18:207–216 (April, 1955).

——. "The Study of State Archival Programs." *American Archivist*, 26:305–306 (July, 1963).

——. "What, Then, is the American Archivist, This New Man?" *American Archivist*, 20:3–11 (January, 1957).

Powell, L. C. "Resources of Western Libraries for Research in History." *Pacific Historical Review*, 11:263–280 (Summer, 1942).

Powers, Z. J. "American Historical Manuscripts in the Historical Manuscripts Room." *Yale University Library Gazette*, 14:1 (July, 1939).

"Property Rights in Letters." *Yale Law Journal*, 46:499–501 (January, 1937).

Quynn, Dorothy MacKay. "The Ecole des Chartes." *American Archivist*, 13:271–283 (July, 1950).

Radoff, Morris L. "A Guide to Practical Calendaring." *American Archivist*, 11:203–222 (July, 1948).

——. "What Should Bring Us Together." *American Archivist*, 19:3–9 (January, 1956).

Reid, Warren R. "Public Papers of the Presidents." *American Archivist*, 25:435–440 (October, 1962).

Richards, Kenneth W. "The State Archivist and the Amateur Researcher." *American Archivist*, 26:323–326 (July, 1963).

Richmond, David W. "How and When to Obtain Bureau Rulings." *Taxes*, 28:46 (January, 1950).

Riepma, Siert F. "A Soldier-Archivist and His Records: Major General Fred C. Ainsworth." *American Archivist*, 4:178–187 (July, 1941).

Ristow, Walter W. "What About Maps." *Library Trends*, 4:123–139 (October, 1955).

Robertson, James I., Jr. "The Civil War Centennial—Archival Aspects." *American Archivist,* 26:11–18 (January, 1963).

Rogers, Henry W. "Literary Property." *Central Law Journal,* 12:338–443 (April 15, 1881).

Rosenfeld, Albert. "The Wild West Lives Again." *Colliers,* 134:48–56 (November, 1954).

Rothwell, C. Easton. "Resources and Records in the Hoover Institute and Library." *American Archivist,* 18:141–150 (April, 1955).

Rowland, Buford. "The Papers of the Presidents." *American Archivist,* 13:195–211 (July, 1950).

Rundell, Walter, Jr. "The Recent American Past v. H. R. 4347: The Historians' Dilemma." *American Archivist,* 29:209–215 (April, 1966).

Runge, William H. "The Madison Papers." *American Archivist,* 20:313–318 (October, 1957).

Russell, Mattie. "The Manuscript Department in the Duke University Library." *American Archivist,* 28:437–444 (July, 1965).

Russell, Mattie and Roberts, Edward Graham. "The Processing Procedures of the Manuscript Department of Duke University Library." *American Archivist,* 12:369–380 (October, 1949).

Sabbe, Étienne. "The Safe Keeping of Business Records in Europe." *American Archivist,* 18:31–45 (January, 1955).

Schad, Robert O. "Henry Edwards Huntington." *Autograph Collectors' Journal,* 2, no. 4:15–19 (July, 1950).

Schafer, Joseph. "Documenting Local History." *Wisconsin Magazine of History,* 5:142–160 (Spring, 1921).

Schell, Edwin. "Methodist Records and History at the Grassroots in Northern Virginia." *American Archivist,* 27:381–385 (July, 1964).

Schellenberg, T. R. "Arrangement of Private Papers." *Archives and Manuscripts,* 1, no. 4:1–17 (August, 1957).

——. "Description of Private Papers." *Archives and Manuscripts,* 1, no. 5:1–19 (August, 1958).

——. "The Future of the Archival Profession." *American Archivist,* 22:49–58 (January, 1959).

Schiller, Irving P. "A Program for the Management of Business Records." Business History Society, *Bulletin,* 21:44–48 (April, 1947).

——. "The Archival Profession in Eclipse." *American Archivist,* 11:227–230 (July, 1948).

Scott, Peter. "Developments in Rapid-Copying Machines." *American Archivist,* 20:239–251 (July, 1957).

Scriven, Margaret. "Chicago Historical Society." *Illinois Libraries,* 40:287–288 (April, 1958).

——. "They'd None of 'em be Miss'd." *Manuscripts,* 7:114–116 (Winter, 1955).

Sellers, James L. "Before We Were Members." *Mississippi Valley Historical Review,* 40:3–24 (June, 1953).

Shaw, Edward B. "Calendar of the Shane Papers: A Preliminary Report." *Presbyterian Historical Society Journal,* 19:183–192 (December, 1940).

Shelley, Fred. "Ebenezer Hazard: America's First Historical Editor." *William and Mary Quarterly,* 3rd series, 12:44–73 (January, 1955).

——. "Manuscripts in the Library of Congress, 1800–1900." *American Archivist,* 11:3–19 (January, 1948).

——. "The Interest of J. Franklin Jameson in the National Archives, 1908–1934." *American Archivist,* 12:99–130 (April, 1949).

——. "The Presidential Papers Program of the Library of Congress." *American Archivist,* 25:429–434 (October, 1962).

Shiff, Robert A. "The Archivist's Role in Records Management." *American Archivist,* 19:111–120 (April, 1956).

Shipton, Clifford K. "College Archives and Academic Research." *American Archivist*, 27:395–400 (July, 1964).

———. "The American Antiquarian Society." *William and Mary Quarterly*, 3rd series, 2:164–172 (April, 1945).

Shoemaker, Floyd C. "Forty-five Years as Editor and Author of Missouri History." *Missouri Historical Review*, 54:225–230 (July, 1960).

Shores, Louis. "Audio-Visual Dimensions for an Academic Library." *College and Research Libraries*, 15:393–397 (October, 1954).

Silver, Harry M. "The Publication of Original Research Materials." *American Documentation*, 1:13–23 (Winter, 1950).

Sioussat, St. George L. "After Fifty Years: A Review of the Beginnings." *Maryland Historical Magazine*, 50:273–279 (December, 1958).

Smith, Louis Charles. "The Copying of Literary Property in Library Collections." *Law Library Journal*, 46:197–204 (August, 1953), and 47:193–197 (August, 1954).

Smith, Russell M. "Item Indexing by Automated Processes." *American Archivist*, 30:295–302 (April, 1967).

Society of American Archivists, Committee on Uniform Legislation. "A Proposed Model Act to Create a State Department of Archives and History." *American Archivist*, 7:130–133 (April, 1944).

[Sparks, Jared]. "Materials for American History." *North American Review*, 23:275–294 (October, 1826).

Spear, Jack B. "Films and Sound Recordings." *Library Trends*, 5:406–416 (January, 1957).

Special Libraries. Vol. 45 (September, 1954).

[Stanard, William G.]. "History of the Virginia Historical Society." *Virginia Magazine of History and Biography*, 39:292–362 (Fall, 1931).

Stauffer, A. P. and Porter, C. W. "The National Park Service Program of Conservation for Areas and Structures of National Historic Significance." *Mississippi Valley Historical Review,* 30:25–48 (June, 1943).

Stevens, Sylvester K. "Cooperation for the National Societies." *Autograph Collectors' Journal,* 1:25–27 (April, 1949).

————. "The Present Status of Organizations and Aid for Local History in the United States." *Proceedings of the Conference of State and Local Historical Societies* (Chapel Hill, 1940), 21–31.

Stevenson, Grace T. "Films in Libraries—The Library Use of Films." American Library Association *Bulletin,* 50:211–214 (April, 1956).

Stewart, William J. "The Sources of Labor History: Problem and Promise." *American Archivist,* 27:95–102 (January, 1964).

Stone, C. W. "The Place of the Newer Media in the Undergraduate Program." *Library Quarterly,* 24:358–373 (October, 1954).

Storm, Colton. "Maps as Historical Documents." *Publisher's Weekly,* 146:2,060–2,065 (November 25, 1944).

Storm, Colton, *et al.* "What to Do With My Collection." *Manuscripts,* 5:16–17 (Summer, 1953).

Striker, Laura Polanyi, and Smith, Bradford. "The Rehabilitation of Captain John Smith." *Journal of Southern History,* 28:476–481 (December, 1962).

Suelflow, August R. "The Struggle of Church Archives for Respectability." *American Archivist,* 24:403–308 (October, 1961).

Swain, Donald C. "Problems for Practitioners of Oral History." *American Archivist* 28:63–69 (January, 1965).

Sweet, William Warren. "Church Archives in the United States." *American Archivist,* 14:323–331 (October, 1951).

————. "Church Archives in the United States." *Church History,* 8:43–53 (March, 1939).

Tarleau, Thomas N. "Tax Problems in the Valuation of Property." *Taxes,* 25:520–524 (June, 1947).

Tate, Vernon D. "An Appraisal of Microfilm." *American Documentation,* 1:91–99 (Spring, 1950).

———. "From Binkley to Bush." *American Archivist,* 10:249–259 (July, 1947).

———. "Microphotography as an Aid to Research." American Library Association, *Public Documents.* New York, 1935. Pp. 210–217.

"Taxation—Charitable Deductions . . . Contribution of Right to Air Space. . . ." *Virginia Law Review,* 43:738–740 (June, 1957).

Thomas, Joe D. "Photographic Archives." *American Archivist,* 21:410–421 (October, 1958).

Thomson, Robert P. "The Business Records Survey in Wisconsin." *American Archivist,* 14:249–256 (July, 1951).

Thwaites, Reuben Gold. "State Supported Historical Societies and Their Functions." American Historical Association, *Annual Report* (1897), 63–71.

———. "Report of the Committee on Methods of Organization and Work on the Part of State and Local Historical Societies." American Historical Association, *Annual Report* (1905), I: 251–265.

Tout, Thomas F. "The Study of Medieval Chronicles." *Bulletin* of the John Rylands Library, 6:414–438 (1921–1922).

Trever, Karl L. "The American Archivist: The Voice of a Profession." *American Archivist,* 15:147–155 (April, 1952).

———. "The Organization and Status of Archival Training in the United States." *American Archivist,* 11:154–163 (April, 1948).

Turner, Joseph B. "A Catalogue of Manuscript Records in the Possession of the Presbyterian Historical Society." *Presbyterian Historical Society Journal,* 8:13–22 (March, 1915).

Turner, Robert W. S. "To Repair or Despair?" *American Archivist,* 20:320–325 (October, 1957).

Tyler, Moses Coit. "The Neglect and Destruction of Historical Materials in This Country." *American Historical Association Papers* (New York, 1888), II:20–22.

Ubbelohde, Carl. "The Threshold of Possibilities—The Society, 1900–1955." *Wisconsin Magazine of History,* 39:76–84 (Winter, 1955–1956).

Ullman, Morris D. "Contemporary Trends in the Production and Use of Social Data." *American Documentation,* 4:137–196 (October, 1953).

U. S., District Court of Minnesota. "In the Matter of the Lewis and Clark Papers." *Manuscripts,* 9:1–18 (Winter, 1957).

U. S., National Archives. *Accessions,* No. 51 (June, 1954), 1–49.

———. *Bulletin,* No. 7 (1952), 8–15.

———. *Staff Circular,* No. 5 (July, 1939).

———. *Staff Information Circular,* No. 8 (1940), 1–4.

———. *Staff Information Papers,* No. 16 (1950).

University of London Institute of Historical Research. *Bulletin,* I:6–28 (June, 1923).

Utley, George B. "Walter Loomis Newberry." *Dictionary of American Biography,* XIII:447–448.

Vail, R. W. G. "Manuscripts and Archives, Introduction." *Library Trends,* 5:309–310 (January, 1957).

Van den Eynde, Damian. "Calendar of Spanish Documents in the John Carter Brown Library." *Hispanic American Historical Review,* 16:564–607 (November, 1936).

Van Schreevan, William J. "Information Please: Finding Aids in State and Local Archival Depositories." *American Archivist,* 5:169–178 (July, 1942).

Varieur, Pascal Marie. "The Small, Limited, or Specialized Church Archives." *American Archivist,* 24:451–456 (October, 1961).

Walker, Mary. "The Archives of the American Board of Foreign Missions." *Harvard Library Bulletin,* 6:52–68 (Winter, 1932).

Wallace, Carolyn Andrews. "The Southern Historical Collection." *American Archivist* 28:427–436 (July, 1965).

Wallace, Paul A. W. "The Moravian Records." *Indiana Magazine of History,* 48:141–160 (June, 1952).

Walton, Clyde C. "Manuscripts in the Illinois State Historical Library." *Illinois Libraries,* 40:305–313 (July, 1958).

Washburn, Wilcomb E. "Manuscripts and Manufacts." *American Archivist,* 27:245–250 (April, 1964).

———. "The Great Autumnal Madness: Political Symbolism in Mid-Nineteenth Century America." *Quarterly Journal of Speech,* 49:417–431 (December, 1963).

Weicht, Carl. "The Local Historian and the Newspaper." *Minnesota History,* 13:45–54 (March, 1932).

Weis, Margaret M. "The Case for Microfilming." *American Archivist,* 22:15–24 (January, 1959).

Wesley, Charles H. "Racial Historical Societies and the American Heritage." *The Journal of Negro History,* 37:11–35 (January, 1952).

"Western Historical Manuscripts Collection." University of Missouri Library, *Bulletin,* No. 5 (1949).

Whatley, William A. "The Historical Manuscript Collections of the University of Texas." *Texas History Teachers' Bulletin,* 9:19–25 (November, 1920).

White, H. L. "Trends in Archival Administration." *Historical Studies, Australia and New Zealand,* 1:102–115 (October, 1940).

White, Helen Mc. "Thoughts on Oral History." *American Archivist,* 20:21–28 (January, 1957).

Whitehill, Walter Muir. "In My Father's House Are Many Mansions." *American Archivist,* 24:133–139 (April, 1961).

Whitehill, Walter M., ed. "Publishing the Papers of Great Men." *Daedalus,* Academy of Arts and Sciences, *Proceedings,* 86:47–79 (1955).

Wik, Reynold M. "Adventures in Business Records: The Vanishing Archives." *American Archivist,* 14:190–200 (July, 1951).

Wiley, Bell I. "Historians and the National Register." *American Archivist,* 17:325–330 (July, 1954).

Williams, Howard D. "Records Salvage After the Fire at Colgate University." *American Archivist,* 27:375–380 (July, 1964).

Wilson, Dwight H. "Archives in Colleges and Universities." *American Archivist,* 13:343–350 (October, 1950).

Wilson, O. G. "Bank of America's Archival Program." *American Archivist,* 29:43–48 (January, 1966).

Wilson, William J. "Manuscript Cataloging." *Traditio,* 12:457–555 (1956).

———. "Manuscripts in Microfilm: Problems of Cataloger and Bibliographer." *Library Quarterly,* 13:216–226 (October, 1943).

Wilson, William K., and Forshee, B. W. "Preservation of Documents by Lamination." National Bureau of Standards *Monograph 5.* Washington, 1959.

Winfrey, Dorman H. "Protestant Episcopal Church Archives." *American Archivist,* 24:431–433 (October, 1961).

Wolkins, George G. "The Prince Society." Massachusetts Historical Society, *Proceedings,* 4th series, 46:223–254 (1936–1941).

Wood, Elizabeth B. "Pots and Pans History: Relating Manuscripts and Printed Sources to the Study of Domestic Art Objects." *American Archivist,* 30:431–442 (July, 1967).

Wright, Louis B. "For the Study of the American Colonial Heritage [Huntington Library]." *William and Mary Quarterly,* 3rd series, 1:201–209 (July, 1944).

Wroth, Lawrence C. "Source Matcrials of Florida History in the John Carter Brown Library of Brown University." *Florida Historical Quarterly*, 20:3–46 (July, 1941).

Wyllie, John Cook. "Pamphlets, Broadsides, Clippings and Posters." *Library Trends*, 4:195–202 (October, 1955).

Yonge, Eva L. "The Map Department of the American Geographical Society." *The Professional Geographer*, 7:2–5 (March, 1955).

Young, James H. "Alexander H. Stephens Papers in The Emory University Library." *Emory University Quarterly*, 2:30–37 (March, 1946).

UNPUBLISHED WRITINGS

Brubaker, Robert L. "The Tibraiy ot Congress Versus the State Historical Societies: The Problem of Competitive Collecting." Unpublished research paper, 1962, in the possession of the present author.

Lisio, Donald J. "The Development of Wisconsin Archives." Unpublished research paper of February 17, 1961, in the possession of the present author.

Marten, William C. "Hanging Together: The Problem of Evaluating Manuscript Collections for Tax Deductions." Unpublished research paper, 1961, in the possession of the present author.

Special Libraries Association, Geography and Map Division. *Keys to Map Evaluation*. Multilith, Washington, 1953.

U. S., Library of Congress. Librarian's Letterbook, No. 7, f. 6, at Library of Congress, Manuscript Division.

U. S., National Archives and Records Service. *Records Management Bibliography*. Mimeographed, Washington, 1954.

INDEX

Abbreviations: Ar — archives; MSS — manuscripts

Academic libraries. *See* Manuscripts, and specific institutions
Acetate lamination. *See* Lamination
Adams, Charles Francis, 163, 353, 378
Adams, Herbert Baxter, 50
Adams, John, MSS, 162–163, 239
Adams, John Quincy, 9; MSS, 163, 239
Adams Family Papers, 99; publication of, 162–163, 239
Adams (James Taylor) Library, MSS, 202
Adhesives, qualities of, 372–373
Administrative Services Act of 1949, 29–30
Afro-American. *See* Negro, American
Agriculture, Department of, films, 319
Ainsworth, Fred C., 8–9, 296
Alabama: Ar, 54; MSS, 173; statehouse fires, 51
Alabama, University of, MSS, 219
Alabama Department of Archives and History, 52
Alabama Historical Society, 52
Alaska: Ar, 54; MSS, 173
Albemarle County (Virginia) Historical Society, MSS, 188
Alger, Russell A., MSS, 221
Allen, Ethan, MSS, 234
American Antiquarian Society, 171, 274
American Association for State and Local History, 184
American Federation of Labor, Ar, 91, 93–94
American Heritage, 359–360
American Historical Association, 12, 13–14, 93
American Legion, 17
American Monthly Register, 169
American Philosophical Society, MSS, 149, 202
American State Papers. See Hazard, Ebenezer
Ames, Herman V., 16
Ames, John G., 348
Anderson, George, 315
Andover-Newton Theological School, Baptist Ar, 85
Angle, Paul M., 244
Anne, Statute of, 252
Antiquities Act of 1906, 337
Appraisal: of mass documentation, 297–298; of records and archives, 34
Archival agencies, with MSS, 172

Archival buildings, design, 377–378
Archival profession, 33, 371, 378
Archival transcripts, 49–50
Archives: business and corporate, 104–105, 106–115, 124–129; church, 75–89; college and university, 89–90; colonial, 45; definition, 4; European origins, 3–6; in libraries, 100–101; local, 61, 67–73; state, 44–60, 71–72; quasi-public, 74–103. *See also* specific agencies and administrators
Archives act, model, 60
Archives and Records Service, 30. *See also* National Archives
Archives Nationales (France), 5, 35
Arizona: Ar, 54; MSS, 173
Arizona, University of, MSS, 223
Arkansas: Ar, 55; MSS, 173
Arkansas History Commission, 52
Army Map Service, 329
Arthur, Chester A., MSS, 153, 242
Arthur, Chester A., III, 153
Artifacts, 337–339
Asbury, Francis, MSS, 355
Associated Press, 272
Associations, historical, 172
Atlantic Monthly, The, 273
Auburn Theological Seminary, Presbyterian Ar, 80
Audio-Visual Committee (ALA), 321
Audiovisual documentation, 316–339
Augustana College, Lutheran Ar, 86
Austin, Moses, and Stephen F., MSS, 220
"Autograph" collecting, 231

Backus, Isaac, MSS, 355
Baker, Ray Stannard, 154
Baker Library, Harvard University, 112, 124; MSS, 212
Ballinger, Richard, MSS, 224
Baltimore, Catholic Diocese of, 77
Baltimore Public Library, maps, 329
Bancroft, George, 152, 170
Bancroft Library, University of California, 223
Bank of America, Ar, 128–129
Baptist Church, Ar, 84–85
Baptist Historical Society (Chester, Penn.), Ar, 85; (Rochester, N.Y.), Ar, 85
Barkley, Alben W., MSS, 218
Barrow, William, 374
Bassett, John Spencer, 346

Baylor University, Baptist Ar, 85
Belknap, Jeremy, 133
Bemis, Samuel Flagg, 161
Benjamin, William Evarts, 142
Berkeley, Francis L., Jr., 227
Berkeley Family, MSS, 217
Bestor, Arthur, 180
Bethel Theological Seminary, Baptist Ar, 85
Bethlehem, Pennsylvania, Moravian archives, 87
Bevan, Joseph Y., 49
Bibliothèque Nationale (France), MSS, 132
Bierce, Ambrose, 213
Binkley, Robert C., 63, 361, 364, 370
Birmingham Public Library, maps, 329
Birney, James G., MSS, 221
Blair, Francis Preston, 150
Blegen, Theodore C., 58
Board of Trade (London), 50
Bodley, Thomas, 131
Boeing Aircraft Corporation, Ar, 128–129
Boell, Jesse E., 59
Bolton, Hubert E., 223
Boston Athenaeum, 171
Boston Massacre, 332
Boston Public Library, maps, 329
Boutin, Bernard L., 177
Boyd, Julian P., 177, 356
British archival tradition. *See* Public Records Office
British Museum, MSS, 131
British royal house, MSS, 131
Broadsides, 336
Brown, E., 333
Brown, John Carter, 213
Brown (John Carter) Library, MSS, 213
Brymner, Douglas, 141, 353
Buchanan, James, MSS, 163–164, 241
Budget, Bureau of, 32
Buffalo and Erie County (N.Y.) Historical Society, MSS, 149, 163
Buffalo Public Library, maps, 329
Burns, James McGregor, 325
Bush, Vannevar, 370
Business and corporate archives, 104–105, 106–115, 124–129
Business History Society, 112
Business records, appraisal of, 115, 123
Butler, Ladson, 290
Butler, Nicholas Murray, MSS, 215
Butterfield, Lyman H., 163, 177

Calhoun, John C., MSS, 219, 355
California: Ar, 55; MSS, 173
California, University of: MSS, 223; maps, 329

Calvin College, Christian Reformed Ar, 89
Cambridge University, MSS, 131
Campbell, Alexander, 82
Campbell, John W., 356
Camus, Armond-Gaston, 5
Canada, United Church of, Ar, 88
Canfield, James Hulme, 214
Cappon, Lester J., 217
Carbon paper, 111, 294
Carnegie Institution, Department of Historical Research, 13, 353
Carroll, John, MSS, 355
Carter, Clarence E., 33, 358
Carter Family, MSS, 217
Cartoons, political, 333
Castillo de San Marcos, 188
Cater, Douglas, 275–276
Catholic Archives of America, 78
Catholic Historical Association, American, Ar, 79
Catholic University of America, MSS, 94
Cellulose. *See* Paper
Census Office, 17
Charleston Library Society, MSS, 203
Cherokee Seminaries Student Association, MSS, 200
Chicago, Burlington, and Quincy Railroad, Ar, 204
Chicago, University of: MSS, 222, 357; maps, 329; records, 323; religious Ar, 89
Chicago Historical Society, MSS, 149–151
Chicago Public Library, maps, 329
Chicago Theological Seminary, Congregational Ar, 82–83
Chicago (McCormick) Theological Seminary, Presbyterian Ar, 80
Christian Reformed Church, Ar, 89
Church archives, 75–89; finding aids, 102–103
Church Historical Society, Ar, 79
Church Mission House, Episcopal Ar, 79
Cincinnati Public Library, maps, 329
Cist, Louis J., 233
Civil War, 8–9, 41, 219, 270, 278
Clark, Joseph C., 65
Clark, Meriwether Lewis, MSS, 213
Clay, Henry, MSS, 218, 355, 357
Clemens, Samuel L. *See* Twain, Mark
Clements, William L., 220
Clements (William L.) Library, MSS, 220–221
Cleveland, Grover, 156; MSS, 153, 242
Cleveland Public Library, maps, 329
Clinton, George, MSS, 221
Clinton, Sir Henry, MSS, 221
Cockrell Commission, 11

Colgate-Rochester Theological Seminary. *See* Baptist Historical Society (Rochester)
College and university archives, 89–90
Colonial Records Project, 227
Colorado: Ar, 55; MSS, 173
Columbia University: Ar, 90; MSS, 214–215; maps, 329
Commager, Henry Steele, 160
Commons, John R., MSS, 94
Competitive collecting, 183–185, 224–225
Computers, 312–313
Confederate States of America, records of, 7–8
Confederation government, records of, 7
Congo, International Association of the, MSS, 224
Congregational Association, American, Ar, 83
Congregational Church, Ar, 82–83
Congregational House, Ar, 83
Congregational Library, Ar, 83
Congress: and the press, 282; debates on National Archives, 13–19
Congress, Annals of, 350
(Congress), *Register of Debates,* 350
Congress of Industrial Organizations, Ar, 91, 93–94
Congressional committees, 277
Congressional Globe, 350
Congressional Record, 350
Connecticut: Ar, 55; MSS, 173
Connor, R. D. W., 19–20, 155–156
Constitution of the United States, 253
Contarini, Matteo Giovanni, 327
Continental Congress, records of, 7, 354
Coolidge, Calvin, 17; MSS, 154, 243
Coolidge, Mrs. Calvin, 154
Copying: heat-sensitive, 366; methods of, 361–362; office machines, 366
Copyright Act of 1643, 252
Copyright law, 251; American, 253–254; English Common, 251–252; English Statute, 252–253; reforms, 260
Corarrubias, José Maria, MSS, 189
Cornell, Ezra, MSS, 214
Cornell University: industrial and labor records, 113; MSS, 94, 214
Corporate and business archives, 104–105, 106–115, 124–129
Corporate form and organization, 107–109
Correspondence, corporate, 118
Corrigan, Michael, 78
Cortelyou, George B., 13, 153–154
Cosa, Juan de la, 327
Cotton, Sir Robert Bruce, 131
Council on Library Resources, 171

Crane Theological School, Unitarian-Universalist Ar, 89
Creek Indian Memorial Association, MSS, 200
Crepeline document preservation method, 373
Crerar (John) Library, MSS, 204
Cross, William L., MSS, 213
Crozer Theological Seminary. *See* Baptist Historical Society (Chester)
Culver-Stockton College, Disciples of Christ Ar, 82
Curti, Merle, 325
Cuvelier, C. J., 308

Daly, L. J., 198
Danner, John Benjamin, 367
Daniels, Josephus, MSS, 119
Danish Society, Royal, 168
Dartmouth College: Ar, 83, 89; maps, 329
Data processing, 314–315
Daughters of the American Revolution, 15
Daunow, Pierre-Claude-Francois, 5
Davis, Jefferson, 8; MSS, 355
Daybook, business, 119
Declaration of Independence, "Signers," 134–135, 233
Delaware: Ar, 55; MSS, 173
Democratic National Committee, Ar, 95–96
De Tocqueville, Alexis, 45–46, 285
Detroit Public Library, maps, 329
Deutscher Pioneer-verein: Cincinnati, 198; Philadelphia, 198
Dewey, Melvin, 90; MSS, 215
Diazo copying process, 366
Dickinson, John, MSS, 355
Disciples of Christ, Ar, 82
Dissertations, in academic libraries, 90–91, 210
District of Columbia, MSS, 173
Documania, 50, 346
Documents: care and preservation of, 370–378; government, 348–350; publication of, 340–370; reproduction of, 360–370
Dodds, Arthur, 45
Douglas, Stephen A., MSS, 222
Douglass, Frederick, MSS, 200
Dramatic Museum (Brander Matthews), 338
Draper, Lyman C., 57
Duke University: industrial records, 113; church Ar, 89; MSS, 218
Dulles, John Foster, MSS, 215
Du Pont Family, MSS, 207–208
(Dutch) Reformed Church, Ar, 89

Ebeling, Christoph Daniel, 211
Eden Theological Seminary, church Ar, 89
Edgehill-Randolph Papers, 217
Edwards, James Farnham, 78
Ehrle, Franz, 374
Eisenhower, Dwight D., 280; MSS, 31, 162, 243
Eisenhower Library, 31, 162
Eleutherian Mills-Hagley Foundation, Inc., MSS, 207–208
Eliot, John, 269
Ellis, Elmer, 222
Ely, Richard, 105
Emerson, Ralph Waldo, MSS, 212
Emery, Francis W. R., 373
Emmet, T. A., 232
Emmons, George Foster, MSS, 213
Emory University, MSS, 219
Ephemera, 335–337
(Episcopal) Church Historical Society, Ar, 79
Episcopal Church leaders, MSS, 205
(Episcopal) Church Mission House, Ar, 79
(Episcopal) Theological Seminary of the Southwest, Ar, 79
Essex Institute, MSS, 187
Ettwein, John, MSS, 196
Evangelical and Reformed Church, Ar, 89
Evangelical and Reformed Church, Historical Society of the, Ar, 83
Evans, Luther H., 63
Evarts, William H., 138
Evidential values (archives). See National Archives, appraisal criteria

Facsimiles, 360
Fair use, doctrine of, 261
Fairbanks, Charles Warren, MSS, 221
Fall, Albert B., MSS, 223
Fall, Mrs. George W., 151
Federal Mediation and Conciliation Service, 92
Federal records, cost of maintenance, 27. See also National Archives
Federal Records Act of 1950, 29–30
Federal Records Administration, 28
Federal Reports Act of 1942, 24
Federal Trade Commission, 39
Feldman, Lew M., 255
Felt, Joseph Barlow, 48
Field, Eugene, MSS, 233
Field, Marshall, 150
Fields, James T., MSS, 206
Fighting words, doctrine of, 261–262

Filing systems: alphabetical, 296; Amberg, 295; numerical, 295; "Railroad Classification," 296; register, 293; self-indexing vertical, 293; Woodruff, 294–295
Fillmore, Millard, MSS, 163, 240
Films, motion picture, 319–323
Finnian, Abbot of Moville, 251
Finnish-American Historical Society, 201
Fire, damage to documents, 376, 377
Firestone, Harvey S., 126
Firestone Tire and Rubber Company, Ar, 126–127
Fish, Carl R., 57
Fiske, John, 178; MSS, 233
Fitzgerald, F. Scott, MSS, 215
Florida: Ar, 55; MSS, 173
Florida, University of, Ar, 125
Fonds (French archival practice), 5
Forbes, William Cameron, MSS, 212
Force, Peter, 47, 136, 345
Ford, Henry, MSS, 127
Ford, Worthington C., 183, 232
Ford Motor Company, Ar, 127–128
Foreign Missions, American Board of (Congregational), Ar, 82
Foreign Relations of the United States, 352
Forest history, MSS, 214
Forest History Society, MSS, 206
Forrestal, James V., 281; MSS, 215
Foster, Mrs. Sophia V. H., 258
Foster (Stephen Collins) Memorial, 338
France, Academy of Inscriptions, 168
Franklin, Benjamin, MSS, 137, 202, 348
Franklin and Marshall College, church Ar, 89
Freeman, E. A., 178
Freidel, Frank, 325
Frémont, John C., MSS, 355
French-Americans, MSS, 199
French archival tradition. See Archives Nationales
French Revolution, 5
Frick, Helen, 262–264
Frick, Henry Clay, MSS, 262
Friedenwald, Herbert, 138–139
Friends, Society of, Ar, 87
Friends Library, Philadelphia, Ar, 87
Frontier thesis, 43
Furman University, Baptist Ar, 85

Gable, William E., 235
Gage, Thomas, MSS, 221
Gales and Seaton, Publishers, 345
Gallatin, Albert, 135
Garfield, Harry, 153
Garfield, James A., MSS, 153, 242
Garrett, John W., 235

Gascoigne, Richard, 131
Gates, Paul W., 214
Gay, Edwin F., 105
Genealogical societies, MSS, 201–202
General Land Office, 70
General Services Administration, 29
Georgia: Ar, 47, 55; archival transcripts, 49–50; MSS, 173
Georgia, University of, MSS, 219
Germain, Lord George, MSS, 221
German-American Historical Society (New York), MSS, 198; (Chicago), MSS, 199
German-Americans, MSS, 198–199
German archival tradition, See Prussian State Archives
German documents, captured (W. W. II), 302
German settlers, in Wisconsin, 190–191
German Society of New York, MSS, 198
Gettysburg Lutheran Seminary, Lutheran Ar, 87
Gilmore, Robert, 233
Gilpin, Henry D., 356
Glass, Carter, MSS, 217
Godkin, E. L., 273
Gompers, Samuel, MSS, 93–94
Goodland, Walter S., 59
Goodyear, A. C., 234
Gorgas, William C., MSS, 219
Goshen College, Mennonite Church Ar, 89
Government Printing Office, 278
Grant, Ulysses S., MSS, 151–153, 241, 355
Grant, Ulysses S., III, 153
Graphics, 326–335
Gras, N. S. B., 105–106
Gratz, Simon, 232
Green, Belle da Costa, 205
Green, J. S., 48
Green, William, MSS, 93
Grew, Joseph C., MSS, 212
Grinnell College, Congregational Church Ar, 83
Grover, Wayne C., 160, 177
Guizot, Francois, 5
Gustavus Adolphus College, Lutheran Ar, 86

Hacker, Louis, 187
Hakluyt Society, 168
Hall of records (American archival concept), 10–13
Hamer, Philip M., 72
Hamilton, Alexander, MSS, 136
Hamilton, J. G. deR., 218
Hammond, George P., 223

Hampton, Wade, MSS, 219
Handlin, Oscar, 325
Harding, Warren G., 279–280; MSS, 164, 243
Harding Memorial Association, MSS, 164
Harlan, John M., 177
Harmon, Josiah, MSS, 221
Harper's New Monthly Magazine, 273
Harrison, Benjamin, MSS, 153, 242
Harrison, Mrs. Benjamin, 151, 153
Harrison, William Henry, MSS, 151, 240
Harvard University: Ar, 89–90, 323; Graduate School of Business Administration, 106; MSS, 211; maps, 329; newspapers, 274. See also Kennedy Library
Hawaii, Ar, 55; MSS, 173
Hawthorne, Nathaniel, MSS, 212
Hay, John, 152
Hayes, Benjamin, MSS, 223
Hayes, John, MSS, 94
Hayes, Rutherford B., 10, 99–100, 164; MSS, 241, 355
Hayes, W. C., 164
Hayes Memorial Library, 99–100
Hazard, Ebenezer, 45, 133, 344–346
Hearn, Lafcadio, MSS, 233
Hearst, William Randolph, 17
Hebrew Union College, Jewish Ar, 87
Heckewelder, John Gottlieb Ernestus, MSS, 196
Heflin, James T., MSS, 219
Historic Sites Act of 1935, 337
Historical Manuscripts Commission (AHA), 51, 140–141, 353
Historical Publications Commission, 354–356
Historical Records Survey, 62–64
Hobbs, Samuel F., MSS, 219
Hockett, Homer C., 283
Hoes, Lawrence M., 150
Hollister, W. W., MSS, 189
Holmes, Oliver Wendell, MSS, 212
Home Owners Loan Corporation, 312
Hoover, Herbert, 19, 280; MSS, 100, 164–165, 243
Hoover Commission, First (1947), 27–28, 287; Second (1953), 32
Hoover Institution on War, Revolution, and Peace, 100, 165
Hoover Library, Stanford University, 100, 337
Hoover Presidential Library, 100, 165
Hopkins, Harry, 63
Hower, Ralph M., 123
Huguenot Society of America, MSS, 199
Humidity, optimum for archives, 376
Hunt, Gaillord, 16, 357, 373
Huntington, Henry Edwards, 205, 234

Huntington Library, MSS, 206
Hurley, Robert, Earl of Oxford, 131

Idaho: Ar, 55; MSS, 173
Illinois: Ar, 55; MSS, 173–174
Illinois, University of, maps, 329
Illinois Central Railroad, Ar, 204
Illinois Historical Collections, 359
Immigration and Naturalization, Bureau of, 40
Income tax: corporate documentary requirements for, 116–117; and manuscripts, 245–251
India, National Archives of, lamination method of, 375
Indian Affairs, Bureau of, 312
Indian Office transcripts (Wisconsin), 58
Indiana: Ar, 55; MSS, 174
Indiana Historical Collections, 359
Indiana University, MSS, 221
Indians, American, MSS, 200–204
Informational values (archives). *See* National Archives, appraisal criteria
Inks, qualities of, 372
Internal Revenue, Bureau of, 246–247. *See also* Income tax
International Ladies' Garment Workers Union, Ar, 93
Interstate Commerce Commission, 40, 123
Iowa: Ar, 55; MSS, 174
Irish Historical Society, American, MSS, 199
Italian document preservation method, 374
Ives, Irving M., 113

Jackson, Andrew, MSS, 150, 240
Jackson, Andrew, Jr., 150
Jackson, Sheldon, MSS, 195
Jameson, J. Franklin, 12–18, 51, 76, 141, 352–353
Jay, John, MSS, 355
Jefferson, Thomas, 133, 135, 178; MSS, 136, 149, 205, 216, 239, 347, 356
Jewish-Americans, MSS, 199–200
Jewish Archives, 87
Jewish Archives, American, MSS, 199–200
Jewish Historical Society: Ar, 87; MSS, 199
Jewish Publication Society of America, 199
Jewish Theological Seminary: Ar, 87; Museum, 338
Johns Hopkins University, 50
Johnson, Andrew, MSS, 152, 241, 355
Johnson, Lyndon B., 280; MSS, 31, 162, 243

Johnson, O. R., 290
Johnson Library, 31, 162
Jones, John Paul, MSS, 234
Jones, Paul C., 147–148
Josephson, Matthew, 325
Judicial decisions, 350–351

Kansas: Ar, 55; MSS, 174
Kendall, Amos, 150
Kennan, George, 325
Kennedy, John F., 280; MSS, 31, 162, 243
Kennedy Library, 31, 162
Kentucky: Ar, 55; MSS, 174
Kentucky, University of: 357; MSS, 218
Kern, Jerome, 235
King, Ernest J., 281
King, Martin Luther, Jr., 188
Knox, William, MSS, 221
Korean War, and federal records, 32

Labor, Department of, 92
Labor movement, Ar, 91–94
Labor Union Archives, Committee on (SAA), 92
Lafayette, Marquis de, MSS, 221
La Guardia, Fiorello, 66
Lamination document preservation method, 374–375
Lamont, Daniel, 153
Land records, 62, 70, 290
Larkin, Thomas O., MSS, 223
Lasker, Albert, 325
Latter-Day Saints, Church of Jesus Christ of: Ar, 83–85; microfilms, 196–197
Laurens, Henry, MSS, 188, 355
Lawrence, David, 278
Leahy, Emmett J., 28, 32, 299, 303
Lee, Arthur, MSS, 212
Lee, Richard Henry, MSS, 216
Lee, Robert E., MSS, 245
Legal documentation: corporate, 117; in federal archives, 40
Legare, Hugh S., MSS, 219
Lehmann, Max, 6
Leiber, Francis, 8
Leland, John, 131
Leland, Waldo G., 15–16, 195
Lewis, John L., MSS, 93–94
Lewis and Clark Papers, 258–260
Libby, O. G., 57
Libel, law of, 261–264
Libraries, public, with MSS, 172
Library of Congress: battle art, 332; competitive collecting, 184; film, 322; graphics, 330; MSS, 11; maps, 329; newspapers, 274; recordings, 323
Library Resources, Council on, 171
Light, effect upon records, 376

Lincoln, Abraham, 8; MSS, 151–152, 241, 244, 355
Lincoln, Robert Todd, 152
Lincoln Museum (Washington), 338–339
Lindley, Ernest K., 281
Linotype, 272
Lippmann, Walter, 276
Literary property, law of, 251–264
Literary rights, in corporate archives, 126
Lloyd, Daniel D., 159
Lodge, Henry Cabot, 12
Lomax, John A., 324
London Society of Antiquaries, 168
London Times, 271
Long Island Historical Society, MSS, 187–188
Longfellow, Henry Wadsworth, MSS, 212
Longwood Library, business Ar, 125
Lord, Clifford L., 59
Los Angeles Public Library, maps, 329
Loudoun, Fourth Earl of, MSS, 206
Louisiana: Ar, 55; MSS, 174
Louisiana State University, MSS, 219–220; Historical Museum, 338
Louisville Theological Seminary: Baptist Ar, 85–86; Presbyterian Ar, 81
Lowden, Frank O., MSS, 222
Lowell, James Russell, MSS, 212
Loyalists, MSS, 136
Lundeen, Ernest, MSS, 100
Lutheran Church, Ar, 86–87
Lutheran Conference (American), archives of, 86
(Lutheran) Synodical Conference, Ar, 86
(Lutheran) Wisconsin Synod, Ar, 86
Lutherans, in Wisconsin, 190

McClellan, John, 276
McCormick Historical Association Library, 112–113
McDonald, William, 274
McElhone, Philip, 138
McElvoy, Robert, 153
McKenzie, Lewis, 138
McKinley, William, MSS, 153–154, 242
McLaughlin, Andrew C., 353
McMaster, John B., 14
McNutt, Paul V., MSS, 221
McReynolds, James Clark, MSS, 216
Madison, Mrs. Dolley, 136, 149, 356
Madison, James, 135; MSS, 136, 149–150, 239, 347, 356
Magazines, American, 273–274
Mahan, Alfred T., 14
Maine: Ar, 55; MSS, 174
Manitowoc County (Wisconsin), 189
Manning, James H., 235

Manuscript: dealers, 235–236; definition, 231; forgeries, 244; values, 236–243, 247–249
Manuscript collections: in academic libraries, 208–225; definition, 130; Library of Congress, 135–140; local, 178–192; Medieval, 131; origins of, 131–134, private, 229–238; proprietary, 202–208; quasi-public, 225–228; in religious, ethnic, and genealogical agencies, 194–202; state, 167–177
Manuscripts, National Union Catalog of, 186–187
Manuscripts Department, Library of Congress, 138, 139–140
Manuscripts Division, Library of Congress: arrangement, 145; catalog, 143; finding aids, 141–144; history of, 140–147; use and access, 143–144
Maps, 327–330
Maritime history, MSS, 203
Marshall, George C., 281
Marshall, John, MSS, 355
Marston, George White, 189
Maryland: Ar, 55; MSS, 174
Maryland Diocesan Library, Episcopal Ar, 79
Mass communications, 282–283, 364–365
Mass documentation, 285, 315
Massachusetts: Ar, 55; colonial records, 47; MSS, 174; state and local records, 48
Massachusetts Diocesan Library, Episcopal Ar, 79
Massachusetts Historical Society, 133, 171; MSS, 99, 149, 163
Meadville Theological School, Unitarian-Universalist Ar, 89
Meissner, H. O., 35
Mennéndez de Avilés, Pedro, 188
Mennonite Church, Ar, 89
Mereness, Newton D., 358
Methodist Church, Ar, 81–82, 219
Methodist Historical Societies, Association of, Ar, 81
Methodist Publishing House, Methodist Ar, 81
Michigan: Ar, 55; MSS, 174
Michigan, Lake, 190
Microfilm: costs and application, 361–363, 367–369; high-bulk records, 307–309; Mormon project, 196–197; National Archives publications, 33
Middle West: state archives in, 53–54; historical societies in, 169
Military history, 337
Miller, David Hunter, MSS, 224
Miller, Samuel, 269
Milwaukee Public Library, maps, 329

Mimeograph, 361–362
Minnesota: Ar, 55; MSS, 174
Minnesota Historical Society, MSS, 258
Mississippi: Ar, 55; MSS, 174
Mississippi Department of Archives and History, 52
Mississippi Valley, Presbyterianism in, MSS, 195
Missouri: Ar, 56; MSS, 174
Missouri, University of, MSS, 222
Missouri Historical Society, MSS, 149
Mitchell, John, MSS, 94
Mitchell, Mrs. L. R., 153
Mitchell, Samuel Chiles, MSS, 219
Modern Art, Museum of, 321, 331
Monroe, James, MSS, 136, 150, 239
Montana: Ar, 56; MSS, 175
Monumenta Germaniae historia, 169
Moore, John Bassett, MSS, 216
Moravian Church, Ar, 87–88
Moravian Church, Northern Province, MSS, 195–196
Moravian Church, Southern Province, MSS, 196
Moravian Provincial Archives, Ar and MSS, 88
Morgan, J. Pierpont, 205, 234, 258
Morgan Library, 205
Mormon Church. *See* Latter-Day Saints, Church of Jesus Christ of
Morris, Mrs. Ellen James Van Buren, 151
Morris, Stuyvesant Fish, 151
Morse, Jedidiah, and Samuel F. B., MSS, 212
Motion Pictures and Sound Recordings, Division of, National Archives, 320
Mumford, L. Quincy, 177
Murphy, Archibald DeBow, 46
Museum of Modern Art, 321, 331
Museums, historical, 338
Music Library Association, 324
Musical recordings, 323–324
Mutual Life Insurance Company of New York, records management at, 305–306

Nation, The, 273
National Archives: appraisal criteria, 34, 36–42; building, 18–19; contemporary development, 32–33; early history, 20–25; establishment of, 17–20; origins, 9–11
National Archives, Division of Records Management, 28
National Archives Act of 1934, 19
National Historical Publication Commission, 33
National Labor Relations Board, 39, 92
National Park Service, 337–338

National Press Club, 278
National Quarterly Review, The, 273
National Records Management Council, 28
National Union Catalog of Manuscripts, 186–187
Navy Department: films, 319; records, 301
Nebraska: Ar, 56; MSS, 175
Negro, American, MSS, 200
Negro Academy, American, 200
Negro Historical Society, American, MSS, 200
Negro history, MSS, 219
Negro Life and History, Association for the Study of, MSS, 200
Negro Society for Historical Research, 200
Netherlands Pioneer and Historical Foundation, 201
Newark Public Library, maps, 329
Newberry, Walter Loomis, 204
Newberry Library, MSS, 204
New Brunswick Theological Seminary, Dutch Reformed Ar, 89
New Deal, 278, 363
New England, historical societies in, 169, 180
New England Historic Genealogical Society, MSS, 201
New Hampshire: Ar, 47, 56; MSS, 175
New Jersey: achival card index, 50; Ar, 47, 56; MSS, 175
New Mexico: Ar, 56; MSS, 175
New Mexico, University of, MSS, 223
New York: archival transcripts, 50; Ar, 56; Dutch colonial records, 47–48; MSS, 175
New York, Catholic Diocese of, 78
New York City, Ar, 66–68
New-York Historical Society, MSS, 359; newspapers, 274
New York Public Library: graphics, 330; MSS, 94, 150; maps, 329; newspapers, 274
New York State Library, MSS, 151
New York Times, The, 271
Newspapers: clippings, 335; colonial, 269; as historical sources, 265–284; partisan, 269–270; "penny-press," 270
Newton Township, Manitowoc County (Wisconsin), 190
Nevada: Ar, 56; MSS, 175
Nevins, Allan, 128, 215, 275, 325
Nicolay, John, 152
Niles, Hezekiah, 269
Niles' Register, 346
Notre Dame University. *See* Catholic Archives of America

North American Review, The, 273, 346
North Atlantic Treaty Organization, 302
North Carolina: Ar, 56; MSS, 46, 175;
    statehouse fires, 51
North Carolina, University of, MSS, 113,
    218
North Carolina Historical Commission,
    19
North Carolina Historical Society, MSS,
    46
North Dakota: Ar, 56; MSS, 175
Northeast, state archives in, 53
Northwestern University, maps, 329
Norton, Robert C., 235
Norwegian-American, MSS, 200–201
Norwegian-American Historical Associa-
    tion, MSS, 200–201

Oakland Public Library, maps, 329
Oberlin College, Congregational Ar, 83
Ochs, Adolph, 271
O'Connor, Basil, 160
O'Dwyer, William, 66
*Official Records of the War of the Re-
    bellion,* 362
Ohio: Ar, 56; MSS, 175
Ohio Historical Society, MSS, 99–100,
    164
Ohio Oil Company, 305
Ohio State University, recordings, 323
Oklahoma: Ar, 56; MSS, 175
Oldroyd, Osborn H., 339
O'Neill, Eugene, MSS, 215
Oral History Project, Columbia Univer-
    sity, 215, 325–326
Oregon: Ar, 56; MSS, 175
Oregon, University of: business Ar, 126;
    MSS, 224; recordings, 323
Oswald, Richard, MSS, 221
Otero, Miguel Antonio, MSS, 223
Owen, Thomas McAdory, 52
Oxford University, MSS, 131

Paintings, 330–333
Paltsits, Victor Hugo, 16
Pamphlets, 336
Panic of 1873, 273
Paper, qualities of, 371–372
Paperwork management (American ar-
    chival practice), 32
Paraffin-silk   document   preservation
    method, 373
Parker, David W., 358
Parkman, Francis, MSS, 233
Patterson, Andrew Johnson, 152
Patterson, Mrs. Andrew Johnson, 152
Peabody Museum of Salem, Massachu-
    setts, MSS, 203

Peale, Charles Wilson, MSS, 203
Pearson, Drew, 278
Peck, Frederick S., 235
Pelham, Henry, 332
Pennsylvania: Ar, 48–49, 56; MSS, 175
Pennsylvania, Historical Society of, 171;
    MSS, 149, 164
Pennsylvania, University of, recordings,
    323
Pennsylvania German Historical Society,
    MSS, 198
Perry, Bliss, 274
Perry, James W., 314
Perry, Matthew, 333
Pertz, Georg, 169
Pico, Pío, MSS, 189
Picture collections, 334
Pierce, Franklin, MSS, 151, 240
Pinchot, Gifford, MSS, 142
Philadelphia, Pennsylvania, Ar, 65–66
Philadelphia Lutheran Seminary, Ar, 87
Philadelphia Public Library, maps, 329
Photocopied historical materials, 186
Photographic journalism, 279
Photographs, historical, 333–334
Photostat process, 365
Plantation Office (London), Ar, 46
Poe, Edgar Allen, MSS, 233
Poindexter, Miles, 14; MSS, 217
Political History, Ad Hoc Committee to
    Collect the Basic Data of American
    (AHA), 72–73
Political parties, Ar, 95–96
Polk, James K., MSS, 151, 240, 355
Populist newspapers, 271
Portland, Oregon, Ar, 68
Posters, 336
Powderly, Terrence, MSS, 94
Presbyterian and Reformed Churches,
    Historical Foundation of the, Ar, 80–81
Presbyterian Church, Ar, 79–81
Presbyterian Historical Society, MSS, 195
Prescott, W. H., MSS, 233
President, Messages and Papers of the,
    351
Presidential Archives Act of 1955, 98
Presidential Libraries, 30–32, 97–99. *See
    also* under Hoover, Roosevelt, Tru-
    man, Eisenhower, Kennedy, and John-
    son
Presidential messages, 165
Presidential news conferences, 279–280
Presidential Papers Program, 313
Press-copying, 294
Priestly, Herbert J., 223
Prince, Thomas, 133
Prince Society, MSS, 201
Princeton Theological Seminary, Presby-
    terian Ar, 80

Princeton University: MSS, 215; maps, 329; recordings, 323
Printing: letterpress, 361–362; photo-offset, 361–362; presses, 272
Prints, historical, 332–333
Protestant Episcopal Church, Ar, 79
Provenance, principle of, 22
Provenienzprinzip (German archival practice), 6
Prussian State Archives (Berlin), 5–6, 35–36
Public Archives Commission (AHA), 14, 16–17, 50
Public Building Act of 1913 (National Archives), 15
Public Buildings Act of 1926 (National Archives), 17
Public Record Commission (Great Britain), documentary publication, 45
Public Records Office (London), 6, 36
Public relations, corporate, 118
Publication: definition, 255; of manuscripts, 177
Publications Commission, National Historical, 352–358
Puerto Rico: Ar, 56; MSS, 175
Pulitzer, Joseph, 271
Puritan Revolution, MSS, 206
Pussey, Edwin, 374
Putnam, Herbert, 139–140, 141–142, 184
Putnam, Israel, MSS, 234

Quaife, Milo M., 58
Quaker Meeting House, New York City, Ar, 87
Quakers. *See* Friends, Society of

Randolph, Thomas Jefferson, 149
"Rebel Archives." *See* Confederate States of America
Reconstruction Era, 273
Record group (American archival practice), 21–22
Records, business, 118–124
Records Centers, 29, 308–309
Records disposal, 9, 11, 26, 302
Records management, 26–28, 110–111, 289–310
Records Management Bureau, Office of General Services, 303
Records Management Council (AHA), 125
Records schedules (American archival practice), 28–29
Republican National Committee, Ar, 96
Reston, James, 278, 281
Revere, Paul, 332

Revolutionary War, 46–47; MSS, 221
Rhenisch Westfälische Wirtschaftsarchiv (German business archives), 105
Rhode Island: Ar, 56; MSS, 176
Rhodes, James F., 266
Richmond, University of, Baptist Ar, 85
Richmond Theological Seminary, Presbyterian Ar, 81
Riley, Franklin L., 179
Riley, James Whitcomb, MSS, 221
Rochambeau, Marquis de, MSS, 137
Rochester, University of, recordings, 323
Rolls (British archival practice), 6
Roman Catholic Church, Ar, 77–79
Roosevelt, Franklin D., 280; MSS, 30, 155–159, 243, 355
Roosevelt, Theodore, 11, 279; MSS, 154, 212, 242, 355
Roosevelt Library, 30, 155–159
Root, Elihu, 11
Rosenman, Samuel, 30, 155
Rosenwald, Julius, MSS, 222
Rush, Benjamin, MSS, 203
Rymer, Thomas, 45

St. Augustine Historical Society, MSS, 188
St. Columba, 251
St. Louis Public Library, maps, 329
St. Louis University: Catholic Ar, 79; Knights of Columbus Vatican Microfilm Library, 197–198
Sampling, mass documentation, 311–312
San Diego Historical Society, MSS, 189
San Francisco Theological Seminary, Presbyterian Ar, 80
Santa Barbara Historical Society, MSS, 188–189
Saturday Evening Post, The, 273
Saturday Review of Literature, The, 346
Scandinavian Historical Research Committee, University of Washington, 201
Schafer, Joseph, 58, 189–190
Schlesinger, Arthur M., Jr., 325
Schlesinger, Arthur M., Sr., 177
Schoolcraft, Henry R., MSS, 136, 355
Schurz, Carl, 199
Scotch-Irish Americans, MSS, 199
Scotch-Irish Society of America, MSS, 199
Scotland, Royal Society of Antiquaries, 168
Scripps-McRae Press Association, 272
Security programs, 280–281
Selective Service System, 41
Serra, Junipero, 188; MSS, 198
Sessional Laws of the United States, 350
Seventh Day Adventist Church, Ar, 88
Shadbolt, George, 367

Shafer, Boyd C., 160, 177
Shambaugh, Benjamin F., 179
Shane, John D., MSS, 195
Shelburne, Earl of, MSS, 221
Sheppard, Morris, 14
Sholes, Christopher Latham, 272, 294
Sibley, John Langdon, 211
Sinclair, Upton, MSS, 221
Sloane, Sir Hans, 131
Smith, Alice E., 248–249
Smith, Joseph, 83, 196–197
Smith, Lloyd W., 235
Smith, Sidney L., 332
Smith, T. C., 153
Smith (Edgar Fahs) Memorial, 338
Smithsonian Institution, MSS, 130, 184, 204
Social Security (Bureau of Old Age and Survivors Insurance), 41
Societies, historical: local, 179–192; with MSS, 167–192; private, 172; state, 170–172
Society of American Archivists, 26
Society of Antiquaries (London), 168
Sons of the American Revolution, 15
Sorting systems, 313
South: archival developments in, 51–53; historical societies in, 169, 182; newspapers in, 271
South Carolina: Ar, 48, 50, 56; MSS, 176, 203; statehouse fires, 51
South Carolina, University of, MSS, 219
South Dakota: Ar, 56; MSS, 176
Southern Baptist Convention, Historical Commission of the, Ar, 86
Southern Historical Collection, University of North Carolina, 218
Spain, Royal Academy of History, 168
Spangenberg, Augustus Gottlieb, MSS, 196
Spanish-American War, 271
Sparks, Jared, 7–8, 47, 89, 134, 148, 170, 211; MSS, 212
Spencer, Herbert, 266
Spofford, Ainsworth R., 12, 136–138
Sprague, William B., 134, 232
Spring, Robert, 244
Stanford University, maps, 329
Stanley, Henry M., MSS, 224
Stanton, Edwin, 8
Star Chamber, Court of, 252
State, Department of: MSS in, 136, 149–150; publications of, 352; restricted documents, 24
State archives, 44–60
Stationer's Company of London, 252
Steffens, Lincoln, 65
Stein, Baron vom und zum, 169
Stephens, Henry Morse, 223
Stevens, B. F., 360

Stevens, Henry, 137, 373
Stevens, Sylvester K., 183, 262–264
Stevens Mill Company, Ar, 112
Stiles, Ezra, MSS, 212
Stilwell, Joseph, MSS, 100
Stimson, Henry L., MSS, 213
Stratton, William F., 323
Sumner, Charles, MSS, 212
Supreme Court Reports, 351
Survey of Federal Archives Outside of Washington (WPA), 21
Surveyor General's Office, 70
Susquehannah Company, MSS, 355
Swanson, Claude A., MSS, 217
Swarthmore College, Society of Friends Ar, 87
Swarthmore Friends Collection, 97
Swedish-American Historical Society of Chicago, 201
Swem, Earl G., 217–218
Swiss-American Historical Society, 201
Sybel, Heinrich von, 6

Taft, Robert A., MSS, 213
Taft, William Howard, 13, 15; MSS, 154, 243
Taft Commission (1910), 21
Takoma Park, Maryland, Seventh Day Adventist Ar, 88
Taner, Joseph M., 137
Taylor, Zachary, MSS, 151, 240
Teachers College, Columbia University, films, 322
Tefft, Israel K., 232
Telephone, and historical records, 272
Temperature, optimum for records, 376
Tennessee: Ar, 56; MSS, 176
Tennessee Valley Authority, Ar, 300–301
Tenney, S. M., 80
Territorial Papers of the United States, 357
Texas: Ar, 56; MSS, 176
Texas, University of: MSS, 220; recordings, 323. See also Johnson Library
Thacher, J. B., 232
Theological Seminary of the Southwest, Episcopal Ar, 79
Theses, in academic libraries, 90–91; 210
Thompson, Alphus Basil, MSS, 189
Thompson, David, 258
Thomson, Charles, 7
Thorton, William Mynn, 217
Thwaites, Reuben Gold, 57, 179
Tocqueville, Alexis de. See De Tocqueville, Alexis
Todd, John Payne, 149
Torrens, Sir Robert Richard, 290
Townshend, Marquis George, MSS, 221

Transylvania University, Disciples of Christ Ar, 82
Trent, William P., 141, 353
Trinity College, Ar, 79
Truman, Harry S., 276, 280; MSS, 30–31, 159–162, 243
Truman Library, 30, 31, 159–162
Trumbull, Benjamin, MSS, 212
Tulane University, MSS, 220
Tully, Grace, 30
Turner, Frederick Jackson, 141, 353; MSS, 206
Turner Thesis, 179, 333–334
Twain, Mark, 255; MSS, 233
Tyler, John, MSS, 151, 240
Tyler, Lyon G., 151
Typewriter, 111, 272, 294

Union Catalog of Manuscripts, 146–147, 226
Union Theological Seminary, church Ar, 89
Unitarian-Universalist Association, Ar, 89
United Mine Workers, Ar, 93
United Press, 272
United States of America: contemporary records, 286–287; early records and archives, 7–11; as map publisher, 328. *See also* National Archives
United States Code, 350
United States Navy, MSS, 206
University and college archives, 89–90
Upsala College, Lutheran Ar, 86
U. S. Rubber Company, 306
Utah: Ar, 56; MSS, 176

Vallejo, Mariano Guadalupe, MSS, 223
Van Buren, Martin, MSS, 150, 240
Van Buren, Mrs. Smith Thompson, 150
Van Name, Addison, 213
Van Tyne, Claude H., 220
Vandenberg, Arthur, 276
Varick, Richard, 148
Vatican manuscripts, microfilmed, 197–198
Vermont: Ar, 56; MSS, 176
Veterans' Administration, 41
Victoria University (Toronto, Canada), United Church of Canada Ar, 88
Virginia: Ar, 57; MSS, 176; statehouse fires, 51
Virginia, University of: business Ar, 113; MSS, 149, 188, 216, 357; films, 322
Virginia Diocesan Library, Episcopal Ar, 79
Virginia Historical Society, 171; MSS, 357
Virginia State Library, lamination method, 374

Wachovia Historical Society, MSS, 196
Wage and Salary Stabilization Boards, 92
Waite, Thomas, 345
Waldseemüller, Martin, 327
Walker, Frank, 155
War Department, records, 301–302
War Documentation Center, 336
War of 1812, destruction of Library of Congress during, 135
Warren, Sir Peter, MSS, 221
Wartburg Theological Seminary, Lutheran Ar, 86
Washington, Booker T., MSS, 142
Washington, George, MSS, 136, 148 149, 205, 239, 347
Washington, George Cochin, 148
Washington, Martha, MSS, 258
Washington: Ar, 57; MSS, 176
Washington, D.C., MSS, 215–216
Washington, University of, MSS, 224
Water damage to records, 376–377
Watt, James, 294
Webster, Daniel, MSS, 212, 355
West, state archives in, 54
West Virginia: Ar, 57; MSS, 176
West Virginia Department of Archives and History, 52
Western Historical Manuscripts Collection, University of Missouri, 222
Wetmore, George P., 12, 14
Whistler, James, MSS, 261
White, Andrew, MSS, 214
Whitehill, Walter Muir, 171
Wilbur, James Benjamin, 142
William and Mary, College of, MSS, 217–218
Williams, Talcott, 141, 353
Wilson, Woodrow, 51, 279; MSS, 142, 154, 215, 243, 355
Wilson, Mrs. Woodrow, 154
Winsor, Justin, 211
Winston-Salem, North Carolina, Moravian Ar, 87–88
Winterthur, Delaware, MSS, 207
Wire services, 272
Wisconsin: Ar, 57–60; local history, 189–191; MSS, 176
Wisconsin, State Historical Society of: Ar, 57–60; business history collection, 113; MSS, 176
Wisconsin, University of, maps, 329
Wisconsin Centennial, 58–59
Wisconsin Legislature, 58–60
Wisconsin Manufacturers Association, 113
Wise, Carl S., 314
Withington, Lathrop, 12
Woodson, Carter G., 200
Woolsey, John Monro, MSS, 216

Worde, Wynkyn de, 251
World War II, impact upon National
  Archives, 22–23, 25–26, 320–321
World War II Records Division, Na-
  tional Archives, 302
Writings in American History, 33
Wyoming: Ar, 57; MSS, 176

Xerox, 365

Yale University: MSS, 149, 212; maps,
  329
Yellow Journalism, 271

Zapone document preservation method,
  374
Zeisberger, David, MSS, 196
Zinzendorf, Count Nicholas Louis, 195

O. Lawrence Burnette, Jr., a native
of North Carolina, was educated in the
public schools of Richmond, Virginia,
and at the universities of Richmond
(B.A., 1945) and Virginia (M.A., 1948;
Ph.D., 1952). In his professional career,
he has combined research and teaching
in the special fields of American diplomacy, constitutional history, and historiography, with editorial service on the
staffs of Charles Scribner's Sons and The
State Historical Society of Wisconsin. He
has taught at the University of Virginia,
Virginia Military Institute, the University of Wisconsin, and Birmingham-
Southern College (where he is currently Professor of History). He is the author
or editor (jointly or singly) of: *A Soviet
View of the American Past; Wisconsin
Witness to Frederick Jackson Turner;
Life in America* (elementary school
text); and several articles in his fields
of interest.

Dr. Burnette served in the U. S. Navy
during World War II, and he currently
holds the rank of Commander, U. S.
Naval Reserve. He is active in several
professional historical organizations and
the American Association of University
Professors.